WOMEN SAINTS

Lives of Faith and Courage

WOMEN SAINTS

Lives of Faith and Courage

KATHLEEN JONES

ORBIS BOOKS
Maryknoll, New York 10545

First published in the U.S.A. in 1999 by
Orbis Books
PO Box 308
Maryknoll, New York 10545-0308
www.orbisbooks.com

First published in Great Britain in 1999 by
BURNS & OATES
Wellwood, North Farm Road,
Tunbridge Wells, Kent TN2 3DR

ISBN 1-57075-291-5

Library of Congress Cataloging-in-Publication Data
Jones, Kathleen, 1922–
  Women Saints : lives of faith and courage / Kathleen Jones.
      p.   cm.
  Includes bibliographical references and index.
  ISBN 1-57075-291-5 paper
    1.   Christian women saints Biography.   I. Title.
BX4656.J66   1999
282'.092'2—dc21
[8]   99-23367
                                                                                           CIP

Typeset by Shelleys The Printers, Sherborne
Printed and bound in Great Britain by
MPG Limited, Bodmin, Cornwall

CONTENTS

PREFACE

THERE ARE some well known and much loved women saints. Joan of Arc rides courageously into battle; Teresa of Avila walks with God among the saucepans, Bernadette kneels at the rock of Massabielle; the Little Flower suffers in heroic silence. The lives of these great saints have generated an enormous literature and much heated debate, and it would be presumptuous to attempt to summarize them in a few thousand words, but there are many others who are less well known, or whose traditional Lives can benefit from fresh scrutiny. Recent scholarship and new insights into human behaviour can illuminate some obscure corners of history. Forty of these women are the subjects of the present study.

There may have been as many holy women as holy men in the centuries since Christ walked in Galilee; but the numbers of those whose acts have been recorded and recognized by the Church are less. In most of the standard works on the subject, the proportion is about one woman to six or eight men, and more of them are "Blessed" rather than having the full status of canonized saints in the Universal Roman Calendar. The reasons for this are related to the historical "invisibility" of women. Until comparatively recent times, women have tended to be hidden from public view. Most of those "in the world" have lived out their lives within the privacy of the family circle—often in societies in which women were not allowed to own money or to make their own decisions. Their possessions passed from their fathers to their husbands on marriage, and they themselves *were* property, handed over with their possessions. They were valued as breeders, as the potential mothers of sons, rather than in their own right as individuals. Women in religious Orders avoided these family pressures. There is a good deal of truth in the contention that the Church gave women a new freedom by allowing them to refuse marriage and to live in community with one another, but freedom from mating and procreation involved other restraints. Nuns were usually much more strictly enclosed than monks and frequently worse-educated. In many religious houses for women, right through the medieval period, there was no nun sufficiently literate to keep chronicles. There are no female equivalents of Bede or William of Malmesbury, and few monastic records from women's monasteries or convents (unless kept by a chaplain or other priest) on which to base claims to holy lives.

Nearly all the accounts we have of holy women have been written by men. From the great historians of the early Christian centuries—Eusebius, Theodoret, Socrates, Sozomen—through to the eminent religious historians of the nineteenth and early twentieth centuries, they have usually taken for granted a framework of society in which women played a minor part. Some have tried to fit women into the kind of biographical structure designed for men—and found this difficult, because women in earlier centuries lived radically different lives from men. Others tried to create a different biographical structure, and ended by approving women with "feminine" virtues—women who were passive, submissive, undemanding. They had a liking for frail women—martyred virgins, sickly nuns. Women compilers of Victorian "treasuries" of women saints tended to follow the same pattern, often in works of dismaying sentimentality. The accounts are often so stereotyped that they make dreary reading. The subjects are almost always described as beautiful and virtuous, but they do not behave like real people, and we are given very little idea of what makes them tick. Women's spirituality is often trivialized by such accounts.

Christians have a special commitment to belief in the uniqueness of each human being as God's creation and the fundamental equality that implies. The early Christians, banded together in a hostile and brutal society, accepted the new understanding of Galatians 3:28: "There are no more distinctions between Jew and Greek, slave and free, male and female, but all of you are one in Christ Jesus." This was a direct challenge to the social structure of the Greco-Roman world, which was based on tenaciously held views of social inequality and heavily biased power relationships. Pope John XXIII echoed this understanding in the encyclical *Pacem in Terris* (1963): "The part that women are now playing in political life is everywhere evident. . . .Women are gaining an increasing awareness of their natural dignity. Far from being content with a purely passive role, or allowing themselves to be exploited, they are demanding, both in domestic and in public life, the rights and duties which belong to them as human persons."

Though the conciliar and post-conciliar documents of Vatican II (1962-5) did not always reflect this insight, some referring to "brotherhood," "sons of God," and even to the saints as "our *brothers* who are in the glory of heaven," the usage was probably stylistic rather than substantive. Other documents already used the more cumbrous "men and women," or "brothers and sisters," which make it clear that reference is to all human beings. Since Vatican II, women have become increasingly visible.

In recent years historians of calibre (both men and women) have begun to produce more soundly based analyses of women saints. Some of these saints, particularly those who lived in the early Christian period, have all but disappeared under the weight of legend and pious fantasy; but we do not (or should not) venerate our own inventions and wishful thinking. We need to look for the humanity, the devotion and the sheer courage that many of their lives exemplified: their relationships with relatives, friends, and fellow-workers; the ways in which they dealt with frustration and fear and opposition; their capacity for seeing God and the purpose of his universe more clearly than other people, and for praising him as they went singing through the valley of the shadow.

This approach may be disconcerting to people who prefer quaint legends and esoteric cults to contact with reality; but the saints are not remote icons, untroubled by the sweat and pain of ordinary human life. Their lives involve the same problems as those of the rest of us. The difference is that they tackled them at an exceptionally high moral and spiritual level.

Traditionally, women saints have been classified as virgins, matrons and widows—that is, by family status rather than by their own achievements. Yet we do not write of "St Jerome, bachelor," or "St Peter, married man," and if a male saint became a widower, we assume that the loss was his private affair, not a description of his personality. Women have been treated by ascription, men by achievement; but a holy life is essentially a matter of achievement. Women do not become saints by being somebody's wife, somebody's daughter, or somebody's mother. They become saints by the way in which they deal with the problems of living.

The women saints whose lives are discussed in this volume had varied careers and varied achievements. They were visionaries, martyrs, collaborators in scholarly works or in the foundation of religious organizations, wives and mothers, penitents, social outcasts, innovators, missionaries. These classifications are by no means exhaustive, but they do have the merit of drawing attention to the variety of women's contribution to the Church's life. Because these are real people, their lives were often complex and many-sided, and the chapter headings do no more than indicate some outstanding features. Their lives are rich in many kinds of spiritual experience and understanding. Some are virgins, and some are married women with responsibilities for husbands and children. Some are members of religious Orders, and some are laywomen. They come from all social classes and all walks of life.

If this interpretation of the lives of these holy women provides a new perspective and promotes discussion, it will have served its purpose. They are interesting and often remarkable people, each constrained by the time in which she lived, but not encapsulated by it; for their fulfilment lies not in time, but in eternity.

1

VISIONARIES

VISIONARY writings represent a strand in Christian experience that was expressed first in the Eastern Church and reached the West largely through the translation of the *Mystical Theology* of Pseudo-Dionysius from Greek to Latin in the ninth century. Earlier Western concepts of the Godhead focussed primarily on the positive attributes of might, majesty, dominion, and power. The Dionysian concepts focussed on the mystery of God—unreachable through human reason, but knowable intuitively through love.

The visionary way is surrounded by dangers, not only the obvious ones of arrogance and attention-seeking. Because it is literally super natural, more than the common understanding of God's action in the world or the laws of the universe as we understand them, it may become confused with occultism, superstition, or hysteric states. The problems relate in particular to mystical phenomena such as ecstatic prayer, levitation, stigmata, or tears of blood. Earlier generations, lacking a twentieth-century knowledge of medicine and abnormal psychology, were prone to see supernatural activity where modern theologians would find a natural explanation. We are very much less easily convinced than our predecessors.

The Church accepts the possibility of supernatural manifestations, but the Holy Office has been properly cautious. As long ago as 1738 the Promoter of the Faith, the future Pope Benedict XIV, laid it down in *De Beatificatione et Canonizatione Servorum Dei* that no supernatural phenomenon was to be attributed to the power of the Holy Spirit unless all possible natural or diabolical explanation had been excluded. It is often the mark of a true visionary that he or she doubts the experience at first and, so far from welcoming it, shrinks from the singularization and the public attention it brings.

Fr J. Aumann comments that "the history of spirituality shows that women are more prone to illusion than men, and more women among the saints have been remarkable for extraordinary phenomena." This may have been true in earlier centuries. The conditions of life for women enclosed in medieval monasteries—the darkness, the few flickering candles, the poor food, the lack of sleep and exercise and fresh air—may well have encouraged

1

illusion. There is a category of women sometimes referred to in the literature as *beatae/delusae* because it is not clear whether their manifestations are divinely inspired or psychosomatic in origin. Among these must be numbered Elizabeth of Schönau, who was included by Cardinal Baronius in the Roman Martyrlogy. Even before her visions began she was constantly tormented by illness and depression. Her visions were terrifying. Monks and demons came out of the shadowy corners of the monastery to mock and deride her, and Christ appeared to her as a figure of wrath, not of compassion. A modern biography by A. L. Clark makes it clear that her visions were not approved in Rome and that she was not regarded as a candidate for sainthood.

Physical deprivation may heighten the spiritual consciousness, but it can also have effects similar to those of the neuroleptic drugs. There is a growing understanding of these mechanisms, but it should not lead to the rejection of the visionary tradition. Both in and out of monastic life, there have been notable men and women visionaries, people who have shown extraordinary spiritual gifts that can still be recognized in the more sceptical context of the twentieth century. Perhaps the only real test is that of Christ himself: "By their fruits ye shall know them."

The writings of Julian of Norwich and Teresa of Avila are now well known and widely available to readers. Julian, a fourteenth-century anchoress of Norwich, had a direct experience of the passion of Christ, her account of which has become a spiritual classic, and there are other christocentric writings of this kind, notably the experiences of Mechtild of Helfta, who first had "a clear revelation" of Christ when she was twenty-five. Her visions were personal encounters with Christ as he was at various times during his earthly life. St Teresa's visionary writings are more concerned with the state of the human soul on its journey to God. This most practical of saints uses analogies: the soul is an interior castle to be cleansed and made ready for the Lord's occupation or a garden to be watered. The five women whose experience is described here represent other insights and other traditions.

Hildegard of Bingen, the most celebrated of the Rhineland visionaries, is probably better known today for her music than for her perceptive and luminous writings, but she had an intuitive understanding of the whole of Creation and God's purpose in the world. In the *Liber Divinum Operum*, she saw the creative power of the Trinity pulsing through the universe and the great struggle between good and evil as its central drama. Hildegard's characters are Platonic absolutes—Reason, Chastity, Divine Wisdom—and she sees the power of the Godhead swirling through the world like a flame, searing and illuminating. She makes it clear that her visions are mental images.

She does not write of dreams or hallucinations, but of what she has seen "with a clear mind . . . in open places according to the will of God."

Juliana of Mount Cornillon in the Low Countries had a dream, many times repeated. Dreams can show in symbolic form what the fully conscious mind is unable to accept; and Juliana's led her to understand that there was one necessary feast missing from the liturgical year: the feast celebrating the gift of the Body and Blood of Christ as manifest in the Eucharist. Corpus Christi was originally decried by many clergy as a "women's feast," and efforts were made to ignore or suppress it, but Juliana's vision eventually enriched the life of the Church by celebrating this most central aspect of its worship.

Catherine of Siena came from the Street of the Dyers in Siena, and her multicoloured visions have inspired much prayer and meditation. In an age before films and television people had to make their own pictures, and Catherine's vivid dreams and symbols helped her to express her own intense spiritual experience. Her austerities were extreme and might today be classified as pathological self-mutilation, though they were not exceptional for the age in which she lived, but when she had worked through her own problems she turned her spiritual energies out to the world, helping lepers, cancer patients, and condemned criminals. A key point in her development was learning to read and write. Once literate, she acquired the power to express her ideas in words rather than pictures and became a spiritual adviser and confidante to many of her contemporaries.

Catherine of Genoa, rather more than a century later, was a very different character. She was a married woman: a Guelph married against her will to a Ghibelline during a brief interlude in the internecine struggles of these two great Italian families. Her difficulties with her husband shaped her life and her spiritual understanding. For seventeen years, with only minimal contact with the Church, she managed the women's side of a hospital for chronic and aged patients. Her husband's death in some way freed her to express the results of prayer and contemplation, and her writings on purgatory and the relationship between the soul and the body have inspired many theologians. Baron von Hügel's monumental work on *The Mystical Element of Religion as studied in St Catherine of Genoa and Her Friends* has become a classic on the subject; but there have been considerable advances in psychology and the understanding of women's lives since it was published nearly a century ago, and some new inferences are suggested from a study of her life.

The final study in this section is concerned with the life of the German philosopher **Dr Edith Stein**, who became a Carmelite nun as Sister Teresa Benedicta of the Cross. Edith Stein was an academic, highly literate and well able to express her ideas, but she came through an arid discipline to the belief

3

that there was an area of human experience beyond academic understanding. Her vision of the human condition, inspired by her reading of St John of the Cross and St Thomas Aquinas, took her from a Jewish family background to acceptance of Christianity, from the sophistication of philosophical analysis to the simplicities of a Carmelite convent, and ultimately to death as a Nazi war victim in a concentration camp. Few people have been less "prone to illusion." She thought in concepts, not in pictures; but her conviction of the necessity for suffering and sacrifice gave her the strength to live out a parable in her own life.

These five women were all practical, energetic, intelligent and disciplined. They were not credulous, and they did not deal in magic or inexplicable phenomena. They were not "mystics" in the sense that they flouted the laws of nature and dabbled in extrasensory perception. They were "seers," or more properly see-ers, who saw further into the interaction of divine purpose and human existence than most other people do, in a way which other people could follow. Their visions were not in conflict with the capacities of human nature. They fulfilled and extended those capacities, enabling us to reach a fuller understanding of the possibilities of religious experience.

HILDEGARD OF BINGEN
(1098-1179)

Hildegard writing down her visions under divine inspiration, with the monk Volmar watching.

From Liber Scivias, *copy of the former Rupertsberg Codex, c. 1180.*

HILDEGARD—abbess, scholar, poet, musician, healer, prophet, adviser to popes and kings—recorded on a number of occasions her belief that all her other activities derived from the power of her visions. She tells us that from early childhood she saw the whole world as a reflection of the "living Light" of God: "My soul, as God would have it, rises up high into the vault of heaven and into the changing sky, and spreads itself out among different peoples, although they are far from me in distant lands and places."

She was the tenth and last child of Hildebert of Bemersheim and his wife, Mechtild, and apparently a sickly child as well as a strange one. She was sent at the age of eight to be taught by the anchoress Jutta, who lived in an enclosure by the Benedictine monastery of Disibodenberg, between Mainz and Trier in the Rhineland. Perhaps, as the tenth child, she was given to the Church as a tithe. Jutta, an exceptional woman and something of a scholar, became her mother: she taught the child reading and writing, in Latin as well as the Low German of their district; she taught her the Psalter and the scriptures, in which she was exceptionally well grounded; she taught her the

5

Benedictine Liturgy and poetry and music. Hildegard said of her, "This woman overflowed with the grace of God like a river fed by many streams."

In 1112, when she was fifteen years old, Hildegard took the veil. She continued to live the frugal and dedicated life of the Benedictine Rule with Jutta until her mid-forties; but even within their enclosure, life was not without change. The monastery was in a constant state of expansion and rebuilding, and as other women came to join the two the enclosure developed into a convent. Hildegard frequently uses building metaphors in her writings, describing the foundations, the towers, the living stones of God's world.

When Jutta died in 1136, Hildegard became prioress. She kept her visions largely to herself for a further five years after that, partly because she doubted what she saw and partly because she was afraid of what people would say if she made them known. Only Jutta and a monk named Volmar had been told of them, but she became increasingly convinced that she was being told to write them down. Volmar went to the abbot and was given permission to help her transcribe some of her visions. The archbishop of Mainz and his theologians read some early drafts and approved them, saying, "These visions come from God." With Volmar's help she began work on *Scivias*—an abbreviation of *Nosce vias Domini* or "Know the ways of the Lord," but she was still concerned at the weight of responsibility thrust upon her. She wrote to St Bernard of Clairvaux, saying that she had been greatly troubled by her visions, that she was wretched "and more wretched in bearing the name of woman." Should she speak of her visions or maintain silence? Bernard, the most powerful churchman of his age, approved her writings, and in 1147-8 the Pope, Bd Eugenius III, who had been one of Bernard's monks at Clairvaux, read extracts from *Scivias* to the Council of Trier. Hildegard was assured that her visions came from God and that she was right to communicate them to others.

In *Scivias* she makes it clear that her visions are not hallucinations:

> The visions which I saw I did not perceive in a dream nor when asleep nor in a delirium nor with the eyes and ears of the body. I received them when I was awake and looking around with a clear mind, with the inner eyes and ears, in open places according to the will of God.

She was the instrument of God, almost against her own will. She accepted what she was given and dictated it in her idiosyncratic and sometimes obscure Latin to Volmar and his successors. They merely took dictation. So she remained in her enclosure, recording her visions, expressing the glory of God in music and poetry, and writing to her many correspondents. Under her Rule, her learned maidens sang her musical compositions in church.

In an account of one vision Hildegard expresses their exalted status as virgins:

I saw a layer of air, pure beyond the clarity of the finest water, purer than the rays of the sun. It had life, and contained the vital force of all the herbs and flowers of earth and paradise, filled with the fragrance of life-giving power, just as the summer is filled with the scent of green plants and flowers. As though in a mirror, I saw in that layer of air those blessed women. They too were as fragrant as sweet-smelling herbs.

They wore golden crowns, interwoven with roses and lilies, and "When the voice of the Lamb resounded, the wind stirred the stems of the roses and lilies, till they rang out like the strings of harps." Hildegard's visions stir all the senses.

When she was over sixty the "heavenly voice" told her to leave her beloved enclosure and preach in other monasteries. She undertook four trips through the Rhineland in all, speaking to the monks and nuns who crowded into their chapter houses to hear her. When she was sixty-seven she founded another community at Rudesheim.

During this busy life she experienced three occasions of great sadness. The first was in 1150, when the monks of Disibodenberg tried to appropriate some of the lands and property of her community and she had to move it to a desolate and forbidding area at Rupertsberg. The second was in 1151, when Richardis of Stade, her friend and sometime secretary, left to become abbess of a convent near Bremen. She told Richardis in a letter than she felt abandoned "like an orphan." The third was in 1178, when the community at Rupertsberg was placed under interdict by the Church authorities of Mainz because Hildegard had allowed the burial in the convent cemetery of a nobleman who had been excommunicated. She maintained that he had become reconciled to the Church before his death and refused to exhume the body. The archbishop of Mainz was absent in Rome at the time, and some months elapsed before he returned and lifted the interdict. While it lasted, the members of the community could not receive the sacraments nor have music in church. The latter was a particular deprivation to a musician who had composed "songs of the heavenly homeland" and experienced "heavenly harmonies." Hildegard defended her community vigorously and left the clergy of Mainz in no doubt that she considered their action vengeful and unjust. She died a year later at the age of eighty-one.

Scivias took her ten years to complete. She describes thirteen visions, which develop a complete cosmology, rich with symbolism, describing the essential and dynamic unity of all living things under God: the heavens and the earth, the elements, mountains, rivers and seas, plants and trees. She sees the Holy Trinity like a flame: the shining brightness represents the Father, the "purple vigour" represents the Son, and the fiery glow is the Holy Spirit, poured into the heart of believers.

In *The Book of Divine Works*, completed in 1174, Hildegard tells how her voice from heaven addressed her:

> O poor little figure of a woman, you who are the daughter of many troubles, plagued by a multitude of bodily infirmities, yet steeped, nonetheless, in the vastness of God's mysteries ... Write these things not according to your heart but according to my witness—for I am Life, without beginning and without end ... I flame above the beauty of the fields, I shine in the waters; in the sun, the moon and the stars, I burn.

She describes the power of the Holy Spirit in sheer exaltation:

> I am the supreme and fiery force who has kindled all sparks of life and breathed forth none of death and I judge them as they are. I have rightly established that order, encircling it with my upper wings, that is, embracing them with wisdom. I, the fiery life of the divine substance, blaze in the beauty of the fields, shine in the waters, and burn in the sun, moon and stars. . . . I am also Reason, having the wind of the sounding word by which all things were created, and I breathe in them all, so that none may die, because I am Life.

She sees Chastity "clothed in a tunic, purer, more full of light than a crystal," and Divine Wisdom with her head "shining like lightning."

Hildegard did not experience trances, wounds, tears, or other supernatural manifestations. Her visions were cerebral, unaccompanied by emotions except those of weariness and infirmity; but she visualized the whole theology of Creation and Redemption and then reported her apocalyptic vision. Like St John the Divine she says, "And I heard a voice from heaven, saying . . ." and insists repeatedly, "These things are true."

The Book of Life's Merits, written between 1158 and 1163, is concerned with sin, punishment, and penance. The central figure is that of a man superimposed on the world, turning to the points of the compass to observe the interaction of good and evil. In the fourth vision she sees a menacing apparition, which gathers "like a cloud of thick smoke, and [it] took on human form, but without arms or legs—only huge black eyes that stared, unblinking. Perfectly still, it remained out there in the dark, motionless. It spoke: its name was HARDNESS OF HEART." Mercy told it that it was "a creature of stone." Even plants offer fragrance from their flowers, and precious stones reflect their brilliance to others: "All you are is a pitiless stare, an evil cloud of smoke in the darkness!"

Hildegard's poetry, often dedicated to saint and martyrs, has been compared to that of Dante or Blake. Among her poems is an antiphon to St Boniface, which celebrates his union with the natural world:

O Boniface,
The living light looked upon you,
As on a wise man, who returned
To God the pure streams
That flowed from him,
When you watered the flowers' green.

And so you are a friend of the living God,
A luminous crystal
In the benign intent
Of the righteous ways
In which,
Wise,
You ran.

Hildegard composed seventy-seven pieces of church music, strikingly original, for her nuns to sing in church and echo the celestial melodies. These, with the musical play *Ordo Virtutem*, make up the *Symphonia* or "symphony of the harmony of heavenly revelations." She wrote many letters of advice and counsel to prominent people, including four popes and the emperor Frederick I (Barbarossa). She met the emperor on one occasion. To Pope Anastasius IV she wrote bluntly, "So it is, O man, that you who sit in the chief seat of the Lord hold him in contempt when you embrace evil, since you do not reject it but kiss it by silently tolerating it in depraved men." Writing to King Henry II of England before the murder of Becket, she warned him about the abuse of power. Her letters were always accompanied by protestations of her own unworthiness, but they were written in the vein of an Old Testament prophet: "Thus saith the Lord."

She also wrote to the tormented Elizabeth of Schönau at the request of Elizabeth's abbess. Elizabeth had many dark and terrifying visions. She prophesied that Satan would receive power to create violent havoc on earth, the sun would appear blood red and streaked with shadows, and Christians would cry out in tribulation. She suffered much physical distress and mental depression. Hildegard counselled her gently, calling her "my troubled daughter" and warning her against the operations of the devil:

For when the serpent sees a pretty jewel, he hisses at once and says "What is this?" And he torments it with the many afflictions of a mind that burns with

9

desire to fly above the clouds . . . as though mortals were gods . . . Those who desire to bring the work of God to perfection should pay attention, for being mortals, they are vessels of clay. And let them always have regard to what they are, and what they will be, and leave the things of heaven to him who is heavenly. For they themselves are outcasts, knowing nothing of the things of heaven.

Hildegard's reputation as a healer rests on her *Causes and Cures* and *Natural History*, written between 1150 and 1158, but she makes no claim that these works come from divine revelation. Each book is a compendium of existing knowledge—the first a medical textbook and the second a description of the healing power of plants, trees, animals, and metals. They show her reverence for the created world and her inexhaustible curiosity. As her fame spread, many sick people must have come to the nunnery to seek cures, miraculous or natural, and the books were probably written for the use of her nuns. Though they are of historical interest, historians of science suspect that both books have been subject to interpolations over the centuries.

Hildegard's music, which includes many dissonances and passages in a minor key, appeals to modern musical taste and has become widely available through audiotapes and compact discs. Her writings had a brief vogue with "New Age" readers, but feminists have generally been unenthusiastic about her work, perhaps because of her habit of referring to herself as *paupecula feminea forma*, a poor little woman. Did she do so from personal humility or was she attempting to deflect masculine criticism of her public mission? She was certainly not afraid to speak with authority and clarity when reporting her visions.

The canonization process was started not long after Hildegard's death but never formally completed—for reasons that had more to do with the vicissitudes of the papacy than with Hildegard's acknowledged merit. In 1324 Pope John XXII gave permission for her "solemn and public cult," and her name is included in the Roman Martyrology.

JULIANA OF MOUNT CORNILLON

(1195-1258)

Juliana holding a monstrance and a book.

Nineteenth-century engraving.

JULIANA had a vision that led to the institution of the feast of Corpus Christi. In her own day this was opposed and ignored by many of the clergy of the Low Countries, being dismissed as "the dream of a silly woman," but it has now become one of the major feasts of the Church, celebrated generally on the Thursday after Trinity Sunday but on the following Sunday in North America.

Juliana was left an orphan at the age of six. We do not know whether her parents died in war or in one of the many plagues that swept the European continent in the early thirteenth century. They evidently came of a noble family, for they left a considerable inheritance, but there were no other relatives who could care for Juliana and her sister Agnes. The children were sent to the convent of Mount Cornillon, near Liège, founded at the end of the twelfth century as a hospital for lepers. Leprosy, which had come from the East during the Crusades, was thought to be highly infectious. It was much dreaded, and lepers in the advanced stages were thought to be no sight

11

for children, so the nuns sent the children to their dairy farm, in the Amescoeur district, where they were lovingly brought up by Sister Sapientia. Agnes died young. Juliana gave all her great inheritance to the convent, which was previously very poor, and took the veil. She was very moved by the liturgy from an early age—she loved Venantius Fortunatus' hymn "The royal banners forward go" on Passion Sunday. After she entered the Order she spent her time in ministering to the lepers and reading St Augustine.

In 1208, before she was sixteen, she had a vision while saying her prayers, and it was repeated many times. She saw the full moon in splendour but with a dark stain on one side. She consulted her superior, but neither could understand its significance. Two years later the explanation came to her in her sleep: the moon represented the Church Militant, and the stain represented the one feast of Our Lord which was lacking in the Church's liturgical year: there were solemn feasts for the Incarnation, the Manifestation to the Gentiles, the Atonement, the Resurrection, the Ascension, and the Coming of the Holy Spirit, but not for the gift of the Eucharist.

About 1225 or 1230 Juliana became superior, following her beloved Sapientia in the office. She felt that she must speak out and consulted a recluse named Isabella who lived nearby. At first Isabella was doubtful about the need for a special feast, pointing out that the Mass commemorated the gift of the Eucharist every day; but after some months she too had a vision. She saw the company of saints pleading the cause of the festival and became convinced that it was God's will. She consulted a canon of St Martin's Church, John of Lausanne, and he in turn consulted a number of people including the provincial of the Dominicans, the archdeacon of Liège, Bishop Jacques Pantaléon of Cambrai, and teachers at the University of Paris. While they were initially cautious, they all replied that such a festival was not in any way contrary to Catholic doctrine and was calculated to increase the devotion of Christian people; but no one was willing to undertake the task of composing an office. Eventually John of Lausanne agreed to draft an office if Juliana would pray for the completion of the task. So the office was composed, "the virgin praying to Christ, the brother composing, and God wondrously assisting." Some of the clergy supported Juliana, but Roger, the prior of Cornillon, seems to have taken advantage of the situation to try to stir up trouble and gain control of the convent. Juliana's advocacy of the new feast was dismissed as just an idle whim. She was "mocked, hooted, scorned by all."

A few of her Sisters were induced to complain to the magistrates that Juliana had misappropriated money belonging to the leper hospital and had bribed the bishop so that he would support her feast. A mob, excited by this allegation, actually violated the enclosure and broke into the convent searching for Juliana and the accounts and title deeds, but she escaped to St Martin's Church and took refuge with a recluse named Eve, now Bd Eve of Liège. Juliana's women friends evidently served her well. The bishop investigated and found the allegations without foundation. He sent Roger away to be head of a house at Huy and returned Juliana to Mount Cornillon.

In 1246 Bishop Robert of Liège announced the establishment of the new festival in his diocese, but he died in the same year, and the clerical opposition to this "women's feast" was not yet over. The clergy ignored his ruling and the festival: only the chapter of St Martin's resolved to keep it on the Thursday after Trinity Sunday in 1247. The festival of Corpus Christi was celebrated in the "extreme western chapel of the right aisle" for the first time on that date. The new bishop wanted to restore Prior Roger to Mount Cornillon, but this could be done only with Juliana's consent—and she refused, no doubt with good reason. There were public riots. The mob invaded the convent again, and she and three other Sisters, Isabella of Huy, Agnes, and Ozilia, had to flee—first to Val-Benoît on the Meuse, and then right out of Liègeois territory, to Namur.

The festival of Corpus Christi found a new champion in Cardinal Hugh of Saint Cher, whom John of Lausanne had consulted when he was originally drafting the office. Cardinal Hugh was sent by Pope Innocent IV to attend the marriage of William of Holland at Aix-la-Chapelle. He heard of the controversy at Liège, confirmed the institution of the feast, and announced that he himself would celebrate it in St Martin's. This he did, and another apostolic legate, Peter Capocci, subsequently issued an order that the feast should be celebrated in accordance with the decree of Hugh of Saint Cher. But when Peter left the feast fell into disuse again, except in St Martin's.

Juliana was desperately poor for some time, but the abbess of Salzinne, sister of the archbishop of Cologne, took up her cause, offered her shelter, and shamed the prior of Cornillon and the bishop of Liège into making her an annuity from the great possessions she had given to the abbey and hospital at Mount Cornillon. In 1256 Namur was besieged by Henry II of Luxembourg. The country around was laid waste, and the abbey of Salzinne was burned down. Juliana and the prioress, Hymenea, found refuge in Fosses. Juliana asked John of Lausanne to go and see her, saying that she had a secret to tell him; but he did not succeed in reaching Fosses, probably being prevented from making the journey by hostile troops. She died on 5 April 1258 without revealing her secret.

Three years later there was a new Pope: Jacques Pantaleon, patriarch of Jerusalem and former bishop of Cambrai, became Pope Urban IV. Juliana's old friend Eve the Recluse urged the bishop of Liège to ask for a recognition of the feast. Pope Urban remembered the consultation in 1230, when John of Lausanne had asked for an opinion on the validity of the feast. He authorized the celebration in 1264 by the papal Bull *Transiturus de hoc mundo*. Bartholomew of Lucca credits the liturgy of the Mass and the divine office to St Thomas Aquinas, but it appears that the present office is an amalgam of several compositions. The Bull of Urban IV was confirmed by the Council of Vienne in 1311.

The main credit for the introduction of Corpus Christi has often been given to John of Lausanne, but it seems clear that, though John was always her loyal supporter, the initiative for the feast came from Juliana, and it was she who suffered from the dissent that it caused in Liège.

CATHERINE OF SIENA

(1347-82)

*Detail from an altarpiece,
by Fra Angelico, c. 1437.*

CATHERINE has the reputation of being a "difficult" saint: her life is full of marvels and wonders, written in the idiom of Tuscany in the early Renaissance. Even in her lifetime people in her native Siena found her behaviour odd and her claims hard to believe. Her friend, confessor, and principal biographer, Bd Raymond of Capua, learned the early part of the story from Catherine and her mother and lived through the later years with them.

Catherine was the daughter of Giacomo Benincasa, a prosperous dyer of Siena, and his wife, Lapa. She was the couple's twenty-third child, one of twins, and the other twin died. She was five or six when she had her first vision, while walking home with her brother Stefano from seeing their married sister, Bonaventura. As they walked back to the Street of the Dyers, she looked up at the sky above the church of San Domenico and saw Christ in glory. He smiled at her and gave her his benediction. From that moment she was his. Stefano, who had gone ahead, came back, shouting at her. She came to slowly, saying, "If you could see what I can, you would not be so

15

cruel and disturb me out of this lovely vision." And she cried bitterly for the loss of it.

Catherine would have wandered in and out of her father's dyeing sheds, full of the heraldic colours of the early Renaissance, the colours of Duccio, who was painting at the same time in the same small town—gold and sapphire and verdant green and glowing red, flaming and swirling about the dark sheds. These were the colours of heaven, and where pragmatic Stefano saw only sunset, Catherine saw heaven itself.

She was a child with a very strong pictorial imagination, and this was early gripped by the central tenets of the Christian faith. She had frequent trances or ecstatic states, and these worried her mother, who nearly broke the child's limbs trying to bend them from their rigidity. As she grew older she also developed a very strong sense of guilt and frequently scourged herself, lamenting her sins. There may have been two influences at work. She was a surviving twin, and it is not uncommon for the twin who lives to feel guilt for the death of the other. In addition she was influenced by the Dominicans from her earliest years: the Benincasa home was almost opposite the church of San Domenico. Catherine would have seen the friars going to and from their convent, and some of them came to the house. Though the gentle Francis of Assisi collected up all the hair shirts and disciplines used by his followers and made a bonfire of them, the Dominicans had a sterner tradition based on the subjugation of the flesh. Catherine's foster-brother Tommaso della Fonte hoped to enter the Order of Preachers, and she would have learned a good deal from him of their practices. Catherine and her small friends were much impressed with the Dominican way of life and practised their prayers and penances.

Raymond tells us that Catherine once dreamed she could see the Christ-child with a vine growing out of his heart bearing ripe heavy grapes. From every side came big, beautiful white dogs with black spots, who ate the grapes and pulled off great bunches to carry to the little dogs who could not reach them. The Dominicans, in their black and white habits, were often called *Domini canes*, the dogs of the Lord.

Lapa had a conventional woman's conviction that her daughter's greatest happiness would lie in marrying young and settling down to have children. Catherine was made to rouge her cheeks, lighten the colour of her distinctive golden hair, and go to festivals where she might meet young men. She obeyed for a time—but then refused, determined that she would never marry. This short period of "faithlessness" deeply impressed her. She was still repenting of it many years later when Raymond of Capua knew her.

She consulted her foster-brother Tommaso della Fonte, who by this time was a Dominican, and he advised her to cut off her hair, which was the traditional sign of a girl's determination to remain a virgin. When her parents saw her shorn head, there was, even by Italian standards, an almighty altercation, in which poor bewildered Lapa must have played a large part. No doubt other members of the family, and neighbours, joined in *fortissimo*. Catherine had to be made to behave like other girls. The upshot was that she was denied a room of her own (a precious possession, because she needed her privacy). A servant was dismissed, and she was made to do the housework. She did this gladly and joyfully; but she was still to be found, rapt and rigid, in odd corners of the house, in the ecstatic communion that was the basis of her life.

At this time she entertained quite serious thoughts of dressing as a man and becoming a Dominican. Then she dreamed that St Dominic himself was holding out a habit to her—not that of a Dominican friar, but the habit of a *Mantellata*, the female Third Order of the Dominicans. The *Mantellate* were older women, who served the sick and the poor. With a new authority, Catherine called her family together and told them, "If you mean to drive me away, I have a bridegroom so rich and mighty that he can give me all I need, and who will never let me want for anything." There was a long silence. Then her father Giacomo stopped all the argument by saying, "She is to be left free and in peace to serve her Bridegroom, and continually pray for us. We could never get a Bridegroom of mightier kindred."

She was given a small room in the Villa Benincasa, where she lived her simple life, sleeping on the floor with a log for a pillow and depriving herself of sleep. She used the discipline frequently—another biographer, Caffarini, saw it hanging in her room, coagulated with blood. She ate so little that she was unable to eat normally for the rest of her life and was said to subsist for long periods on the Host alone. If she tried to eat she was physically sick.

As we now know, self-mutilation and anorexia can affect young women who have a very low sense of their own worth. Another source of guilt for Catherine was her inability to behave like a conventional daughter. Lapa was openly distressed. She "performed all sorts of strange acts, such as scratching her face and tearing her hair," according to Raymond; but eventually she admitted defeat. She went to the prioress of the *Mantellate* and asked that Catherine might be admitted. The prioress refused, saying that the *Mantellate* admitted only widows, respectable older women of maturity, not girls of sixteen.

Catherine became ill: some accounts suggest that she had a violent form of chicken-pox and others that she was herself responsible for the blisters that covered her skin. Raymond says that Lapa had taken her to the baths— perhaps in one last attempt to make her attractive to young men. Catherine lay under a conduit of boiling water, "afflicting her body more than she had ever done, even by beating it with an iron chain." Lapa went back to the *Mantellate*, pleading with the prioress to admit her daughter. When the prioress asked her if Catherine was attractive, she replied "Come and see for yourselves." With her wasted body, shorn hair and blistered skin, she was quite different from the healthy girl of a year or two earlier. The *Mantellate* accepted her without further argument. She was clothed in 1363, when she was still only sixteen, but she continued to be a deeply unhappy and very sick girl. Even the *Mantellate* grew irritated with her endless prayers, her noisy weeping in church, and her habit of going into trances. Fr Tommaso asked her to restrain her tears, but she said she could not. When she received Holy Communion she sweated violently, and some people said that she literally sweated blood. Sometimes her trances lasted so long that when it was time for the church to be closed, she would be carried out into the street and left there, to be kicked by passers-by. At other times she was troubled by sexual excitement and had visions of naked girls dancing with the devil, until she cried, "*Confido in Domine Nostro Jesus Christo!*" and the tormenting sights disappeared.

The crisis came on Shrove Tuesday 1367, when she was nearly twenty years old. Shrove Tuesday was a day of revelry and riotous indulgence before the austerities of Lent. It must have been a day of particular trial for Catherine, with her strong sexual instincts and her even stronger sense of denial; but her richly creative imagination was the means of spiritual understanding. In a vision she had a magnificent wedding to Christ himself, conducted by the Blessed Virgin his Mother, with St Paul, St John the Evangelist, and St Dominic as witnesses and King David playing the harp for wedding music. Her troth was pledged with a gold ring with a large diamond—"the diamond of truth, which nothing can scratch"—and four pearls signifying purity in mind and thought and word and deed. She could feel this ring on her finger for the rest of her life.

She had fought her spiritual battle and won. Now with the Spiritual Espousal came a new energy. The Lord commanded her to go out and mix with the people, to serve the poor, and she obeyed. Never one to do things by halves, she gave away her father's goods so enthusiastically that even the servants began to lock up the family's possessions to save them from her depredations. She took wine, eggs, bread, oil, and grain and left them by stealth at the doors of poor families. Sometimes the burdens were so heavy and her strength so little that she could only crawl. She went to the *lazaretto*, where she nursed a cross old leper woman named Tecca, who never had a kind word for her and taunted her with being uncommonly fond of friars. She continued to nurse Tecca until the old woman finally died; then she washed the sad and wasted body and (presumably because no one else would do so) buried it with her own hands after the funeral rites had taken place. She nursed many other patients, some of them grateful and some as ungrateful as Tecca. One cancer patient named Andrea, whom Catherine had nursed long and patiently despite the terrible stench of her ulcer, viciously alleged publicly that Catherine had lost her virginity. She was called to answer to the *Mantellate*. She could only say, "I assure you, ladies and sisters, that by the grace of God I am a virgin." Her sincerity was so patent that the charges went no further. When the plague came to Siena in 1374 she was in the hospitals with her followers, organizing, soothing, and doing the humblest nursing tasks tirelessly and prayerfully.

She made regular visits to prisons to be with condemned men. On one occasion, as she recounts in a letter, she went with a prisoner to Mass and accompanied him to the scaffold. He smiled at her prayers and murmured "Jesus and Catherine" as the axe fell. She received his still-smiling head into her hands. Catherine was never afraid to get her hands dirty.

Some time in her early twenties, she had received a great blessing. She taught herself to read with the aid of a simple ABC. She read Holy Scripture, the Psalms, the Divine Office, and the works of the early Fathers. The Dominicans came to consult her, and she began to be greatly respected in Siena. People came to her for counsel and arbitration. She was said to be able to see into the heart of a sinner, and many who came to her went away repentant. She acquired a circle of friends and disciples, who called themselves the *Caterinati*. Some of them were Dominicans, some *Mantellate*, and some lay people from the city, attracted by her growing spirituality. She had become what she was clearly fitted to be, a scholarly and wise woman.

Letters requesting advice came pouring in from other cities. Catherine was acquiring a wider ministry. Early in 1375 she went to Pisa, where she settled disputes and brought about a religious revival. It was at this time that she received the stigmata, though others could not see the wounds. The invisible marks of Christ crucified were a sign of vicarious suffering gladly undergone for the sins of the Church and the state of the world.

She wrote to the English mercenary captain, Sir John Hawkwood, who fought for Pisa and later for Florence, begging him to stop killing Italians and go on a Crusade against the Saracens. She addressed him as "Messer John, the Soldier of Fortune and Head of the Company that came in Time of Famine":

Now my soul desires that you should change your way of life, and take the pay and the cross of Christ crucified, you and all your followers companions; so that you may be in Christ's company, to march against the infidel dogs who possess our Holy Place, where rested the sweet Primal Truth and bore death and pains for us ... You take such pleasure in war and fighting, you should not make war against Christians any more—for this is a wrong to God—but go against the infidels! For it is a great cruelty that we who are Christians, and members bound in the Body of Holy Church, should persecute one another. We are not to do so; but to rise with perfect zeal, and to uplift ourselves above every evil thought.

There was no Crusade for Sir John to join; but he promised that thereafter he would carry only "regular arms."

Catherine heard that the Pope, Gregory XI, who had his court in Avignon, was in conflict with Florence and other cities in northern Italy. She wrote to all the insurgents. She wrote to the Pope six times about the mismanagement of his officials and the neglect of his responsibilities, not mincing her words. In one letter she urges him to come back to Rome:

Most holy and reverend my father in Christ Jesus: I, Catherine, your poor and unworthy daughter, servant and slave of the servants of Christ, write to you in His precious Blood, with desire to see you a good shepherd. For I reflect, my Babbo, that the wolf is carrying away your sheep, and there is no one found to help them . . . Raise swiftly, Babbo, the gonfalon of the most holy Cross, and you will see the wolves become lambs. Come, come, and resist no more the will of God which calls you; the hungry sheep await your coming to hold and possess the place of your predecessor and champion, Apostle Peter. For you, as Vicar of Christ, should rest in your own place. Come then, come and delay no more; and comfort you and fear not for anything that might happen to you, since God will be with you.

Babbo is the diminutive of the Italian *papa*. In the end she went to Avignon herself. Raymond of Capua went with her as her interpreter, for she could speak no Latin, and the Pope (a Frenchman, Pierre Roger de Beaufort) could speak no Italian. She was involved in many negotiations for peace, not all of them successful; but the Pope did leave Avignon for Rome in 1377, and Catherine went back to Siena.

Surrounded by her friends and disciples, she settled down to write her *Dialogue*. This mystical treatise, known to the *Caterinati* simply as "The Book," is her own synthesis of Christian belief and doctrine. Though attempts have been made to trace the influence of great Christian writers, notably St Thomas Aquinas and St Augustine of Hippo, in her thought, it seems to be based less on literary sources than on her own unceasing search for truth. Her letters, of which some four hundred survive, give a livelier picture of her personality and activities. During this period Pope Gregory XI died, and Christendom was again divided: this time between Pope Urban VI in Rome and an antipope in Avignon. Catherine wore herself out supporting Urban—preaching, exhorting, cajoling, sending letter after letter.

Raymond tells us that people in Siena still misunderstood her. "What does she want to go traipsing about for?" they asked: "She is a woman! If she wants to serve God, why doesn't she stay at home?" Raymond insists that everything she did was to the glory of God; but this loyal friend and confessor was in Genoa, on his way to the annual Dominican chapter, when her strength finally failed early in 1380.

In February and March of that year Catherine lay in bed, tackling the task of dying with the same thoroughness that she had shown all her life and offering her sufferings as reparation for the sins of the Church. One of her disciples saw her looking up to heaven and murmuring "*Grazie, grazie*" because her offer was being found acceptable. A Dominican who came to hear her confession said, "I drew near and saw her poor little body so emaciated that one could count every bone and every nerve." She made her last testament to her friends and disciples and called them in one by one to discuss their future. On 21 April she had a paralytic stroke, and eight days later she died, still gently talking to her Saviour. She was thirty-three years old.

Raymond of Capua became general of the Dominican Order in that same year. Catherine was canonized in 1461 and declared a Doctor of the Church in 1970. There are portraits of her by Veronese and Fra Bartolomeo in the Pitti Gallery in Florence, and in most Dominican churches. Her usual attribute is a lily, though she is also found holding a heart and a book and wearing a crown of thorns. Her house in the Street of the Dyers may still be seen in Siena, and there is an early portrait in the Pammatone Hospital.

CATHERINE OF GENOA
(1447-1510)

The earliest known portrait of Catherine of Genoa, by Tommasina Fieschi, 1510.

FOR MUCH of her adult life, Caterinetta Fieschi, born a century later than Catherine of Siena, into a very wealthy family with papal connections, had very little contact with the institutional Church. She was not a member of a religious Order, or even a tertiary. She was a married woman, caught in an unhappy, childless marriage—and women of her time who did not please their husbands and produce children usually bore all the blame for both failures. For many years she had no spiritual director and did not go to Confession. She never sought plenary indulgences for herself, nor did she ask other people to pray for her, nor invoke the saints. She did not practise popular and obvious means of devotion, such as the use of the rosary or the scapular, but her contemplative life was intense and interior, expressed outwardly in hard physical work and poverty. Her writings are of such a quality that other spiritual leaders such as St Francis de Sales, Cardinal Bellarmine, *Barbe Acarie and Cardinal Manning learned from them and used her teachings. Cardinal Newman's great poem *The Dream of Gerontius* (1865), expressing the soul's journey to God, is based on her sayings on the afterlife; and Baron Friedrich von Hügel used her life and work as the focus for his monumental work on *The Mystical Element in Religion* (1908).

Catherine was a member of the great Guelph family of the Fieschi, then at the height of its power, owning land in Liguria, Piedmont, and Lombardy and as far south as Naples. Her father was descended from Robert, brother of Pope Innocent IV, and there were at least two cardinals in the family in Catherine's day. She was born in Genoa, probably in the autumn of 1447, the last of five children, and her baptismal name, Caterinetta, is a diminutive that suggests she was the little one, to be loved and protected. Her elder sister Limbania became an Augustinian nun. Catherine is said to have "received the gift of prayer" at the age of twelve, and soon after that she asked her confessor, who was the chaplain of the Augustinian convent, if she too could enter the Order. He told her that she was too young. In 1461 her father died, and the protected child became a pawn in a complicated series of negotiations between the feuding Guelphs and Ghibellines. She was married against her will in 1463, at the age of sixteen, to Giuliano Adorno, a Ghibelline. He came from an equally distinguished family: there were six Doges of Venice in the line, including Giuliano's own grandfather; but he had a reputation as a weak and wayward character.

The marriage ceremony in the cathedral at Genoa, conducted by Cardinal Napoleoni Fieschi, was a splendid affair, but the marriage seems to have been doomed from the start. There were no children, and Catherine passed ten years of her life in loneliness and despair. Giuliano was seldom at home. He was repeatedly unfaithful and spent money wildly, dissipating his patrimony. Catherine's misery lasted until early in 1473. On 20 March, while she was praying in distress, she asked that God would make her stay "three months sick in bed." The prayer was not answered. Two days later she went to consult the chaplain to the Augustinian Cannonesses, on her sister's advice. When she knelt before him she was suddenly uplifted and overwhelmed with the love of God. Soon after that she had a vision of the Passion. She was clear that it happened "in the spirit," not through physical sight. She saw Christ carrying his cross and dripping with blood, which ran in rivulets along the floor.

About the same time Giuliano's affairs reached crisis point, though we are not told what form the crisis took. He seems to have been ill and to have lost much of his inheritance. Catherine cared for him, and with help and support from her he turned to religion and a life of service. He agreed to live with Catherine in continence and eventually became a Franciscan tertiary. The *palazzo* in Genoa was let and their large country mansion sold. They went together to live in two bleak rooms for a time and then moved into a small house in the grounds of the Pammatone Hospital, where they both worked as nurses.

The Pammatone was a hospital of last resort—many of the 130 patients were lepers, and all were incurable. From 1473 to 1496 husband and wife worked together at their own expense and without pay. Catherine went out into the poor homes of the neighbourhood, undertaking the most unpleasant tasks, cleaning the rooms and washing clothes stiff with dirt and vermin. In 1490 she was placed in charge of the female side of the hospital and became a very competent administrator, responsible for the direction of staff, for patient care, and for financial management. An epidemic in Genoa in 1493 killed four-fifths of the population, and the work must have become a nightmare. Catherine herself was ill for a time, and it was said that she caught the plague by kissing a dying woman, but whether her collapse was due to the plague or to strain and overwork is not entirely clear. Through all this time her own intense spiritual life grew and developed. Her one link with the Church was her daily Mass, which was a lifeline. She often walked to a distant church where she would not be noticed, to avoid drawing attention to her practice. She said later that she had a certain envy of priests, who could receive the Sacrament "as many days as they would without anyone wondering on it." She wore a hair shirt and never ate meat or fruit. Her fasts were prodigious. It was said that she ate hardly at all in Lent and Advent. Her body would not receive the food, though she made light of the matter and claimed no spiritual merit from fasting. Sometimes people would find her stretched out on the floor in prayer, apparently insensible. She went through great pain and violent emotions, in which it seemed to her that a fire of love consumed her body.

Giuliano became ill in 1496 and died in 1497. The director of the men's side of the hospital was Fr Cattaneo Marabotto, a secular priest and member of a noble family. Catherine turned to him and expressed her terrible loneliness. He was a good priest, gentle and understanding. She told him that she had been "guided and taught interiorly by her tender Love alone, without the means of any (human) creature, either religious or secular" through the long years she had worked at the Pammatone. Then she made her confession, which he said was as blameless as that of a young and blushing boy; and he became her spiritual director for the last eleven years of her life.

A group of noble Genovese, both men and women, gathered round to become Catherine's disciples. Among them were Fr Marabotto and Ettore Vernazza, a wealthy notary who became her "spiritual son." Catherine was ill for some years before her death in 1510, and it may have been during this period that she dictated her *Vita*, the *Purgatorio* (originally a chapter in the *Vita*), and the *Spiritual Dialogue*.

A major difficulty in assessing Catherine's writings is that she did not actually write down any of them herself. Baron von Hügel made an intensive search for anything written in Catherine's own handwriting, as a clue to her character, but could find nothing. Even the records of the Pammatone, which she must have kept, had been destroyed in a fire. Fr Marabotto and Ettore Vernazza were her main scribes; devoted though they were, they interspersed her dictation with their own comments and interpretations. They often seem to have made a brilliant and original series of ideas appear positively mediocre, and the organization of the works leaves much to be desired—von Hügel calls it "curiously infelicitous." As a result scholars are presented with many problems in trying to disentangle Catherine's ideas from the well-meaning efforts of her uninspired secretaries.

The *Dialogue*, written in the form of a debate between two people who are travelling round the world, expresses her theology most clearly. She explores the conflicts arising between the soul, which is given the freedom to choose good or evil; the body, drawn to evil by its appetites; the pressures of a society longing for what is forbidden; self-love, putting the self before God; and the life of the spirit, fortified by reason, illuminated by faith and strengthened by divine grace. God is Wisdom, Justice, infinite Charity, and Omnipotence. Human beings are born for blessedness in God's kingdom, but she stresses the transcendence of God rather than the immanence. God is the Absolute—not a father or a friend and certainly not a spiritual bridegroom. She is overwhelmed with a sense of evil in the world, of the great distance between sinful human beings and their Creator.

In the *Purgatorio* Catherine expresses her belief that there is continuity between this life and the next: human beings can begin to expurgate their sins on earth, and after death they will contemplate them only once before turning to God and joyfully undergoing whatever pains are necessary to bring them to salvation. Despite the solemnity of her eschatological work, there is joy in Catherine's vision of the continuity between this world and the next and in her reverence for all the works of the Creator. She had the sympathy with the natural world that is often found among the saints and is a mark of the followers of St Francis of Assisi. It was said of her that "if an animal were killed or a tree cut down, she could hardly bear to see them lose that being which God had given them."

Commentators have devoted much effort to finding the sources of Catherine's spirituality, which are generally thought to have been of three kinds. First, she often alludes to the New Testament, usually to the Gospel of St John and St Paul's Epistles, seldom to the synoptic Gospels, but there is little in the way of direct quotation. It is probable she is making reference to what she has heard in church or from the clergy rather than working from first-hand study of the Bible. Second, her ideas are very similar to those of Pseudo-Dionysius, whose thought had a profound influence on medieval theology. It combined Christianity with Neoplatonism and was much concerned with the subject of the soul's journey to God, one of Catherine's main themes. Catherine's cousin Tommasa, who was a nun and probably the Tommasina who painted her portrait on page 22, wrote a devotional treatise on Pseudo-Dionysius. A first printed edition of his works was published in Florence in 1492, so Catherine would have been familiar with the thought of this philosopher whose ideas so well matched her own. Third, she was well acquainted with the *Laudi*, or popular spiritual songs, of Jacopo Benedetti, better known as Jacopone da Todi. Jacopo, a prosperous Umbrian merchant of more than a century earlier, became half-crazed by the tragic early death of his young wife. He spent years in bizarre forms of penitence for his sins before he was finally accepted by the Friars Minor. Later, as a result of his criticisms of the papacy, he suffered severely in prison, experiencing great spiritual darkness before reaching a new understanding of the love of God. There are no less than twenty references in Catherine's works to Jacopone's *Laudi*.

When Catherine died, no books or manuscripts were found in her room. It seems that she learned not from books but from other people, re-working the ideas they discussed in her own spiritual experience. It is this ability that gives her work, poorly as it is presented, a freshness and immediacy that has appealed to later generations.

Catherine's works were placed on the Index in 1523, and for a time the faithful were forbidden to study them. Whether this was because of her unusual life or because they were written in the vulgar tongue and not in Latin is not clear. Even when the quality of her writings was acknowledged, her cause was very critically examined during the lengthy canonization procedure begun in 1630. Particular difficulties were her lack of spiritual direction, her failure to come to regular Confession for many years, and her failure to seek the intercession of the saints or the Blessed Virgin. She had not sought the company of eminent churchmen, or the approbation of the church authorities, though her family connections would have made this easy enough. She had made no outward show of faith. It was as if she had avoided the clergy and the ministrations of the Church. The fact that she had exerted a good influence on Giuliano and saved a very precarious marriage would hardly have counted in her favour: women were expected to follow their husbands, not to take the lead.

The Congregation of Rites was careful to make no judgment on the facts of Catherine's unorthodox life. It was finally concluded that her writings alone were sufficient cause for sanctification, and she was canonized in 1737. Baron Friedrich von Hügel has given Catherine a reputation as one of the great Christian mystics, but he bases his analysis on his own theories about the nature of mysticism rather than on the facts of her life. He admits that she had only one vision, and that "in the spirit." She made it plain that she did not see the bleeding Christ with her bodily eyes. Despite his great respect for her spiritual experience he stresses what he regards as her "neurasthenic" symptoms. "Neurasthenia" was a very popular explanation for odd female behaviour at the beginning of the twentieth century, but the term has long since fallen into disuse among psychiatrists. In an extensive consideration of her long final illness he classifies her sufferings as "psycho-physical phenomena" because the Genoese doctors of her day could not pinpoint a physical cause. The descriptions in the *Vita* of great heat, great cold, inability to digest food, frequent vomiting, and acute bodily pain might well find a medical diagnosis today.

Von Hügel shows very little interest in Catherine's relationship with Giuliano, concluding that she had no instinct for physical love and that she was lacking in "innocent and normal sensuality." Since she was forced into marriage with a promiscuous man at the age of sixteen, her lack of response seems understandable enough. He also criticizes her on the grounds that she did not love children. There were no children of the marriage, and her many years of compassionate work for lepers and old people with incurable conditions may have been a way of sublimating her motherly instincts. Her work was no less commendable for that. When von Hügel commends her for her "staunch *virility*" (he lived in London and was writing in English), his own restricted concepts of appropriate feminine behaviour become plain. Catherine simply did not fit the stereotypes of his world any more than she fitted those of the Church in her own day.

In 1979 Fr Benedict J. Groeschel, a Capuchin friar with qualifications in psychology and pastoral counselling, wrote an introduction to Catherine's writings, pointing out that von Hügel, while he used the best psychiatric theory of his day, was "not aware of the insights of psychodynamic theory," which were then not widely known. Fr Groeschel considers whether Catherine would now be classified as psychotic, possibly schizophrenic; whether she suffered from *anorexia nervosa*; whether she was in a state of denial. He comes to the conclusion that the consistency and integrity of her work, her highly organized and practical nature, do not suggest a pathological state. They indicate a healthy personality adjusting to great stress. Catherine was "exceptional, but not eccentric."

27

Catherine's life still presents us with a puzzle. What led a noblewoman from one of the proudest families in northern Italy to lead a life of such material poverty—not in a religious Order, but unsupported? The Franciscans cared for Giuliano but not for her. Why did she avoid the ministrations of the Church, apart from her daily Communion, for so long? How could she have reached the heights of contemplation in a life so filled with the day-to-day cares of administration and without the usual apparatus of scholarship? As so often the case in accounts of the lives of the saints, we are given very little in the way of hard facts about her human relationships and her day-to-day life; but the *Vita* does provide some clues which suggest a tentative explanation.

There were two periods of major change in Catherine's spiritual life: the first occurred in March 1473, when she had her spiritual illumination, and the second was at the time of Giuliano's illness and death in 1496-7. Von Hügel calls the first of these occasions her "conversion," but she was already a devout young woman who had wanted to enter a religious Order, so the term seems unsuitable. The prayer that she might "stay three months sick in bed" suggests that she needed to escape from a human situation that she found intolerable. She very much wanted to make her Confession but felt unable to do so. Two days later, on her sister Limbania's suggestion, she went to see the Augustinian chaplain, again with the intention of making her Confession; but "at the moment that she was on her knees," before she could begin, her heart filled with love, and she thought, "No more world! No more sins." She was not able to make her Confession on this occasion either. Soon after that she had the vision of the bleeding Christ carrying his cross, and—as far as can be ascertained—she did not make a Confession again until after Giuliano's death, twenty-three years later.

"About the same time" as she prayed for an illness that would keep her in bed for three months, Giuliano came to the point of crisis. The timing is inexact, and it is unclear which came first. The only explanation that von Hügel suggests for a crisis in his life is that he was near to bankruptcy, but since he and Catherine both came of very wealthy families and they went to the Pammatone with the comparatively large income of £1,200 a year (which they spent on others, not on themselves), that does not seem to be the whole story. Something sufficiently serious had happened to lead them both to a drastic change in their way of life. It seems likely that Catherine's spiritual experiences were a result of Giuliano's problems rather than occurring independently.

One suggestion is that she discovered the existence of his natural daughter Thobia at this time. Giuliano named the child after his own mother, which suggests that she was the result not of a casual infidelity but of a serious relationship of considerable significance for him. When he died he left Catherine to administer his estate, which included bequests both to Thobia and Thobia's mother, and she carried out his wishes. By then Thobia was in her twenties. Her mother, who is not named, is thought to have become a Franciscan tertiary, as Giuliano himself did.

It is difficult to see why the discovery of Thobia's birth should have had such a marked and lasting effect on Catherine. One account says that Giuliano already had five illegitimate children when he and Catherine were married, and he was frequently unfaithful after the marriage took place. If his relationship with Thobia's mother was a deep and significant one (as the bequests so many years later indicate), why did Catherine, his wronged wife, find it impossible to go to Confession? If she felt hurt or angry, Confession would have helped her to deal with her destructive emotions.

Another suggestion put forward by Von Hügel is that Catherine had a secret sin that she was afraid to confess; but this does not explain a series of well-established events. When Giuliano's health broke down in 1496 Catherine completely changed her way of life. She resigned her hospital post to look after her husband, and she ended her lengthy fasts and her long periods of ecstatic prayer. Giuliano was "languishing" and "infirm in body" for over a year. He made a good death, which greatly affected Catherine. "About the time" of his death—again there is no precision in the timing—she at last felt able to go back to Confession, telling Fr Marabotto, "Father, I know not where I am, either as to my soul or my body . . . I should like to confess, but I cannot perceive any offence committed by me." Fr Marabotto, who knew her well, thought that she had little or nothing to confess. Later she said, "I have persevered for *twenty-five years* in the spiritual way without the aid of any creature"—that is, any other human being. This suggests that her anguish of mind began before March 1473. Her knowledge of Giuliano's crisis came before her inability to make a Confession and the spiritual experiences that gave her an alternative source of courage. The sense of being filled with love and the vision of the bleeding Christ made it possible for her to carry her own cross—and Giuliano's—but with his death she was free of it. She had no secret sin to confess.

The logical conclusion is that it was not her sin, but Giuliano's, and that it may have been something with far wider repercussions in the society in which they lived than an extra-marital affair. Guelph and Ghibelline were still enemies, and in that time of murderous feuds almost any crime was possible. Back-street assassinations were common, and violence flared up daily. If Giuliano was involved in some Ghibelline action against her own family, the Guelphs, she could not possibly speak of it, for man and wife were one flesh in the eyes of the Church. So she kept the Church at arm's length. Though she was married against her will, she took her husband's sins on herself and joined him in his search for redemption, but she guarded her marital privacy. For the rest of her life the burning desire to make theological sense of what had happened occupied her mind and her heart.

If this was the case, it helps to explain Catherine's abiding sense of the evil in the world and her preoccupation with Purgatory, which she insists can begin in this life. She learned from many sources and made a unique and valuable synthesis of what she came to understand. It is difficult to see how these major themes in her writings could have come from her own personal life, which Fr Marabotto found to be as innocent as that of a child when she finally made her Confession, but they could very well have come from knowledge of the internecine feuds that split late-fourteenth-century Genoa. Only a very high view of marriage gave her the spiritual power to make the sacrifice of identifying with her husband's long and costly expiation.

EDITH STEIN (TERESA BENEDICTA OF THE CROSS)

(1891-1942)

Edith Stein as Sister Teresa Benedicta of the Cross, shortly after she joined the Carmelites in 1933.

DR EDITH STEIN was a distinguished German Jewish philosopher who pursued a singular intellectual and spiritual journey, with St Thomas Aquinas and St John of the Cross as her guides. It led her through school teaching to university research, into Carmel, where her academic reputation counted for nothing, and in the end to the gas-chambers of Auschwitz.

She came from an Orthodox Jewish family. Her mother, left a widow when Edith, the youngest child, was two, took on the tasks of reorganizing the family timber business and bringing up six children with determination and efficiency. When Edith went to school she proved to be a brilliant pupil. Despite her intelligence and application she was never able to come first in class, though she was a consistent second. In later life she attributed this to her headmaster's anti-Semitic prejudice.

From the ages of thirteen to twenty-one she was an atheist: though she continued to accompany her mother to the synagogue she took no part in worship. Judaism had become meaningless to her. At university she was not really fired by her early studies at the University of Breslau, where the professor wanted her to pursue experimental psychology. This was not at all to her taste; but when she moved to Göttingen she was to find her way to Catholicism through the agency of two men, her philosophy professor, Edmund Husserl, and Dr Max Scheler. Husserl was the author of *Logical Investigation*, a work that greatly attracted Edith because of its honesty and its search for truth. Ever since Kant, German philosophers had taught that human beings could not know the nature of ultimate reality, only the "phenomena" of experience. Husserl went back to the medieval schoolmen, asserting that objective truth exists and that we can know the objective world around us. Though he was not a Catholic, so many of his students became Catholics that he joked that he ought to be canonized. "Without knowing it," Edith wrote, "I had grown up within the barriers of rationalistic prejudices, which now broke down so that the world of faith suddenly rose before my eyes."

Edith was not yet a Catholic, but study at Göttingen opened a new intellectual world to her. She began to understand for the first time that religious experience is part of the human experience to be studied and that it has its own validity. She became Professor Husserl's assistant; but unfortunately she was to find that this post left her little time for her own work. In the conventions of the German university system, the post simply meant working for the professor, not following her own studies. She taught preliminary classes for him, found the work boring and elementary, and called the students "the philosophical kindergarten." She organized the professor's notes—a difficult task, since he committed all his thoughts to odd pieces of paper and frequently discarded the effects of her patient work. She put up with the frequent intrusions of Frau Husserl, who, jealous of her husband's interest in his assistant's intellectual powers, would frequently interrupt conversations, bringing them down to a pedestrian level. Edith succeeded in completing her doctorate *summa cum laude*, but much of the work she undertook during this period went unacknowledged, and the financial rewards were meagre.

Early in 1919 she left to seek academic work on her own terms. The parting was an amicable one: Husserl praised her "far-reaching as well as profound philosophical knowledge" and her "capacity for independent historical research." He added, "If the academic career should be made available for ladies, I could most warmly recommend her in the very first place for admission."

But the academic career was not available for ladies. In the shattered conditions of post-war Germany there were few university posts available for men either. Edith was unable to secure a lectureship, and the next three years were a time of rethinking and upheaval for her as well as for her country. In the early days of the Weimar Republic she joined the Social Democratic party, avoiding the political extremes of both right-wing nationalism and near-Communism. She began to write and speak publicly on mildly feminist topics, and she became a Christian.

It was a time of great mental and emotional exhaustion, and afterwards she was reluctant to speak of it, but we do know that in the summer of 1921, while staying with Lutheran friends, she picked up the autobiography of St Teresa of Avila. Edith's cool, cerebral approach to faith could not have been more remote from Teresa's vivacious enthusiasms, but she read it and said, "This is the Truth." With characteristic clarity of purpose she wasted no time. On the following morning she went out to buy a catechism and a missal, went to the parish priest, and asked to be baptized.

Her baptism took place on New Year's Day 1922. She had kept up a vigil through from the previous night, and she made her profession of faith in Latin. On 2 February she was confirmed, and then she faced the trauma of telling her mother. She had expected her to be angry, but the older woman covered her face with her hands and wept. For an Orthodox Jew, acceptance of Christianity was a stark betrayal of family and tradition. Edith went regularly with her mother to the synagogue and joined in the psalms and the prayers as far as she could, but their mutual incomprehension was painful to both of them. Many years later, when her mother died of cancer, well-meaning friends told Edith that they were sure the old lady had become a Catholic before her death. Edith retorted, "My mother has remained true to her faith to the last ... I am confident that she has found a very gracious Judge and is now my most faithful helper, so that I, too, may reach my goal."

After her reception into the Catholic Church she wanted to become a Carmelite, but her spiritual director, Canon Schwind, counselled against it, thinking that her main value to the Church was as an academic writer and public speaker. Since she could not obtain an academic post, he found her a post as a teacher in a girls' school in Speyer, run by the Third Order Dominican Sisters. She had a small, bare room of her own, taught German language and literature to the upper forms, and had time to study Catholic philosophy at weekends and in vacations.

Edith was not a great success as a school teacher. The girls found the Fraülein Doktor distinctly forbidding. She taught standing motionless, without gestures, speaking in a low monotone, and she made scathing remarks about their work. An inspector of schools, watching Edith at work, concluded, "She knows much, but she cannot teach." This comment upset her considerably. She was used to unqualified admiration and saw no lack in her own performance. At this stage of her life she was unapproachable, a narrow and rigid personality. She spent long hours at prayer in the school chapel, always kneeling upright and motionless, and she said that she could not understand why others found long periods of prayer tiring. A Jesuit theologian, Fr Przywara, encouraged her to translate Cardinal Newman's *Letters and Journals* into German. She did it by being "severely objective . . . even aiming at preserving the rhythm of the sentences and the order of the words." Since German sentence rhythm and word order are quite different from those of English, the result was precise, but almost unreadable. She translated Newman's *Idea of a University* in the same mechanical way.

Then Fr Przywara directed her to translating Thomist texts, telling her not to bother with commentaries, but to go straight to the mind of St Thomas Aquinas himself. This was very good advice. Her own clear and logical mind met another of first-class calibre and with a powerful grasp of Christian orthodoxy. She began to translate the *Quaestiones disputatae de Veritate*, for which there was no German translation. In *Wahrheit der Dinge* (The Truth of Things) she describes the meeting of the discourse of contemporary German philosophy with that of the medieval schoolmen. For modern philosophers, the bases of their study are the natural world and the power of reason; but this framework unduly limits their field of operation. For the medieval schoolmen, following Aristotle, both the natural world and the power of reason came from the First Principle, the Creator. Wisdom came not only from logic but also from religious experience: it could be validated by an appeal to the scriptures or the works of the early Fathers of the Church.

Edith was venturing into a new field, and she made some mistakes. Thomist scholars objected to some of her translations, but she had achieved a powerful, if flawed, work of synthesis. From 1928 she began to lecture on Thomist thought and on the position of women in modern society. She still wanted to enter Carmel, but her new director, Abbot Walzer of the Benedictine abbey of Beuron, thought her work in the world too important. She applied for university posts but was unsuccessful at both Freiburg and Breslau. This may have been due to prejudice against women or to rapidly-mounting anti-Semitism; but she probably did not interview very well. She was still very stiff and judgmental in her contacts with others. She criticized other women for vanity, curiosity, gossip, indiscretion, and frittering away energy; and when she went to Vienna for the first time to give a lecture she ignored the Danube, the cathedral, the art galleries, the palaces, the cafés, and the Vienna Woods entirely until the last day, when her host's wife insisted on a quick tour of the city. Eventually, in 1932, she was given a post in the Educational Institute at Münster—not as prestigious a post as her intellectual capacity warranted, but more congenial to her than teaching schoolgirls.

From this basis Edith began to express her ideas on the position of women in the Church. There was always an acute contrast between her modest and reserved manner and the trenchancy of her discourse. She asked that the Church should study the problems of educating women and not simply ignore them. She contested the Encyclical on Marriage of Pope Pius XI, which stated that a woman's primary task was to be a wife and mother. She brushed aside St Paul's views on women keeping silent in churches, arguing that this might be local regulation, but it was not divine law; she contested statements in canon law which precluded women from taking any part in the sacred offices of the Church, pointing out that there were deaconesses in the early Church, and that teaching, nursing, and social work were all professions that had had their origin in Church activities; and, incidentally, she came into open opposition with the Nazi view of women as the breeders of Aryan heroes.

By this time Hitler was in power, and his brownshirts were marching in the streets of German cities. Slogans were posted over shopfronts, and Jews were beginning to be driven out. Even Edith's students were affected by anti-Semitism, and she knew that she would soon be forced to give up her post. On her way to Beuron to visit Abbot Walzer she stopped at Cologne and prayed for guidance:

> I spoke to Our Lord and told Him that it was His Cross that was being laid on the Jewish people. Most of them did not know that, but those who did ought to embrace it willingly in the name of all. This I desired to do. He should only show me in what way. When the devotions were finished, I had the interior certainty that my prayer had been answered. But in what manner I was to bear the Cross, this I did not yet know.

She then went to a church that was celebrating its patronal feast with thirteen hours of prayer. When she came out, she knew it was time to go to Carmel.

She was forty-two years old, Jewish, and had no dowry. Even her academic reputation did not recommend her, as it might have done if she had gone to the Dominicans or the Benedictines. She sent the Carmelites the only dowry she had, her considerable library of books, carefully catalogued and annotated. She arrived to find that "when they were unpacked, everything was gaily muddled up." The nuns had no great interest in books. One of the older nuns was heard to express the hope that the new postulant would be good at sewing.

The provost of Münster Cathedral had written on her behalf, "She will be an example to all in deep piety and zeal of prayer, a joy for the community . . . and she will walk among you in silence like a ray from God." But the nuns were more interested in her capacity to do the work that was expected of any other postulant. She was slow at housework and dishwashing: any country girl could do better than this middle-aged scholar. All her intellectual gifts counted for nothing. But this was what she wanted. Edith had embraced the way of the Cross: complete abandonment to the will of God. She was reading St John of the Cross, and echoed his *Nada, nada, nada*. Nothing else was necessary to her. She had no visions, no revelations. She was "led by the safe road of dark faith" with a childlike acceptance quite unlike her previous tough, searching intellectual inquiry.

It was at this time that she learned to laugh. She was no longer the Fräulein Doktor but a simple beginner in the religious life. Her former harsh austerities gave way to a peaceful obedience. Abbot Walzer asked her bluntly whether she could be at home in this community of simple women. She replied that she felt completely at home. On the Sunday of the Good Shepherd, 1934, the Fräulein Doktor ceased to exist, and she became Sister Teresa Benedicta of the Cross.

She might have disappeared entirely from public view in the peaceful life of her convent, but the provincial of her Order directed her back to scholarship. She wrote one or two minor pieces before getting back into her stride. Before long she wrote *The Prayer of the Church*, in which she treated Christianity as the fulfilment of the Jewish Messianic hope and reminded her readers that "Christ prayed as a believing Jew." She insisted that mysticism was the life-blood of the Church: "If it breaks through the traditional forms, it does do because the spirit that blows where it listeth is living in it." A sombre piece on *The Mystery of Christmas* (written at the time when the Nazis were trying to replace Christmas with the pagan *Julfest*) told her readers that there was no peace possible with the children of darkness. The white altar frontals of Christmas, she reminded them, were almost immediately replaced by the red of martyrdom and the purple of sorrow. "The mystery of the Incarnation and the mystery of iniquity are closely related."

When her mother died she stayed close to St John of the Cross. She writes of the dark night of the soul, "when the Divine light no longer shines and the voice of the Lord no longer speaks;" but she knew that she was still part of the Mystical Body of the Church. She could still find a means of grace through the Eucharist. It was in these circumstances that she wrote her great work, *Endliches und Ewiges Sein* (Finite and Eternal Being). In this she rejected the Thomist distinction between theology and philosophy, arguing that there was no true philosophy without revelation: revelation was one of the sources of knowledge with which philosophy had to deal. She explored the linguistic roots of German words in order to elicit their meanings—and German is probably the only language in which such a powerful work could be expressed. The book was refused by one publisher after another because the author was Jewish. Eventually she had an offer of publication from a small publishing firm in Breslau, which had handled some of her earlier work, and she spent much time in the laborious correction of proofs.

Sister Teresa Benedicta made her profession on Easter Day 1935 and found it a deeply spiritual experience. She was already aware that the Nazis would not leave her in peace, and her superior reported that "she said it was clear to her that she was going to suffer for her people, that she was meant to bring many home." She made her final vows in 1937. Jewish shops and homes were being plundered, Jews were being murdered and synagogues burned down. Even the convent walls could not protect a Jewish Carmelite. She would have liked to go to Israel, but her superiors thought that she should finish her book; at the end of 1937 she was sent to a convent at Echt in the Netherlands for her protection. It was not entirely a happy move. She continued correcting proofs—only to have the manuscript returned to her in 1938 because by that time even the firm in Breslau could not publish a work by a Jewish author. It was not published until some years after her death. The Dutch nuns were even less aware of her academic reputation than the German nuns. She found there were tiresome local restrictions particular to this convent but treated as part of the Carmelite way of life, and she had to speak Dutch, which is not a precise language for a philosopher.

She accepted all this as part of the burden she must bear. In 1939 the Nazi forces invaded the Netherlands, and before long the German bombers were roaring overhead on their way to England. In the Carmelite convent at Echt, Teresa Benedicta worked on Pseudo-Dionysius and St John of the Cross. There were plans to transfer her from Echt to a convent at Le Paquier in Switzerland. She had already been interviewed once by the Gestapo and had greeted them defiantly with "Praise be to Jesus Christ!" instead of the required "Heil Hitler!" She refused to go into hiding, because there would have been repercussions on her convent. "There are negotiations going on with Le Paquier," she wrote, "but I am so deep in our Father John of the Cross that nothing else matters to me."

The *Kreuzeswissenschaft, or Knowledge of the Cross*, was to be her final work. She never lived to revise it, and it was evidently written under great difficulty, when she lacked access to libraries and discussion with theologians; but in it, without any academic props, she follows St John into the mystery of the Cross, knowing that her own Calvary is near. She writes:

The darkness which leads to God is faith. It is the only means leading to union, for it presents God to us as he is, as the infinite Triune One. Faith resembles God in that it blinds human reason and appears to it as darkness.

... This darkness hides the light of truth which will only shine forth unveiled when faith and life will end together. ... God communicates himself to the spirit rather than to the senses; the soul is more secure, and makes greater progress in the former, whereas experiences communicated to the senses are normally very dangerous. For in that case, the senses would presume to judge spiritual things, whereas they are as ignorant of these as a donkey is of reason.

She goes instinctively to the poems rather than to the prose works, as St John himself recommended, asking, "How can it be proved that John actually achieved himself the perfect spiritual detachment he demanded of others? For the inner life of this silent saint seems closed to us ... the purest impression of his personality is probably to be gained from his poems. Here he speaks from his heart, and in some of them with unearthly purity." She follows him through to his death in obscurity and disgrace at Úbeda. There the manuscript breaks off.

On 11 July 1942 all the Christian communions in the Netherlands protested to the German authorities about the persecution of the Jews. The Archbishop of Utrecht followed this protest with a pastoral letter. Three weeks later, on 2 August, all non-Aryan Catholics and other Christians were arrested in reprisal. The Gestapo went to the convent and forced Teresa Benedicta to leave in a police van. In the next week she was seen in Westerbork concentration camp by a businessman who subsequently went free. He said she "walked about among the women, comforting, helping, soothing like an angel." A former student saw her standing at the window of a train in Schifferstadt station. Teresa Benedicta said, "Give my love to the Sisters at St Magdalena. I am travelling eastwards." She died in Auschwitz on 9 August.

Her beatification by Pope John Paul II took place at Cologne on 1 May 1987, and her canonization in Rome on 12 October 1998. There were protests from Jewish groups that she had died not because she was a Catholic, but because she was Jewish; it seems clear that if she had remained the Jewish philosopher Dr Edith Stein, she would have been free to leave Europe, as many other Jewish academics did, and seek refuge in the United States. It was because she was a Carmelite nun, Sister Teresa Benedicta, that she was under obedience and remained in Europe. Her writings testify to the intensity of a Christian sacrifice made for people of all faiths.

2

MARTYRS

IN POPULAR LEGEND women martyrs are almost always young, noble, beautiful, and virginal. The images are still with us, on stained-glass windows, in Books of Hours, and on ecclesiastical banners. They never age and never change. The names of the virgin martyrs of the Roman persecutions read like a roll of honour: Agnes, Lucy, Agatha, Anastasia, Catherine, Cecilia, Faith, Irene, Scholastica, Barbara, Christina, Pudentiana, Victoria, Anatolia, and many more. Only Agnes, Lucy, Agatha, and Cecilia now remain in the revised Universal Roman Calendar. The cults of the rest have been quietly relegated to history because the evidence is unreliable. If there is a true story behind the legend of these virgin martyrs, it has been obliterated by the telling and re-telling of increasingly fanciful accounts.

Basically, the story is that of a young Christian girl who refuses to marry or to sacrifice to the Roman gods. She is insulted, and attempts are made to violate her. When these fail she is subjected to horrifying tortures (which became more gruesome as the story was repeated) before dying for her faith. The tradition that some of these girls were placed in brothels is so persistent that it must have represented a brutal but deeply-felt reaction to their stand from Roman men. This female defiance, as they saw it, struck at the basis of the existing order, for the whole of Roman society was built on *patria potestas*—the power of the head male of the family over his household. He had the power of life and death over his wife, children, servants, and slaves. He could accept or reject a child at birth, divorce his wife and keep the children of the marriage, give his daughters in marriage to whom he pleased, and name a male guardian for his wife and children after his own death. Women and children did not have the status of citizens. Male adultery was taken for granted, while female adultery was punishable by death. Christianity offered women a new and enhanced status, giving them the right to choose virginity rather than marriage. The result was a massive culture-clash that was to continue for centuries, in which the traditional power of the father was countered by young girls supported and encouraged by the Church.

Perhaps the popular stories about these girls satisfied the instincts now served by the tabloid or "yellow" press and what are somewhat misleadingly called "adult" films, but with the fascination with pornography and sadism there is often an odd sort of respect and protectiveness. The girls are sent to brothels, but they are not violated. Lucy cannot be moved from the spot where she stands, even by a thousand men and teams of oxen. Irene of Salonika is shot with a bow and arrow by a guard who pities her plight. Agnes, stripped of her clothes, finds an angel (or several angels) standing by with a tunic to cover her. By the time Aldhelm, abbot of Malmesbury, wrote his *De Virginitate* in the eighth century (unfortunately on some very dubious evidence) the virgin martyrs were already celebrated throughout Europe. Their legends were preserved, to be reproduced in Archbishop Jacobus de Voragine's *Golden Legend* in the fourteenth century and to take their place in the *Acta Sanctorum* in the seventeenth. Only the remorseless historical scholarship of the Society of Bollandists, Jesuits devoted to separating fact from fiction, has enabled us to come closer to the truth. Fr Delehaye, the most celebrated of these scholars, complains that his predecessors in studying the Lives of the saints suffered from "a certain sluggishness of mind." Confronted, for example, with the legend of St Ursula, who was said to have sailed about the North Sea with eleven thousand virgins in the reign of Pope Cyriacus before finally landing at Hamburg, they did not think about the logistics of transporting this unlikely passenger load, nor did they check whether there was a Pope Cyriacus. He is not to be found on the papal rolls.

Other less celebrated virgin martyrs of the early Christian period have better attested Acts than many of the celebrated ones. Blandina, a young slave girl, was one of the Martyrs of Lyons in the year 177. Her martyrdom is vouched for in a letter written by eyewitnesses, and reproduced in the *Ecclesiastical History* of Eusebius. She was exposed to the beasts in the amphitheatre and could only say repeatedly, "I am a Christian, and nothing vile is done among us." Potomiaena died in a persecution in Alexandria in 202 with such patience and courage that her executioner was said to be converted and to have suffered a similar fate. Her martyrdom is described in the contemporary *Historia Lausiaca* of Palladius. However, little is known about either Blandina or Potomiaena apart from the fact of their martyrdom, and there is no physical evidence in the shape of tombs, relics, or churches. Religious relics in Lyons were vandalized and destroyed during the French Revolution, when it is said that the skull of Bishop Pothinus, martyred at the same time as Blandina, was kicked through the streets like a football. Early Christian relics in Alexandria have long since disappeared under the attacks of invaders. Consequently, neither of these saints has become the subject of a cult in the West.

Not all the women martyrs of the early Church were young virgins. There were married women martyrs, too. Crispina, who had several young children, defied the proconsul Anulinus at Theveste in North Africa in 304 and conducted a long and courageous defence of her faith. Perpetua and Felicity, a young Roman noblewoman and her slave, died at Carthage in the same persecution. Perpetua was the mother of a young child, whom she was breast-feeding. Felicity was pregnant and was kept alive until the child was born, being executed soon after a painful confinement. These two are mentioned in Eucharistic Prayer I in the revised Order of the Mass.

Little is known about the witness of older women in the classical world; but there is the story of Apollonia, an aged deaconess of Alexandria, who had her teeth knocked out by an angry mob during a riot and who threw herself on the flames of the fire prepared for her execution. Her martyrdom was described in a letter, still extant, from Dionysius, bishop of Alexandria, to Fabius, bishop of Antioch. Mediaeval schoolmen debated whether she was morally justified in committing suicide rather than leaving the mob to cause her death; but popular accounts soon transformed her into a king's daughter, a beautiful girl whose teeth were torn out as a form of torture. Curiously, she became the patron saint of dentists.

Since the Roman persecutions, which ended with Constantine's Edict of Milan in 314, there has been a long and honourable roll of Christian martyrs in many lands. Nearly all of them are men. Europe was Christian, and until the colonial expansion of the nineteenth century very few women travelled to non-Christian countries. The missionaries who set out to convert the German tribes, the Saracens, the Moors, and the people of India, China, and Japan were all men. Women were shut away from such perilous work, but with greater freedom for women came greater physical danger.

Of the early virgin martyrs, **Agnes** is well known, and her story is exceptionally well validated. She died in Rome, probably in the persecutions of Diocletian in 305. By the end of the century she had been cited in the writings of Ambrose and Jerome, Pope Damasus I had written an inscription for her, and the poet Prudentius, on his travels from his native Spain, celebrated her life in verse in the year 400. She is represented in many paintings by great artists, and her tomb, two miles outside Rome, has been a centre of veneration through the centuries. She was only twelve or thirteen (accounts vary), but in Rome in her day that was a marriageable age: she chose virginity and martyrdom.

Margaret Clitherow was an English martyr of the sixteenth century—one of the many women who concealed priests during the reign of Elizabeth I when it was declared treasonable to owe allegiance to the papacy. They were often housewives or housekeepers who gave shelter to priests who came on the English Mission, arranged for Mass to be celebrated in their houses in secret, and in many other ways put their own lives at risk. Margaret Clitherow, the butcher's wife of York, is listed among the Forty Martyrs of England with thirty-seven men and two other women—Anne Line, who was housekeeper to Fr John Gerard's secret house for seminarians, and Margaret Ward, who helped Fr William Watson to escape from prison, smuggling a rope into his cell.

Madeleine Fontaine and three other Sisters of Charity went to the guillotine during the brief but bloody period of the Terror in the French Revolution. Their only offence was that they refused to take the oath to Robespierre's anti-Christian government and were therefore deemed "enemies of the Republic." These Sisters of Arras are venerated with the Sisters of Compiègne, who were also martyred at this time.

Women missionaries began to enter the mission field in the second half of the nineteenth century. By 1900, when **Hermina Grivot** and her Companions were martyred in Taiyuan in northern China in the Boxer Rebellion, they were serving in many countries. The Taiyuan martyrs were killed because they were teaching what was seen as a foreign creed to Chinese children. The cry of "Drive out the foreigners" led to the deaths of many missionaries, who were easy targets, often working in areas far from any protection the European powers could provide. When the Boxers came to Taiyuan bishops, priests, catechists, and nuns, European and Chinese alike, were all killed without discrimination and without mercy.

In Africa, as in India and the Far East, the first missionaries were white; but their aim was always to teach local men and women so that they could take on responsibility and become fully active members of the Church. In the colonial territories of Africa, Africans became catechists and in time priests and nuns. **Anuarite Nengapeta** was a Congolese teaching nun killed by the Simbas, a terrorist group, as a result of an attack on an outlying mission in 1964. She died because she was an African Christian, following what her killers thought were European ways instead of the tribal ways of her ancestors. The attempted rape of this young virgin brings us full circle to the circumstances of Christian virgins in the Roman Empire so many centuries ago. The number of women martyrs may be few, but they show the same courage and conviction as the many men who have died for their faith.

AGNES

(? 292-305)

St Agnes with her lamb.

Detail from Duccio's Maestà, *in the Museo dell'Opera, Siena.*

ST AGNES is probably the best known of the virgin martyrs of the early Church, and certainly the best attested of those who died in Rome. She is thought to have died in the last weeks of the persecutions of Diocletian, which began with an edict in February 303 and lasted less than two years. Her traditional date of death is 21 January, so the year was probably 305. Her parents must have been wealthy, since they erected a marble tomb for her on a burial plot belonging to the family. This stood on the via Nomentana, about two miles outside the Aurelian Wall of the city of Rome. Attempts to identify Agnes as a member of one of the noble Roman families whose names have survived have been unsuccessful, but a Roman noblewoman named Constantina, possibly the daughter of Constantine the Great (emperor 306-37), built a basilica over the tomb. Agnes was evidently venerated not long after her death. The church of St Agnes-Without-the-Walls stands on the same site today. It contains an early alabaster statue of Agnes, and a seventh-century mosaic of her martyrdom.

Agnes is mentioned in the *Depositum Martyrum* of 354. St Ambrose, writing in about the year 377, says in his *De Virginibus* that Agnes "lived a virgin and suffered martyrdom." She was threatened with torture but would not renounce her faith. She was only twelve years old at the time of her death, and she was absolutely fearless. He marvels at her courage, saying that "maidens of that age are unable to bear even the angry looks of parents, and are wont to cry at the pricks of a needle as though they were wounds." Since he was writing for his sister Marcellina, a consecrated virgin, on Agnes' birthday, he may well have been recalling incidents from their own childhood. St Jerome, writing to the virgin Eustochium toward the end of the fourth century, cites Agnes as an outstanding example of virginity and martyrdom. He writes, "The life of Agnes is praised in the literature and speech of all peoples, especially in the churches, she who overcame both her age and the tyrant, and consecrated by martyrdom her claim to chastity." Jerome was secretary to Pope Damasus from 382 to 385, and he would have had a close knowledge of the pope's work in excavating and preserving the tombs of the Roman martyrs and composing inscriptions for them. The inscription Damasus wrote for Agnes is still extant. It mentions her age and records that, though her parents kept close watch over her, she confessed her faith and died for it. This epitaph was lost for centuries and was discovered beneath the floor of her church in 1728, when the flooring was being restored. The architect noticed the ancient lettering and saved the stone from being cut up and used for other purposes.

About the year 400 the celebrated Spanish-Roman poet Prudentius was in Rome and composed his poem to Agnes, now listed as Hymn 14 in his *Peristephanon*. Prudentius found a living oral tradition, which is conveyed in the poem with a certain amount of poetic licence. Agnes, he tells his readers, deliberately challenged the persecutors and, when brought before a magistrate, refused to sacrifice to the Roman gods. She was stripped of her clothes and exposed naked in the Piazza Navona (the earliest mention of the place where the confrontation occurred). The crowd, embarrassed, looked the other way, apart from one young man who stared at her and was struck blind by a flash of fire like a bolt of lightning. Agnes prayed for him, and his sight was restored. Then she went forward to her execution in triumph, singing a hymn to God and to Christ. Here Prudentius puts some magnificent poetry into the mouth of his young martyr: "Eternal sovereign, open to me the gates of heaven; O Christ, call my soul to come . . . it is a virgin soul, sacrificed to the Father."

Prudentius goes on to say that "Her soul, set free, leapt into the air, and was escorted on its dazzling way by angels." She saw the world spread out beneath her, and laughed with joy to see the whole universe and everything that was in it. "Oh happy virgin, new splendour . . . noble dweller in the city of heaven," sings Prudentius; "I will be purified by the glow of thy face . . .

whatever thou deignest to visit, whatever thy foot blesses with its touch, can no longer lack purity."

Agnes is one of the twenty-two virgins in the mosaics of the Procession of Virgins in the church of San Apollinare Nuovo in Ravenna, which date from the first quarter of the sixth century. All the virgins are richly dressed and adorned with pearls, carrying the crowns of their martyrdom. Agnes is fourth in the procession behind the Three Kings and has a lamb at her feet. Unusually, she appears as a fully grown young woman and not a child. Possibly the mosaicist required all the virgins on the wall of the north aisle to be of equal height, like the male martyrs on the south aisle, to make an artistically satisfying frieze. Another explanation is that the mosaics are Byzantine, not in the tradition of Roman art. In the sixth century the Exarch of Ravenna was the representative of the Byzantine emperor in Italy, and the Byzantine legends of Agnes would have been known and accepted there. These legends do not mention her youth but describe her as a Christian teacher who instructed young matrons.

How Agnes died is not clear. Beheading was the traditional form of execution for Roman citizens and their families. Pope Damasus mentions flames, but it seems that she did not actually die by fire. Ambrose says that she "bent her neck" to receive the final blow. This may have been the sword thrust in the throat that was a common means of execution in the fourth century.

From the time of Prudentius the legends began to proliferate. In the early Latin texts by pseudo-Ambrosius (not St Ambrose of Milan) it was said that Agnes had rejected the son of Symphorian, the prefect of Rome, as a suitor. In these early legends all the authority of the imperial power is often attributed to a single well-known figure. It is significant that a girl was given a feminine reason for facing martyrdom, rather than being credited with doing so as a matter of conviction. She was said to have been dragged before the statues of the gods and told to sacrifice. Even when offered the opportunity of becoming a vestal virgin she had refused to do so. The prefect's son tried to rape her and was stricken dead but revived by her prayers. When Jacobus de Voragine wrote the *Golden Legend* in the fourteenth century the story had been further elaborated: the prefect of Rome himself wished to marry her and promised her "diamonds and great riches if she would consent to be his wife." The prefect's son tried to force her, and she replied spiritedly, "Begone, sting of sin, food of crime, poison of the soul, for I am already given to another lover!" When she was taken to a brothel her hair grew at once to cover her, and an angel stood before her with a tunic. The prefect's son became very ill and accused her of witchcraft, but he was saved by her prayers. The crowd, instead of being sympathetic, howled for her death. The two traditions of her death were conflated: it was said that she was led out to die by fire, but that the fire miraculously went out, and the executioner dispatched her with a sword. There is a certain difficulty in believing in miracles that are of such very limited duration.

All that is certain is that Agnes was a very young martyr, that she died bravely for her faith, and that she was buried on the via Nomentana. A gold and enamel cup showing her martyrdom was made for the Duc de Berry, whose *Très Riches Heures*, a celebrated Book of Hours still in print, was commissioned some time before his death in 1416. The cup passed through the Duke of Bedford to King Henry VI and is now in the British Museum. Agnes appears frequently in Renaissance paintings by Duccio, Fra Angelico, Tintoretto, and others, and she was the subject of many rood paintings and stained-glass windows of the medieval period, when the virgin martyrs attracted great popular devotion. There were five ancient church dedications in England. She is often depicted with a lamb in her arms or at her feet. Her heraldic emblem is a white lamb seated on a gold book, on a red field, signifying martyrdom.

On 21 January, her feast-day, a choir in her church on the via Nomentana sings the anthem *Stans a dextris ejus agnus nive candida* (On her right hand a lamb whiter than snow). Two white lambs are offered at the altar rail, and later, when they are sheared, their fleece is laid on the high altar in the basilica of St Peter on the vigil of the feast of SS Peter and Paul (29 June). It is then spun and woven by the nuns of St Cecilia in Trastevere into the *pallia* or collars sent to archbishops "from the body of the Blessed Peter" and worn as a symbol of their office. This ancient custom rests on the association between Agnes and *agnus*, a lamb: both Agnes and the lamb are white and pure. Her name, however, probably derives from the Greek *agneia*, meaning pure, and not from *agnus*.

Agnes' association with other virgin martyrs of the period, such as St Margaret of Antioch, St Faith, and St Barbara, whose acts are now thought to be spurious or of very doubtful authenticity, has led to renewed efforts to validate her martyrdom. In 1605 a silver reliquary containing a body thought to be hers was found under the altar of her church in the via Nomentana, but it was without a head. This does not indicate that she was beheaded: it was common custom for some centuries to separate the head from the body for burial. In 1901 further excavations again uncovered the reliquary, and it was measured. It was four and a half feet long, one and a half feet wide and a foot high: about the right size for a young girl's coffin. Soon after this a French investigator, Fr Jubaru, claimed to have discovered the reliquary of her skull in the treasury of the Sancta Sanctorum of the Lateran Palace. The reliquary was opened with the permission of Pope Leo XIII on 19 April 1903 and found to contain a head. A medical practitioner, Dr Lapponi, examined the teeth and concluded that they were those of a child of about twelve years of age.

Some commentators, unimpressed by the weight of documentary, archaeological, and medical evidence, regard Agnes as an archetype rather than an individual martyr. In this view, she is a symbol and memorial of many virgins who died in the persecutions, rather than a girl with a known history. Such a view does not lessen her significance, nor does it affect the devotion and veneration which her example has attracted through the centuries.

MARGARET CLITHEROW
(? 1553-86)

MARGARET'S father was Thomas Middleton, a leading citizen of York and sheriff of the city in 1564-5. He was a wax chandler and had a vested interest in the continuance of full Catholic ritual because of its use of many candles, but he and his wife Jane conformed to the Elizabethan Settlement, which required them to attend the established Church. Margaret was about eleven years old when her father died. He asked in his will that there should be prayers for his soul, which suggests that he was still a Catholic at heart. Four months later Margaret's mother, in her early fifties, married a young man in his early twenties named Henry May. He was a "foreigner"—not a York man and not even a Yorkshireman. Marriage to this wealthy widow gave him an entrée into the closed circle of prosperous tradesmen who ruled the city. He was granted a licence as a tavern-keeper (there were only eight taverns permitted in the city) and was appointed a city chamberlain. The Middletons' large house became an inn. Henry May prospered greatly and had ambitions to become lord mayor of York.

In July 1571 Margaret became the wife of John Clitherow, a prosperous butcher. John Clitherow was a widower with children and much older than his young wife. We do not know the date of her birth, but she was probably between fifteen and eighteen years old at the time of her marriage. It is thought that Henry May arranged the marriage. By tradition, butchers in York did not hold office in the city, and so John Clitherow was not a rival candidate for the mayoralty. Those initiated into the butchers' craft kept to themselves: they had their own Butchers' Company and Butchers' Hall, and they lived close together in the Shambles, the traditional butchers' street in the city. So Margaret went to live "between the blood and the sawdust," as a modern biographer, K. M. Longley, puts it. Her husband, like her mother and stepfather, attended the parish church, but three years after her marriage Margaret became a Catholic.

The Act of Supremacy of 1559, which declared Queen Elizabeth I to be the head of the Church of England and required Sunday attendance in the reformed Church, was not pursued with great vigour. It was a political move, to keep Mary Queen of Scots and Philip of Spain (both Catholics) at bay, not a religious one. People were required to conform outwardly, but some left before the end of the service, some went only to Morning or Evening Prayer, and not to Communion, and others received Communion, but went to Mass secretly afterwards. No questions were asked about belief, and when one recalls that many of the officiating clergy of the Church of England at that time had served under Henry VIII, Edward VI, Mary Tudor, and then Elizabeth in the twenty-five years since Henry VIII's Act of Supremacy in 1534, religious allegiances must have become somewhat blurred for many. Protestants had killed Catholics, Catholics had killed Protestants. There was a good deal of support for an easygoing settlement that would reconcile the two.

It was precisely the success of this policy that alarmed Catholic Europe and forced the Pope into action. In 1570 Pope Pius V issued a papal Bull formally deposing Queen Elizabeth I from the English throne and declaring her excommunicate. Those who obeyed the English law of 1559 were similarly declared excommunicate. The English parliament responded in 1571 by declaring it to be high treason to affirm that Elizabeth was not, or ought not to be, queen, or that she was a heretic, schismatic, tyrant, infidel, or usurper of the crown. Loyal Catholics in England were thus faced with a stark choice: to conform or to take the penal consequences. Some chose to conform; others secretly helped the seminary priests sent over from the English College at Douai, later moved to Reims. The seminarians were trained in a very heady atmosphere for the glories of martyrdom. They were strictly forbidden to engage in politics or to discuss politics—which meant that they had little understanding of the political situation into which they were being sent. The Catholic heiress to the English throne, Mary Queen of Scots, was in an English prison, and Philip of Spain was preparing an armada to conquer England. The work of the English Mission was regarded by the English government as treasonable.

Margaret came into contact with the family of Thomas Vavasour, a Cambridge disciple of the great Bishop John Fisher, who had been martyred in the reign of Henry VIII. Vavasour refused to conform and spent periods in prison in Hull, eventually dying there in 1585. His wife, Dorothy, assumed the leadership of the York Catholics, and she probably recruited Margaret to their number. Dorothy Vavasour's eldest son trained at Douai with a young man named John Mush, who was to become Margaret's spiritual director in the last two years of her life and later her biographer. By the time the young priests returned to England after their training Margaret was serving her third term of imprisonment for refusing to attend the parish church. She had become an outspoken critic of the Elizabethan Settlement and a great embarrassment to her ambitious stepfather.

Margaret had been given the sort of education thought suitable for a tradesman's daughter: she was an excellent housewife, skilled in baking and all household tasks, but it was not thought necessary to teach her to read. She learned this skill during her time in prison, and when she was allowed home she organized a small school for her own and her neighbours' children, in which she taught them full Catholic doctrine.

The Council in the North was composed not of the easygoing Elizabethans of the south but of men with strong Protestant beliefs, Puritans rather than Anglicans, determined to root out Catholicism. Between July 1582 and November 1585 six seminary priests were executed for treason on the Knavesmire at York. This became a place of pilgrimage for Margaret and her friends, who would go by night (it was not safe to go in daylight) and kneel in prayer at the gallows. Margaret's thoughts centred on martyrdom. She consulted John Mush as her spiritual director on a matter of conscience: was she justified in helping priests without the knowledge of her husband? Fr Mush replied that her actions were justified, even meritorious, but warned her, "You must prepare your neck for the rope." "God's will be done," she said, "but I am far unworthy that honour."

It is hard to believe that John Clitherow did not know what was going on in his house. Though he was careful to keep the law himself, he had one brother who was a priest and another who was imprisoned in York Castle for recusancy. The house in the Little Shambles had been adapted to provide a secret priest's room, in which priests were regularly harboured, and he and Margaret had sent their son Henry abroad to a Catholic college. In 1586 John was summoned to court to explain his son's absence and consigned to prison. While he was away the house was raided by the sheriff of York and his men. They found Margaret composedly organizing her household. One "ruffian with a sword and buckler" (the description comes from John Mush) broke into the schoolroom, where a schoolmaster was quietly teaching the children. While the sheriff's man called for reinforcements, thinking that he had discovered a priest, the schoolmaster managed to escape into the priest's chamber, which had a way out through the house next door. The children were interrogated. A Flemish boy, eleven years old, who had been staying with the family, was stripped and threatened with a flogging. Terrified, he gave away in his broken English the secret of the hidden room, where vestments and Communion vessels were found. Margaret was arrested and charged with harbouring priests, "traitors to the Queen's Majesty and her Laws." She went gaily to prison in York Castle, where she told her cell-mate, Anne Teshe, "Before I go, I will make all my brethren and sisters on the other side [of] the hall merry." Then she made a pair of gallows with her fingers and "pleasantly laughed at them."

At this time only Catholic priests faced certain death: lay Catholics usually received a prison sentence, but Margaret was determined to be a martyr. She wrote to John Mush "desiring him to pray earnestly for her, for it was the heaviest cross that ever came to her, that she feared she should escape death." Her trial was held in the York Guildhall before two judges from Westminster, Judge Rode and Judge Clinch (or Clench: John Mush's handwriting is very difficult to read). With them sat the Vice-President of the Council in the North, two legal members of the Council and its secretary, the lord mayor of York, the whole bench of aldermen in their scarlet robes, and two sheriffs and their officers: a formidable masculine array against one young woman denied counsel. The lord mayor was Margaret's step-father, Henry May. K. M. Longley suggests that Henry, who had at last fulfilled his ambition, may have been involved in her arrest and arraignment. He was anxious to be rid of this troublesome stepdaughter. Margaret's mother, Jane, had died not long before, and Henry had married Anne Thomson, who had long been his mistress. He made no move to save Margaret. The jury was composed of local people who would have known the family history, and no doubt his reactions were being carefully observed.

Clergy of the established Church visited Margaret in prison before the trial, urging her to save her life by conforming to the law and arguing that Christ himself and his apostles had fled from their persecutors, but she replied, "God defend that I should favour my life in this point. As for my martyrdom, I am not yet assured of it, for that I am yet living; but if I persevere to the end, I shall be saved." At her trial she refused to plead, saying, "Having made no offence, I need no trial." This stand enabled her to avoid testifying against other people—her friends, relatives, and children, and the inhabitants of the house next door to her own, which could be reached through the priest's chamber. They were relatives of John Clitherow. It also meant that she would not reveal the hiding places of seminary priests. She must have known of the whole network in the York area.

Judge Clinch seems to have done his best to save Margaret's life. He examined her at some length and pleaded with her: "Consider on it, you have your husband and children to care for, cast not yourself away." She was unmoved by this appeal to her family responsibilities, being quite determined on martyrdom. The evidence against her was thin: the only witness, apart from the sheriff and his men, was the Flemish boy, still terrified and hardly able to understand the proceedings; but the Council members were determined to secure her conviction—not to bring about her death but to make her recant.

The judge warned her in detail of the penalty for refusing to plead. This, prescribed by an ancient statute, was the *peine forte et dure*—death by being crushed by heavy weights. She would be taken to the lowest part of the prison, stripped, and have as much weight laid upon her as she was able to bear. There she would stay for three days, with only "a little barley bread and puddle water"; at the end of three days her hands and feet would be tied to posts, a sharp stone placed under her back, and more weights laid upon her till she was crushed to death. Margaret was found guilty of refusing to plead and reluctantly condemned to this terrible punishment. She was not sentenced on the original charges. The *peine forte et dure* was designed as a way of extracting information rather than as a means of execution. Very few people would survive for three days without telling all that they knew.

John Clitherow, when he heard of her sentence, "fared like a madman, out of his wits." He had violent nose-bleeds and said, "Alas, will they kill my wife? Let them take all I have, and save her, for she is the best wife in England, and the best Catholic also." However, he had no intention of joining her in martyrdom. He was set free and banished six days before his wife's execution. Margaret was sent back to prison, where Sir Thomas Fairfax and members of the Council in the North went to see her, saying that if she would hear one sermon by an Anglican cleric she would be reprieved. She was offered a sermon by the Bishop of Durham, but she refused to see him. Casting around for ways of saving her life, they asked her if she was pregnant again. She replied that she did not know for certain. Four "honest women" were sent to talk to her and find out if she were pregnant or not. They came back to say that they thought she was, and Judge Clinch pleaded that she should be reprieved on that account; but sentence had been passed. Her friends and relatives pleaded with her but to no effect. She spent her last hours in prison in making herself a symbolic linen shift in which to die, and sewed into the sleeves "inkle strings" or tapes for her hands to be secured. After a night of spiritual preparation she went cheerfully to her execution on Lady Day, 25 March 1585. It was Lady Day in the Old Calendar, which England still used; in the Gregorian Calendar, by which Catholics reckoned, it was Good Friday.

Two sheriffs, an Anglican clergyman, four serjeants, and a small group of men and women witnesses attended her execution. It was carried out by beggars who had been hired for the purpose. It seems that the authorities had despaired of extracting information from her or of persuading her to recant. They did not make her suffer for three days. Her executioners were instructed to proceed directly to the sharp stone and the heavy weights, and she died within fifteen minutes.

John Mush's *True Report of the Life and Death of Mrs. Margaret Clitherow* was the main contemporary evidence for Margaret's beatification in 1929 and her canonization in 1970 by Pope Paul VI as one of the Forty Martyrs of England and Wales. Anne Line and Margaret Ward, who are also numbered among the Forty Martyrs, were both hanged. Only the merry butcher's wife of York suffered the barbarous punishment of the *peine forte et dure*.

Margaret is not the female protomartyr of England: the first known woman martyr is Margaret Pole, mother of Cardinal Pole, who died in 1541, but she was the first in the north of England, and commentators have compared her to St Alban, who was also martyred for harbouring a priest.

MADELEINE FONTAINE

(1723-94)

MARIE-MADELEINE FONTAINE of the Daughters of Charity suffered during "the Great Terror" in revolutionary France. She was born at Etrépagny, south-east of Rouen, in the reign of Louis XIV. Her father Robert was a shoemaker, and the family, like many of the French peasantry of that time, was desperately poor. She was the eldest of eleven children, of whom only three survived infancy. When his first wife died Robert Fontaine married again, but his second wife lived only long enough to produce a son who died at birth and twin girls who died with her. Eleven children and her mother and stepmother had died in their family home before Madeleine was sixteen. Marriage had no attractions for her. She had been taught by the Daughters of Charity, and in 1748 she entered the Congregation, leaving a brother and a sister at home to look after their father.

The Daughters of Charity, founded in 1656 by "Mademoiselle Le Gras" (*Louise de Marillac), were much respected. They wore secular clothing and made only yearly vows, so they were free from enclosure and able to visit the sick and poor in hospitals or in their own homes. Madeleine became a nursing Sister and followed her vocation for over forty years. When the French Revolution broke out she was in her late sixties, in charge of a small mission of seven nuns in Arras, where they ran a hospital and a small school for children. For a time their work went on as usual. They can have had no idea of the lengths to which the revolutionaries would go in suppressing religion.

In "the Terror," the period from the assassination of Marat in July 1793 to the death of Robespierre in July 1794, priests and nuns went in danger of the guillotine, and many died when they refused to take an oath of loyalty to the new régime and to abandon their vocations. Churches were closed by troops who removed church bells, smashed altars and crucifixes, and made bonfires of vestments and confessional boxes. A popular spectacle was that of a priest abjuring his vocation, and a ceremony of "debaptization" was invented for the laity. All public and private worship was forbidden. On 10 August 1793 the artist Jacques-Louis David, a strong supporter of the Revolution, organized a secular ceremony for the acceptance of the new Constitution. An enormous statue of the goddess Nature, spurting water from her breasts into a pool, was erected on the site of the Bastille, which had been razed to the ground. There was a new calendar, which began not with the birth of Christ but with the proclamation of the Republic. The months had new names (now surviving only on the names of Paris Métro stations) and there was a ten-day week, the *décadi*. Christmas, Easter, Pentecost, and the harvest festival, together with saints' days, were abolished. There were thirty-six new festivals, one every *décadi*, celebrating reason, courage, motherhood, temperance, hatred of tyrants, and similar ideals of the régime. On 10 November a great Festival of Reason was held in the cathedral of Notre Dame in Paris, where sixteen Louis Capets had walked to their coronations as kings of France. The secularized Notre Dame was re-named the Temple of Liberty.

The rest of France varied in its expression of the new system: local administrators organized events varying from mildly pagan ceremonies to the active stirring-up of public hatred against religion of any kind. In Le Havre a girl of good morals was made the goddess Reason for a day, with floral tributes and dances; in Poitiers, farther south, there were grotesque ceremonies in which people dressed as sorcerers, priests, popes, monks, angels, and nuns were chased through the church of Saint-Porchade.

Robespierre and David seem to have decided that the nation needed something more than secularism to hold it together. In May 1794 Robespierre laid down the new creed: the existence of a Supreme Being and the immortality of the soul. David organized another ceremony "in good taste, in the mould of classical antiquity." Robespierre, who appears to have been born without either compassion or a sense of the ridiculous, agreed to honour it, dressed in sky blue and carrying a bouquet of berries, grain, and flowers. And meanwhile the tumbrils rolled.

Arras was sufficiently far from Paris to have escaped the worst of the persecution but for two factors: it was Robespierre's home town, and he frequently visited it to stay with his sister and her husband, who lived in the rue des Rapporteurs; then on 1 November 1793 a new mayor of Arras, Joseph Lebon, arrived in the town. He was a fanatical apostate priest, a former Oratorian and Robespierre's personal friend. Only days after his arrival, his commissioners were sent to the Daughters of Charity. In accordance with their bishop's direction, the four had refused to take the oath demanded of clergy and religious by the Revolutionary Convention. Now they refused again. On 23 November they were told that their hospital, the Maison de la Charité, was to become the Maison de l'Humanité, and they were forbidden to wear their habits. Then their possessions were seized, and the school was placed under a lay director. Robespierre congratulated Lebon on "the energy with which he had suppressed the enemies of the Revolution" and gave his sanction to the full operation of a terrorist policy in the town.

For a time the nuns were permitted to continue their nursing duties in secular dress. There was a good deal of public sympathy for them, but, realizing that worse was to come, Madeleine Fontaine sent the two youngest nuns to Belgium disguised as peasants. One Sister returned to her family when her yearly vow expired, and only three of the older nuns remained in the hospital. Madeleine was seventy-one years old. The other Sisters were Françoise Lanel, forty-nine; Thérèse Fantou, forty-seven; and Jeanne Gérard, forty-two.

On 5 February 1794 (*17 pluviôse an II* in the new anti-Christian calendar) they were expelled from their house. Nine days later they were arrested as suspects. Joseph Lebon's injunction was: "*Ne laissez point multiplier les ennemis de la liberté,*" "Don't let the enemies of liberty multiply," and it was clear that the fact that the four were religious would be sufficient to condemn them. Evidence of their so-called "counter-revolutionary activity" was fabricated. They were moved from prison to prison (some of which were former monasteries), thrown in with other prisoners in appalling conditions, and given nothing to eat except black bread. Over four months later they were arraigned in Cambrai, where Joseph Lebon was carrying out a policy of mass arrests and summary executions. They arrived on 26 June and were brought before a tribunal on the same day. They bore themselves with dignity, but there was no hope of a fair trial. There was no counsel for the defence and no chance of replying to the accusations that were hurled against the four. They were all condemned to be executed, the sentence to be carried out on the following day. The Sisters went to their death singing *Ave maris stella*. Madeleine Fontaine was the last to go to the guillotine, and as she approached it she turned to the crowd and shouted, "Listen, Christians! We are the last victims. The persecution is going to stop. The gallows will be destroyed. The altars of Jesus will rise again gloriously."

Commentators have raised doubts as to whether Sister Madeleine actually made this speech or whether it was attributed to her, with hindsight, after her death. Fr Lucien Misermont, who wrote a study of the martyred Sisters in 1900 when he was chaplain to the Mission at Arras, is emphatic that these were her actual words and that many local people testified to them. The prophecy came true. France was weary of persecution. Robespierre, the architect of the Terror, was dragged to the guillotine in July of that same year, and Joseph Lebon followed him in August. Nobody was enthusiastic about the new secular ceremonies, and they disappeared very quickly. Madeleine Fontaine and her Sisters were beatified with the Ursulines of Valenciennes on 13 June 1920 by Pope Benedict XV.

HERMINA GRIVOT

(1866-1900)

Hermina Grivot (Mother Marie Hermine of Jesus).

From a Life published by her Order in Quebec, 1910.

A SMALL CONTINGENT of nuns of the Order of the Franciscan Sisters of Mary went out to Taiyuan, in the Shansi province of China, in 1898, to run an orphanage for Chinese children and a public dispensary. During the Boxer rebellion of 1900 the entire Franciscan mission was wiped out. All seven Sisters were martyred.

Mother Marie-Hermine of Jesus, born Irma Grivot, was the superior of the small convent of St Paschal—named for a ninth-century pope who had been devoted to the veneration of the early Christian martyrs. She was born in Beaune, in the Burgundy region of France, in 1866 and had joined the Order as a young woman. The Franciscan Sisters of Mary were (and are) Third Order Regulars of St Francis, distinguished by their white habits and known as the "White Franciscans." Their Congregation was founded in India in 1877 by Mother Mary of the Passion (Hélène de Chappotin de Neuville) specifically for work in foreign missions.

In 1898 Mgr Fogolla, the coadjutor bishop of the Franciscan Mission in Shansi, came to Europe for a great exhibition in Turin, which had a section devoted to overseas missions. He visited Rome and asked Mother Mary of the Passion for Sisters for his mission. He specified that they must have certain skills: they must be able to make bread and to cook in clay ovens; they must be skilled in embroidery, music, painting, nursing, and surgery (specified in that order). They must be "calm, self-possessed and obedient," with "no sign of insubordination or disobedience."

This job specification did not in fact match either the needs of the situation or the abilities of the nuns. Embroidery, music, and painting would have been more appropriate as subjects in a school for Western-educated young ladies than for the abandoned and neglected little girls who were to be the nuns' care. The Chinese value boy children, and girls were often sold, given away, or simply left to fend for themselves. The nuns were not to be teachers, apart from giving religious instruction. The orphanage was already established, with Chinese women to look after the children; but the friars could not manage the Chinese women, and the children were getting out of hand. Mgr Fogolla's insistence on the nuns' absolute obedience was a reflection of his anxiety that they should follow the policy of the Mission in all respects and not become embroiled in the daily arguments. Presumably the requirement that the nuns should make bread (in a country where rice is the staple food) was an indication that the friars, like most Europeans in China at that time, firmly adhered to their Western diets. The Sisters were also to run a dispensary using Western medicines. They knew little of nursing and less of surgery, and Mother Hermina's only equipment for this task was a few months spent as infirmarian in the Order's house in Marseilles.

The nuns knew nothing of Chinese language or customs. Though the first regional synod of the Church at Peking had urged in 1880 that "every vicariate should show care for the study of the Chinese language and books," the friars did not speak the local dialect but used catechist-interpreters. The nuns would have women interpreters to enable them to communicate with the Chinese workers in the orphanage.

By modern standards, the Sisters were ill-equipped for their work, but they did not lack devotion and courage. They were going out "to convert the heathen"—the phrase recurs in the literature. Their models were St Francis of Assisi, who had longed to go to Jerusalem to convert the Saracens, and St Francis Xavier, who had died on the coast of China. They knew that China was a dangerous and difficult missionary area, and they longed for the grace of martyrdom. Hermina, who had been secretary to one of the superiors of the Order in France, was chosen to lead this small mission. When the nuns played games, drawing lots to see who would be the first martyr, she was chosen. She told the others that she was sorry that the days of martyrdom were probably over.

While she was at Marseilles, learning what she could of the work of an infirmarian, she ventured on a ship for the first time in her life, to see what it felt like, but this can have been little preparation for the fearsome journey ahead: the ship did not leave port. Then she made her final retreat at the motherhouse in Rome and received a pontifical audience and blessing. She and her Sisters, together with ten members of their Order destined for other parts of China, sailed from Marseilles on 12 March 1899.

The journey to China took them six weeks. The voyage through the Mediterranean was so rough that they were all seasick, but Mother Hermina reported bravely that "they bore it without complaint and tried to find an amusing side to their experience as they were tossed to and fro in their berths." The priests on board were seasick, too, and unable to say Mass until they reached the calm of the Suez Canal and the Red Sea. The ship called at Colombo, Singapore, Saigon, Hong Kong, and Shanghai before the Sisters finally disembarked at Tientsin (now Tianjing). From Tientsin, they travelled in palanquins—chairs of rushes and rope slung between mules. They were awed by the towering grey-green limestone mountains and the rushing waterfalls of their new country. At last they reached Taiyuan, a major commercial city in a coal-mining area about 250 miles south-west of Peking (now Beijing). The population consisted of several hundred thousand Chinese, of whom only some six hundred were Christian. There were six Franciscans and two hundred Chinese children waiting for them at the mission.

There were very few European women in Taiyuan, and the Sisters found it disconcerting to be constantly watched by people to whom their appearance and behaviour were so strange. The Chinese women were astonished by their large feet, for they considered unbound feet the height of vulgarity, and they were intrigued to see the nuns eating with knives and forks. The nuns for their part were appalled by the "terrible lack of cleanliness." The children were verminous and covered in sores, the local people slept with all their clothes on and considered baths bad for the health, and there were piles of rotting rubbish everywhere. There were difficulties with the "strange diet" — "vermicelli in hot water without salt," "pork hash, Chinese sauce impossible to describe," "tea without sugar or hot water for beverage." The Sisters' boxes and trunks did not arrive for weeks. There were long waits for mail, which sometimes did not arrive at all. Despite all these difficulties they set to work with a will.

The Chinese workers in the orphanage apparently had little idea of discipline. They let the little girls "fight and roll in the mud like animals," and the nuns had to show much tact in helping them to keep better order. The children were made clean, the vermin were banished, and the sores dressed.

They "ceased to live like little beasts." They had religious instruction and were set to work. They were taught to sew, to knit, to do the laundry, to weave, to spin, and to clean the compound. "This to put an end to their playing about, from morning till night all summer or sleeping all day in winter," reported Mother Hermina. There was no possibility of teaching them to read or write, though they appear to have learned a few anthems in Latin.

The dispensary was a great success. "Chinese, foreigners, heathens, Protestants and Catholics" flocked to it every day "with the fullest confidence." The Sisters' medical and nursing skills must still have been very limited, because when one of their own number, Sister Marie de Ste Nathalie, developed typhoid fever, Mgr Grassi thought them too inexperienced to deal with her case and insisted that she should be treated by Chinese medicine. Her body was rubbed with pure alcohol, and to the Sisters' horror, her flesh was "pierced again and again with needles." Whether her recovery was due to their fervent prayers or to acupuncture, or to a combination of the two, she survived. Four other Sisters suffered severely from dysentery, and for a time Mother Hermina and Sister Marie de St Just were the only members of the community fit to work.

As well as running the orphanage, where the number of children rose to 260, and the dispensary, where the demands increased daily, the Sisters furnished their own chapel. It was swept and cleaned and made spotless; altar hangings were made, linen brought from Marseilles became altar linen, and a piece of Chinese satin became a veil for the tabernacle. Mass and Benediction were said daily from the time of the Sisters' arrival, and great preparations were made for the Feast of the Assumption. Mother Hermina, with more faith than artistic experience, found an engraving of the Blessed Virgin in a prayer book, and copied it in water colours to hang above the altar. On 15 August 1899, less than four months after the Sisters arrived, a joyous procession carrying green boughs and lighted candles bore the statue of the Virgin into the chapel while the clean and tidy orphans sang *Ave maris stella* and the *Magnificat*.

So much had been achieved in a very short time, but this was the first and the last time than the Feast of the Assumption was to be celebrated in the chapel of St Paschal's convent. China, closed to foreigners for over a century, had been opened up by force by the European powers. After the Opium Wars of 1839-42 and 1856-60 all the major Chinese ports, from Tientsin in the north to Hong Kong in the south, passed into European hands. By the end of the century the Europeans, principally the French and the English, controlled virtually all China's external trade. The Chinese called it "squeezing the melon." National humiliation led to bitter popular resentment.

In inland China the missionaries often bore the brunt of this resentment. They were blamed for foisting foreign ways and foreign values on the people. Christianity was regarded as no more than the faith of the Europeans, and missionaries were more vulnerable than other "foreign devils." There had been sporadic persecutions ever since the first Western missionaries went to China, and Mother Hermina had told her Sisters: "There is a need for real victims in China." In 1899, even as the Franciscan Sisters of Mary were beginning work, the situation deteriorated. There was a severe drought through a long, hot summer. Seeds did not germinate, and by the autumn people were dying of starvation. There was dust everywhere, hanging like a pall over Taiyuan and obscuring the sun. Mother Hermina wrote home to say that "terrible calamity, unspeakable misery and death" were everywhere. The friars and the nuns did what they could. Food was handed out, even if it was no more than a cup of water with some millet seed. The nuns outdid one another in austerities so as to have more to give to the local people.

Hardship led to political unrest. In January 1900 Mother Hermina wrote home to tell her community that the road to Peking had been blocked and the railway line cut, and saying: "The insurgents are gradually hemming us in on every side." She added that a German priest and seven Christians had been martyred in a nearby town. In Peking, some 250 miles to the north-east, the ageing dowager empress Tzu Hsi had bowed to foreign power but secretly supported the secret societies dedicated to driving the foreigners out. Prominent among these organizations were the *Yi Ho Chuan* or "Righteous Harmony Fists," known as the Boxers. The desperate state of the country gave them their opportunity. Late in 1899 the Boxers openly took up arms. Foreign legations in Peking were besieged, and European missionaries and their supporters in many towns and villages were indiscriminately massacred. The total death-roll of Christians, which includes European missionaries of other Churches as well as Catholic Chinese priests, nuns, and catechists, was between twenty and thirty thousand.

The work at the Franciscan Mission continued through the winter. At Christmas the cold was so intense that Mother Hermina told the Sisters to wear blankets over their habits, and the Chinese admired their new festal attire. The orphans sang *Adeste fideles*. When the Chinese New Year came at the end of January the Sisters "joined heartily in the celebrations," holding a service of Thanksgiving in the cathedral so that the orphans should not feel cut off from their own culture. The feast of St Paschal was celebrated in the nuns' chapel on 11 February, and there was a note from Mother Hermina: "The Chinese love processions and ceremonies, but walking is difficult for their bandaged feet." Easter passed quietly; but during April a new viceroy was appointed to the province, to reside in Taiyuan. He was Yu Hsien, notorious for his fanatical opposition to Europeans and Christians. In June he gave an order to pillage and burn all the houses of the Christians in Taiyuan.

When news came, Mgr Grassi told the Sisters, "The hour of combat is here." He procured some carts, telling the Sisters to dress in Chinese clothes and take the children to safety. They knew what would happen to the mission and were unwilling to leave, saying, "Don't stop us dying with you, Monsignor." The bishop tried to insist that they should go, but they were surrounded. A day or two later armed men took the children away, much to the nuns' distress. Many of the children cried and tried to cling to them. The Europeans were placed under guard. Christian houses in the city were being sacked and looted, and the air was thick with flames and smoke. Mother Hermina's chief anxiety was for the children. The other nuns begged her to rest, but she said, "Rest! Time enough to rest in heaven." Mgr Grassi wrote to the viceroy and twice tried to see him, walking through the streets with a howling mob at his heels screaming, "Death to the devils from Europe!" The viceroy refused to see him. He later sent a message requiring all the Franciscans to renounce Christianity and promising to arrange rich marriages for the nuns if they did so.

On 5 July, following their refusal, they were all taken to a mandarin's house named the Inn of Heavenly Peace, adjoining the governor's residence. There the two bishops said Mass daily until 9 July. On that day Bishop Grassi had just pronounced absolution when the soldiers broke in and dragged them all before a tribunal. On the way they were beaten and kicked by the mob. Yu Hsien asked Mgr Grassi, "Why did you come to China?" and the old bishop answered calmly, "To save souls." The crowd screamed "Kill them!" Yu Hsien drew his own sword and personally killed Mgr Grassi and Mgr Fogolla. Three friars, five Chinese seminarians, nine Chinese catechists, a priest, and a lay brother were killed by the soldiers in an orgy of slaughter. The nuns remained calm in the face of taunts and insults, kneeling and singing the *Te Deum*. Then they embraced one another and one by one presented their heads to the executioner. The other Sisters who died with Mother Hermina were Marie de St Just (Anne Françoise Moreau, French), Marie de Ste Nathalie (Jeanne Marie Kerguin, Breton), Marie Amandine (Pauline Jeuris, Belgian), Marie Adolphine (Anne Catherine Dierkx, Dutch), and two Italians, Maria della Pace (Marianna Giuliani) and Maria Chiara (Clelia Nanetti).

The mission was completely wiped out. There are no records apart from Mother Hermina's letters to her motherhouse. Two young Chinese boys witnessed the martyrdoms and were later able to give evidence of what had occurred. Four days later thirty-three Anglican and Free Church missionaries were also murdered.

The seven nuns are the Chinese protomartyrs of their Order. They were all beatified, together with the two bishops and the other male martyrs, on 24 November 1946, when the courage and steadfastness of men and women alike was celebrated. Among the missionaries who attended the beatification ceremony were the two boys who had witnessed the executions as children. Both had become Franciscan friars.

A century later, after many political upheavals, China is still closed to foreign missions, and the Church maintains only a token presence in a society of 1,200 million people. Officially, there is religious toleration, but proselytizing is strictly forbidden and punishable by imprisonment. China remains potentially one of the great mission areas of the world. The death of the Taiyuan martyrs is a focus for prayer and devotion, a sacrifice to be built on when the memory of the tragic consequences of nineteenth-century European intervention in the affairs of a proud people is finally erased.

ANUARITE
NENGAPETA
(d. 1964)

Nun Reading.

*From a wood figure by
an artist of the Congo.*

THE EUROPEAN colonial powers who explored and dominated Africa in the second half of the nineteenth century began a mass withdrawal after the Second World War. Much effort was invested, particularly by Britain and France, in trying to secure peaceful handovers and relatively stable governments. Few transfers of power were as catastrophic as that in the Congo, where the former Belgian administration had faced violent opposition. In this huge equatorial territory, with its scattered population of a little over two million, there were many small French and Belgian Catholic missions, which had set up hospitals and schools to improve the condition of a desperately poor and sickly population; but these missions were identified with the departing Europeans. Those that had made attempts to Africanize, recruiting Congolese priests and nuns, attracted the special hatred of the Simbas (Lions), a rebel force that was to destabilize the country for many years. Violent and murderous attacks were made on isolated and unprotected missions. The story of Marie-Clementine Anuarite Nengapeta, a young Congolese nun martyred at Isiro, commemorates the witness of many other Catholics who were loyal to their faith in the dark period that followed the setting up of the Republic of Zaire (now once again known as the Congo).

Anuarite was a teaching Sister of the Congregation of the Holy Family, known locally as the *Jamaa Takatifu*. She taught in the school at Bafwabakka, where the nuns were well aware of the dangers of their position and their vulnerability to Simba attacks. Only a short time earlier their own diocesan, Bishop Wittebols of Wamba, had been murdered, and they knew that their faith and the religious habit were no protection against these violent guerillas, who regarded both as evidence of their collaboration with the Europeans. Their minds must have been concentrated on thoughts of martyrdom in October 1964 when St Charles Lwanga and the Uganda Martyrs—the Catholic proto-martyrs of black Africa—had been canonized. The Ugandans had been cruelly executed in 1886 at the hands of Mwanga, the irrational and debauched *kabaka*, for their faith. Before he died Bruno Serenkuma, one of their number, told his brother: "A well which has many sources never runs dry. When we are gone, others will come after us." Others had come, and now the Church was under threat again in neighbouring Zaire.

The attack at Bafwabakka came suddenly and without warning only seven weeks after the canonization—at lunch-time on 29 November 1964. A lorry packed with Simba troops broke into the compound, and guerillas swarmed into the mission house through doors and windows. The officer in charge seemed to have control over his men at this stage. He told the Sisters not to be afraid: the Simbas had to come to save them from the Americans. This may have referred to an American mercenary force in the area—the government in Kinshasa was recruiting former military personnel from wherever it could find them—or it may have been complete fantasy. Mother Kasima and the Sisters were told that they must leave the mission and that the soldiers would escort them to Isiro, where the Simbas had their headquarters. They packed and were herded into the lorry, sitting on the floor while armed Simbas stood over them. The journey took a long time, and the troops got increasingly out of control. They stopped at villages, terrorizing the local people, looting and drinking heavily. As they became increasingly drunken, and the lorry lurched and jolted on its way, they menaced the Sisters with their guns and threatened to rape them. After dark they stopped at an abandoned mission, where the Sisters were pushed into a room but left unmolested. In the morning they were put back into the lorry, and the journey continued.

Before they reached Isiro the lorry was stopped by a car in which the commanding officer of the Simbas was travelling. The troops became very excited: there were cheers, and bullets were fired into the air. This officer was enraged to see one Sister saying her rosary. He ordered the nuns to be stripped of all religious objects, and crosses, rosaries, and medals were snatched from them and thrown into the bush. He told the Sisters furiously that they would soon be taken back to Bafwabakka and made to dress like "proper African women," not like Europeans. Then the lorry went on to Simba headquarters in Isiro, where they were to be taken to a house—all except the youngest, Anuarite. She was to be taken to the officer's quarters for the night.

Rape is often an act of aggression rather than a matter of simple lust. The officer must have known that the Sisters had taken a vow of virginity, and this order was a deliberate assertion of power, a crude way of denying everything that the nuns stood for. Mother Kasima at once acted to protect Anuarite, telling the officer that it was "not possible" for the girl to go with him: her vows could not be violated. She put her arms round Anuarite and refused to let her go. Anuarite clung to her superior, telling the officer, "What you are asking is impossible. I cannot commit this sin. Kill me instead." Though the soldiers tried to pull them apart, hitting out wildly at them both, they refused to be separated. After a distressing and exhausting physical struggle they were allowed to go and rejoin the other Sisters. At this point they must have hoped that their ordeal was over; but another officer, who had been drinking heavily, tried to force Anuarite and another of her companions, Sister Bokuma, into his car. When they resisted he drew his revolver and began to beat them both with the butt. Sister Bokuma's arm was broken. Anuarite told him that she would rather be killed than go with him. She was beaten to the ground, gasping "*Naivyo nilivyotaka*," "This is what I wanted." At this point the officer panicked and cried out to the watching Simbas to kill Anuarite, shouting wildly that she had attacked him. Two of the guerillas rushed up and stabbed her repeatedly. Then the officer shot her through the heart.

This might have been the signal for a general massacre of the nuns, but some kind of reason seems to have prevailed among the guerillas, and the sudden death sobered some of them. The other Sisters were allowed to take Anuarite's body into the house, and a Sister who was a nurse set Sister Bokuma's arm in a splint. The officer who had shot Anuarite came back several times to see her body, blustering and threatening the others. Another Simba came into the house and attempted to rape several of the nuns, but they clung together in spite of beatings and further threats.

At last the mood of murderous and drunken fury passed. The nuns were not molested further; some days later Government forces took the town, and they were released. There were many other incidents in which nuns were raped or killed, but the story of young Anuarite and her acceptance of martyrdom was an outstanding example of courage and fidelity. In 1980 her body was taken to Isiro cathedral, where it rests in a special tomb. In that year Pope John Paul II made his first visit to Zaire, where so many Catholics had suffered, and approved Anuarite's cause. She was beatified on the Pope's second visit to Zaire in 1985, during a solemn High Mass. During his address, the Pope stressed four aspects of her martyrdom: her commitment to her Congregation, her fidelity to her vows, the intense prayer life that made it possible for her to resist her attackers, and the support of Mother Kasima and the other Sisters. He reminded his listeners that a martyr is literally a witness and that Anuarite had accepted the opportunity to witness to her faith, giving her life for it.

The story of Anuarite's death is not a simple and straightforward one: perhaps the deaths of women martyrs are seldom simple. It was the result of heavy drinking, brute rage at being defied by women, and a nascent nationalism that saw all the outward signs of Christianity as identified with the hated colonial power. Her death was a message to Africans that Christianity is not merely a European faith, to be discarded with political independence. It is universal truth for all peoples. The life of the Church in Central Africa is developing in a truly African context, strengthened by her witness.

3

COLLABORATORS

CIRCUMSTANCES in which a man saint and a woman saint have been able to form a sustained working partnership are comparatively rare, for four reasons: through most of Christian history women were not free to meet men with similar theological interests; men had more experience of the world, and were better educated, so they tended to take the lead; women had a comparatively low status, so that even when one of them made a contribution to a joint enterprise, the man was likely to get the credit for it; and fears of gossip and scandal were likely to damage the most disinterested and spiritual partnership.

In most of the modern world (though not in some Muslim countries), co-education in schools and universities and working partnerships between men and woman in many settings are now the norm, but for most of the Church's history women, even Christian women, even celibate women, have been regarded primarily as a source of sexual temptation to men rather than as fellow-workers for Christ. Many great churchmen have seen them as strange and alien beings, best kept at arm's length—or not encountered at all. The double monasteries that had been renowned from the seventh to tenth centuries had ceased to operate by the time of Francis and Clare of Assisi, and some male saints of the later medieval period were highly regarded for their avoidance of women. Louis the Pious (King Louis IX of France) in the thirteenth century was venerated for his inability to relate to women of any age and any status. Aloysius Gonzaga in the sixteenth century refused to look at any woman, even his own mother, and said that he would not recognize any of his female relatives if he happened to meet them. Any meeting with a woman was regarded as an occasion of sin. This attitude, which many women have found offensive and prurient, was supported by reference to the third chapter of the book of Genesis, the story of Eve and the apple. God tells Eve that as punishment for her sin in eating the apple and giving it to Adam, she shall be cursed:

> I will multiply your pains in childbearing,
> you shall give birth to your children in pain.
> Your yearning shall be for your husband,
> yet he will lord it over you.

The perpetuation of this ancient curse on the female sex depends on a literal interpretation of the Genesis text. Eve's subordinate position and the pains of childbirth are explained as God's punishment for Adam's fall and thus the fall of the human race. Adam's punishment is hard labour: "With sweat on your brow shall you eat your bread." Even in the early Church there was some argument on the question of whether this story was to be interpreted literally or allegorically. The school of theology at Alexandria maintained that it was a literal historical record of how the world was created and how the first man and woman behaved; the school of theology at Antioch regarded it as an allegory of the human situation. In the Western Church the literal view prevailed, and it now comes as something of a shock to realize that most of the great Fathers of the Church were biblical fundamentalists. It was not until the time of Pope Pius XII that a papal decree, *Divino afflante spiritu* (1943), officially commended the insights of biblical scholarship to Catholic scholars and the way was opened for the publication of papers and commentaries based on textual analysis.

The notes in the Jerusalem Bible, first published in English in 1966, reproduced in an abridged form in the popular edition of the New Jerusalem Bible (1988), indicate how far biblical criticism has changed traditional views of the Genesis stories. The editors comment that the early chapters "visualize the situation of all mankind in the persons of Adam and Eve" rather than giving literal accounts of historical events. The Creation stories in Genesis are purer and more spiritually meaningful than the Creation stories of the Assyrians, the Persians, or the Egyptians, but we can now recognize that they were based on the experience of a nomadic Middle Eastern people many centuries ago. Men were stronger than women and had to toil at heavy tasks. The making of a child was a brief and pleasurable activity for men, but a long and painful process for women. (The pains of childbirth must have been well enough known to a desert people, living close to one another in tents and with no anaesthetics.) In struggling with the problem of original sin, the priests of Israel came to the conclusion that, since God was good, the punishment of the daughters of Eve must be just. Women must therefore be weak, sinful, and subordinate to men.

Pope Pius XII not only commended biblical scholarship; he issued two papal encyclicals designed to rescue women from these ancient strictures and followed them with a series of addresses on the subject of women's status. In 1945 he stated that, "As children of God, man and woman have a dignity in which they are absolutely equal; and they are equal, too, in regard to the supreme end of human life, which is everlasting union with God in the happiness of heaven." In 1950 he emphasized spirituality in women: while men often followed Jesus Christ as a leader and were loyal to the external organization of the Church, many of the world's mystics have been women. While Pope Pius deprecated the labour-saving devices that freed many married women from domestic burdens (it was the peasant pope, John XXIII, who realized how heavy those burdens were), his pronouncements gave women a new status in the eyes of the Church.

Men have always instructed women, directed women, made decisions for women; but examples from the lives of the saints of circumstances in which they have found it possible to work with women as equals and to learn from them are very limited. Three of the examples that follow relate to a relatively short period of time, in which women in the Roman Empire were given something approaching equal status with men, being able to own money and property and to make their own decisions about how to use it. Constantine the Great relaxed the imperial laws laid down by Augustus Caesar some two centuries earlier, allowing single or widowed women control of their own lives and their own resources. Relations between men and women were probably less constrained in the fourth century than in any other period until the twentieth century. Women were able to study, to travel, and to devote their lives to Christian causes.

Macrina the Younger was a consecrated virgin living in Asia Minor, the sister of three great bishop-saints. As the eldest daughter in a large family she taught her brothers and sisters the Christian faith, firmly based on the Nicene Creed. The Council of Nicaea had been held in Asia Minor only six years before her birth, and its teachings were well understood by educated Christian families. When the children had grown up she entered a women's community. Her brother Gregory of Nyssa gives a detailed account of how, when their brother Basil of Caesarea died, he went to her for counsel and advice in his grief, and she expounded Christian doctrine on death and the afterlife for his comfort. Women were able to attend lectures in the great schools of theology in Antioch and Constantinople at this time, and Macrina's exposition shows a thorough grasp of doctrine and dialectical method: so distinguished is her contribution that it has sometimes been credited to Gregory himself and not to her, but Gregory calls her "The Teacher," and his respect and admiration for her learning and piety are evident.

Paula was a wealthy Roman widow, one of St Jerome's circle of aristocratic women who studied the scriptures under his direction, and she became his assistant. His enemies, wishing to make him leave Rome, publicly accused this most misogynistic of men of an improper relationship with her. Jerome's response was swift and emphatic. Later, in Bethlehem, where he was pursuing his Latin translation of what are now the Old and New Testaments, Paula and her daughter Eustochium continued to advise and assist him. Paula had the advantage of a Greek father, so that she spoke Greek as well as Latin, and she studied Hebrew for years—first in Rome and then in Jerusalem. Jerome mastered Greek, but he found Hebrew difficult and grumbled about the idioms. His biblical text, later known as the Vulgate, forms the basis of modern translations of the Bible, and it may owe a good deal to Paula's scholarship. Jerome was generous in acknowledging his debt to her, and she founded two monasteries in Jerusalem, but she is often regarded as a sort of housekeeper for the great Father of the Church rather than as a colleague in scholarship.

Olympias was a deaconess of the Church in Constantinople and a powerful ally of St John Chrysostom, the bishop, during his battles against corrupt churchmen and a corrupt imperial power. A very wealthy woman, she supported his work for the poor and sick of the city and backed him openly in his epic struggles against the Empress Eudoxia. She was herself arrested and persecuted after he went into exile. During the last four years of John Chrysostom's life, when he was frequently moved to wilder and more dangerous regions of Armenia and Bithynia and harried by the imperial troops, she sent funds for his support, and they kept up a unique correspondence, of which John's letters are still extant.

By the thirteenth century, when **Clare of Assisi** dramatically left her family home to take the habit, women's lives were very much more constrained. Francis of Assisi had intended from the first that his movement should be open to women as well as men; but his vision was not shared by the society in which they lived. Elaborate precautions had to be taken to chaperone both Clare and Francis at their meetings in order to avoid scandal and gossip in the locality. The men of the Offreduccio family, Clare's relatives, were outraged that she was escaping from their control and broke into the Benedictine nunnery where she was staying to drag her home again. After a short period in which friars and nuns worked together in the kind of partnership that had been common in earlier double monasteries, the bishop, fearing scandal, forbade the friars to visit or help the nuns, and Clare did not see Francis again until his funeral cortège passed her convent door on its way into Assisi.

Louise de Marillac lived in seventeenth-century France, and the Church in France was then notably more liberal in its attitude to women than the Church in Italy. St Francis de Sales, Bishop Pierre Camus of Belley, and St Vincent de Paul all acted as her spiritual directors at different times, and it was with Vincent de Paul's help that she founded a Congregation complementary to his own Order for priests. Vincent had set up associations of noblewomen, known as the Ladies of Charity, who gave money and time to helping the sick and poor people who were his first concern, but these ladies could not do the practical work of nursing and caring. Louise recruited sturdy and sensible country girls, who could be trained and sent out to do this work. They were known first as the Daughters of Charity and later became the world-wide Congregation of the Sisters of Charity of St Vincent de Paul. At a time when women religious were still unable to work outside the cloister they succeeded in doing so, because they took only yearly vows. Vincent's great reputation made the work possible; but it was Louise's sheer competence in organization and in training her young women that made the movement a success. Vincent gradually withdrew from the work, leaving Louise to manage the Congregation. They were still in close touch by correspondence in their final years, and the relationship between them was clearly one of friendship and personal affection.

These examples of partnership and the meeting of mind and spirit—of relationships based on *agape* rather than *eros*—provide models for Christian partnerships between men and women, based on common purpose.

MACRINA THE YOUNGER

(c. 330-379)

with

ST GREGORY OF NYSSA

MACRINA was the sister of three bishop-saints—Basil the Great, Gregory of Nyssa, and Peter of Sebaste. They came of an illustrious Christian family living in Cappadocia in Asia Minor. Their parents were St Basil the Elder and St Emmelia. Emmelia's father, whose name is unknown, was a great landowner and a martyr. Basil the Elder's parents fled to the mountains near the Black Sea during the the persecutions of the emperors Galerius and Maximian. His mother, Macrina the Elder, was a student of the great bishop St Gregory the Thaumaturge (Wonderworker) of Neo-Caesarea, of whom it was said that when he came to the city there were only seventeen Christians, and when he died there were only seventeen pagans. Gregory's methods of teaching included much use of feast-days and merrymaking, so when Macrina joined her son Basil and his wife Emmelia to help bring up their large family the children would have received good Christian teaching in an atmosphere of rejoicing.

By this time the persecutions were over, and Constantine, who had introduced religious toleration throughout the Roman Empire, had moved his capital to Byzantium. What this meant to Christians in Asia Minor is lyrically described by Eusebius of Caesarea in the closing passages of his

Ecclesiastical History. Eusebius says that Constantine "wiped the world clean from the hatred of God":

> Men had now lost all fear of their former oppressors, day after day they kept dazzling festival. They danced and sang in city and country alike, giving honour first of all to God our Sovereign Lord.... Old troubles were forgotten, and all irreligion passed into oblivion; good things present were enjoyed, those to come were eagerly awaited.

Basil the Elder was a celebrated teacher of rhetoric in Caesarea. He and Emmelia had ten children, five boys and five girls. Macrina the Younger was the eldest daughter and possibly the eldest child: the year of her birth is variously given as 327, 329, or 330. She shared with her mother and grandmother the upbringing and education of the younger children, as many elder daughters did in the days of large families. Since Macrina the Elder is thought to have died in 340, when young Macrina was only ten or eleven years old, a considerable burden must have fallen on the girl. Like her grandmother, she was scholarly, and she became a devout and learned Christian. She is said to have influenced Basil and Gregory to a religious vocation.

Basil went on to study at the great teaching institutions of the Eastern Mediterranean—in Caesarea, where Eusebius was his teacher and later bishop, then in Constantinople and Athens. He disliked student life, which was rowdy and promiscuous, but he made a close friend in Gregory of Nazianzus, son of the bishop of that city. Macrina the Younger is said to have been betrothed to a brother of Gregory Nazianzen; but he probably died, for when Basil completed his studies he and Macrina, who were much of an age, held long discussions on whether to make vows of celibacy. They both did so: Basil became a monk and then for some years a hermit, before being called from his retreat to defend the Church in 365. In 370 he became bishop of Caesarea. He and Macrina were much of an age, and when he came home puffed up with his new responsibilities she is said to have reproved him for vainglory (or, in the parlance of most sisters to their brothers, taken him down a peg). When the youger children had grown up Macrina became a consecrated virgin, living an ascetic life in her own home.

Gregory, who was five years younger than Melania, followed Basil in studying at Athens, married, and became a teacher of rhetoric. It is not known whether his wife died or became a nun, but after some time he became a monk. In 371 he was made bishop of Nyssa. Basil of Caesarea, Gregory Nazianzen, and Gregory of Nyssa are all named as Doctors of the Church and are known as the Three Cappadocian Fathers, champions of orthodoxy in a period when the basic tenets of Christianity were under attack from Arianism and the many other unorthodox beliefs that flourished in Asia Minor. Basil was renowned as a great administrator, Gregory Nazianzen as a theologian, and Gregory, whose mind was more speculative, as a philosopher. A younger brother, Peter, became bishop of Sebaste in 380.

While her brothers travelled and were active in the world, Macrina stayed with her mother and her family until she was about thirty years old. After Basil the Elder died in 370, Emmelia established a religious community on the banks of the river Iris, near Pontus, and Macrina moved there to become a nun and later a spiritual director. Basil, as bishop of Caesarea, was also exarch of Pontus, and the community was under his jurisdiction and protection.

After Basil the Great died in 379, Gregory, who had attended a synod in Antioch, visited Macrina on his way back to Nyssa. He had not seen his sister for eight years, and he was "yearning for an interchange of sympathy" over their joint loss. He says: "My soul was right sorrow-stricken by this grievous blow, and I sought for one who could feel it equally, to mingle my tears with. ... The mind, in time of bereavement, craves a certainty gained by reasoning as to the existence of the soul after death." He found Macrina very ill, lying on two planks and breathing with great difficulty; but she roused herself sufficiently to enter into a long exploration of the Church's teaching on life after death. He says:

> Basil, greatest among the saints, had departed from this life to God: and the impulse to mourn him was shared by all the churches. But his sister the Teacher was still living, so I journeyed to her.
>
> The sight of the Teacher wakened all my pain, for she too was lying in a state of prostration even unto death. Well, she gave in to me for a little while, like a skilful driver, in the ungovernable violence of my grief, and then she tried to check me by speaking, and to correct with the curb of her reasonings the disorder of my soul.

Throughout, Gregory the bishop speaks of his sister as "the Teacher" in tones of deep respect for her learning and piety. Their beloved brother has died; she comforts him and expounds the hope of the Resurrection to him. Gregory asks questions; she answers, and it is evident that she had some of her father's skill as a rhetorician, for he says her handling of his own ungovernable emotions and wild questionings was like a chariot driver handling a team of horses. Gregory's account of their discussions, *On the Soul and Resurrection*, is also known as the *Macriniae*.

"She quoted the Apostle's words about not being 'grieved for them that sleep' because only 'men without hope' have such feelings," Gregory recalls. She spoke at length on Christ's words, "Unless a wheat grain falls on the ground and dies, it remains only a single grain; but if it dies, it yields a rich harvest" (John 12:25). She recalled St Paul's letter to the Corinthians, in which he promised them that what was sown corruptible should be raised incorruptible (1 Cor. 9:53); and she spoke of her own vision of the life to come:

> She told her brother, "The Divine power, in the superabundance of Omnipotence, does not only restore you that body, once dissolved, but makes great and splendid additions to it." After death, all the features of the personality deriving from dishonour and corruption and weakness would be lost, but the personality would survive. When the negative aspects had been "purged from it and utterly removed," it would be "furnished in a manner more magnificent:"
>
> Then every one of the things which make up our conception of the Good will come and take their place: incorruption, that is, and life, and honour, and grace, and glory, and everything else that we conjecture is to be seen in God; and in his Image, man as he was made.

It is unlikely that Macrina could have made the long eschatological expositions attributed to her on a single occasion: probably brother and sister met several times, and her words were treasured all the more because it was evident that she also had not long to live. There were other people present with them, listening to her discourse and probably taking notes. Even in the few sentences quoted above we can catch the echo of the voice of the nun who was speaking in short sentences, controlling her breathing, for the sake of the brother she wanted to help through his grief. The suggestion of some commentators that these were really Gregory's ideas and that he put them in the mouth of his sister as a literary device is really not tenable. This great bishop would not have treated his memories of his last meeting with his beloved sister in such a way, and Macrina, like her mother and grandmother, was a learned and scholarly woman. She had taught Gregory when he was a child; he went back to her in the convent on the banks of the Iris in his hour of need.

Macrina died soon afterwards. Her possessions were so few that she had not even a shroud to be buried in, and Gregory provided one for her. He later wrote a brief panegyric on her life at the request of a monk named Olympus. The number of manuscript copies of this Life that have come from the Pontus district suggests that there was a considerable cult.

The separation of the Eastern Church from Rome in the ninth century and the fall of Constantinople to the Ottoman Turks in 1453 have left the West with a very limited knowledge of the glories of the Church in Asia Minor in the fourth century. Macrina's Life and the *Macriniae* were not known at all in the West until the eleventh century, when they were finally translated into Latin.

PAULA (347-404)
with ST JEROME

St Paula and a group of women studying the scriptures with St Jerome.

PAULA was born ten years after the death of Constantine the Great. She was a Roman noblewoman of illustrious stock. Her mother was descended from the Scipios and the Gracchi, and her father, a senator, traced his Greek ancestry back to King Agamemnon of Troy. Her husband, Toxotius, claimed descent from Aeneas, celebrated by Virgil as the founder of Rome.

Paula was a Christian, and Toxotius was not, but there was religious toleration, and such mixed marriages were common at the time. Rome in their day was only partially christianized. There were new churches, such as the basilica of St Peter, where Constantine had brought down twelve baskets of rubble with his own hands, in memory of the twelve apostles, and *Helena's church of Santa Croce, said to house a piece of the True Cross. The pope sat in the Lateran Palace; but Christian Rome existed side by side with a much older and pagan Rome, represented by the Pantheon and the temples, where the old Roman gods were still worshipped, and the Coliseum, where so many Christian martyrs had died in the days of persecution. Paula and Toxotius lived in a style suited to their time and status, and it was a time of great luxury for the wealthy. The homes of the senatorial class were palaces, with great courtyards and extensive gardens, pools and fountains, galleries

79

with marble statues and marble columns, rich wall-hangings and many slaves to do the work. Long hours were spent in the baths, and more at splendid banquets. The women wore many jewels, their hair was dressed elaborately, and they were carried through the streets in closed litters, which protected them from the sight and the stench of the poor. All the spoils of the known world had come to Rome, and Rome enjoyed them.

Paula probably took this kind of life for granted. It was all she had ever known. She and Toxotius were happy together, and they had five children, four daughters named Blessilla, Paulina, Eustochium, and Rufina, followed by a much-wanted son, named after his father. When her husband died, she was overwhelmed with grief. The attentions of friends and relatives, the sympathy of other noble families, meant nothing to her. She was intensely lonely, but she had no wish to remarry, as so many Roman women did. She was only thirty-two years old, and she had to decide, when the first grief was spent, what to do with the rest of her life. It was at this point that she turned to St Marcella, a woman ascetic whom St Jerome called "the glory of the ladies of Rome." Marcella had been widowed only seven months after her marriage, and Jerome writes of her:

> In those days, no high-born lady in Rome had made profession of the monastic life, or had ventured—so strange and degrading did it then seem—publicly to call herself a nun. It was from some priests of Alexandria and from Bishop Athanasius . . . that Marcella heard of the life of the Blessed Antony, then still alive, and of the monasteries in the Thebaïd [founded] by Pachomius, and of the discipline laid down for virgins and widows.

St Antony, the most prominent of the Desert Fathers, is thought to have died in 356, so Marcella and her friends must have been leading an ascetic life in Rome for more than twenty years when Paula turned to her for help. Her life was devoted to prayer and study, she slept on sackcloth, fasted, and drank no wine. She had given up all social engagements and amusements, and she devoted much of her wealth to the poor of the city. Paula joined Marcella and her circle, who were living a modified version of the lives of the Desert Fathers in their own homes and studying the scriptures. Through Marcella she met two bishops from the East: St Epiphanius, bishop of Salamis in northern Cyprus, and St Paulinus, bishop of Antioch. Pope Damasus I had convened a council in Rome, and the visiting bishops needed hospitality. Paula offered them accommodation, and through them she met Jerome.

Jerome, secretary to the aged Pope Damasus, had instructed Marcella's group in the Bible. He called them "the senate." All Jerome's writings suggest that he avoided contact with women. He was impatient of their triviality—

their preoccupation with dress and social life and domestic affairs; but this little group of ascetic widows attracted his notice. They were wealthy, they were influential (and Jerome had need of wealth and influence to help him in his great task of translating the Bible from Hebrew and Greek into Latin); but more than that, they were well-educated, and they wanted quite desperately to learn. They met regularly with Jerome for Bible study and made devotional visits to the martyrs' tombs, newly excavated under the supervision of Pope Damasus. Jerome advised them in chaste living, which involved the neglect of personal appearance, wearing coarse clothing, and not going to the baths. In return, the members of the study group bombarded him with questions: What were the ten names given to God by the Jews? What did "Selah" mean in the Psalms? Who were the Montanists, and why were they wrong?

Paula was looking for theological guidance: she asked Jerome about the nature of God, the life of Jesus Christ, the operation of the Holy Spirit, the work of the apostles. She already read Latin and Greek. Under Jerome's tutelage, she learned Hebrew, and he was astonished that she did so more quickly and easily than he had done. She developed a great love of the Psalms; and he must have found, as teachers often do, that an exceptionally bright pupil was turning into an assistant.

Their relationship did not pass unnoticed by the gossips of Rome. When Pope Damasus died in 384, Jerome was rumoured to be a possible candidate for the papacy; but he was a prickly and sarcastic man, often devastating in his comments on others. He had made many enemies, and allegations were made that he and Paula were lovers. Rome was still a very cynical and profligate society, and the story easily gained credence among those who could not imagine a man and a woman meeting for any other reason. A slave was induced, probably bribed, to swear to the allegations. In spite of Jerome's theological standing and his erudition, this slur effectively removed his name from the list of possible papal candidates, and Siricius was elected; but the case against Jerome dragged on. Jerome had to fight hard before an official clerical enquiry to clear his name and Paula's. He protested that Paula was chaste, and insisted that their work together was entirely innocent. He wrote afterwards in one of his letters:

The only woman who could give me delight was one whom I never so much as saw at table; yet when I had begun to revere, respect and look up to her, as her conspicuous chastity deserved, at once all my former virtues were held to have deserted me.

Paula, as a woman, was a non-citizen and could not defend herself, but Jerome brought the slave before the magistrates and forced him publicly to retract the allegations. The case ended in an acquittal, but Jerome was made to sign an undertaking that he would leave Rome. In August 385 he left in disgust at the debased morality and the malice of his enemies and went to Jerusalem.

Paula's daughters Eustochium and Blessilla, learned like their mother, had joined Jerome's study circle—the first of the noble virgins of Rome, the next generation of Christian women, to do so. Blessilla died in 383. Rufina had died young, Paulina was married to a Christian layman named Pammachius who was a friend of Jerome's, and Paula had no rights with regard to her son Toxotius, since a male member of her husband's family had become his legal guardian. Eustochium was the only one of her children left. Some months after Jerome's departure, mother and daughter sailed for the Middle East.

She and Eustochium were both still studying Hebrew, and they longed to see the Holy Land for themselves. They travelled with a small group of consecrated virgins and widows and went first to Cyprus, to see Bishop Epiphanius, who had stayed with Paula in Rome. Cyprus then had eleven bishoprics, and Epiphanius, as bishop of Salamis, was the metropolitan. They had long discussions with him and with other holy men on the island. They walked in the steps of St Paul, who was flogged at Paphos, and of St Barnabas, who was a Cypriot, martyred at Salamis. They visited monasteries and made a pilgrimage to the tomb of St Hilarion, though they found the tomb empty. After that they sailed for Antioch, to-visit Bishop Paulinus and to hear of the work of the Church in the East. Then they went overland to Jerusalem.

They travelled on mules, through the worst part of the winter, to Caesarea. There they visited the Centurion's House and the house where St Philip had lived with his four virgin daughters, before taking the Roman route through the plains of Sharon to Jerusalem. It was nearly sixty years after *Helena's pilgrimage and the finding of the True Cross. Paula felt a great attraction to the small church of the Holy Cross, which had been built on the site. She saw the stone on which Christ's body had reputedly lain when he was taken down from the cross, walked the Via Dolorosa, and visited the House of Caiaphas. She visited St Melania the Elder, who had gone in her widowhood from Rome to Jerusalem and built a community there for women. She was a relation by marriage, and Paula had been inspired by hearing of her travels.

Jerome, who had met the little group of women in Jerusalem, said of Paula, "She would see everything, and one could only drag her from one place to lead her into another." They went on to Bethlehem, about six miles to the south, where St Helena had built a small church over the place of the Nativity and restored the grotto in the cave below. Paula was greatly affected by the place where Jesus of Nazareth was born, already venerated by four centuries of Christians. She recreated in her mind the arrival and adoration of the Magi and the massacre of the Innocents, whose tiny stone sarcophagi rested in a nearby cave. She knelt and quoted from Psalm 131: "This is my rest for ever and ever. Here will I dwell, for I have chosen it."

The party went on to Bethphage, to Jericho, and to other places associated with the earthly life of Christ; and wherever they went, Paula sought out the poor and distributed alms. They went down into Egypt, to visit Alexandria, the great centre of learning where theologians, philosophers, historians, and other scholars studied the Gospels. They pressed on into the Thebaïd, to visit the monasteries and the hermits, the successors of the Desert Fathers. They were exhausted, and the journey was difficult: they encountered hostile Arabs and crocodiles, they suffered hunger and thirst, they endured tempests and sand storms. Once they lost their way and wandered about the desert for five days and nights. When they reached the hermits of Nitria, a wild desert place, Paula gave thanks to God who had "made the desert to flourish like a rose-garden." She knelt at the feet of the monks, asked about their daily lives, and listened eagerly to all that they had to say.

It was a year before she and Eustochium returned to Bethlehem and she took up her Hebrew studies again. A monk named Barabbas was her teacher. Jerome had settled in a cave very close to the place of the Nativity: it now lies beneath St Catherine's church, and there is a passage-way through the rocks into the grotto. In art, Jerome is often represented with an attendant lion in a rocky landscape, or in a well-stocked library with a cardinal's hat, but both images are remote from the facts. There were no printed books in his day and no cardinals. He certainly lived in a cave, but the area round the site of the Nativity was already well-populated with monks and hermits. Paula and Eustochium found him working at his usual furious pace, surrounded by manuscripts and copyists, and still having trouble with his Hebrew. He said that he "went creeping slowly through the darkness of the idioms, which to a Roman seemed so barbarous." Palladius says that Paula and Eustochium "cared for" Jerome, which suggests that they brought him his frugal meals and did his infrequent washing; but they were not housekeepers, they were fellow-scholars. Paula helped him with his Hebrew translations into Latin, and had better Greek than his for the New Testament, from her Greek father. We do not know the extent of her influence on his text, which became the basis of the Vulgate, but Jerome's continued respect for her and gratitude to her suggest that it was considerable. She also urged him to write his Biblical commentaries, which supplemented the textual works.

Paula founded two monastic communities, one for men with the help of Jerome, one for her own little band of virgins and widows. She also built a hostel for pilgrims, commenting, "If Mary and Joseph came back to Bethlehem, they would at least find a decent inn to receive them." She governed the women's community, which no man was allowed to enter. The nuns ate sparingly of simple food, made their own garments, and worked with their hands. They spent much time in silence. If any nun was talkative or passionate, she was told to walk last in procession, to pray outside the church, and to eat alone. They studied the scriptures with a new under-standing, in the land where Christ himself lived. Paula returned again and again to the mystery and wonder of the Incarnation, and she loved walking in the fields, picking wild flowers and thinking of the shepherds, and the heavenly host praising God, on the night when the Word became flesh. She wrote to Marcella in Rome, asking her to come and join the community:

> Certainly here we have no grand porticos, no gilded ceilings, no palaces built with the sweat and blood of the poor; neither have we our glorious basilicas with their arched roofs and avenues of columns. No; here there is but a cavern—a little fissure in the rock, a little recess in the earth; but it is here that he was born who made the heavens.

Marcella was too committed to her teaching in Rome to leave; but another future woman saint did come for a time: the lively and wealthy Fabiola, who had founded a hospital in Rome and who thought that she would settle in Bethlehem; but the life of a consecrated widow was not for her: she was too active and too tempestuous. Jerome commented that she would have expected the stable at Bethlehem to be in constant touch with the inn, and persuaded her to go back to Rome.

Paula spent nearly twenty years in the peace of Bethlehem. One of her joys was in educating her granddaughter. Her son Toxotius had married Laeta, the Christian daughter of a priest of the old Roman gods, and the couple sent their daughter Paula the Younger to be educated in Jerusalem. This Paula entered the community and succeeded her grandmother in ruling it.

In 407, when she was dying, Jerome asked Paula if anything troubled her. She replied in Greek, which had become her main language, "Oh! No—neither pain nor regret. I feel, on the contrary, a supreme peace." She died on 26 January 404, just after the setting of the sun.

People flocked to her funeral. Her body was reverently carried by bishops, and the poor came in their hundreds, crying that they had lost their mother; but it was Jerome who wrote her epitaph:

The daughter of the Scipios, of the Pauli, of the Gracchi, of the illustrious blood of Agamemnon, rests in this spot. She bore the name of Paula. She was the mother of Eustochium. The first in the series of noble Roman matrons, she preferred the poverty of Christ and the humble fields of Bethlehem to the splendours of Rome.

OLYMPIAS (? 361-408)
with ST JOHN CHRYSOSTOM

Fresco from Kariye Cami, Istanbul.

OLYMPIAS, one of the great benefactors of the Church in Constantinople in the late fourth century, became a deaconess and was persecuted for her support of St John Chrysostom when he fell from imperial favour. She was born in Constantinople, where her grandfather Abbabibios was in favour with Constantine, and became a consul and a prefect. Her father was also at court and became chamberlain, or master of the palace. Palladius says that his name was Seleucus, but Cardinal Baronius thought that this was a gloss introduced by a copyist.

Olympias was born some time between 361 and 368 and orphaned when she was very young. Her uncle, the prefect Procopius, a friend of St Gregory Nazianzen, entrusted her to the care of Theodosia, sister to St Amphilochius. Theodosia had formed a group of Christian women who studied the scriptures together and were taught by both saints. The historian Palladius, marvelling at their powers of intellect and sanctity, called them "manly women," which he no doubt meant as approval.

Olympias wished to remain a virgin and to stay with this group, but she was a great heiress, and Procopius instructed Theodosia to prepare her for marriage and life at court. She was married to Nebridius, sometime prefect of Constantinople, with great pomp and ceremony. Nebridus must have been much older than she was. Gregory Nazianzen approved the marriage and wrote apologizing because age and bad health (he had gout) kept him from attending the wedding. Nebridius died soon after: some accounts say that the marriage lasted two years, but Palladius says that it lasted only four days and that Olympias remained a virgin. Her uncle Procopius wanted her to make a prestigious remarriage, and the emperor Theodosius proposed that she should marry his cousin Elpidius; but Olympias determined to remain celibate, saying, "If my Lord had wished me to live with a man, he would not have taken away Nebridius."

The emperor, incensed and convinced that a young woman was incapable of managing such great wealth, placed her fortune in the hands of the urban prefect, with orders that he was to act as her guardian until she was thirty years old. The prefect prevented her from seeing the bishop or from going to church. She worked among the poor and lived simply. It was not until 391 that the emperor, observing her quiet and steady life, restored her liberty and returned her property.

St Nectarius, bishop of Constantinople, made her a deaconess soon after. This was a considerable mark of trust and respect. She was about thirty years of age, and the usual custom at the time was that only women over the age of sixty should be deaconesses, on the assumption that younger women might be a source of scandal. Olympias had a large house built, where she welcomed visiting bishops and clergy, pilgrims, travellers, and the sick and poor— anybody in need of shelter. Many early institutions were of this undifferentiated kind, serving the functions of hotel, hostel, hospital, and hospice. Other single women who wanted to devote themselves to the service of God came to staff the house. They dressed plainly, lived simply, and established a regular pattern of prayer and Bible study. John Chrystostom, who first met her when he was assistant to the bishop of Constantinople, shared her belief that Christians should be devoted to the relief of poverty and sickness and helped her to establish an orphanage and a separate hospital for sick poor—similar to the *ptokhotropheia* established by Basil the Great in Caesarea. Olympias was so liberal in giving that John thought she was attracting spongers. He advised her to be more cautious in giving alms, so that she would have money for those who needed it most: "You must not encourage the laziness of those who live upon you without necessity. It is like throwing your money into the sea."

In 398 John Chrysostom succeeded Nectarius in the see of Constantinople. He took Olympias and her disciples under his protection, and she supported his work; but John incurred the enmity of Theophilus, patriarch of Alexandria, a man greedy for money, who had been one of the chief spongers on Olympias. When four monks known as the Tall Brothers on account of their height were expelled from Nitria and came to Constantinople to appeal against Theophilus, Olympias sheltered and fed them at her own expense.

John was a forthright bishop, prepared to speak out against the corruption of both the Church and the Eastern Empire. He became surrounded by enmity, jealousy, and rancour. Theophilus intrigued against him, holding lavish banquets and promising honours to his own supporters. The empress Eudoxia favoured Theophilus, taking some of John's preaching against vain and luxury-loving women as personal criticism. In 403 Theophilus convened a synod of three disaffected bishops to hear forty-six charges against John. He was accused of having carried out irregular ordinations; of eating alone (hardly an offence: he had a delicate stomach, and ate sparingly); of receiving women without a chaperone; of taking his bath alone. John's contemptuous reply to these trumped-up charges was that he was not insane: he had no intention of appearing before a synod composed of his enemies, but if he was called to answer before a general synod of the Church he would do so. The synod condemned him in his absence, and the emperor exiled him to Bithynia, though he was soon called back to Constantinople when there were popular demonstrations in his favour. There was an earthquake during his brief exile, and this may have affected both the attitude of the empress and that of the populace, being taken as a mark of divine disfavour; but the empress was still determined to be rid of him. She had a large silver statue of herself placed opposite the great cathedral of Hagia Sophia and deliberately arranged games and races on Good Friday and Holy Saturday. She refused to receive Communion from John. During this time of tribulation Olympias openly supported John and went to the cathedral to hear him speak. The empress claimed that he had referred to her as "Jezebel," and he replied with an outspoken sermon. He was seized and exiled again, being moved from place to place, ever further from Constantinople, until his death in 407.

John's exile greatly distressed Olympias. She wrote to him repeatedly (though unfortunately only his side of the correspondence has been preserved, not hers) and supported him generously with funds for the rest of his life. Meanwhile, she, like his other friends, was also at risk in the persecution of his supporters that followed his departure. There was a riot at the cathedral, during which the building caught fire. John's supporters claimed that their persecutors had deliberately set fire to it in order to burn them alive. The authorities accused John's friends of starting the blaze. Olympias and others were arrested and brought before a tribunal headed by Optatus, the prefect of the city. She defended herself energetically, telling Optatus that he was her accuser and was not competent to act as judge in the case: his real role was as prosecutor. She said contemptuously that she was not in the habit of burning churches—she had used her wealth to build them. Told to recognize Arsacius, John's replacement as bishop of Constantinople, as his lawful successor, she refused to do so, protesting against the injuries which had been done to a faithful bishop and his supporters.

She was very ill all winter and kept to her room. In the spring, she was heavily fined for her refusal to accept Communion from Arsacius and exiled to Cyzicus. Atticus, successor to Arsacius, broke up her community and put an end to all her charitable works. She was frequently ill, and the outrageous slanders and persecutions continued. John Chrysostom comforted her from his own places of exile by his letters, of which seventeen survive.

"To my Lady, the Deaconess Olympias, greatly blessed and beloved of God," he writes. The letters contain many enquiries about her health and advice about how she should deal with adversity. She is not to abandon herself to the tyranny of sorrow, but to conquer the tempest of her emotions by calm and rational thought. He tells her how he has seen the results of a fierce storm at sea—the wrecked ships, the bodies of the drowned sailors; but as God calmed the storm, so he will calm the storms in their lives. He quotes Isaiah 51, verses 7-8:

> Listen to me, you who know what integrity means,
> people who take my laws to heart;
> do not fear the taunts of men,
> nor be dismayed by their insults,
> for the moth shall eat them like garments,
> the grub devour them like wool,
> but my integrity will remain for ever,
> and my salvation for all generations.

He says very little about his own tribulations, though we know that he suffered on long and painful journeys by sea and land. These are the letters of a man under great pressure, but they are protective and caring, the meditations and exhortations of a Father in God.

John Chrysostom died in September 407 while he was being harried by soldiers to move to yet another place of exile. He wrote to Olympias in what was probably the last of his letters:

> Can you not see the enabling power of God? Can you see his wisdom? Can you see his unfathomable ways? Can you see his love and care for mankind? Do not be perturbed, do not be troubled, but stay where you are, giving thanks to God for all things, glorifying him, calling upon him, praying to him, entreating him. Even if the storms break in front of your eyes, do not fear them. . . . He can raise up them that are fallen, guide those who are lost, reassure those who are shocked and disgusted . . . bring to life the dead, render more radiant those who have been destroyed, and make young again those who have grown old.

The historian Palladius tells the story of how these two lonely people sustained each other from their places of confinement. Olympias died in the year after John. She was less than fifty years old. She had endured the loss of her fortune, the destruction of her community and her charitable work, and chronic illness, but she was fortified by John Chrysostom's burning faith. Gregory Nazianzen called her "the glory of the widows of the Eastern Church." Palladius says that she "engaged in no mean combat for the truth's sake" and that the people of Constantinople reckoned her life among those of the confessors, "for she went away to the Lord in the midst of her struggles for God's honour."

CLARE
OF
ASSISI

(1194-1253)

with

ST FRANCIS

Detail from St Clare and St Elizabeth *by Filippo Memmi, in Assisi.*

CLARE was eighteen years old when Francis of Assisi, who had dramatically and publicly renounced his family inheritance in the same city in his youth, preached in the church of San Giorgio in 1212. By then, Francis had developed his brotherhood of friars devoted to poverty and simple Christianity and drawn up his Rule.

Little is known of Clare's girlhood. Her family was aristocratic and bore famous names: her father was Faverone Offreduccio, and her mother Ortalano di Fiumi. She had two younger sisters. Their father was dead by the time she first heard Francis preach, and their male relatives—brothers, uncles or cousins—were pressing Clare to marry. At eighteen, she was well beyond the usual age of marriage for a girl, and it is probable that she was already contemplating a vow of virginity. We do not know what earlier efforts had been made to marry her off, but she had evidently resisted them. Now her relatives were impatient. Custom demanded that the eldest daughter should marry first, so she was blocking the marriage prospects of her sisters. Clare listened to Francis as he talked of abandoning the world and serving God, and the conviction grew that she was called to a similar way of life. Her contemporary biographer, thought to be Thomas of Celano, says that "The love and flower of earthly things seemed to her but smoke, and a false painting of short durance."

On Palm Sunday, 1212, Clare went to the cathedral at Assisi for the service of the Blessing of Palms. When the rest of the congregation went to the altar rails to have their palms blessed, she held back, but the bishop saw her praying and went down to her and gave her a palm branch. That night she left home and went to the small Franciscan community about a mile from the town. In a simple service attended by the friars, Francis cut off her hair before the altar, and she exchanged her rich brocaded clothes for a robe of sacking, tied at the waist with cord. Since the friars had no accommodation for women, she was taken to the Benedictine nunnery of St Paul.

This dramatic story, re-told many times, is a compression of what actually happened. It is recorded that Francis, when he was labouring to rebuild the church at San Damiano, before he had any companions, addressed the interested crowd that had gathered to watch, saying, "Come and help me in my work on the monastery of San Damiano, since there will one day be ladies here, and by their celebrated holy way of life, our Father in heaven will be glorified in all his holy Church." It seems that Francis had decided from the first that his movement should be open to women as well as men and was seeking a woman who would develop a parallel women's Order.

Though there were Benedictine monasteries for women and some double monasteries, such as that established at Fontrevault in 1099 by Robert of Arbrissel, women were considered something of an embarrassment in the reformed monasteries. The Cistercians refused to recognize women's communities, and the Praemonstratensians, who had over ten thousand women by the mid-twelfth century, ceased to recruit them and became a wholly male Order. This was less a denial of women's spirituality than a fear of sexual scandal. The Benedictine Rule, by which women were strictly enclosed, was considered the only appropriate Rule for them: the male Orders could be left to initiate new forms of monasticism, untroubled by female concerns and female frailty.

Thomas of Celano tells us that before Clare was received by the Franciscans, "Francis visited Clare, and she more often visited him, so ordering the times of their visits that their meetings might neither become known by men nor disparaged by public rumour." Clearly the utmost discretion was necessary. She never went alone. She always took one trusted friend with her—probably her aunt, Buona Guelfuccio, or one of her sisters—and Francis met her in the company of other friars. While this procedure had the merit of avoiding gossip, it must have made the kind of close collaboration they needed somewhat difficult.

Both Clare and Francis would have had to be very sure that her acceptance was God's will for the Order before she made her public gesture. It was Francis who told her to go to the cathedral on Palm Sunday, and he must have consulted the bishop before making any public move. The fact that the bishop went down to Clare where she knelt in her pew in the cathedral on Palm Sunday and gave her the palm branch in full view of the congregation suggests a mark of approval for this new beginning.

Clare's female relatives probably knew about her plans. Her widowed mother, her aunt, and her two sisters Agnes and Beatrice joined her community soon after its establishment, but her male relatives were certainly not informed in advance. When her commitment became known they were outraged. Whatever the standing of Francis in the eyes of the Church, he must still have been regarded as something of a maverick in Assisi. Quite apart from their belief that they alone had a right to determine Clare's future, Francis was not one of their own kind: he was the son of a local merchant, not a nobleman; he was not even a priest: he remained a deacon all his life. These factors, which seem so unimportant now, must have weighed heavily at the time. For a well-born young woman to join this dubious character and his friends, even under the chaperonage of Benedictine nuns, was unthinkable. Her brothers and uncles went in a body to the nunnery to carry her home, violating the enclosure and pursuing her into the chapel. Bribes and threats did not move her, and they turned to force. When she clung to the altar they tried to drag her out of the sanctuary, pulling off the altar cloths with her. Perhaps this act of sacrilege finally made them hesitate, for Clare, freed for a moment, took off her head-covering. She "showed them her head all shaven and affirmed that never would she depart from the service of God."

Then, it seems, they admitted defeat, and she was left free to begin her new life. She remained with the Benedictines until Francis was able to offer her and her companions a small house close to the church of San Damiano. By that time she had been joined by her female relatives, and other women came, including members of the illustrious Ubaldini family from Florence. There was a further explosion of male disapproval when her sister Agnes entered the community: at one point, Thomas of Celano tells us, twelve of her kinsman went "all furious" to the place where they were, and Agnes was dragged out by her hair, but Clare's prayers saved her.

In 1215 Clare was appointed abbess of this small community—against her will, for she had no desire to take authority. Thomas says: "The more that prelacy seemed a great thing, the less did she assume it, and it seemed to her a thing vile." After three years she tried to lay down the office, but Francis persuaded her to return to it. It was not an easy assignment. Francis did not obtain final papal recognition for his own Rule until 1223, three years before his death, and Clare was to wait much longer for her own. She had to do most of the negotiations without his support. She had promised obedience to Francis, and she needed his help and inspiration both in spiritual matters and in obtaining recognition of the Rule. After a short period in which the friars visited frequently and the nuns nursed a sick friar, the two groups were firmly separated by ecclesiastical authority. The friars were instructed to keep away from the nuns' convent. Francis was not allowed to help in the development of the parallel Order and, no doubt under pressure from his superiors, rejected all familiarity with women. In his later life he said that he never looked directly at them, and that he knew only two women by sight. If his mother was one, we may hope that Clare was the other.

Pope Gregory IX (1227-41) imposed a ban on visits to the convent by the Franciscan friars without his special permission. Whether the real cause was a disagreement between the friars and the nuns, as was alleged, or whether the ban was due to the Pope's own belief that the sexes should be strictly segregated, is not clear; but this caused considerable problems for the women. In double communities it was customary for the nuns to depend on the friars not only for the priestly services of Confession and the celebration of the Eucharist but for doing heavy work and for contacts with the outside world. Clare and her Sisters did not have farms or household servants, and they were left very much to their own resources. Attempts were made to impose the Benedictine Rule on them. For a time they suffered total enclosure, so that they could not beg, or visit the sick and poor, or even attend the church in San Damiano. Benedictine clergy were sent into the convent to hear their Confessions and celebrate Mass instead of the Franciscan friars. They were not allowed any contact with the friars.

The community had five different Rules imposed upon it in Clare's lifetime, but she clung to her ideal of poverty and was not prepared to own property. Pope Gregory IX offered the Sisters a yearly revenue, which would have given them an income without the need to beg, but this was firmly refused. They were determined to live in daily dependence on God, like the birds of the air and the lilies of the field (Matt. 6:25-34). It was not until 1228 that the Pope at last granted the nuns of San Damiano the *privilegium paupertatis*, or privilege of poverty, which meant that they were under no obligation to accept rents or possessions. Despite all the hardships, Clare had her own very clear vision of her Rule and the pattern of life involved. The constant pressure from the hierarchy to assimilate it to existing patterns of monastic life for women must have been a heavy burden to bear.

During these long years of conflict Clare was faithful to her vision. A basic principle of her community was the practice of "holy silence." The Sisters spoke only when necessary. Clare thought that silence would avoid many sins of the tongue and aid recollection. She herself never left her enclosure, but when the Sisters left the convent to beg for the poor and for their own sustenance she would wait for them to return, washing and kissing their bare feet. She was the servant of servants—waiting at table, nursing the sick, ringing the bell and lighting the first candle in the morning, praying late into the night.

This simple and caring movement for women soon spread to other parts of Italy, to Germany, and to France. Clare's contemporary, Cardinal Jacques de Vitry, who had been the confessor and disciple of Bd Mary of Oignies when he was a Canon Regular at Liège, wrote with much sympathy of the Franciscan movement for both men and women:

> Many of both sexes have left the world, called *Fratres Minores et Sorores Minores*. They are revered by popes and cardinals, but have no care for temporal things, labouring for the cure of souls. They live according to the pattern of the primitive Church ... by day they enter cities and towns, giving practical help that they may benefit some; by night they return to a hermitage or lonely house, devoting themselves to contemplation. The women live together near the cities in separate hostels: they receive nothing, but live by the toil of their hands, and are greatly upset and troubled because they are honoured by clergy and laity more than they wish.

It is understandable that the rapid development of the Order, in which women had a much greater degree of freedom of movement than under the Benedictine Rule, must at first have been alarming to those who believed that all women bore the taint of Eve's sin and could only be granted a place in the Church under conditions of close confinement and masculine authority, and it must have been equally alarming to those of a more protective nature who believed that women needed to be sheltered in what was undoubtedly a very harsh world, but it was attractive to many women who wanted to live a simple Christian life without being hampered by restrictions.

In 1236 Agnes, daughter of the Bohemian king Ottokar I, was allowed to form a convent in Prague on the lines of that at San Damiano. Agnes, like Clare, had been subject to pressures to marry, and she was twenty-eight before the royal family of Bohemia finally abandoned their dynastic plans and consented to her wishes. Clare sent Agnes five nuns from Assisi and a series of wise and affectionate letters, of which four are still extant. One included advice to restrain from excessive austerity, "since our bodies are not of brass and our strength is not the strength of stone, but rather we are weak and subject to corporal infirmities." Agnes and her Sisters were encouraged to continue "living and hoping in the Lord," so that they might offer him "a reasonable service and a sacrifice seasoned with the salt of prudence."

The Sisters became known as the Poor Ladies of St Clare, and then the Poor Clares for short. Clare herself remained abbess at San Damiano for forty years. Francis of Assisi died in 1226, but she lived on, increasingly frail, until 1253. She found a more sympathetic pontiff in Pope Innocent IV, who succeeded Pope Gregory in 1243. He drew up a new Rule for the Order, much closer to the Franciscan ideal but still providing that the nuns should accept rents or property. Clare was not willing to accept it and drew up her own Rule—she was the first foundress to do so. Pope Innocent visited San Damiano and gave Clare absolution, saying, "Would to God I had as little need of it." He visited her again two days before her death, to give final confirmation of her Rule in the form she had designed.

In her long final illness Clare was determined still to be of service to the Church. She spent many hours in devotion to the Blessed Sacrament and made corporals and altar-cloths for the churches of the area. Among the people who came to her death-bed were her sister Agnes and three of the original group of Franciscan friars—Brother Juniper, Brother Angelo, and Brother Leo—as well as many bishops and cardinals. When she was dying Clare was heard to say to herself, "Go forth in peace, for you have followed the good road. Go forth without fear, for he that created you has sanctified you, has always protected you, and loves you as a mother. Blessed be thou, O God, for having created me."

Clare was canonized in 1255, two years after her death. Her Life was written about the same time by order of Pope Alexander IV, who, as Cardinal Rainaldo, had been her friend and a frequent visitor to San Damiano in her later years. Thomas of Celano was the biographer of Francis of Assisi, and though the authorship of Clare's Life has been queried, it is now generally agreed that it comes from the same hand. He writes of her life at San Damiano with gentle understanding and affection:

> In this little house, which seemed like a cloister, the Lady Saint Clare enclosed herself. And for her, the tempest of the world ceased, and she secluded her body as long as she lived. She may be called a silver dove, for thus does the dove make her nest and her walls, and thus did she build herself in with other such little ones, there where she brought forth to God a great company of virgins.

After Clare's death her sister Agnes became the superior of the Order, and the community was removed from San Damiano to the convent of Santa Chiara, high above the town of Assisi, where her body still lies in its shrine.

LOUISE de MARILLAC

(1591-1660)

with

ST VINCENT de PAUL

*Portrait by
Gaspard Duchange.*

LOUISE DE MARILLAC, co-founder of the Daughters of Charity with St Vincent de Paul, shared Vincent's deep Christian concern for the poor and oppressed and worked with him in an unique partnership. Vincent came from a peasant family in Gascony and combined a ministry to the rich and fashionable with the foundation of the Society of mission priests that bears his name. Priests could cross the social barriers of a highly stratified society, but women were seldom able to do this. It is necessary to know something of Louise's mysterious background to understand how she became able to relate to aristocratic ladies, to the country girls who formed the Daughters of Charity, and to the sick and poor people whom she served.

She was almost certainly illegitimate. Her father, Louis de Marillac, was the son of a distinguished family in the Auvergne. Louise was born on 12 August 1591, between the death of his first wife, who was childless, and his re-marriage in 1595. The pages for 1590 to 1595 have disappeared from the local birth register, and there is no trace of another marriage in those years; but though we do not even know the name of Louise's mother, Louis acknowleged her as his daughter. She bore both his baptismal name and the patronymic, and he made provision for her when she was born: an annual sum of one hundred *livres* and a field on his estate at Ferrières. She was given a larger pension when he remarried and a still larger one in his will. He kept her in his own household for some years. When a legitimate child was born of his second marriage, he settled on Louise the sum of a thousand *livres*, family jewels, and household goods such as she might bring to a marriage of her own. He died before her marriage, but she was described in the marriage certificate as his daughter, though there was no mention of her mother. He seems to have done everything he could to give her full recognition as his daughter and his first child. At this time there was a sharp social distinction between the child of an unknown father and the child of a father who honourably acknowledged his responsibilities. While today reproach would be attached to the irresponsible father, then it was the child of such a father who incurred the full stigma. The child of a father who acknowledged paternity and provided maintenance was acceptable in society.

Who was Louise's mother? Biographers have speculated that she may have been a girl from the de Marillac estate. Pehaps she died when the child was born; but there is another possibility. Louise was thirteen when her father died, and about that time she was taken away from the fashionable royal convent at Poissy, where she was acquiring an excellent education, and sent to the household of "a poor spinster" who ran a small residential establishment for girls without homes of their own. It seems fairly clear that the de Marillacs, including her stepmother, were unwilling to pay the high fees for Poissy; but the "poor spinster" may have been her natural mother. Louis de Marillac may have protected the reputation of his former mistress and provided the funds to give her a home and an income.

Whatever the limitations of the house of the "poor spinster," it was a Christian background and a respectable one. Louise read the *Imitation of Christ* and St Francis de Sales' *Introduction to a Devout Life*, developed a devotion to St Luis of Granada, and learned to meditate. She spent much time in churches, listening to the sermons of Jesuits and Capuchin friars. It was a time of spiritual renewal in France, after the end of the Thirty Years' War and the accession of the newly Catholic Henry of Navarre. Louise made a vow in her prayers that she would enter a religious Order. She wanted to become a Capuchine, but her confessor, Fr de Champigny, thought that she was not physically strong enough for the rigours of the religious life.

There was only one alternative: marriage. Though Louise had only a relatively small dowry, she now had a considerable social advantage in her de Marillac relatives, who had become prominent in court circles. Belatedly, they helped to settle her. She was married to Antoine Le Gras, a court official. In seventeenth-century France only ladies of rank were addressed as "Madame," and her husband's status was not such as to give her that title. All other women, married or single, were "Mademoiselle," so Louise was, somewhat confusingly, often referred to in her own day as "Mademoiselle le

Gras." Antoine held the post of secretary to the Queen's Household. He was apparently rather a dull man, in poor health and with a sharp temper; but a young woman in Louise's position had no choice. It seems that she and Antoine tried to make a good Catholic marriage—they asked jointly for permission to read the Bible in its unabridged form, a privilege seldom granted to the laity. Then Antoine's health deteriorated, and so did his temper. They had a child—a son named Michel, of whom we know little except that he was backward and unstable and that Vincent de Paul later helped him to marry and settle down. It sounds like a loveless and unrewarding marriage.

Louise continued to care for her husband until his death in 1625, but she went through a long period of profound depression, in which she thought that she was being punished for not keeping her vow of virginity. She received some spiritual help from Pierre Camus, bishop of Belley, but his diocese was far away. Francis de Sales advised her, but he died in 1622. She invoked Francis in her prayers for a new spiritual director, and on the feast of Pentecost 1623, in the Paris church of S. Nicolas-de-Champs, her prayer was answered. She met Vincent de Paul, and he agreed to act as her spiritual mentor. At first she found him hard and cold—he lacked the gentle manners of Pierre Camus or Francis de Sales and was reluctant to take on the burden of directing a woman when there was so much to do in setting up his mission for the poor. Vincent's principle was that " the poor man comes first in the Church; he is prince and master there. . . . The sick man is a suffering member of the Body of Christ." By degrees, however, he and Louise developed a close mutual trust and understanding. Through his help she was able to care for Antoine Le Gras, to cope with the burning fevers and the haemorrhages, to make his last days bearable and turn him to God.

When Antoine died on 21 December 1625 Louise was resolved not to marry again. She moved into a small apartment. She had to decide what to do with her life, and she consulted her spiritual advisers, who told her that the decision had to be her own. Pierre Camus wrote to her from Belley, and told her that she relied too much on spiritual direction: "Behold, Monsieur Vincent is now eclipsed (*i.e.* busy with other things), and Mlle le Gras is out of humour, she has lost her bearings and is bewildered. It is very necessary to see God in our guides and directors, and to look at them as they are in God; but sometimes it is necessary to look to God only, for he can cure our paralysis and other disorders without the help of man."

Mlle le Gras stayed in her small apartment, praying. She painted watercolours, sewed and knitted for Monsieur Vincent's poor, and made vestments and an altar frontal for him. He begged her not to work so hard, not to load herself with pious practices and rules. She was in her late thirties.

She had never known real affection, and her life was joyless, but she had to find herself. Wisely, Vincent also refused to tell her what to do. It took her over two years to find her calling.

Vincent had developed associations of aristocratic women, the Ladies of Charity, who had a concern for poor and sick people. In 1628 he asked Louise to inspect the growing number of his charities, and she discovered skills and talents she had never known she possessed. She would set out by public coach with a friend or a servant, taking a basket of linen, clothing, and medicines. She made detailed reports, some of which still exist, of what she found, which services were efficient or inefficient, which were in debt and needed extra assistance. In every centre she found a teacher to teach the children to read, believing that literacy was the first step to improving their situation. She went to Montmirail, Asnires, Saint-Cloud, Villepreux, Saint-Germain, Verneuil, Beauvais, and into Burgundy revitalizing the local organizations, rallying support. She was out in all weathers and learned how to address groups of people. Often the men came to hear her as well as the women. Sometimes there was opposition: in one place she was denounced for "subversive activities," and in another the curé complained that she was trying to do his work, but in the main she was welcomed and found support.

She discovered that although the Ladies of Charity were prepared to give money and time to this work, few of them had the capacity to do the practical work of caring on a regular basis. It required physical strength and a knowledge of how the poor lived. After a time the aristocratic ladies tended to send money or a servant instead of giving personal service. Louise saw a need for a regular body of women who would devote themselves to the work on a full-time basis. She decided to recruit stalwart country girls with plenty of common sense, who could be trained in religion and nursing care. On 26 November 1633 she accepted the first four, housing them in her own apartment.

Vincent de Paul worked with her every step of the way, keeping the clergy and public authorities informed of the plans. So great was his reputation and that of the priests he trained that there was no opposition. He gave her personal support too. Her son Michel, intended for the priesthood, had left the seminary and got into difficulties. Vincent found him a post as a bailiff and later induced the de Marillac relatives to find enough money for him to marry. Within a year Louise had moved to larger accommodation and there were twelve members of her organization. She named them the Daughters of Charity and drew up statutes, which Vincent approved. They were taught prayer, meditation, basic nursing, and how to meet the needs of the very poor, whose life was a continual struggle to survive. They wore peasant clothes—the white cornette, the grey stuff gown and clogs—so that they could pass unnoticed in a crowd. Before long Vincent wrote to Louise: "You are in demand everywhere! Just imagine! Good-natured servants, content with little in the way of board and lodging—the whole world is looking for them."

By May 1636 there were fifteen Daughters, and they moved into a large house near Saint-Lazare. Three years later they moved again, into a big house opposite the priory of Saint-Lazare, Vincent de Paul's headquarters. The Ladies of Charity supplied funds. The house was bought by the Mission and resold to the Daughters of Charity. There were none of the financial problems that beset so many new foundations for women. Louise did not run into debt. She chose the postulants and trained them. She looked for prudent and sensible girls, rejecting those of a dour or melancholy nature (the sick poor needed cheerful people around them) and those liable to be discontented or flighty. They were accepted only with the consent of their parents and a recommendation from their parish priest. They had to come with a new set of suitable clothes—and their fare home, in case they decided not to stay.

Soon suburban foundations were made: at Saint-Germain-en-Laye in 1638 and at Richelieu in 1639. At Angers, many miles to the south, the Daughters of Charity were invited to take over the hospital. Louise went to Angers with the girls, drew up a contract with the magistrates, and discovered an excellent ally in the vicar general, the Abbé de Vaux. At Nantes the Daughters cleaned and equipped a decrepit hospital and were promised the support of ladies "many in number and high in rank." Inevitably there were problems: at Nantes there were some misunderstandings over the use of funds; at Liancourt the Daughters were accused of being flighty and were excluded from Communion; at Char there were wordy battles with a Jansenist curé. Louise seems to have sorted out all these situations and many others. There were problems with the girls too: despite all the care she took in selection, one was much too enthusiastic about wielding the lancet and bleeding patients, another stole the community money-box, a third left and took some of the poultry with her. Most of the Daughters worked very hard; indeed some of them are thought to have died of exhaustion in the early years.

In 1634 Louise made her vows and drafted a Constitution for the Daughters of Charity, and in 1642 the first four were allowed to make annual vows of poverty. Vincent told the girls: "Your convent will be the house of the sick; your cell, a hired room; your chapel, the parish church; your cloister, the streets of the city or the wards of the hospital; your enclosure, obedience; your grating, the fear of God; your veil, holy modesty."

In 1647 Vincent de Paul and Louise constructed the Rule: it was to be a secular Congregation of women devoted to the sick and the poor. In 1658

Cardinal de Retz, archbishop of Paris, transmitted official approval from Rome: Vincent was appointed director and Louise superior general.

Most of the work of nursing in the Hôtel Dieu in Paris was taken over by the Daughters of Charity. Louise also took on the terrible problems of the *enfants trouvés*—the four hundred children abandoned each year on the Paris streets—and set up a foster-care scheme and a foundling hospital. She started schools for girls in Paris before John Baptist de la Salle started equivalent schools for boys. Many of the Daughters were not well educated when they joined the Congregation, and Louise trained them herself. She and Vincent de Paul held "conferences" for the Daughters in Paris once or twice a month. All attended unless they had urgent business with the sick. The subject was announced by letter in advance, and the girls were asked to meditate on it. When the conference took place Monsieur Vincent would make his meditation, then Mademoiselle; then the girls would be asked to speak and to "contribute to the common spiritual treasury." The youngest and shyest of the postulants would be encouraged to express their ideas, and the two discussion leaders would pick up and enlarge on their thoughts, making them feel that their contributions were valued. Notes were taken during these sessions and transcripts circulated to other houses. Though some of the transcripts have been lost, a large number have survived (and are still available in Pierre Cost's edition of the *Conferences*). The discussions were simple, straightforward, and in familiar terms.

Vincent gradually withdrew from the work of the Congregation, leaving Louise to run it. She developed a gift for organization. Perhaps because of her somewhat ambiguous background, she was able to move between the social classes: she could talk to aristocratic ladies, teach the postulants, chat with children, talk to the poor. She had married and had a difficult child; she had experienced suffering and understood suffering in others.

Louise and Vincent de Paul continued to correspond until her death. They discussed theological issues, exchanged prayers and meditations, sent reports on their ailments, and offered each other remedies. It was a long and affectionate friendship. In February 1660, when Louise had not long to live, she asked to see Vincent for one last time. He lived only across the road, but he was eighty years old and also ill. He sent a Brother to tell her that she should depart in peace and that he would soon be joining her in heaven. She died on 16 March 1660 and he on 27 September of the same year.

Louise de Marillac was canonized on 4 March 1934, and the Daughters (now Sisters) of Charity today number some fifty thousand in foundations all over the world. They still take annual vows, though these may be repeatedly renewed. The original Act of Consecration of 1658 is still read out every year and ratified by the Congregation.

At a time when women in religious Orders were still unable to leave the cloister and work in the community the Daughters of Charity succeeded in doing so. They had four advantages: the patronage of aristocrats, sufficient funds for their work, the support of the charismatic and much respected Vincent de Paul, and the fact that they took only annual vows, so that they could be regarded as in the world and not in the cloister. They were allowed the freedom that other women with a religious vocation—notably *Mary Ward—sought in the seventeenth century and failed to obtain.

4

WIVES AND MOTHERS

ST PAUL, in response to queries from members of the Church in Corinth, told them that it was better to marry than to burn—or, in the less memorable phrase of the *New Jerusalem Bible*, better to be married than tortured. He proceeded in 1 Corinthians 7 to set down some guidelines for married life. Marriage involves mutual rights and responsibilities: "The husband must give the wife what she has a right to expect, and so too the wife to the husband." Each has rights over the other's body. They should not refuse each other "except by mutual consent, and then only for an agreed time, to leave yourselves free for prayer," and they should be faithful to one another.

This much Paul is certain is the will of God. He then proceeds to add what he makes clear is his own opinion. He himself is unmarried, and he thinks that "in these present times of stress . . . it is good for a man to stay as he is."

> If you are tied to a wife, do not look for freedom. If you are free of a wife, then do not look for one. But if you marry, it is no sin, and it is not a sin for a young girl to be married. They will have their troubles, though, in their married life, and I should like to spare you that.

He goes on to say that time is growing short: "The world as we know it is passing away." It is because he wants the members of the Church in Corinth to concentrate on the things of God that he wishes them to be free of the "worldly affairs" that are inevitably involved in marriage. "Trust . . . that you give your undivided attention to the Lord."

Four points stand out from this much-quoted passage. First, Paul expects the Second Coming to take place at any time. He is not thinking of future generations. Christian men and women have to be alert, ready for action, and to concentrate on personal holiness. Second, he thinks of marriage as a tie, a loss of liberty—as it would have been for him in his apostolic work. Paul's missionary activities were to take him to many countries and through many dangers: it was no life for a married man. Third, he is a man talking primarily to men. He does tell the women of the Corinth congregation that they will "have their troubles" if they marry, but he does not specify what these troubles are or how married women are to deal with them. That is simply not the point of his discourse. Fourth, he is thinking here of marriage primarily in terms of sexual satisfaction, not as a lifelong and developing relationship between a man and a woman. Against this, we can set his superb hymn to love in 1 Corinthians 13, which is so often read or quoted at wedding ceremonies.

There was no tradition of consecrated virginity as a permanent state in the Jewish literature that now forms the Old Testament. Marriage was almost universal for both sexes; but from the earliest days of the Christian Church there were men and women who kept to the single state, awaiting the coming of the Lord. By the late fourth century, when St Ambrose collated his sermons on virginity in *De Virginibus* for his sister Marcellina, the argument that the virgin state was superior to the married state had some strong advocates. Ambrose echoed St Paul when he wrote that "she that is married taketh thought for the things of the world," and his own celibate distaste for marriage is evident from a comment about "the painful ministrations and services due to husbands from wives."

St Jerome, writing a few years later, was even more specific about the trials of marriage. Writing to the virgin Eustochium, daughter of *Paula, he refers to "the drawbacks of marriage, such as pregnancy, the crying of infants, the torture caused by a rival, the care of household management, and all those fancied blessings which death at last cuts short." "Not that married women as such are outside the pale," he adds hastily, no doubt thinking of Paula, who by that time was a widow, "they have their own place, the marriage that is honourable and the bed undefiled," but he warns Eustochium that "great inconveniences are involved in wedlock" and advises an ascetic way of life that will preserve her from this "inconvenient" state. When he added, "I gather the rose from the thorns, the gold from the earth, the pearl from the shell," the married women represented by the thorns, the earth, and the shell must have felt that they were being offered a very low status in the Kingdom of Heaven.

The result of these and similar statements by the early Fathers of the Church was to leave married women with relatively little in the way of guidance. The special honour paid to the virgin Mother of Jesus obscured all other wives and mothers, and the Church, in a desire to pay honour to those who kept the virgin state, tended to overlook married women—even though many were married against their will, often to men who were complete strangers and whom in some cases they feared and disliked. As records of the lives of the saints developed, there were very many virgin saints, some widowed saints (chiefly celebrated for what they did after the death of their husbands), and very few married women saints. There is Helen of Bologna, who is said to have lived an uneventful life, happily married to a citizen of

Bologna, for thirty years and to have been considered a saint by general acclaim from those who knew her. There is Frances the Roman, who "contrived in forty years never to annoy her husband," but we do not know how annoying he was, or whether this total deference made for a good marriage. Nothing is known about the dynamics of their marriage relationships. There are queens, such as Cunegund, Radegund, and Bathild, but they were relatively visible. There are outstanding women of spiritual gifts, such as *Catherine of Genoa and Mary of Oignies, who were childless and lived for many years in continence with husbands who respected their special abilities; accounts of their lives concentrate on their spiritual experiences, not on their marriages. We have very little information on women saints who lived a normal family life. Locked in the privacy of the family, women were exhorted to submit to their husbands and to raise their children in the Faith, but their problems and their achievements were not known outside that closed circle.

Though the Church has placed increasing emphasis on the importance of family life in recent years, there have been very few new canonizations or beatifications that offer models to women in the complex tasks of relating to a husband and bearing and raising children. The Abbé Thierry Lelièvre lists the canonization of eleven women and the beatification of a further twenty-five between 1963 and 1984. All but one, Bd Kateri Tekakwitha, an American Indian maiden who lived in a Christian village, were members of religious Orders.

It is not difficult to see why this should be so. In a religious community women are well known by their superiors, and their spiritual formation is carefully evaluated, so that a judgment on the sanctity of their lives can be made with relative confidence; few married woman receive this degree of attention to their spiritual development. What happens in the closed circle of the family often goes unnoticed and unknown. There may be many unrecognized saints among Catholic wives and mothers, but their chances of public recognition are necessarily limited.

Further, the life stories of married women are seldom recorded in any detail. For most of human history marriage has been a full-time occupation for almost all women, and many have not lived beyond the years of child-bearing. Their lives have been secondary to those of their husbands, occupied, as St Jerome informed Eustochium, with pregnancy, crying infants, and household management. It is only in the twentieth century that child-rearing and home-making have been fully recognized as the foundation of Christian family life and the all-but-invisible mother has been given dignity and status.

It is not surprising, therefore, that the choice of married women saints celebrated for the quality of their family life is limited and that the selection should include an empress, the mother of one of the great Fathers of the Church, a queen, a wealthy Parisian, and only one poor woman. The first four were visible because of their ecclesiastical or social status; the last happened to live in Rome and to be married to a servant of the one of the princely houses.

Helena was the mother of the Emperor Constantine. Despite all the legends that have tended to obscure her name, there is enough solid history to indicate a lively and devout woman who brought up her son when she was a single mother in Asia Minor, who made the transition to the imperial court at Rome and was named Augusta, or empress, and who had a considerable influence on the establishment of Christianity as the religion of the Roman Empire. She was prepared to let her son go his own way, but her support was always available to Constantine, and the relationship was always a strong and affectionate one on both sides.

Monica was the mother of St Augustine of Hippo, and all we know of her comes from Augustine's *Confessions*. A writer of outstanding honesty and perception, he makes it clear that her family life had many problems and that he often found her interventions in his own life irksome and unwarranted, but he gives a memorable and compassionate picture of her difficult life with her husband and of the tangled and conflict-ridden mother-son relationship that followed. Their final tranquil reconciliation at Ostia before her death is not just a happy ending; it is a logical outcome of his search for faith and of her prayers for him.

Queen **Margaret of Scotland** was an unwilling bride. She wanted to enter a religious Order, but since she and her brother and sister were exiles in the hands of the bloodthirsty and fearsome Malcolm Canmore of Scotland, she had no choice. The story of how she taught Malcolm to love books, even if he could not read them, and to serve the poor, has its humorous moments, but it is an interesting account of the dynamics of an unusual and successful marriage. As the mother of three kings and two queens, she exerted a Christian influence that lasted long after her own lifetime.

Barbe Acarie combined an intense spiritual life during her marriage with thoroughgoing practicality, caring for her husband and children, pacifying her mother-in-law, running her household, sorting out the family's financial affairs, and still finding time to be a spiritual director, to help in the reform of some very lax convents, and virtually to act as novice-mistress to the first Reformed Carmelite Sisters in Paris. "Time Management" is now a regular subject of study for managers: Barbe was an expert. Despite poor health and chronic pain she put thirty-six hours' work into every twenty-four. She nursed her husband through his final illness and then entered Carmel—at her own insistence as a lay Sister—for her final four years. She took the name of Mary of the Incarnation, but it is as Madame Acarie that she is chiefly remembered and venerated.

Anna Maria Taigi was the wife of a servant in the Chigi Palace in Rome. Had she lived anywhere else, her life of poverty and devotion to a rough husband and a growing brood of children and grandchildren in cramped quarters might have passed unnoticed. There are many such women. They become drudges and attract very little attention because the world is not interested in them, but Anna Maria discovered in this drab and overworked life opportunities for holiness in prayer and spiritual vision. She found time to bring healing and spiritual peace to a variety of people, rich and poor. The rich included the Queen of Etruria, who offered her gold, which she refused, and the sorrowing Letitzia Bonaparte, mother of the exiled and dying emperor Napoleon. The poor included battered women in her own locality, and she was often asked to act as a marriage-counsellor, bringing calm and clarity to passionate and angry relationships.

Virginity is a vocation: so is marriage. One conclusion that emerges clearly from these five lives is that marriage and motherhood have always involved multiple roles, pressure on time, and involvement in the deepest human relationships. "Wife" and "mother" are not simply descriptions of social status; they are indicators of continuous activity, year in and year out, which can be raised to the highest levels of sanctity.

HELENA
(c. 250-330)

*Presumed portrait bust of
Helena, in Vienna Museum.*

THE TWELFTH-CENTURY CHRONICLER Geoffrey of Monmouth
recorded that Helena was the daughter of Coel or Coelus, king of the
Britons. Her marriage to the Roman general Constantius Chlorus was one of
the terms of a treaty by which Coel continued to rule Britain and agreed to
send tribute to Rome. Eleven years later Constantius, by then the Roman
Emperor, died at York, and Constantine, his son by Helena, succeeded him.
Geoffrey's history was often imaginative rather than accurate, and he seems
to have been misled by a panegyric to Constantine, which said that he
"ennobled the British by arising there." *Oriendo*, arising, probably refers to
the fact that Constantine was in England when he was proclaimed emperor
and does not imply that he was born there. Evelyn Waugh's *St Helena* makes
use of the legend of Helena's English birth, but the novel is, as the author
makes plain in his introduction, based on legends rather than historical fact.

Coel was king of East Anglia, not of Britain, and Helena was not his
daughter. According to Eusebius of Caesarea, who was a contemporary and
friend of Constantine and a much more careful historian than Geoffrey of
Monmouth, she was born at Drepanum in Bithynia, Asia Minor, and was
probably the daughter of an inn-keeper. In or about 270 she married
Constantius Chlorus, then a Roman general. She must have been a beauty

and had a strong personality. A later mosaic from Trier shows her as dark-haired, with huge compelling dark eyes. The eyes might be an effect of the mosaic mason's art, but there is no mistaking the passionate mouth, the firm chin, and the elegant hands. Whether or not her marriage to Constantius was according to Roman law has been disputed. The pagan writers Zosimus and Orosius, who attacked the growth of Christianity in the empire, alleged that she was a prostitute and that she was only Constantius' mistress, but this was almost certainly anti-imperial propaganda. Constantius had a reputation as a steady, restrained man with a respect for the old Roman virtues of dignity and honourable behaviour, and he always treated Constantine as his true son and heir. Helena may have travelled with Constantius on his campaigns for some years, for Constantine was born in 274 at Naissus (now Nis in Serbia), a military headquarters on the Danube. According to Eusebius the boy "grew up joyous of heart and cheerful of countenance," and Constantius seems to have been much attached to both mother and son through the years of his rise to imperial status. Constantine was brought up by his mother at Drepanum, a fact that has a bearing on his later decision to move the capital of the Roman Empire from Rome to Byzantium: Asia Minor was home to him. When he was about twenty-one his father had to send him to the court of the emperor Diocletian in Rome. Nominally, he was to be trained in warfare and politics, but in fact he was a hostage. Constantius repeatedly asked for his son to be sent back to him, but Diocletian and his successor Galerius refused to let him go. Galerius apparently tried to kill Constantine, goading him to fight with wild beasts. Constantius formally separated from Helena in order to make a dynastic marriage with Theodora, daughter-in-law of the emperor Maximinian, some time before 289. He had six children by Theodora, including three sons, but none of them supplanted Constantine either in his affections or in public recognition.

Constantine fled from Rome in 306 and joined his father at Bononia (Boulogne). By that time Constantius Chlorus had become the western emperor. Father and son were together in Britain on a brief military expedition to suppress the northern tribes when Constantius died in York later that year. Constantine was immediately acclaimed as his father's successor. He was then thirty-two years old—a sturdy, thick-set man of great vitality. The troops were intensely loyal to him and called him "Bull-Neck." Eusebius tells us that "he so far surpassed his peers in personal strength as to be a terror to them." He returned to Rome, ousted Galerius, and having reunited the eastern and western parts of the Roman Empire, invited his mother to Rome to be with him. He wished the Roman world to know that he thought highly of Helena. Later, he proclaimed her Augusta, or empress (which would have silenced any comments about the status of her marriage), and had medals struck in her honour.

Helena became a Christian in about 312. Her adoption of the Faith was whole-hearted. She became very devout in prayer and church attendance, dressing in plain and simple clothes and giving generously to the needy. Rome was not a large city then. She must have known all the churches and all the clergy and made her son aware of their needs.

In 312 Constantine raised the *Chi Rho* symbol in front of his troops before the battle of the Milvian Bridge against his rival Maxentius. Most of his army was Christian, and it was a potent symbol of victory. It is not clear whether Helena's conversion preceded this battle and so inspired his action or whether she became a Christian in thanksgiving when the battle was won. There may have been a third factor: according to the historian Philostorgius, Helena had a special devotion to St Lucian, a famous biblical scholar who had a school in Antioch, said to be second in learning only to the great school at Alexandria. Lucian was imprisoned in Nicomedia in the persecutions of Diocletian in 303, and he died, still in captivity, early in January 312. The traditional date of his death and so of the observance of his feast is 7 January. The circumstances of his death are obscure, but he is reckoned as a martyr.

Much later, when Constantine renamed Drepanum, the city where Helena was born and he grew up, as Helenopolis, Lucian's body was taken to this city to be honoured. Helena and Constantine may have known Lucian—she was said to have been learned for a woman, speaking Latin and Hebrew in addition to her original Greek. In the years when they were still in Drepanum they may have met this great Christian teacher. Helena had been in Rome for six years when Lucian died. Both she and Constantine had been preoccupied with the affairs of the western empire, and the news of his death would have shocked and distressed them. It may have played some part both in Helena's decision to become a Christian and Constantine's raising of the *Chi Rho* symbol at the Milvian Bridge.

In 314 Constantine promulgated the Edict of Milan, relegating the religious persecutions of Diocletian's reign to the past and guaranteeing liberty of practice to Christians and other religions. He did not commit himself exclusively to Christianity and seems to have seen no great distinction between Christianity and popular solar monotheism: he was a practical soldier, not a theologian. Despite some fairly fanciful medieval stories, which said that he suffered from leprosy and attributed his recovery and subsequent baptism to Pope Silverius, he was not baptized until 337—in Byzantium, when he was on his death-bed, and by an Arian bishop. However, his astounding munificence to the Church in Rome in the years when he and

Helena lived in that city is a matter of record. To some extent this may have been due to his understanding that Christianity was the cement that would hold his empire together, but it must also have owed much to his mother's influence. He gave Pope Silvester the palace of the Lateran, which became the first cathedral church of Rome, enriched with gold and silver images. He built the first church of St Peter on the Vatican hill, where Peter himself and other martyrs had died in the reign of Nero. He built the church of the Holy Cross in the Sessorian Palace and St Laurence-outside-the-Walls. The *Liber Pontificalis* lists many gifts to the Church from the emperor, including heavy silver chalices and patens, candlesticks, chandeliers, and the endowment of farms and properties.

Constantine called the bishops of the Church together for the great Council of Nicaea in 324-5. This was held not in Rome but in what is now Izmir, in north-west Turkey. The letters of invitation went out in the emperor's name; he placed imperial transport at the disposal of the bishops; and the conference ended with a magnificent banquet at his imperial palace at Byzantium. He attended some of the sessions himself—asking the assembled bishops' permission to be seated, and himself taking a small stool (though the stool was made of wrought gold: there were limits to imperial modesty). Nicaea was the first ecumenical or general council of the Church, of major doctrinal importance, since it drafted the Nicene Creed, condemned the Arian heresy, and promulgated a number of important canons. Some 220 bishops attended—nearly all from the Eastern Church. Pope Silvester of Rome did not attend and sent only two priests and two deacons as legates. In the same year Constantine marked out the perimeters of the new city he proposed to build at Byzantium, moving the capital of the Roman Empire from Rome. Other people called the splendid new city he built "Constantinople," but he preferred the old title. His roots and Helena's were still in the eastern empire rather than the west.

Mother and son worked closely together, and her piety seems to have been a major influence in his growing support of the Church. She was also much involved in his family life, and he evidently trusted her judgment. In 326 there was a major imperial scandal involving his eldest son, Crispus (by his first wife, Minervina) and his second wife, Fausta. Whether this was a political plot or adultery or both is not known, but Crispus was tried, sentenced, and executed. Ten days later Helena approached Constantine in mourning for her grandson. It must have been a difficult interview. She seems to have convinced Constantine that the main guilty party was his own wife Fausta. This time there was no trial. Fausta went to the baths and was suffocated in the steam. She was not executed, but she committed suicide under compulsion. The names of both Crispus and Fausta were excised from all public inscriptions. In the following year Helena went on a pilgrimage to Jerusalem, perhaps in reparation for the sins of her family.

Eusebius says that "though now advanced in years, yet gifted with no common degree of wisdom, [she] had hastened with youthful alacrity to survey this venerable land." She went in state, taking her court with her, and with the full authority of the Emperor to back her. She released criminals from the prisons and from mines, ordered people to be brought back from exile, talked to bishops and priests and scholars and communities of virgins, and made magnificent gifts to churches, even in the smaller cities she passed through.

The story that she was personally involved in the discovery of the True Cross in Jerusalem has a very long history. The fourth-century historians Socrates and Sozomen mention it, and they took it from Galatius of Caesarea, who in turn heard it from his uncle, Cyril of Jerusalem, who was a boy of only twelve in 327. Some commentators suspect that Cyril may have invented the link with Helena in order to validate the discovery: the involvement of an empress made a good story; but Helena was certainly in Jerusalem at the time. Constantine had sent a letter to the bishop of Jerusalem, asking him to destroy the temple of Venus on Mount Calvary and to search for Christ's cross of nearly three hundred years before. Three crosses were found, though whether Helena was agile enough at nearly eighty to climb the mound of earth left after the destruction of Hadrian's temple on the site and to delve into the excavations herself, as legend has it, is doubtful.

Socrates says that the excavators did not know which cross was Christ's, but the three were tested on a sick noblewoman, and the True Cross healed her infirmities. Neither a pilgrim lady named Egeria or Etheria, who visited the Holy Land at the end of the fourth century, nor St Jerome, who lived in Bethlehem from the same time to his death in 420, mentioned Helena's involvement. Some later commentators have concluded that Cyril of Jerusalem's story is a pious invention, but Egeria was writing a travelogue rather than a history, and Jerome was absorbed in his manuscripts. The omission of this story is hardly conclusive evidence of a non-event.

The Anglo-Saxon poet Cynewulf describes the legend of Helena as it was known in his day: how men "delved for the tree of glory in the earth" and found the crosses twenty feet down from the surface; how Helena had "men dowered with skill" sought out and charged them to rear a temple unto God on the spot; how the cross was graced with "gold and gems, with fairest precious stones":

113

And there since that day the cross of life has rested, best of trees of triumph, not to be broken in its excellence. There it shall ever be a ready succour unto those afflicted of any torment, any sorrow or strife; and by that holy sign they shall soon find help and grace with God.

Helena is said to have taken three nails from the True Cross and sent them to Constantine, who wore one on his helmet and the other two on his horse's bit and bridle. She certainly founded a basilica on the Mount of Olives and one in Bethlehem on the site of the Nativity, where Constantine later built a splendid church. The mosaic floor of his church can still be seen in the Church of the Nativity today.

Helena became ill in the Holy Land in 329 or 330, but she managed to reach the imperial court, which was then at Nicomedia, before she died. Eusebius says that "her son was in attendance at her side, caring for her and holding her hands," and Theodoret adds that she gave him "a fervent parting blessing." Her body was transported back to Rome, and the remains of her tomb can be seen about two miles outside the Porta Pia. The sarcophagus was removed in the time of Pope Pius VI. There are relics under the altar of the Capella Sant'Elena in Rome, and on the island of Sant'Elena in the Venice lagoon. One of the piers supporting the dome of St Peter's is dedicated to her. The church of Santa Croce-in-Gerusalemme is said to have been built by Helena in gratitude for her discovery of the True Cross and to contain a fragment of the cross and one of the nails. She was a woman of piety and considerable personality, and through her influence on her son she made Christianity central to the structure of a great empire.

MONICA

(332-87)

The Death of St Monica.
*Detail from a fresco by
Gozzoli in S. Agostino,
San Gimignano.*

MONICA had a difficult marriage, and after her husband died she spent
most of her later years worrying about an unsatisfactory and profligate son,
who became a heretic and had an illegitimate child. We know about her life
from the unsatisfactory son, who gives a detailed picture of her abrasive
family life in his *Confessions*. He became St Augustine of Hippo, one of the
great Fathers of the Church.

Augustine, writing after his own conversion and his mother's death, is still
trying to come to terms with her. He gives an honest account of his own side
of a difficult relationship. He describes his mother as a mild and sweet-
tempered woman who influenced others by prayers and tears, not by
reproaches and angry accusations, but he makes it clear that she possessed a
steely determination to shape his life. It would be interesting to have Monica's
side of the story—but, as so often, the son was literate and the mother was
not.

Monica was born in Tagaste, in what is now Algeria. She was the child of
Christian parents. Augustine says that when she was of marriageable age,
which probably means about thirteen or fourteen, "her parents gave her" in

115

marriage to a man named Patricius. We might wonder why they did so, for Patricius was not a rich man, he was not a Christian, and he had no inclination to cherish a young wife. Augustine does not have much to say that is good of his father. Patricius frequently flew into violent rages. He was repeatedly unfaithful and became furiously angry with Monica when she protested, but he never struck her, because she always gave way to him meekly when he raged at her. If she wanted to put her own point of view she would wait until he was calm. When she went into the market place and met battered wives—and Augustine gives the impression that there were many with black eyes and bruises—she would tell them that it was their own fault because they should give way to their husbands. We cannot know whether this comment was resigned or merely practical.

Apart from Patricius' violent outbursts and his unfaithfulness, she had to put up with constant carping from her mother-in-law, who lived with them. The servants carried malicious gossip to the older woman, who used it to berate Monica. This also she bore without words of reproach. The only areas she kept to herself were her prayer life and her care for the children. We do not know how many children she bore in this sad household, but three survived: Augustine, Navigius, and a daughter. Apparently Patricius did not object to the children becoming Christians. Augustine says that his father was the only non-Christian in the household, though Navigius' hold on Christian beliefs seems to have been as tenuous as his own at this stage.

In the year 370, when his marriage to Monica had lasted for some twenty years or more, Patricius finally became a Christian—perhaps under the pressure of mortal illness as much as his wife's constant tears, for he died in the following year. By this time Augustine was a student at Carthage sixty miles away. His parents had found enough money to give this clever son a good education, but his student circle consisted of young men who were "proud of their slick talk, very earthy-minded and loquacious." They were impudent to their teachers and ready to twist any honest beliefs into a perversion of the truth. They thought themselves superior to the other students, who were "foul and uncontrolled," given to committing acts of vandalism "with an astonishing mindlessness." Augustine says that he was brilliant, wayward, and idle. He was a highly-sexed young man, and, he says, "all around me hissed a cauldron of illicit loves." He looked for love in women but was "flogged with the red-hot iron rods of jealousy, suspicion, fear, anger and contention." Perhaps he exaggerates his adolescent waywardness, for he was only seventeen when he cut himself off from these undesirable friends and settled down with a mistress. She was a girl from Carthage, of low social standing and no education, and he was faithful to her for fifteen years. Such an arrangement was not uncommon among young men in North Africa, or for that matter in Rome. It minimized the risks of promiscuity and enabled him to keep his mind on his studies. After that his brilliance overcame his idleness.

By his mid-twenties he was known in North Africa as an outstanding teacher. He had his own schools of rhetoric and grammar in Tagaste and Carthage, and he was searching for a faith to live by. Perhaps in reaction against Monica's religious certainty, he became a Manichee. The basic tenet of the Manichaean religious system was that good and evil were equal and conflicting forces. Manichaeism had its own rituals and missionary activities but denied the omnipotence of God and the divinity of Christ. In North Africa it was one of the major sets of beliefs in opposition to Christianity, and it was condemned by the Church as a dangerous heresy.

Monica, no longer required to be a forbearing wife, had become a grieving mother. She spent nine years praying desperately for Augustine. "My mother, your faithful servant, wept for me before you more than mothers weep when lamenting their dead children." Her horror at Augustine's beliefs and behaviour was so great that for a time she would not allow him to live in her house or eat at the same table. At one point she consulted a bishop, who seems to have had some understanding of Augustine's spiritual and intellectual travail: he had been a Manichee himself but had found Mani's writings intellectually untenable. The advice he gave was, "Let him be where he is, only pray the Lord for him. By his reading he will discover what an error and how vast an impiety it all is." Monica begged him to see Augustine and reason with him, but he said gently, "Go now, I beg of you. It is not possible that the son of so many tears should perish." She told Augustine later that she "had taken these words as if they sounded from heaven."

In 382, still under thirty, Augustine decided to go and teach in Rome. He was tired of the uncouth Carthage students and disillusioned with the Manichees. They had replied to his many questions by praising a Manichee bishop named Faustus and promising that he would make everything plain when he came to Carthage, but when Faustus arrived Augustine found him a smooth talker whose "soft eloquence" concealed ignorance of the classics and the real problems of human existence. Augustine was searching for faith.

Monica was still unable to take the bishop's advice to "let him be where he is," and determined to go with him to Rome. She followed him to the port of embarkation, and he says that "she vehemently held on to me, calling me back," but he was equally determined to leave her behind. He was taking his mistress and their four-year-old son with him. He lied to his mother, saying that he was merely visiting the port to say goodbye to a friend, and he sailed at night while she was at her prayers. In the morning, finding him gone, she was "crazed with grief" and redoubled her prayers with "recriminations and groans." Augustine says: "As mothers do, she loved to have me with her, but much more than most mothers . . . she suffered greater pains in my spiritual pregnancy than when she bore me in the flesh." He thinks there was "something unspiritual" in her possessiveness. She did not understand that God was using their separation to bring him, in his own time, to faith.

Monica was not willing to let him go and made plans to go to Rome. They seem to have been separated for some while, because Augustine was seriously ill for a time in Rome and became disillusioned with the Roman students. They listened to what he had to say but disappeared when it was time to pay their fees. By the time Monica had crossed the Mediterranean and arrived in Rome he had gone to Milan, where there was an appointment for a teacher of rhetoric. There he met Ambrose, archbishop of Milan, who knew of his academic reputation. Ambrose was kind to this scholar from overseas, and Augustine was impressed by him. At first he listened to Ambrose's preaching to appreciate his rhetorical technique, but gradually "what he said began to seem defensible," and "there also entered no less the truth which he affirmed." Augustine found him much more impressive than the smooth-tongued but vacuous Manichee bishop, Faustus. He became a catechumen, though he was still in a state of theological confusion. By the time Monica arrived he was "in a dangerous state of depression," but if he had not attained the truth he was at least "rescued from falsehood."

For a time he thought about "honours, money, marriage," and Monica tried to arrange a marriage to an heiress for him. It appears that his faithful concubine was entirely unsuitable, for Augustine describes her as "a hindrance to my marriage," though he says, "My heart which was deeply attached was cut and wounded, and left a trail of blood." His mistress went back to Africa, "vowing that she would never go with another man." It is not clear whether this implied a religious commitment to celibacy or simple disillusionment with the male sex; but she left the child, who was named (or perhaps re-named) Adeodatus, a gift from God. For a time the marriage negotiations were unsuccessful, and Augustine took another mistress. Eventually, as a result of Monica's efforts, he became affianced to a wealthy girl; but his great mind was working like a pile-driver, forcing him on remorselessly to reading, to meditation, to full acceptance of Christianity and all that it demanded of him. He held many discussions with other catechumens and eventually decided to become celibate. He says very little about the three women he abandoned and does not even give their names, but it seems evident that celibacy did not come easily.

Like her son, Monica found Ambrose a figure to respect, though a somewhat remote and patrician one. He was engaged in major conflict with the empress Justina, who was an Arian, and he probably had little time for these provincials from North Africa. Augustine, though, says that Monica "hastened to church more zealously than ever, and drank in the word of Ambrose as a fountain of water."

Monica, Augustine, and the child Adeodatus went together to stay in a country house at Cassiacarum, near Milan, where they lived in community with some of Augustine's friends. Monica acted as housekeeper. There is no evidence that she could even read, and many of the theological arguments the group indulged in must have passed her by. She must have wondered why they took so long to come to conclusions about matters that seemed straightforward to her. At Easter 387 Ambrose baptized Augustine with several of the others. Augustine then retired from teaching, partly because of poor health but principally because he was tired of being "a salesman of words in the markets of rhetoric." He went with his mother to the port of Ostia, where they were to take a ship back to North Africa. She said to him, "Son, nothing in this world now affords me delight. I do not know what there is now left for me to do, or why I am still here, all my hopes in this world being now fulfilled."

At Ostia they had a long and tranquil talk together, "leaning in a certain window, which looked into the garden within the house" while they were "getting ready for the weariness of the long journey back to North Africa." When he wrote the *Confessions* years later, Augustine remembered it vividly: "Then conferred we hand to hand very sweetly," he writes. They discussed silence. What if the whole world were silent? What if the tumult of the flesh subsided, and there was no sound from earth, air, or water; if "dreams and tongues and signs" ceased, and even the voices of angels? Then it would be possible to hear the voice of God. "This one exaltation should ravish us and swallow us up." They experienced together a timeless moment of complete understanding.

Five days later Monica fainted, and when she came round she said to Augustine, "Bury your mother here." She had wanted to be buried in Tagaste with Patricius, but now she no longer thought this important. She told him to "bury my body anywhere you like, let no anxiety about that disturb you. I have only one request to make of you, that you remember me at the altar of the Lord, wherever you may be." When she was dying she called Augustine "a dutiful child." He was thirty-three years old. After her death he said that his very life, "which had been made one of hers and mine together," was torn in pieces; the boy Adeodatus, by then sixteen, cried out in sorrow. She had evidently been a caring grandmother.

Augustine's detailed narrative tells all the facts, but makes hardly any comments on them. Few sons have described their early family life so honestly and directly, or dealt more compassionately with what was clearly at times a very ambivalent mother-son relationship. He ends:

> I pass over many events because I write in great haste. Accept my confessions and thanksgivings, my God, for innumerable things even though I do not specifically mention them. But I shall not pass over whatever my soul may bring to birth concerning your servant, who brought me to birth both in her body so that I was born into the light of time, and in her heart so that I was born into the light of eternity.

Monica brought a great Christian into the Church by her prayers, but she was a very possessive mother who would not allow her son a life of his own. The emotional pressure of her constant prayers and tears must have been very great. She could not understand why her relatively simple faith could not be communicated to this scholarly and complicated son, but he had his own intellectual and spiritual journey to make. On the other hand he must always have been conscious that her prayers were underscoring his desperate search for a faith to live by. If she still thought of him as a child when she was dying, he was by then mature enough to value the love that motivated her.

Monica's bones rested quietly at Ostia until 1430, when they were translated to the church of San Agostino in Rome. The Austin canons, named after her son, have long kept her memorial.

MARGARET OF SCOTLAND

(c. 1046-93)

St Margaret landing in Scotland. *Detail from a nineteenth-century mural in the Scottish National Portrait Gallery.*

MARGARET was not a Scot: she was Saxon and German by birth, and she grew up in Hungary. She was the granddaughter of Edmund Ironside, the king of Wessex who fought a series of spirited battles against Canute. When Ironside died in 1016 the West Saxons, recognizing that the Danes by then held most of England, accepted Canute as their king. Ironside's twin sons, then only a few months old, were sent to Olaf of Sweden, Canute's half-brother, with a hint that he might "rid himself of them without noise." Olaf spared their lives but sent them to the royal court of Hungary, then on the outer borders of Christendom. This was the golden age of Hungary, which was newly Christian. Pope Silvester II had sent a consecrated crown for the coronation of St Stephen, whose wife, Bd. Gisela, was the daughter of Duke Henry of Bavaria. The Benedictines had founded monasteries, Latin was the language of the court and the nobility, and the religious heritage of Rome was fully accessible. Scholars had even found a way of transliterating the difficult Magyar language into the Latin alphabet.

One of the twins, Edmund, died, but the other, known as Edward the Exile or Edward the Stranger, was recognized as the heir to the throne of

121

England and grew up in the court. There he married Agatha, a relative of Queen Gisela, and they had three children, Margaret, Christina, and Edgar.

Margaret, the eldest, was born probably between 1045 and 1048. The place of her birth is not known: though there have been many speculations, the court travelled about the country, and there is no evidence of where it was at the time of her birth. Scholarly searches of Hungarian records have failed to find any documentation of the royal Saxon children's stay in the country, but this is not surprising: in 1073 the country was overrun by the Tartar invasion, and many documents and manuscripts were destroyed. We are dependent on the English monk-chroniclers for the basic facts. We know that Agatha taught her daughters herself, and Margaret was well grounded in the scriptures and the liturgy. She was about twelve when the family returned to England in 1058, to the court of Edward the Confessor, where her education continued under Benedictine influences. She learned French and ecclesiastical embroidery and began to read works of theology: St Augustine and St John Cassian were major influences on her development. Her father died almost as soon as they landed in England, before he reached the court, and Margaret's brother Edgar inherited his claim to the throne.

Edgar unfortunately showed none of the strength of character his two sisters were to exhibit. He was passed over for Harold Godwinson on the death of Edward the Confessor; and when Harold was killed at Hastings in 1066 he first hesitated, then eventually swore allegiance to William the Conqueror. He and Margaret and Christina stayed in England for some time, then took a ship to leave England with other Saxon nobles fleeing from the tightening grip of the Conqueror. They possibly intended to reach the Continent and return to Hungary, but there was a violent storm at sea, the ship was blown off course, and they landed at Wearmouth, which was Border country. There they encountered Malcolm Canmore (Malcolm III of Scotland) who was raiding Northumberland, burning churches, and pitilessly disposing of the conquered. Men of working age were taken captive; women, children, and the aged were killed. The procedure was standard for the time, but Malcolm was a very enthusiastic raider.

This unlikely man became their protector. He already knew Edgar and his sisters, for like them he had been a refugee at the court of Edward the Confessor. He supported Edgar's claim to the English throne, and the three went to his castle at Dunfermline. This was not like the great Norman castles that were beginning to be built in England. It was probably a wooden structure, not much more than a tower. Scotland was poor, wild, and inhabited by a primitive people, nominally Christian, but remote from the civilized courts in which the refugees had grown up.

Malcolm was a widower, and it was not long before he "began to yearn after" Margaret, as the chroniclers put it. She wished to enter the religious life like her sister Christina, but she had little choice. They were entirely in Malcolm's power, and he was not a man lightly crossed. The marriage took place about 1070.

Malcolm Canmore seems to have been fascinated by this calm, learned girl with her sophisticated European background. The Danish Benedictine priest Turgot, who was her spiritual director for a time and wrote her Life, describes how she brought to the court new furnishings, tapestries, clothes, and tableware. He says that the court used vessels of gold and silver—"or at least they were gilt and plated," he adds, being an honest man. This was not a wealthy court, and Margaret did not like excessive show. His description of how she fed orphans "from her own spoon" suggests that there were not many spoons, either, but there was a new elegance, with colour and fashionable clothing in place of the drab Scottish garments, and the courtiers "appeared like a new race of beings." They were taught good manners. There was no more debauchery or drunken rioting at court. Knights who were used to satisfy their hunger and rush from the table were induced to stay and say grace after meat before they left: Margaret introduced the practice of the Grace Cup, a cup of wine from the queen's own table sent down for those who stayed for the grace. This became known as St Margaret's Blessing and for centuries remained a custom followed at Scottish feasts.

The king was devoted to his wife: she showed him a new way of life and a spiritual power he had never known. Though he could not read he would handle her books and examine them. If she had a liking for a particular book he would look at it with special interest, turning it over in his hands and kissing the pages. He had her favourite books ornamented with gold and silver bindings. Sometimes he brought them to her himself after they were bound, as proof of his devotion. While she did not succeed in teaching him to read or stop him from making war, she taught him to pray earnestly and often, with many groans and sighs.

On one occasion a courtier, bent on making trouble, told the king that the queen had been seen going alone into the woods. Malcolm, jealous, followed her—and found her alone, praying aloud for him. Turgot says that "her loving spirit sent him on fire" and that "she added to her prayers the two wings of fasting and alms, that they might more easily ascend into heaven." He thought that she fasted too much, but he records her good works in detail. She founded Holy Trinity Abbey in Dunfermline, enriching the abbey church with gold and silver vessels and giving it a magnificent jewelled gold crucifix, said to contain a fragment of the True Cross. This was kept in a black case and became known as the Black Rood. It probably came from the royal Saxon treasury and was greatly venerated in Scotland. She drew together a circle of ladies of "noble birth and approved gravity of manners," who formed what was virtually an ecclesiastical embroidery school. They were respected and treated with courtesy by the men at court. They embroidered albs, stoles, cottas, and altar frontals with which many churches were beautified.

At Dunfermline poor people, orphans, and widows flocked to her whenever she appeared, knowing that she would distribute alms to all who needed them. When she had exhausted all she had brought with her the courtiers would give what they had, even giving their own cloaks to the beggars. Sometimes she would take the king's gold to give to the poor. He usually pretended not to notice and was amused. Once when he caught her emptying his coffers he laughingly threatened to have her arrested, but she kept the money. Every day after Matins and Lauds she and Malcolm would wash the feet of six poor people and give them alms. After breakfast she would feed nine orphans with "some soft food such as children of that tender age like"; later in the day poor people (Turgot says three hundred at a time, but he may be exaggerating) were brought into the palace, and the king and the queen waited on them with food and wine, he taking one side of the room while she took the other. She also ransomed many Normans who had been taken prisoner after battles. Turgot says that "there was not a village, there was not even a house so poor but could boast of some English captive held in thraldom." Margaret had her "spies," who travelled through Scotland and found the most wretched, so that she could set them free.

Archbishop Lanfranc of Canterbury, whom she had also known at the English court, sent Margaret a friar named Goldwine and two monks to support her work. She decided with them that the Church in Scotland was in need of reform and convinced Malcolm that this was necessary. Though the Scots had kept Christianity in the five hundred years since St Columba, the monks, known as the Culdees, had become lax and their faith lacklustre. They still followed the old Celtic rite, abandoned in England after the Synod of Whitby, but most of them were unlettered, and the rite had deteriorated over the centuries. Turgot called it "barbarous." There were many irregularities in observance. They did not receive Communion, and some did not keep Easter. They kept the Sabbath on Saturday and worked on Sunday. They stood in church instead of kneeling reverently. They did not keep the Lenten fast as they should, and they lacked direction from Rome. Malcolm gave Margaret permission to "choose priests fit to reform the manners of the people; to restore the Divine Office to its first splendour; to re-establish the magnificent reverence and the decency of the Church." She met the leaders herself and explained what she thought fitting, quoting from the scriptures and the Fathers of the Church. Malcolm interpreted for her: she spoke

French, Latin, and the Saxon tongue but could not make herself understood in Gaelic. Whether the Culdees were swayed by her learning, her diplomacy, or the status of her interpreter, they agreed, and the reform was carried out. The Lenten fast was lengthened, the observance of Easter was agreed, and the Latin rite was introduced. The practice of observing the Sabbath on Saturday was changed to Sunday, the Lord's day, and they agreed to kneel in church. The main point of opposition was to Margaret's insistence that they should receive Communion at Mass. This was not their practice, and they objected that they were sinful men and unworthy. They were told firmly that all Christians were sinners and that they must confess, do penance, and receive the body of the Lord for their souls' health. Turgot called her "a second Helena."

Margaret was not bigoted about the Latin rite. She visited many of the Culdee hermits scattered about the remoter parts of Scotland, who kept to the old ways, and offered them alms. When they refused, saying that they did not need money, she asked them to tell her who in the district needed it most. When Malcolm regained the Western Isles from the Norwegians in 1072 she visited Iona with him. They found the monastery in a sad state after waves of Scandinavian raiders had devastated it, and they rebuilt and endowed it. She encouraged pilgrims to visit Iona and also built a hospice on either side of the Firth of Forth for pilgrims to St Andrews, who were carried across free of charge by the Queen's Ferry.

Margaret is regarded by the Church as a patroness of motherhood. She bore Malcolm six sons and two daughters, reared them all, and supervised their early education herself. All we learn from Turgot is that they were given a good religious education and that they were treated severely:

> She took all heed that they should be well brought up, and especially that they should be trained in virtue. Knowing that it is written "He that spareth the rod hateth his son," she charged the governor who had the care of the nursery to curb the children, to scold them, and to whip them whenever they were naughty, as frolicsome children will often be. Thanks to their mother's religious care, her children surpassed in good behaviour many who were their elders.

Turgot was no expert on child care, and doubtless he thought this was the proper way to bring up children; but his description is probably correct. He was writing for Margaret's daughter Eadgyth, whose name was changed to Matilda when she married King Henry I of England, and she would have known the truth of it. Such treatment is a long way from modern theories of child care, but Saxon children were trained and shaped, not indulged. As

Derek Baker points out, Dom David Knowles' statement that Margaret presided over "a nursery of saints" is debatable: she was a distant mother rather than an affectionate one, and most of their education was left to other people—her sister Christina, abbess of Wilton, in the case of the two girls, and tutors for the boys. Edith/Matilda's evidence on her aunt Christina's training suggests that the girls received more slaps and threats than encouragement, but most of the children turned out well. Margaret's other daughter, Mary, married Eustace, count of Boulogne. Three of the sons became kings of Scotland: Edgar (1072-1107), Alexander I (? 1078-1124), and David (1084-1153). William of Malmesbury writes of them that, "No history has recorded three kings and brothers who were of equal sanctity, or savoured so much of their mother's piety." Of the other three sons, Edward was a warrior: he died in battle in 1093 at a place in Jedburgh forest called Edward's Isle in his memory. Ethelred became the first earl of Fife and lay abbot of Dunkeld. Edmund was a problem and is said to have been "degenerate," but eventually he repented of his way of life and died at the monastery of Montacute in Somerset.

In 1093 Margaret and Malcolm were in the castle at Edinburgh. Margaret was ill—worn out with years of hard work and asceticism. Malcolm, accompanied by their sons Edward and Edgar, was about to undertake a military expedition against William Rufus, who had confiscated Edgar Atheling's English estates. Turgot says, "She was most urgent with him (Malcolm) not to go with the army, but it came to pass that he did not follow her advice." Malcolm stopped at Durham, where Turgot had become prior, and they took part in the consecration of the cathedral church. Then they fought the English near Jedburgh. Edgar returned alone and had to tell his mother that Malcolm and Edward were dead.

Margaret prayed continually through her last hours. The Black Rood from Dunfermline was brought to her, and she received Communion before she died four days later. By that time Malcolm's brother Donald Ban (Donalbane) was claiming the Scottish throne and besieging the castle. Her body was taken down the steep face of the Castle Rock in a thick Scottish mist and across the Queen's Ferry to Dunfermline. She was interred at Dunfermline Abbey, opposite the high altar that bore the Black Rood, and there Malcolm's body was also interred later. At the time of the Reformation the bodies of Malcolm and Margaret were translated for safety to a special chapel in the Escorial, near Madrid, though they cannot now be identified. Margaret's head was taken away by the abbot of Dunfermline in a jewelled casket. It became a precious relic, which was passed from Benedictine custodianship to the Jesuits. It was venerated at Douai but was lost during the French Revolution. The tunic in which she died was kept in the abbey church at

Dunfermline, and until the Reformation the queens of Scotland wore it when they were in childbirth. More enduring memorials to Margaret are the cave near Dunfermline where she went for prayer and meditation; her ancient chapel on Castle Hill, Edinburgh; and the arms of the Burgh of Queensferry, which are her personal coat of arms.

Margaret was canonized by Pope Innocent IV on 19 June 1250. She became a patron saint of Scotland in 1673 and is commemorated in the Universal Roman Calendar. What is almost certainly her Gospel Book—which must have been one of those favourite books bound by Malcolm in gold or silver— was discovered, soiled and without its binding, in the parish library at Brent Ely in Suffolk in 1887. It was put up for sale at Sotheby's and bought for £6 by the Bodleian Library at Oxford. It was found to be an eleventh-century document, of the same period as the Canute Gospels in the British Museum, and was eventually identified as being Margaret's book. There is a note in Turgot's Life, telling how a priest had accidentally dropped the book and left it lying in a stream. It was recovered, undamaged apart from water marks at the edge of some pages. These marks are still visible.

Turgot claimed no miracles for Margaret, only "the sweetness of her conversation, the innocency of her deportments, the force of her spirit." As he says, "Signs are common to the good and the bad, whereas works of piety and true charity belong to the good only. The former are sometimes proof of holiness, the latter are that which constitutes it."

BARBE ACARIE (MARY OF THE INCARNATION)

(1566-1618)

Barbe Acarie (Mary of the Incarnation).

Contemporary portrait.

BARBE AVRILLOT, celebrated in Paris as "La Belle Acarie" after her marriage, was the daughter of Nicholas Avrillot, financial counsellor to the *Parlement* of Paris and chancellor to Queen Margaret of Valois. Her father was not a courtier but a senior government official. Though her parents had a number of children, she was the first they were able to rear after several miscarriages and infant deaths.

Barbe was sent to the Franciscan convent at Longchamps, where her aunt was the prioress. This convent usually accepted only girls who were destined for the religious life, but Barbe's mother had no intention of allowing her to become a nun. When, at the age of fourteen, the child expressed an ambition to nurse at the Hôtel-Dieu, the great medieval Paris hospital for the poor, she was summarily taken away from Longchamps and prepared for the marriage market. She was made to wear the elaborate clothes that were then in fashion in Paris and to join in the usual amusements thought suitable for a girl of her age. These had no effect on her at all: she still longed for the convent. Madame Avrillot, impatient to have the girl married off, seems to have decided that the only practical course was to give her a taste of convent-type discipline. For nearly two years Barbe was confined to the house, given coarse food and clothing, and denied a fire in winter. The cold affected her so badly

128

that a chilblain turned septic and she lost a toe. All maternal affection was withdrawn from her: sometimes she did not see her mother for days at a time, and when she did she had to endure reproaches and harsh rebukes.

Two years passed before Barbe finally bowed to her parents' wishes. She was married in 1582, at the age of sixteen-and-a-half, to Pierre Acarie, Viscount of Villemor, a wealthy young lawyer who held a post in the Treasury. She said: "If I am unworthy through my sins to be the bride of Christ, I can at least be his servant." Perhaps she could not hold out any longer—or perhaps she was attracted to Pierre, who was gay and witty and only twenty-two. Pierre was a devout Catholic. He had helped English Catholic refugees after the accession of Queen Elizabeth I. Once she had accepted marriage, Barbe complied with his wishes, wore expensive clothes, and led the kind of social life that went with his position. She was a delightful and charming girl, with abundant chestnut hair. She became very popular in Paris society, and it was in this period that she became known as "La Belle Acarie." In the ten years after her marriage she bore Pierre six children, three sons and three daughters. Unusually for a mother of her social class and time, she spent many hours with her children, bringing them games and toys and enjoying their company.

Pierre thought her almost too worldly when he discovered that she read novels. Shocked, he consulted a priest, who recommended that the offending books should be removed and works of devotion substituted. Barbe obediently read them: and in one she came across a saying of St Augustine: "He is indeed a miser to whom God is not enough." She could not forget it. It reverberated in her mind and shaped the course of her subsequent life. When she was twenty-two years old she had the first of many ecstatic experiences. In the late summer of 1590 she went to High Mass in her parish church, Saint-Gervais, and during the *Sursum Corda* she was transported into a state of ecstasy. The day wore on, and she did not appear at meals. Eventually a search was made, and she was found in church, motionless and scarcely breathing. When she was shaken, she looked up and said, "Is Mass over?" It was evening.

Neither Pierre nor his mother, who lived with them, could understand what was happening to her. Barbe had further ecstatic experiences, but she tried to hide them, playing the spinet or otherwise distracting herself. Her mother-in-law was affronted at what she considered unsuitable behaviour and wailed, "What ails my daughter? My happiness in her did not last long." Doctors were brought in, on the assumption that Barbe must have some obscure disease; but they could find no trace of illness, and their invariable remedy of blood-letting had no effect except to weaken her. Priests were consulted, but they did not understand her experiences. Barbe was very

129

distressed at her husband's and her mother-in-law's disapproval until, on Pierre's manor at Ivry, she met an Englishman, Fr Benet of Canfield, born in Essex as William Fitch. Benet was a Capuchin friar, and he had had similar ecstatic experiences. The assurance that the phenomenon came from God "lifted a stone from her heart."

Pierre did his best to be helpful: he bought more books for Barbe, bound in beautiful morocco covers. Among them were the writings of Bd Angela of Foligno, a thirteenth-century married woman mystic who had extraordinary visionary experiences. Barbe read them obediently, but by this time she was beyond books: she was deeply involved in her own prayer life.

Like many women with intense spiritual experiences she remained very practical in her daily affairs. She continued to care for her husband and her children, to nurse them when they were sick, to take great care over the regulation of her household, and to undertake charitable work in the city, but Pierre's perplexity remained. She had moved into a sphere he did not understand and where he could not follow her.

Pierre had other causes of worry and concern. He was a member of the League—a movement of militant Catholics opposed to the Protestant Huguenots. France was divided by civil war, and in the winter of 1690-1 Paris was besieged. There was famine in the city, and epidemics broke out. Barbe fulfilled her early ambition of nursing at the Hôtel-Dieu, dressing wounds and praying with the dying. Many Parisians were reduced to eating cats and dogs slaughtered and cooked in great cauldrons in the street, while the rich hoarded supplies of food. Barbe gave away as much as she could. She discovered that her mother-in-law had a great cache of wheat, stuffed away in mattresses, and advised the older woman to find a better hiding place if she did not want her supplies to be given to the poor.

Peace came in 1594, when the Huguenot Henry of Navarre became king as Henry IV of France and turned Catholic. There was a general amnesty, and the Edict of Nantes, which gave religious toleration, was to follow. The League had been opposed to Henry's accession, and its members were banished from Paris. Pierre, though he had never taken part in violence, had to leave his home to live at the Charterhouse near Soissons. He was not good at handling business affairs, and as soon as he was disgraced his creditors closed in. Bailiffs arrived at the Acarie house in the rue des Juifs, taking away the furniture, the silver, and all the family's possessions.

Barbe, still in Paris and now homeless, rose to the emergency. She boarded her two elder sons at the Collège de Calvy at the Sorbonne, sent her two elder daughters to the convent at Longchamps, and asked relatives to care for her two youngest children. She herself stayed with a cousin, Madame de Bérulle, and she began to tackle Pierre's tangle of debts and loans. She called together his creditors and arranged his finances. At one point he was taken prisoner by an irregular band of guerrillas, and she even managed to raise a ransom for him. She visited him frequently at the Charterhouse, making the long journey from Paris to Soissons on horseback. On one occasion she was thrown by her horse and broke her leg. It was badly set, and this was only the first of three accidents. Some time later she slipped coming out of the Collège de Calvy, where she had been visiting her sons, and broke her thigh. Later she broke her thigh again, and the bone-setter's work was no more skilled. Perhaps she had become accident-prone through sheer anxiety for her family and the necessity of rushing from place to place to see them all. She endured great pain and weakness, but she continued to interview creditors and carry out negotiations from her bed until Pierre's financial position was sound again. By the time Pierre was allowed to return to Paris in 1599 she was on her feet, but she had to use a stick for walking and was unable to stand for long or to walk any distance. Further, she had been told by doctors that the displacement of her pelvis and hip-bone were so severe that she must not have any more children.

It is understandable that life was not easy for Pierre Acarie when he finally returned to the rue des Juifs. He had been disgraced and was no longer a man of repute and public standing; his wife had taken over his financial problems and dealt with them successfully; as a good Catholic, he knew he would have to live with her in continence because of her physical frailty; and in his absence his home had been turned into a spiritual salon, where many people came to consult her and ask her prayers. It is to his credit that, once he was convinced of the importance of Barbe's work, he raised no objection and became a hospitable, sometimes over-hospitable, host. It cannot be easy to be the husband of a saint.

During the time when she stayed with Madame de Bérulle, and particularly during her long periods of recovery from broken bones, Barbe had become well known in religious circles in Paris. Scholars, friars, and lay people came to her for spiritual direction and discussion. The civil wars had left religious life in France at a low ebb, and now there was a "mystic invasion" coming from Spain, the one country largely unaffected by Lutheranism and Calvinism, where the work of St Teresa of Avila and St John of the Cross had led to the growth of a new spirituality. It was a time for the founding of new religious houses, particularly houses for women, and for the reform of some of the older ones. Barbe's common sense and clear judgment were greatly in demand. With the backing of influential clergy she held many interviews with the superiors of women's communities, quietly suggesting necessary reforms. One was the prioress of the Hôtel-Dieu at Pontoise, who was said to have "made merry every day," dressed in the height of fashion—

but who had no sheets for the sick or shrouds for the dead. Barbe was successful in altering her priorities. She also visited groups of laywomen living without vows, such as the one at Aumâle, which later became the nucleus of an Ursuline foundation; but her chief and most beloved work was the foundation of a house of Discalced Carmelites in Paris.

The spiritual writings of St Teresa of Avila, together with her autobiography, had been published in French. The group of ladies who met at Barbe's house asked her to read some chapters to them, but she was unable to do this herself for fear of becoming rapt in ecstasy. Another member of the group read from Teresa's work. According to her contemporary biographer, Fr André Duval, Barbe listened attentively, but was at first not much impressed. She "wondered that the holy mother had been able to found so great an Order in the Church." At first she was not attracted to Teresa's work, but after discussion with some of her spiritual circle she began to see that it could be of great importance to the religious life of France.

Fr Duval, a doctor in the Sorbonne, was among the group of priests and lay people interested in the Carmelite Reform whom Barbe had met while staying with Madame de Bérulle. She also had many discussions in this period with her young cousin Pierre de Bérulle, then a student at the Sorbonne and later a Capuchin friar. Subsequently she was introduced to Francis de Sales, who became bishop of Geneva in 1602. These three men were influential in encouraging Barbe in her plans for a new Carmelite house.

The matter was not an easy one. Political relations between France and Spain were still strained, for the Spanish court had encouraged the militancy of the League. Bishop Francis de Sales wrote to the Pope asking permission for the new foundation, and Barbe obtained the patronage of the Princesse de Longueville, a prominent member of the court, who was able to persuade the king that six Spanish nuns would hardly be a threat against the body politic. The king stipulated that the new house should be governed (since women could not be allowed to govern themselves) by three French clerics, not by Spanish Carmelite friars. The three selected were Fr Duval, Fr de Bérulle and Fr Jacques Gallemant, parish priest of Aumâle and later vicar general to the archbishop of Rouen. The foundation was authorized by letters patent on 18 July 1602.

The deserted and partially ruined priory of Notre-Dame-des-Champs, on the outskirts of Paris, formerly a Benedictine foundation, was selected for the house. Barbe went frequently to the site, supervised the construction, and, despite her lameness, climbed about on the scaffolding. She interviewed and recruited girls who would be novices when the Spanish nuns came, looking for simplicity and openness and rejecting a number with large dowries and noble backgrounds who lacked these qualities. She took them into her own house and acted as unofficial novice-mistress, training them "in the Teresian tradition."

It was some time before the Spanish nuns arrived after months of patient diplomacy and negotiation. The proposal for a French foundation was not welcomed by the Spanish Reformed Carmelites, chiefly because Henri IV of France, who had himself been a Huguenot before his accession, refused to allow the friars to accompany the nuns. Among the six nuns chosen were Teresa's own close companions, Anne of Jesus, whom she called "my daughter and my crown," and Anne of St Bartholomew, who had accompanied her on her difficult and exhausting journeys, sat at her door while she prayed or slept, and was privileged to hold her while she was dying. The six went reluctantly and with many apprehensions, for it was believed in Spain that France was lost to the Catholic Faith. When their coach passed French peasants on its way to Paris, Anne of Jesus commented, "Nearly all the inhabitants are heretics. That can be seen from their faces. They look like lost souls." The nuns held their crucifixes and rosaries out of the coach windows to confess their faith openly and bring martyrdom closer. As Henri Brémond comments, "Martyrdom did not frighten them: rather they were astonished that the hour tarried."

At last, on 15 October 1604, they reached Paris after a twelve-week journey. They were astonished at the warmth of their reception and the splendours of the Church in France. Anne of Jesus said that the basilica of Saint Denis made the Escorial look like a bagatelle. Perhaps she exaggerated in sheer relief. They were welcomed at the gate of Saint Denis by Barbe and the Princesse de Longueville, who had their coaches turned and escorted the nuns' coach to their new home. When the humble Anne of St Bartholomew, who was a lay sister, slipped out to the kitchen to prepare a meal, Barbe insisted that she should be brought back and honoured as Teresa's chosen companion.

There were many problems: only one of Spanish nuns could speak French, and the novices did not speak Spanish. The two groups could communicate in Latin, but the novices laughed at the lisping Latin pronunciation of the Spanish nuns. Their language, their cultural assumptions, even their diets, were different. There was a particularly difficult incident when Anne of St Bartholomew, who wanted to make peace between the two groups, went to much trouble in cooking a special Spanish meal for a feast-day. It was spiced cod with prune sauce—good country fare in Spain, but the French novices found it uneatable.

Anne of Jesus, despite her great admiration for the basilica of Saint Denis, never really felt at home in Paris. She sent back to Spain for pictures of the Nativity, "for those made here do not please me," and for perfumes for the church, "for there are none to be obtained here, and the supply brought by me from Spain is nearly exhausted." Barbe spent much time in helping the two groups to come to terms, but eventually all the Spanish Sisters went to the Spanish Netherlands, where they were more at home than in France and could again receive direction from friars of their own Order. By that time the Reformed Carmelite movement had taken root in France.

From this first foundation in Paris a number of other houses of Discalced Carmelites were established. The early ones were at Amiens, Tours, Rouen, Bordeaux, Chalons, Besançon, and Dieppe. Within fifteen years the movement was widespread and of considerable influence in France.

Barbe was involved in many other religious enterprises. She helped Fr de Bérulle to found the Oratorian Order, urging him to "supply the bishops with good parish priests and curates." She knew the young Vincent de Paul, who was influenced by de Bérulle and encouraged him in his work with the destitute, and many people continued to come to her for spiritual advice and counselling. She somehow juggled all the elements in a complex life, giving time to her husband, her children, her household, her charities, and her own spiritual life as well, in spite of constant pain and lameness. In 1607 she was seriously ill, and Pierre was much affected, anxiously getting in the way of doctors and nurses as they tried to help her, but she recovered.

Barbe continued to love her children and to care for them when they were adults, but she respected their individuality and left them free to make their own decisions. When they were young she took charge of their religious education, and observers asked whether she was training them for the religious life. Her reply was, "I am preparing them to carry out God's will. A religious vocation can come only from God." Eventually her three daughters all entered the Order of Discalced Carmelites—Marguerite in 1605, Geneviève in 1607, and the eldest, Marie, in 1608, after she had helped to nurse her mother back to health. Of her three sons, Nicholas married and became a lawyer; Jean was in minor orders, then married and settled in Germany; Pierre was a Jesuit for a time, then became a secular cleric and ultimately vicar general of Rouen.

In 1613 Barbe's husband became very ill. She gave up all her other occupations to nurse him, frequently sitting up all night with him. When he died she was worn out with nursing and was very ill for a time. She spent the next two months recovering and disposing of her property to her sons. Her daughters had already been provided with dowries. Then she entered the Discalced Carmelite convent at Amiens as a lay Sister.

She had discussed this step with André Duval and Pierre de Bérulle. Duval said: "The Carmelites owe you too much not to welcome you among them," but she wanted to be a lay Sister, and he thought this unsuitable, because of her physical handicap. Lay Sisters did manual work in the kitchens and gardens, and he thought it would be more appropriate for her to be a choir nun, whose work would be primarily prayer and contemplation. Barbe resisted this suggestion: she wanted the lowliest of occupations and was very anxious not to exert power of any kind in one of the religious houses she had done so much to foster. Duval and de Bérulle, who were now sharing the responsibility of administering the Discalced Carmelite convents, since Gallemant had moved to Bordeaux, sent her to Amiens, where Mother Isabel of Jesus was the prioress. She was clothed on 7 April 1614, as Sister Mary of the Incarnation. She went into ecstasy during the ceremony. Duval, who conducted the clothing, wrote: "When the ecstasy was over, she went into the kitchen to prepare the dinner." She sought obscurity and was, as always, practical. For a time her own daughter Marie was subprioress at Amiens, and Barbe quietly accepted her authority and called her "Mother." When Mother Isabel left for the Low Countries the nuns at Amiens, who understood Barbe's great spirituality, wanted her to become their prioress, but she was unwilling to accept and continued scouring pots and pans. St Teresa would have approved.

A new prioress was appointed—Anne of the Blessed Sacrament, who as Anne de Viole had been one of the postulants trained by Barbe in her own house. Evidently she found it difficult to have her former mentor as a humble lay sister: her attitude to Barbe was consistently severe and unhelpful. She humiliated her in front of the other nuns and forbade her to give them spiritual advice, with the excuse that this was good for her soul. Barbe bore all this without complaint, recalling how St John of the Cross had deliberately chosen to end his life at Úbeda, where he was treated with similar harshness by an unsympathetic prior. Duval and de Bérulle were reluctant to intervene, but when Gallemant returned from Bordeaux and discovered what was happening in the convent, he conferred with them, and Barbe was moved to the house at Pontoise "for her health's sake." Pontoise was her own favourite convent, and the community warmly welcomed her. It was a small house, and she was encouraged to do what she could to build it up. She organized the completion of the building work, the construction of an infirmary, and the purchase of a garden—a great boon to an enclosed community. She was given leave to provide spiritual counsel, not only to the nuns but to the many people who travelled from Paris and other cities to ask her help. With the aid of these visitors the money was soon forthcoming to pay for the improvements to the convent.

Barbe became ill on 7 February 1618 and died some nine weeks later, on the morning of Easter Day, 18 April. Fr Duval was with her in her final hours and gave her the viaticum. She had been married for thirty-one years and had spent only four in the cloister. Her son Pierre Acarie was one of the first to act in her cause. He wrote to his archbishop, asking that steps be taken to have her declared Blessed, and her cause was introduced in Rome in 1627 but postponed because Pope Urban VIII had issued a decree that at least fifty years must elapse after the death of a candidate before beatification procedures could be followed. In fact a century and a half elapsed before King Louis XVI of France and his sister, Madame Louise, who was prioress of the Carmelites of Saint Denis, petitioned in 1782 for the re-opening of the case. The beatification took place on 5 June 1791. It was made clear in the decree of beatification that she was honoured for her work "in the world"—a very unusual endorsement of a married woman.

ANNA MARIA TAIGI

(1769-1837)

Contemporary portrait.

THE LIFE of Anna Maria (or Anne Mary, as she is sometimes called in English texts) is by any standards an extraordinary one. How did a porter's wife with a large family, unable to read or write, come to be the spiritual confidant of cardinals and queens—and even, it is claimed, of popes? She was known as a saint in her lifetime, but she was also the subject of malicious gossip and cat-calls in the streets, and some called her a witch. It is not surprising that the process for her beatification was long and searching, but lengthy and detailed testimony was given by eminent clergy of Rome, by two of her daughters, and by her husband, Domenico, when he was ninety-two years old. Even if Domenico's rough temperament had been softened by the years and he was more appreciative of Anna after her death than during her lifetime, his testimony is still a remarkable tribute to a remarkable wife.

Anna Maria Antonia Gesualda Giannetti was born in Siena on 19 May 1769. Her father Luigi, like his father before him, was an apothecary in the city—a man of moderate prosperity and some standing, but when Anna was six his business failed. Creditors took almost all the family's possessions, and they set out for Rome, where they lodged in a poor quarter. One of their neighbours was St Benedict Joseph Labre, the "holy beggar" from Boulogne, now known as the patron saint of vagrants and the homeless. When he died, Santa, Anna's mother, helped other local women to wash his body and to wrap it in a shroud, and the children cried in the street, "The saint is dead."

Luigi found work as a domestic servant. Santa did rough cleaning in other people's houses. Life was hard. Luigi was bitter about his experience and ill treated his daughter. She had very little education. Though she was sent to a school run by nuns for some two years, her teachers were keener on domestic accomplishments than on study. She learned to sew, but she could barely write her own name. After she had smallpox she was kept at home to help her mother, but she went to church regularly, was confirmed at the age of eleven in the church of St John Lateran, and made her first Communion at thirteen. She had an excellent memory and could recite the Catechism and most of the Psalms. At sixteen she found a post as a silk winder, and she seemed to have the same interests as other girls of her age, enjoying dancing and all the excitement of Rome—the processions, the carnivals, the theatres.

In 1787, when she was eighteen, life changed. Luigi found a domestic post with Madame Serra, a relative or friend of the powerful Chigi family, which had produced several popes. Before long he found a post for Santa in the same household, and for three years Anna became Madame Serra's personal maid. The *palazzo*—scarcely a palace in English terms—was close to the huge Chigi Palace on the Corso, and meals were sent to Madame Serra daily from Prince Chigi's own table. They were brought by a kitchen porter, Domenico Taigi, a young man who began to take an interest in Anna. She for her part had been wondering whether to marry or enter the cloister, but a confessor thought that she had no vocation to the religious life and advised her to marry. She looked for a good, steady husband and married Domenico when she was twenty and he was twenty-eight.

Anna's decree of beatification noted that Domenico's "manners were rough and uncultured, and his temperament unamiable," and people clearly wondered how such a sensitive and gentle girl could have consented to marriage with such a man, but she seems to have been attracted by him, and although he was only a porter, carrying heavy sacks of vegetables and loads of wood to the kitchen, he was a good Catholic and steady and reliable. His wages were small, but there were advantages in marrying a servant in a great house: they had somewhere to live—two rather gloomy rooms in an alley adjoining the Chigi palace—and there was plenty of food to bring home, after the cook had taken his pick of what went uneaten at the Prince's table. Domenico was proud of his young wife. He bought her trinkets and took her strolling on the Corso with the other young couples on summer evenings. He clearly enjoyed what the Italians call *fare una bella figura*—making a good public impression.

But Anna was experiencing great tension. Something profound had affected her around the time of the birth of her first child. She sought help from a priest at one of the city churches, weeping and saying, "Father, you have at your feet a great sinner," but the priest said, "Go away, you are not one of my penitents." She begged him to hear her Confession. He listened impatiently, clearly thought that she was hysterical, gave her a hasty absolution, and slammed the shutter on the confessional. It was some time later that she met a Servite friar, Fr Angelo, who took her problems seriously. She told him that God was calling her to be "a victim of expiation for the sins of the world," and she wanted to undertake exaggerated penances. Fr Angelo thought the penances unwise, reminding her that she was a wife and a mother and that she had duties to her family. She could not be a nun; it was too late for that. After a time, however, he suggested that she might become a tertiary of the Order of the Trinity. Once she was admitted as a tertiary she led a very restricted life. There were no more walks on the Corso and no more carnivals or theatres. She put aside the trinkets Domenico had bought her. A Trinitarian director told her that she must wear the tertiary habit always, even when out with her husband, and that they must live in continence.

Domenico had accepted the rejection of his simple pleasures, and of the trinkets he had bought his wife with such pride, but this was too much. He had no intention of being seen in public with his wife dressed in a white scapular with a red and blue cross, though he said she might wear it when she was on her own if she wished, and he had no intention of living in continence. He said later, "I do not know whether the suggestion came from the priest or from my wife. . . . I emphatically refused, for in that case she ought to have become a religious and not to have been married." The couple went on to have six more children.

It is not clear whether Domenico's outbursts of rage started from this time, but he became a very domineering husband. When he came home from a day's work, the door had to be opened immediately he knocked. His meal had to be ready on the table, and if it was not to his liking he would pull the tablecloth off the table and throw everything on the floor. He swore continually, which Anna hated. He beat the children, and on one occasion, when a child escaped into the street, he threw an armchair through the window after him. Such conduct was probably fairly common among the manual labourers of Rome. Whether his frustrations arose from the way in which Anna had changed from the girl he married, from the strains of heavy physical work and having to be the breadwinner for a growing family, or from their domestic circumstances, is not clear, but the frustrations were real, and his reactions were explosive.

Their domestic circumstances were trying. In the early days of his marriage to Anna, knowing that his in-laws were unhappy together, he had expansively offered to share their two rooms with her mother. Santa moved in but became extremely disagreeable, constantly carping, complaining, and interfering. Luigi, Anna's father, stayed at the *palazzo* of Madame Serra for a time but went to pieces. He would arrive unexpectedly, shouting at his wife and making scenes. He lost his job, and when Anna found him another, he lost that. Anna had to feed him, look after him, and mend his clothes. Whatever the reason for the break-up of Santa and Luigi, its consequences fell heavily on Anna and Domenico. There were babies every two or three years, children crying and children underfoot: Anna had the first of her seven children when she was twenty-one and the last when she was forty-one.

Though they moved to somewhat larger quarters after a time, it was no wonder that Domenico was frustrated and found family life intolerable, but he never struck Anna, and he protected her when he could. Once a soldier pushed her roughly in the street when she was pregnant. Domenico half killed him. Anna, coping with Domenico, Santa, Luigi, and her growing brood of children, always put her husband first. She pacified him, waited on him, soothed him, and gave in to his demands, however unreasonable. She made his coats and trousers and all the children's clothes. All the children were breast-fed. There were no wet-nurses for the poor. Often, she would still be working, pale and exhausted, when Domenico came home late at night.

The children had a sound Catholic upbringing in this city of many churches. They were baptized within two days of their birth and brought to Confirmation and First Communion. There were family prayers in the morning and readings about the saint of the day in the evening, and they always attended Mass on Sundays. Anna disagreed with Domenico in only one respect: when the children were growing up, he made an effort to take part in their education and wanted to take them to visit Rome's museums and art galleries, but she refused to allow this, saying that they should not see "indecent objects." She said that even churches contained pictures of children in "an indecently naked condition." No doubt she was passing on Tridentine strictures. Not everybody in Rome appreciated the work of Titian and Michaelangelo.

In 1799, when the French invaded Italy, the Taigi household's precarious existence was threatened. Rome was occupied, and Pope Pius VI, eighty-one years old and ailing, was driven out of Rome. There was hunger and deprivation, looting and burning; churches were profaned and despoiled.

Prince Chigi and his family left the country, and Domenico, the breadwinner, was unemployed. Anna sewed bodices and petticoats and sold them so that she had money for a little food. Her most recent child, Luigi, died in that terrible year at the age of eighteen months. He was the only one she lost.

It was two years before conditions improved. The French left Rome, and Prince Chigi returned and made an effort to help the family. He knew Domenico personally and thought well of him, and Anna was beginning to be recognized as a woman of unusual spiritual power. The Taigi were moved to bigger and better quarters adjoining the palace, where they provided domestic services for Mgr Natali, an eminent cleric who wished to study her mystical experiences.

Anna was sustained through her difficult and exhausting life by what she called her "sun," a dazzling globe surrounded by a circle of thorns. In the centre sat Eternal Wisdom, through whom she perceived many things not within the normal scope of a poor, uneducated woman living in the back streets of Rome. Cardinal Pedicini, who came to know her well, testified at the beatification process:

> For forty-seven years, day and night, at home, in church, in the street, she saw in this sun, which became increasingly brilliant, all things on this earth both physical and moral; she penetrated to the depths, and rose up to heaven, where she saw the eternal lot of the dead. She saw the most secret thoughts of persons nearby or far off; events and personages of by-gone days. . . . She saw the people who handled affairs, the places concerned, the opinions held, the sincerity or guile of ministers, all the back-door diplomacy of our era, as also the decrees of God for the confusion of these mighty ones. . . . We may say that this gift was one of omniscience, for it was the knowing of all things in God so far as the intelligence is capable of such knowledge in this life. . . . Nor let anyone think that I am exaggerating, for, on the contrary, I find myself incapable of describing the wonders of which I was for thirty years the witness. . . . For her, the world was an open book, consisting of one word, GOD.

These experiences began in 1790, the year in which Anna's first child was born, and continued for the rest of her life. One of the objections raised during the beatification process was that, since Anna could neither read nor write, all that was known of her experiences came from the three clerics, Cardinal Pedicini, Mgr Natali, and Fr Louis-Philippe, who became her amanuenses. Perhaps, in a period of great upheaval and the apparent overthrow of everything the Church stood for, they were looking for a sign of God's presence. All three were convinced that Anna had become a channel for the pain of the world and the continuing grace of God.

141

As her children grew up and she had a little more time, people came to Anna in increasing numbers for counsel and advice. She sheltered battered wives and acted as a marital counsellor, coping with brandished knives and shrill accusations from husband and wife and then saying, "Forgive! Forget!" She practised the laying-on of hands, using oil from a sanctuary lamp—a very old Christian custom. She fed the many beggars in the streets, often taking them home to wash and feed them. She visited hospitals, praying with the sick and tending the dying. She went to cemeteries in all weathers to pray for the repose of the souls of those who had died. She was kind to animals, binding up the wounds of injured horses and regularly feeding the stray cats that congregated in the Forum of Trajan.

As her gifts became known, many clergy came to her for counsel, and the women in the street gossiped, saying that she was a prostitute and, when she was older, that she was prostituting her daughters. Poor Romans, like poor people everywhere, were not accustomed to invite visitors into their homes; but Anna's apartment was open to the world. In his testimony for her beatification Domenico gave a touching picture of her work and her continued care for him:

> It often happened that on my return home, I found the house full of people. At once she would leave anyone who was there—a great lady, maybe, or a prelate—and would hasten to wait upon me affectionately and attentively. One could see that she did it with all her heart: she would have taken off my shoes if I would have allowed it. In short, she was my comfort and the consolation of all. . . . The servant of God knew how to keep everyone in his place and she did it with a graciousness that I cannot describe. I often came home tired, moody, and cross, but she always succeeded in soothing and cheering me.

Among the great ladies who came to Anna for counsel was the former Queen of Etruria, Marie-Louise de Bourbon, daughter of the king of Spain. Anna was said to have cured her of epilepsy. She called Anna "sister" and offered Domenico the post of butler in her own household at a high salary, but Anna refused: she must have known that Domenico was not suited to such an appointment and that her own work could only be done where she was. The queen opened a chest and offered her gold. Anna said, "Madame, how simple you are. I serve God, and he is richer than you."

Another celebrated lady she was able to help was Letitzia Bonaparte, "Madame Mère," who came to live close to the Chigi Palace after Napoleon's defeat at Waterloo. The Buonaparte, to give them their original name, were of Italian stock, not French. While her son became an emperor and her other sons and daughters became kings, queens, princes, and princesses, Madame

Mère stayed in Corsica, where she is still much more respected than Napoleon, who cared little for the island. Letitzia's half-brother was archdeacon of Ajaccio, and Napoleon served him as an altar boy in the great gloomy basilica at Ajaccio when he was young. In the Napoleonic era, the archdeacon became a cardinal, and it was as Cardinal Fesch that he took his sister to live in Rome in 1815. They bought the Rinuccini Palace on the Corso, near to the Chigi Palace. It was their habit to join an unofficial confraternity, which met every Friday evening at the Coliseum to follow the Way of the Cross and to pray for the souls of the early Christian martyrs. Anna was also a member of the group. Cardinal Fesch became her disciple, and they talked much about the meaning of Napoleon's rise and fall and the state of his soul as he sat in exile on Elba. Anna said, "God did not break him. God humbled him, and in humiliation lies his salvation."

Before Napoleon died on Elba in 1821, Madame Mère, surrounded by her surviving and deposed sons and daughters, spent much time in praying for him and trying to send him clothes, books, and food, but the English governor of Elba was unsympathetic and sent the parcels back. Madame Mère lived on for another fifteen years, old, nearly blind, and seeking consolation in the Church. Anna often met her in the church of Santa Maria on the via Lata, where they both attended Mass. When his sister was dying Cardinal Fesch asked Anna to send her a message. By that time Anna was herself bedridden and racked with pain. She said the ex-emperor's mother should meditate on "what she had been, what she was, and what she would be soon; and prepare herself for death." It was simple but penetrating advice.

Madame Mère died in 1836, and a year later Anna followed, ending her life very quietly on 9 June 1837, after talking to Domenico and all her children in turn. Her coffin was taken to lie on the same spot as Madame Mère's in Santa Maria for the Requiem Mass, but Anna's funeral was very simple, because there was a cholera epidemic in Rome at the time and people did not congregate. Her body was buried in the public cemetery, and it was only later that her relics were taken for reinterment in the church of Peace (*della Pace*), but her friends and disciples began to collect material for her beatification almost immediately.

There was a wealth of testimony, including that from Domenico, grown old and feeble and rather sentimental, who said, "I have lost a treasure of great price," and from a number of eminent clerics who knew her well. The testimony of Cardinal Pedicini alone amounted to over a thousand pages. Perhaps the recognition of this holy life was possible only in central Rome, where the great of Church and State lived cheek by jowl with the poor.

Because Anna had spent much of her life unsupervised and unknown, unlike a religious or a noblewoman, it was necessary for her record to be scrutinized in great detail, but all questions were satisfactorily resolved. At her beatification ceremony she was described as a model for wives and mothers, "a soul quite different from that of the virgins, nuns and widows canonized by the Church . . . the glory of this Rome of ours." After the ceremony Pope Benedict XV returned privately to her tomb, to kneel and pray before her relics.

5

PENITENTS

IN THE ancient world there were two very popular stories about penitent women. The first was that of a wealthy and beautiful courtesan who gave up her jewels and her property on being converted. The second was that of a penitent woman who entered a monastery disguised as a man. Sometimes the two stories were combined: no doubt it was thought that a woman whose behaviour was considered shocking in one way might well also offend the mores of the time in the other, but a closer look at these ancient morality tales suggests that there were two distinct groups. Women who dressed as men usually had a good reason for doing so and gave rise to no scandal. They are considered in Appendix II. Courtesans generally did not dress as men: femininity was their stock in trade.

In modern books of saints, stories about courtesans are either omitted entirely or dealt with very briefly and usually pronounced to be spurious. This approach follows the work of Fr Hippolyte Delehaye, the Jesuit hagiographer, whose books *Les légendes hagiographiques* (1903) and *Les origines du culte des martyrs* (1912) supplemented his monumental work on the *Bibliotheca Hagiographica Graeca* and the uncompleted November and December volumes of the *Acta Sanctorum*. Fr Delehaye, a rigorous classical scholar, described how such stories became current in the Middle East and around the Mediterranean Basin, how history became confused with legend, and names and biographies were misappropriated. Early writers on saints were not concerned with exact reportage: their aim was to write edifying stories that would please the listener. They often attribute their own narratives to eyewitnesses of the events they recount or to some well-known and respected contemporary person; and they fail to quote their sources. Fr Delehaye points to a kinship between some of these legends, supported by the names of the saints: for Marina (feast-day 12 Oct. or 12 Feb.) is the Latin form of Pelagia (9 June), and Pelagia the courtesan was also called Margaret (8 Oct. or 20 July); and Reparata (8 Oct.) might mean "the penitent"; and Mary, Marina, and Margaret are forms of the same name. The legends of Euphrosyne (1 Jan.), Marina (12 Feb.), and Theodora (11 Sept.), are often cited as belonging to this family, though none of them was a courtesan: they belong to the group who wore male dress. Reference books on saints often note: "Euphrosyne: see Pelagia," or "Pelagia: see Marina, Euphrosyne, Theodora"; and 8 October recurs so often as their feast-day that it seems successive generations of liturgiologists have despaired of separating their histories.

Margaret of Antioch (20 July) is often treated as a "doublet" of either Pelagia of Antioch in Syria or Marina of Antioch in Pisidia, but she was not a courtesan, and she did not wear male attire. The legend is that she was the daughter of a pagan priest, Aedisius. She became a Christian, and her father drove her out of the house. She became a shepherdess. The governor of Antioch pursued her, and she is said to have endured many picturesque trials, including swallowing a dragon or being swallowed by a dragon. Eventually she was beheaded in the persecutions of Diocletian, 303-4.

Margaret has been an immensely popular saint. She was the source of much prayer and devotion during the Crusades, some two hundred ancient English churches were dedicated to her, and she is one of the Fourteen Holy Helpers of the German devotional tradition. Hers is one of the "voices" said to have inspired Joan of Arc. The legend of Margaret was declared apocryphal by Pope Gelasius as early as 494, and her cult was suppressed by the Holy See in 1969.

According to Fr Delehaye's very rigorous criteria, the Acts of a saint can only be regarded as genuine if there are official written reports to draw on, or accounts by reliable eyewitnesses. The rest he describes as *historical romances*, in which a few facts about a saint may be arbitrarily combined with fictional material; *imaginative romances,* in which even the name of the saint is an invention; and *forgeries*. While his successors admit that some of them are *historical romances*, they seem to find them embarrassing. Such stories may be referred to jocularly as "entertaining," or "lending a little glamour to the cloister," but they are not taken seriously. Yet despite the difficulties of getting at the facts, these accounts contain some interesting feminine spiritual experience.

For many of the early saints, men and woman alike, we do not have documentary evidence that meets Fr Delehaye's stringent criteria; while this suggests a cautious approach, it does not mean that all accounts failing to meet the criteria are equally valueless. Historians and theologians are used to weighing evidence: much of their work is based on judgments about possibility and probability, on content analysis that sorts out the convincing from the merely plausible or the literary flourish. Early accounts of the lives of saints have much to tell us about the customs and attitudes of earlier generations, and even myth can have its own validity. Folk myths are not forgeries: they are often symbolic versions of human experience.

More recent scholarship has in some cases given us a better understanding of these stories. We are now aware of instances where a story about a courtesan has been grafted on to the name of a genuine early martyr and it has been possible to restore the martyr's original reputation. Sometimes we can establish borrowings or overlaps. St John Chrysostom's *Homily 67 in Matthew* is often cited as the original of stories about courtesans. Chrysostom recounts the story of a renowned actress, whose dissolute life made her talked about in Cilicia and Cappadocia. He does not give her name, but he says that she came to Antioch from one of the Phoenician cities. She heard the Christian gospel, suddenly resolved to be baptized, and thereafter lived austerely, wearing a hair shirt and shutting herself up in a cell.

There is no reason to conclude that all these stories had a common source. Probably every great city in the Middle East had its own local story about a repentant courtesan. There are likely to have been many penitent courtesans as the early Christians brought their message to the great and sinful cities of the Middle East: for the first time they were offered the chance of a better way of life. To assume that they were all the same person is rather like insisting that two Jane Smiths are the same because they both acted as check-out staff in supermarkets.

Emphasizing the similarities between these stories may lead to ignoring important differences. Most of this group of saints have now been removed from the revised Roman Calendar and figure only as minor footnotes in the standard Lives of the saints; but before they disappear into the shadows of history, it may be worth considering them again, for two reasons: first, even popular historical romances usually have some basis in fact. They may be borrowed, added to, and embroidered. They may mix two or three earlier accounts in one, but somewhere, at some time, the events related happened. Second, these stories have a particular relevance to the roles of women in a male-dominated world.

Women in the ancient world could seldom find respectable forms of employment. They were expected to be supported by their families—fathers, brothers, husbands; and if family support failed, prostitution may have been the only way of avoiding starvation. A girl's femininity and her looks may have been her only capital—and a capital that would diminish over time. Later, the Church would make provision for neglected girls without family support and save them from a degraded life. Courtesans of the early Christian period may often have been victims rather than flagrant sinners.

Despite Christ's treatment of the woman taken in adultery—"Go, and sin no more"—and his suggestion to her male accusers that they examine their own conduct before casting the first stone, religious stories at the popular level tended to choose courtesans as examples of women sinners, as though women could not commit the other deadly sins; and their repentance had to be lengthy, painful and public, as a deterrent to other women. The reasons for this are biological and social rather than moral. Women's chastity was the safeguard of the family and the system of inheritance, since a father must be sure that his heirs are his and not another man's. Though the Church from its early days demanded the same high standard of chastity from both sexes, a man who failed in this respect might repent and be fairly easily forgiven. A woman suffered permanently—there was no way back to virginity.

These stories almost all come from the Middle East. They often read as though they have been told and re-told many times by weary travellers sitting at night round camp fires; and no doubt when the original story-teller had finished, there were others ready to contribute half-remembered stories from other sources: "I heard she was a courtesan, not a virgin," or, "Surely she went to a monastery dressed as a man? I heard that she was accused of fathering a child," and so on; but they have something to teach us about women's lives in the ancient world. This particular genre of morality tale really belongs to the first five or six centuries of the Christian era, but examples continue to occur well into the Middle Ages.

Eudoxia of Heliopolis probably lived in the second century. The account in the ancient Life of her conversion by a monk and the itemisation of the many rich possessions she gave to the Church are quite detailed and specific. This account may be the origin of St John Chrysostom's illustration in *Homily 67 in Matthew*. Her Life was written at some time after the death of Constantine in 337, and Chrysostom, archbishop of Constantinople, lived from 347 to 407. Heliopolis was in Egypt, near to where Cairo stands today.

Mary of Egypt, naked and shrivelled by the desert sun, covered only in her long hair, is a well-known figure in Books of Hours and on frescoes. One ancient Life gives no explanation of why she sought expiation for her sins in the desert. The other says that she was a child prostitute in Alexandria, abandoned by her family and casually exploited by men in one of the most vice-ridden cities of the ancient world. She heard of the Holy Sepulchre, and some sailors offered to take her to the Holy Land. She says with some bitterness, "They had my body as the price." Her experience in Jerusalem was so overwhelming that she went to live alone in the desert across the Jordan for many years. Though the very popularity of her Life caused it to become festooned with improbable and fantastic legends, the basic story seems real enough.

Pelagia the Penitent also has a distinctive and well-attested story. Her acts were grafted on to those of an earlier Pelagia of Antioch, a virgin martyr; and she was sometimes confused with Margaret of Antioch because she was a dancer and her professional name was Margarita; but her ancient Life has enough human detail to suggest that there is history behind it. The account of how Bishop Nonnus, though strongly attracted to his lovely penitent, succeeded in providing her with good pastoral care, and of how she took his cloak to cover her identity and lived alone as a solitary on the Mount of Olives, has the bite of real experience.

The two medieval cases are quite different from these ancient dramas. **Salome,** in ninth-century Bavaria, sets an interesting problem in detection; and if she was as wicked as the accounts suggest, her penitence was long and hard. She has been identified with a Saxon queen who tried to poison one of the king's favourites and accidentally poisoned her husband instead. She fled to the Frankish kingdom, where she deeply offended Charlemagne, then went to Jerusalem, lost her servants and her possessions, went temporarily blind, and fell into the Danube. After all these disasters she became an anchorite and lived for some years in conditions of total enclosure until her death.

Margaret of Cortona, in the thirteenth century, is known as "the Magdalene of the Seraphic Order." She was probably only twelve when she left home to escape a cruel stepmother and went to live with a young lord of the district. Though she was resented by envious neighbours, her life with her lover seems to have been one of genuine affection and domesticity. They had a child and a dog, which took her to his master's decomposing body after he had been murdered. Margaret's appalling penances, the product of a mind in shock and a society imbued with stories about long-dead courtesans, were mercifully mitigated by the Franciscans of her city.

With the exception of Salome, who was a poisoner and for a time the abbess of a scandalous abbey near Paris, these women do not seem to have been murderous or lustful. Courtesans are generally not highly-sexed women: they are plying a trade, not indulging a vice. Yet all were condemned for Lust, and there was no corresponding condemnation of the men who exploited them. "The woman tempted me" has been repeated many times throughout history.

There appear to be no records of women saints celebrated for repenting of Pride, Anger, Avarice, Envy, Covetousness, or Sloth. These sins were more commonly the results of wealth, power, and warfare, all generally reserved to men. It is a sobering thought that the modern freedoms of women include the freedom to commit all seven deadly sins.

EUDOXIA
of
HELIOPOLIS

(? second century)

EUDOXIA, or Eudocia, was a Samaritan courtesan living in the city of Heliopolis. There is an ancient Greek Life, which says that she lived in the reign of Trajan (98-117), but the phraseology suggests that it was written down after the time of Constantine, who died in 337.

Eudoxia is said to have been very beautiful and to have amassed great wealth through her shameful way of life. "She thought only of how she might gratify the lust of the flesh, the lust of the eye, and the pride of life." However, her living quarters in the city seem to have been comparatively humble. A monk named Germanus lodged in the house next door to hers, and there was only a lath and plaster wall between them. The monk arose in the middle of the night and sang his psalms, and then opened a book and read in a loud voice a "spiritual lecture," which described how Christ would appear as a judge on his Second Coming. Those who had done well would enter into eternal life, and those who had done evil would be cast into the fire. At first Eudoxia was annoyed at having her sleep interrupted, then she became interested, and finally she was alarmed and overwhelmed with remorse for her way of life.

In the morning she sent for the monk and asked him whether what he had said was true. He replied that it was and, looking round her luxurious room,

150

said simply, "What a rich man thy husband must be." At this she blushed and confessed that she had no husband but many lovers. "How hard thy God must be to hate riches," she said, and the monk replied that God did not hate riches, but he hated "gains unjustly gotten." He told her that she should send for a priest to baptize her and prepare herself by fasting and prayer.

Eudoxia closed her house, as though she had gone to the country, and told her servants not to admit anyone. She sent for a priest and told him, "Oh sir, I am a grievous sinner, a sea of guilt." The priest offered her hope: "Be of good cheer, my daughter," he said, "The sea of guilt may be changed into a port of salvation, and the waves tossing with passion sink into an ineffable calm." (We may assume that this literary speech was polished by repeated telling.) The priest told her to put away her silks and jewellery, to wear "a mean gown," and to fast for seven days; before he left, he "diligently taught her what she must believe and do."

When she had eaten nothing for seven days she had a vision, in which an angel led her to heaven and she saw all the blessed ones in white, but a shadow "horrible and black" appeared, shrieking, "This woman is mine. I have used her to destroy many, she has worked for me as a bond slave, and shall she be saved? I, for one little disobedience, was cast out of heaven, and here is this beast, steeped from head to foot in pollution, admitted to the company of the elect. Have done with this: take them all, scrape all the rascals and harlots on earth together, and admit them into your society. I will off into my hell, and grovel there in fire for ever." The devil often has a strong part in these stories and some of the best lines. But Eudoxia withstood the Evil One: she understood that "God willeth not the death of a sinner, but rather that he shall repent of his wickedness and live." Germanus came back to see her and rejoiced to find that she had continued with her repentance.

When she had been fully prepared for entry into the Christian life, the bishop came and baptized her, after which she made an inventory of all her possessions. These are recounted in detail: there was a great store of money and jewels; 275 boxes of silk dresses; 410 chests of linen; 160 boxes of gowns embroidered with gold; 123 large chests of jewelled dresses; twelve boxes of musk; thirty-three of Indian storax, a balsam used in oriental medicine and perfumery; a large number of silver vessels; silk and satin curtains, some embroidered with gold; and many other items, all of which were collected by the church treasurer and used for the relief of the poor, being immediately distributed to the most needy.

Eudoxia, in her white baptismal robe, went off into the desert to a convent of thirty nuns directed by Germanus the monk. She wore a white robe to her dying day, covering it with a sackcloth gown and cloak in the winter.

Thirteen months later the superior died, and Germanus appointed Eudoxia in her place.

One of her former lovers, a young man named Philostratus, was "greatly vexed at her conversion." He decided to go and fetch her back to the city—partly because he desired her, and partly because the enterprise amused him. He went to the convent but was told by the porteress, "Thou art mistaken in coming here. No men are admitted into the house." She told him to go to the monastery and ask for Germanus, and then she shut the window in his face. Germanus received the young man but was doubtful about his motivation. He noticed "a certain wantonness in his eye" and refused to give a decision, saying, "We are all old men here, and are not the proper advisers and guides of a hot-headed, fire-blooded youth." Eventually Philostratus' arguments that if Eudoxia could repent and be saved, so could he, and that Eudoxia could help him to repentance, were accepted. Philostratus was taken to Eudoxia's room, "some of the Sisters standing afar off, according to the rule of the house, to witness the meeting, though out of earshot of the conversation."

Philostratus looked round her poor room and saw her haggard cheeks and sunken eyes, the results of fasting; he passionately implored her to go back with him to the city, saying, "All Heliopolis awaits thee, ready once more to lavish on thee its gold and its adulation; return once more to the raptures and liberty of a life of pleasure." But she refused steadfastly and counselled him gently, so that in the end he went away and led a better life.

Eudoxia's reputation for holiness grew in the city of Heliopolis, and eventually she was martyred, being executed by the sword by order of the governor. Legends accumulated. She was said to have converted a king, to have been arrested and stripped by another king, and to have confronted the governor of the province armed only with a particle of the Host. The Host turned into a blazing fire, which consumed king, governor, and all the bystanders. These stories may be discounted as accretions—there is no record of a king or a governor of Heliopolis having come to such an astonishing end—but the facts of Eudoxia's conversion and martyrdom appear to be well supported. The only reason to doubt whether they occurred as early as the reign of Trajan is that the convent seems too well organized and established for such an early date.

Eudoxia's name was first inserted into the Roman Martyrology by Cardinal Baronius, whose revised Martyrology was authorized by Pope Benedict XIV in 1749. She has now been omitted from the revised Martyrology, but her Life sheds an interesting light on the position of women in the early Church and on the ability of a monk to hate the sin and love the sinner.

MARY
of
EGYPT

(? 344-421)

St Mary of Egypt holding three loaves and a book.

Painted screen at Kenn in Devon.

THIS MARY is described in the *Bibliotheca Hagiographica Graeca* as *Maria paenitans in deserta Jordania*, Mary the Penitent in the Jordanian Desert. A familiar figure on medieval stained-glass windows and in Books of Hours, she is immediately recognizable—a naked woman, covered by her long hair and carrying three loaves. There are two ancient Greek Lives, of which the briefer and more reliable is given in a life of Abba Cyriacus by the monk Cyril of Scythopolis, who died about 558. Cyril went twice to visit the aged hermit Cyriacus, who was living at the *laura* of Souka. A *laura* was a community of monks who lived as anchorites in separate huts, meeting only occasionally for worship and common meals. On his second visit to Souka, Cyril also met Abba John, "bishop and solitary," who told him the following story:

Abba John, accompanied by a fellow monk, Abba Parammon, was travelling from the Great *Laura*, Mar Saba, to see Cyriacus. They were frightened by a lion, but later found that Cyriacus was on good terms with it. Then they saw a curious creature which ran away from them and hid in a cave. When they followed, the creature said, "I am a woman" and told them that her name was Mary. She said, "I became cantor of the holy church of the Resurrection of Christ, and the devil made many scandalized with me. Fearing lest, in addition to being made responsible for such scandals, I should add sin to sin, I entreated God to rescue me from being the cause of such scandals." She had left Jerusalem with a flask of water and a basket of lentils, which remained miraculously full, and she had not seen a human being since. She had lived in the desert for eighteen years. She bade them go and see Cyriacus and to visit her on the way back. When Cyriacus heard their story he said, "Glory to thee, O God, for having such hidden saints. But go, my children, and do as she told you." They went back to the cave and found Mary lying dead. So they went on to their own *laura* and fetched what was necessary for a proper funeral; they then buried her in her cave and blocked up the entrance with stones.

In this version, the nature of Mary's sin is not specified: whatever it was, it was unmentionable and the work of the devil. The other ancient Life says that she was a prostitute from Alexandria, but certain features are common to both: her association with the church of the Holy Sepulchre in Jerusalem, the lion, the lentils, and her death before the second visit.

This second Life is attributed to Sophronius, patriarch of Jerusalem, who died in 639, but the story is much older. The writer says, "The monks continued to hold this tradition, and to hold their narrative by tradition, and to narrate it to those desiring to hear something tending to edification. Possibly others before me have written the life of the holy woman, though I have not met with such a life." He recounts how the solitaries of the Jordanian desert had a custom of meeting together on the first Sunday in Lent. They would receive Communion, eat a light repast together, and go their separate ways into the desert, chanting Psalm 27, *Dominus illuminatio mea.* Each observed Lent in his own way, with God as the only witness of his penance, so that they should not be puffed up by their own austerities. At Easter they met again in Jerusalem. An abbot named Zosimus endured the burning days, shivered through the cold nights for twenty days, and then started on the return journey. He saw a naked creature, blackened by the sun and covered only with its own long white hair. At first he thought that it might be a spirit—the desert was reputedly the home of *afreets* and *djinni*—but when it ran away he pursued it, complaining that he was old and feeble and could not run very fast. The creature stopped and called to him by name, saying "I pray thee, for the love of God, approach not nearer; for I am a woman, and I have nothing wherewith to cover my nakedness. Cast me across thy mantle, and then I will speak with thee." When he hesitated, she said, "May God forgive thee, abbot, for mistaking a poor sinful woman for an evil spirit!" Zosimus gave her his cloak, and when she had covered herself he asked her who she was and what had brought her to live in this desolate place.

She told him that her name was Mary. She had left home for Alexandria at the age of twelve and had spent seventeen years there. We do not know whether she came from a broken home or a cruel one, nor what made her leave; but she made a living as a musician and a prostitute. She sounds like the sort of girl who might drift about with a pop group today. She often saw people boarding ships to make a pilgrimage to Jerusalem, and she asked them where they were going and why. When she was told about Christ she determined to go to the Holy City herself. She asked some sailors if she could embark with them. They agreed readily enough and used her as a prostitute on the voyage.

When she reached Jerusalem, she went to the church of the Holy Sepulchre on the feast of the Exaltation of the Holy Cross with the other pilgrims, but she was unable to enter: an unseen force held her back. She tried many times but was unable to cross the threshold. After wandering about for a time she saw an image of the Blessed Virgin Mary on a wall in the forecourt, and she had a great and sudden consciousness of sin. She threw herself down on the stones, shaken by a paroxysm of sobbing, and prayed to the Virgin, asking pardon for her sins. She promised to renounce her way of life and to live in charity. Then she went back to the church of the Holy Sepulchre, and this time passed through the door without any difficulty. Afterwards, she went to the church of St John the Baptist by the river Jordan, and she washed her face and hands in Jordan water, and received Communion in the church. A stranger gave her three pieces of silver, with which she bought her three loaves, and she heard a voice saying, "Go beyond the Jordan and thou shalt find salvation".

She was ferried across the river and began her isolated life. At first she was haunted by the melodies of popular songs and dances and by vivid memories of her past life, but she stayed in the desert for forty-seven years, living on dates and wild berries. If this chronology is more or less accurate, she must have been in her late seventies when Zosimus met her: the eighteen years specified in the Life recorded by Cyril of Scythopolis seems more likely. In all her years in the wilderness she had seen no one, and her clothes had rotted from her body. She asked Zosimus to bring her Communion and to wait for her on the banks of the Jordan. He is said to have returned on Maundy Thursday, just before the beginning of the Good Friday ceremonies in Jerusalem. She received Communion thankfully and asked him to come again in a year's time. Her offered her food, but she would take only a few lentils. When he returned in the following year he found her body wrapped in the tattered remains of his cloak, and a lion came and dug a hole in which he buried her.

This story was elaborated by Byzantine hagiographers. John Moschus mentioned it in his *Pratum Spirituale*, and it appears in Jacobus de Voragine's *Golden Legend*—where Mary is credited with walking across the surface of the river Jordan. She is also said to have left instructions about her burial written in the sand. As so often occurs, a real and human story has been embroidered with rather pointless miracles to feed the popular desire for sensation: an oral tradition demands constant stimulus for the listeners. However, it seems reasonably certain that there was a woman named Mary living in the desert; that she had been a prostitute; that she went to the church of the Holy Sepulchre in Jerusalem; that she sought a penitential life across the Jordan; that she was discovered after many years by a monk; that she died soon after, and the monk (or monks) buried her. It is possible, of course, that two or more women named Mary took such a course over several centuries, but the identifying details suggest that the stories relate to the same woman.

In the medieval period, relics of Mary were much prized. Pope Hormisdas (514-23) is said to have given relics to St Eleutherius of Tournai. Cyril of Scythopolis is thought to have been born about 525, so his Life could not have been current in Europe during the pontificate of Hormisdas. Possibly Abba John was telling Cyril of events that had happened many years earlier. Alternatively, the story and the relics could have been taken to Europe by other travellers before Cyril wrote his record; or the link with Pope Hormisdas could simply be a matter of later attribution. Other relics of Mary of Egypt are said to be placed in St Peter's basilica in Rome, in other churches of the city, in the cathedral in Urbino, in St Peter's in Cremona, and elsewhere. The popularity of Mary of Egypt in carvings, paintings, and stained glass seems to derive from the oddity of her appearance and the dramatic nature of her long penance rather than from any understanding of the facts of her story.

PELAGIA
THE
PENITENT

(early fifth century)

*Detail from a page of a
Life of St Pelagia of Jerusalem,
who is represented in the margin.*

*From a twelfth century Byzantine
Menologion.*

THERE ARE TWO Pelagias, both from Antioch, whose stories have
become confused by oral tradition—perhaps also by the comparative lack of
interest in Eastern saints in the West after the schism between Rome and
Constantinople. The first was a young virgin martyr in the fourth century. St
Ambrose (340-97) mentions this Pelagia in his *De Virginibus*. She was about
to be arrested as a Christian, probably in the persecutions of Diocletian, went
up to the roof of her house, and jumped off into the river to her death. Like
the story of Apollonia, this became a favourite topic for medieval
disputations on the "death before dishonour" theme: whether the
preservation of her virginity, which would have been violated if she had been
captured, took moral precedence over the sin of suicide.

The second Pelagia, whose story has been immensely popular in both East
and West, was a courtesan in Antioch a century or so later. Some
commentators have dismissed it as fiction. There are two ancient Greek Lives,
one of which, said to be by James the Deacon, is in the *Vitae Patrum*. Helen
Waddell describes this account as a masterpiece of storytelling, but she also
points to features of the story that suggest it had a basis in fact. Bishop
Nonnus, to whom Pelagia made her submission, is an historical character. He
was a monk at Tabbenisi, Pachomius' great monastery in the Upper Thebaïd,
who was called from his secluded life to be bishop of Edessa. He attended the

Council of Chalcedon in 451, and some of the bishops whose names are mentioned in the Pelagia narrative can also be identified as signatories to conciliar documents. The writer is thought not to have been the deacon who attended Bishop Nonnus, though he may have had an earlier manuscript to work from.

It is a compelling story. The writer produced his account for reading aloud, possibly in the monastic refectory. He starts by asking his audience to be silent and consider the story well, because it is one of a "rich repentance."

Pelagia was a dancer and an actress. Her professional name was Margarita, which is why she is sometimes known as Margaret of Antioch. When she was at the height of her popularity she and her associates passed by the basilica of St Julian in Antioch at a time when Bishop Nonnus was expounding the gospel to a group of other bishops. Eight of them had been called to Antioch by their metropolitan, and they were sitting outside the church, in its shade. "A splendid train of young men and maidens clad in robes of price, with torques of gold about their necks" came suddenly into the brilliant sunlight of the square. They were carrying a litter on which Pelagia reclined. In a society where women were veiled in public, she rode shamelessly bareheaded and bare-shouldered. She was graceful and charming, and "of the beauty and loveliness of her there could be no wearying for a world of men." She was covered in gold and silver and precious stones, and she was deliciously perfumed. Her shoes were of gilded leather, studded with pearls.

All the bishops groaned at the sight of her and turned away, shocked— except for Nonnus, who gazed at her intently for a long time. When her train had passed, he turned to the other bishops and asked, "Did not the sight of her great beauty delight you?," but they made no answer. And he sank to his knees and wept, until his book of prayers was stained with tears. He asked them again, "Did not the sight of her great beauty delight you?," but they answered him nothing. Then he asked them how many hours they thought this woman spent in bathing and adorning her body, so that it might be flawless and suitable to her art, and how little time they spent preparing their souls for the riches and beauty of heaven. "We adorn not, we care not so much as to wash the filth from our miserable souls, but leave them lying in their squalor."

Nonnus had a troubled night, in which he prayed "Lord Christ, have mercy on a sinful man, for a single day's adorning of a harlot is far beyond the adorning of my soul. . . . She hath promised to please men, and hath kept her word. Naked am I in heaven and earth, for I have not done thy bidding." When he slept he dreamed of a black dove, which kept flying round him at the altar. It was stained and filthy, and he could hardly bear the stink and squalor of it; but he seized it and dipped it in the font, and it came out white as snow and soared into the sky. He stood watching as it flew higher and higher and was lost to sight in the deep blue of the sky.

The next day was Sunday, and the presence of the synod made it a great occasion for the city of Antioch. The bishops processed into the basilica and sat on thrones prepared for them, and the people crowded in after them. The metropolitan of Antioch held the Gospel book out to Nonnus and bade him speak on the wisdom of God. He did so, expounding on the emptiness of human vanity, and the people were so moved by this that the floor-stones of the cathedral were wet with their tears. Pelagia was there, and this was a great wonder to the congregation, for she was not a catechumen and did not attend church. She was suddenly stricken with the fear of God and fell to sorrowing and despair. After the service she told two of her young men to follow the bishop and find out where he lived; and when she was told that he was staying in St Julian's hospice, she wrote to him on wax tablets, saying:

> I have heard of thy God, who bowed the heavens and came down to earth, not to save the just, but sinners; and that He so humbled Himself as to draw nigh to publicans, He, whom cherubim dare not gaze upon, conversed with sinners. And thou, my lord, who art very holy, although with the eyes of flesh thou hast not seen Jesus Christ who manifested Himself by the well to the Samaritan woman, yet thou art His worshipper, as I have heard from Christians.

She asked if she might come to see Bishop Nonnus, so that she might learn about his God. Nonnus was clearly attracted to her, and he was properly cautious. He wrote back saying, "Seek not to tempt my weakness, for I am a man that is a sinner, serving God." He would not see her alone but was willing to see her in the presence of the other bishops. So she came to the hospice, and the bishops assembled in the courtyard and received her. There she flung herself at the feet of Nonnus, saying, "I pray thee, my lord, imitate thy Master, Jesus Christ, and pour out upon me thy great charity and make me a Christian. For I, my lord, am an ocean of sins and an abyss of iniquity. . . . I pray that I may be baptized." And she washed his feet with her tears, and wiped them with the hair of her head. The bishops said in wonderment that they had never seen such faith and desire for salvation. Nonnus, perhaps rather embarrassed by this dramatic behaviour, sent his deacon to ask the bishop of Antioch to find a woman who would look after his tempestuous penitent. Then he told her to confess her sins. She said they were heavier than the sands of the sea, and the waters were too scant to wash them all away; but she trusted in God, who would loosen the load of her wrongdoing. Nonnus asked her what her name was; she said her father and mother had named her

Pelagia, but the townsfolk of Antioch called her Margarita, which means a pearl, because she was the devil's jewel.

Then Nonnus exorcized her and baptized her Pelagia, and the chief deaconess Romana, whom the metropolitan had sent to be with her, acted as her godmother. The sign of the Cross was set upon her, and she was given the Body of Christ and sent to be with the catechumens. Nonnus rejoiced and bade the bishops to eat and drink well, to celebrate the salvation of the girl; but they were disturbed by the devil, who came shouting and lamenting up and down outside the gates, saying, "Woe is me, for the things I suffer from this decrepit old man! Might not the ten thousand Saracens have been enough for thee, that thou didst wrest from me and baptize and offer to thy God? Might not Heliopolis have been enough for thee, that was mine and thou didst wrest it from me?" And the devil appeared to the girl in the chamber where she and her godmother Roxana slept, and offered her more gold, and more precious stones; but she prayed and made the sign of the Cross, and he vanished.

Three days later she sent for the steward who had charge of her house and told him to make a list of all her possessions—gold and silver and ornaments and rich apparel; she sent word to Nonnus through her godmother, asking him to come to her, and she set all her wealth before him and gave it to him, saying that all she desired were the riches of Christ. Nonnus sent for the senior treasurer of the Church in Antioch and handed it all to him in her presence, saying that it was tainted money, "the hire of sin." It should not be used by the Church but be given to the widows and orphans, so that the wealth of a sinner might become the treasury of righteousness.

According to the story in the *Vitae Patrum*, Pelagia summoned her slaves and gave them their freedom, making them presents of the gold torques they wore as a symbol of her service and saying, "Make haste and escape out of the bondage of this sinful world." Then, on the eighth day after her baptism, she put on the tunic and cloak of Bishop Nonnus and fled; she was seen no more in the city of Antioch. Her godmother Romana wept bitterly, doubtless thinking that she had failed to care for the girl; but Nonnus comforted the deaconess, saying that he was sure all would be well with Pelagia.

Three or four years later James the Deacon made a pilgrimage to Jerusalem. Before he left Antioch, Nonnus asked him to go and see a certain brother Pelagius, a monk who lived on the Mount of Olives; after he had made his devotions in Jerusalem, James made his way to the place where Christ had prayed and been betrayed and found a little cell, closed on every side but with a small window covered by a shutter; he knocked on the shutter, and the monk opened it. James says that the monk knew him, but he did not recognize the monk. All he saw was a face wasted and haggard with fasting. When he said he came from Nonnus, the monk Pelagius said, "Let him pray for me, for he is a saint of God," then closed the shutter quickly and began to sing the Psalms of the third hour. James stayed outside and prayed, then went back to Antioch. On the way he visited many monasteries, where the monks told him of the fame of the holy Pelagius.

Some time later James went back to the Mount of Olives and knocked at the shutter again, but there was no answer. He came a second day, and a third, and still received no reply. So he opened the shutter and saw Pelagius lying dead. He closed the shutter again, fastened it securely with clay, and went back to Jerusalem to give the news that the good monk Pelagius was at peace.

> Then the good fathers came with the brethren of divers monasteries . . . and they carried out the holy little body, reckoning it as precious as gold and jewels. And when the good fathers set about anointing the body with myrrh, they found that it was a woman; and they cried aloud with a shout, "Glory to thee, Lord Christ, who hast many treasures hidden on the earth, and not men only, but women also."

When the story was told abroad, monks and virgins came from Jericho and Jordan with wax candles and flaming torches, chanting hymns, and the good fathers carried her to her grave.

Some elements in this story read like fiction, particularly the splendidly rhetorical speeches attributed to the devil, who is unlikely to have made such a public appearance at the city gates. However, the manager of Pelagia's theatre group may well have done so, for he had lost his leading lady and was probably very angry. Other parts of the story have a definite ring of truth about them. Both the deacon and the bishop were evidently strongly attracted to their beautiful penitent, as other men were; but for them, in Helen Waddell's elegant and sensitive phrase, "religion was not the mask of desire, but the countenance of that eternity which doth ever besiege our life." The careful chaperoning of both bishop and penitent reads like fact, as does the puzzlement of James the Deacon at Pelagia's disappearance and later at the strange behaviour of the monk Pelagius. Pelagia knew him, but he did not know her when her beauty had gone. He says afterwards, when he knows the identity of the person he saw in the brief moment when the shutter was opened, that "her eyes were like trenches in her face." That sounds like recollection, not fiction. So does his final plastering of the shutter with clay—an expedient to leave her body in privacy until it could be properly buried.

It seems clear even from this account that Bishop Nonnus knew a good deal more than he told James. The other ancient Life suggests that Nonnus had always known of Pelagia's flight and the reasons for it. Perhaps she found life with the female catechumens difficult. Until her conversion she had lived her life among men, and the company of virgins and widows may have been strange to her. Did she tell Nonnus of her wish to be a solitary? Did he lend her his tunic and cloak and tell her to go to the Mount of Olives? It is hard to believe that she would have stolen his cloak, when she had such a great respect for him, or that she would have known where to go without his advice; and if there is any truth in the story of his dream, Nonnus understood that the white bird had to be free.

SALOME
(? Ninth Century)

German monastery with early medieval church.

IN A chronicle written by a monk of Ober Altaich in Bavaria there is an account of a woman named Salome who appears out of the blue near Regensburg on the Danube. Perhaps she was named for Salome, the wife of Zebedee and mother of the apostles James and John (Mark 15:4, Matt. 27:6), rather than for the daughter of Herodias, who encompassed the death of John the Baptist, but she had a sinful past of which to repent. The chronicler, who claims to be a contemporary, says that she was a royal princess, a niece of "the king of England," who had been forced to leave her own country because she had committed crimes. She went on a pilgrimage to the Holy Land. On the way back her two servants died, she lost all her possessions, and became temporarily blind. At Regensburg she fell into the river and was rescued by fishermen. They took her to Passau, the great medieval fortified city in Bavaria, where a noble lady offered her shelter for some three years. She recovered her sight and suffered no lasting ill effects from her misfortunes apart from chilblains. Abbot Walter of Ober Altaich, a double monastery, came to hear of her and thought she was his kinswoman. He offered her a

163

place of shelter where she could find peace after her troubled life. A cell was built for an anchoress adjoining the abbey church, and there the English royal lady was enclosed with full rites for the rest of her natural life, with only a small opening to the church through which she might hear Mass and receive Communion.

Later another relative, a widow named Judith, who was Salome's aunt or cousin, came to Ober Altaich. It was said locally that she had been sent by her brother "the king of England" to find out what had happened to Salome, but Judith did not return to England. She decided to become an anchoress, and another cell was built adjoining the monastery church. Judith occupied it until her death, which took place some years after Salome's. It is said that in her last years she had nightmares and that the monks would come running to her cell when they heard her screams. Both Judith and Salome were buried in the monastery church. The monastery was overrun and destroyed by the Hungarians in 907, but it is said that the relics of both anchoresses were safely moved to Nieder Altaich, where they are still venerated.

Searches through records of the royal houses of England in the ninth century have failed to identify a princess named Salome, but Asser, bishop of Sherborne, who compiled his biography of King Alfred the Great in about 893, tells the story of Eadburga or Eadburh, who, he says, was notorious in Mercia "in recent times." He claims that the story was related to him by Alfred himself. It is repeated by the eleventh-century chroniclers William of Malmesbury and Roger de Hoveden, who, like Asser, do not give exact dates but place it in the early ninth century. Eadburga was the daughter of Offa, king of Mercia, and married Beorhtic, king of the West Saxons. After her marriage she began to cause trouble at court by her tyrannical way and her vicious nature, and she was generally hated. She trumped up charges against the nobles and the clergy, forcing Beorhtic to decree their execution or exile. When he refused to listen to her, she turned to poisoning those who lost her favour. She was jealous of anyone who had influence with the king, and when he rejected her accusations against an "illustrious youth" named Worr, she put poison in Worr's cup; the king drank from the same cup, and he and Worr both died. Eadburga, "this most wicked poisoner," fled the country, taking with her "countless treasures."

She went to the court of Charlemagne (742-814). Much impressed by her wealth and beauty, he wished to marry her. To test her, he offered her the choice of marrying himself or his son. Unwisely, she chose the younger man, and Charlemagne was so offended that he decided she should not marry either of them: she should be a nun, and live segregated from men. He gave her a monastery, but she proved a very unsuitable abbess. She had a flagrant affair with a "low fellow," an Englishman. Her behaviour was so scandalous that eventually Charlemagne, in anguish and sorrow, was forced to expel her, and she was reduced to wandering the streets in great penury. Asser says that he knew many people who saw her in this condition, and he ends by recording that she died miserably at *Patavium*, which was the Latin name for Pisa in Italy.

There was of course no king of a united England in this period: the first was Canute in 1016, but a German monk might well have given that title to the king of Mercia. The identification of the unknown Salome with Eadburga, about whom so much is known, seems a strong possibility, particularly if there was a very small copyist's error in the Ober Altaich chronicle. *Patavium* is the Latin form of Pisa, but *Patavia* is the Latin form of Passau, where Salome is known to have stayed before finding sanctuary at Ober Altaich. If Eadburga was seen in the streets of *Patavia*, not *Patavium*, the two halves of the story fit very well.

Doubts about this solution to the mystery of Eadburga's end and Salome's origin have been expressed by M. Holder-Eggar, who maintains that the Ober Altaich manuscript dates from the late eleventh century, about the time of William the Conqueror; but the content makes it clear that Salome is a Saxon princess, not a Norman, and it is quite possible that the eleventh-century monk copied a ninth-century manuscript—including the claim that it was "contemporary." If this is the case, Bishop Asser's satisfaction in Eadburga's miserable end was unfounded, and we have an unusual story of a very wicked woman who genuinely repented and found the peace of God after great hardship.

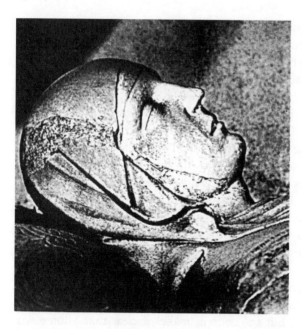

MARGARET OF CORTONA

(1247-97)

Detail from her tomb in the church of S. Margherita in Cortona, by di Pietro.

MARGARET was the daughter of a farmer from Laviano in Tuscany. Her mother was kind and taught her to pray; but she died when Margaret was only seven, and her father married again. According to the Franciscan account, her father neglected his daughter, "being completely engrossed in his agricultural pursuits." Her stepmother was "hard, violent, and passionate." It seems that Margaret was an only child, and she must have had good reason to want to leave home. She "fled in fear in the dusk of evening" to live with the young lord of Montepulciano. Since she was twenty-seven when her lover died, and they had lived together for nine years, she must have been about eighteen when she left home.

It is recorded that "for nine years, she led so criminal a life that she was the scandal of the country." Certainly the neighbours gossiped. There were envious reports, which described her as "riding through the streets of Montepulciano on a superb steed, splendidly attired, and adorned with pearls and sparkling jewels." These bear a distinct resemblance to the ancient stories of courtesans such as Eudoxia and Pelagia, who were described as "flaunting their jewels." In fact Margaret and her lover, who was probably not much older than she was, seem to have lived a quiet domestic existence together. She bore him a son, and they lived together with the child and a dog, which seems to have been a family pet rather than a hunting dog. In the Italian society of the time it was not possible for them to marry. A young man of rank would have to marry a girl of equal rank, so as to unite two noble families: marriage to a farmer's daughter was unthinkable.

166

One day Margaret's lover went out to visit one of his estates with the dog, and she anxiously awaited his return through the evening, the night, and the following day. She sent a servant to search for him, but he could not be found. Then the dog came back alone, tugging at Margaret's skirt and running to the door. When she followed, it led her through hedges and bushes to a spot by an oak tree where there was a heap of leaves and began to scratch at the leaves. To Margaret's horror, she found the badly-decomposed body of her lover, who had been assassinated. We are not told whether he was set upon by robbers or by enemies of his family. The account of these events concentrates only upon the sin and shows no concern for the human tragedy. The shock of her discovery must have been sufficient to unhinge her mind.

Margaret put on penitential dress and went with her young son to Laviano to ask her father for forgiveness. He was willing to receive her, but her stepmother told him than he would be dishonoured if he gave shelter to a woman of such evil repute and drove her away. Weeping, and with her weeping child (described as " the offspring of her unlawful connection"), she walked from Laviano to Cortona, intending to ask the Franciscans for help. On her way she met two ladies, the Contessa Maneria and the Contessa Raneria, who were both devoted to the Franciscan Order. They saw that Margaret was distressed and offered to assist her. She and her son stayed for some time in their house. When they introduced her to the Friars Minor she was placed under the direction of a friar, Fr Giunta Bevegnati, and lived for three years a régime of prayer and penance. The Franciscans were much gentler than the Dominicans of that period and avoided extreme penances, but it was an age for bizarre mortifications of the flesh, and Margaret went beyond any penances prescribed by her director. She lived on bread and water and a few herbs, deprived herself of sleep, slept on the bare ground with a log or a stone for a pillow, and wore a hair shirt. She gashed her body with knives, beat herself savagely, and even threatened to cut off her nose and lips. Today, this self-mutilation would be recognized as symptomatic of grief and unbearable stress. Fr Giunta was concerned and finally forbade her to undertake these extreme acts, though he seems to have been unable to prevent her from going back to Laviano, her birthplace, barefoot and with a rope around her neck, to ask pardon of the congregation during Mass. He did manage to deter her from another penitential project: she proposed to wear a halter and to be led through the streets of Montepulciano by another woman who would cry out her sins to those who passed by. In time she became less frenzied, and eventually she was admitted to the Third Order of Franciscans. The two benevolent contessas paid for her son's education at a school in Arezzo, and later he entered the Franciscan noviciate.

Margaret moved to a cell near the convent of the Friars Minor and for a time devoted herself to attending noble women in confinement, in order to earn her living. Most of what she earned she gave away. Later she devoted herself wholly to prayer and contemplation, begging her bread.

She prayed that she might share the sufferings and the passion of Christ: she saw the treachery of Judas, the fury of the mob, the denial of Peter, the scourging and the crowning with thorns, and the pains of crucifixion. She "writhed like a worm, and became ashy pale. At length, her pulse ceased to beat, and she remained speechless and cold as ice." So she remained from None until Vespers, until she looked up to heaven with a joyful countenance "as though she had risen from the dead." This experience began at the end of Mass and was witnessed by the friars. She had many other revelations. She did not tell her director of these unless she felt obliged to do so, either because she had a message for him or because she wanted to be sure that she was not the victim of a delusion.

Margaret had a prayer she used frequently:

Oh, Lord! Thou art the life of my life, thou art my treasure without whom all riches are poverty to me. How joyfully, O Lord, do I offer myself to endure willingly all sorts of torments for thy love. Thou knowest that I seek and desire nothing but thee, who art inexhaustible sweetness, without whom I should seem to be in hell.

Fr Giunta tells us that Margaret bore the name of Jesus always graven in her heart. Whenever she pronounced it, she would break off the discourse, and, melting into tears, would exclaim, "O Name, sweet to my heart above every other name, whose virtue has called me to a life of grace. Name which has attracted me by love and which has brought me to attach myself to Jesus alone!" Again, she would say, "O my Saviour! Thy name is so sweet to my soul, that I never refuse any gall or bitterness, since thou wert drenched with gall for my sake."

Apparently the holiness of her life did not exempt her from public censure. Some people in Cortona accused her of madness or hypocrisy, and "the public veneration for the Saint was turned to universal contempt." Her critics were scandalized at the care given to her by the Friars Minor and regarded those who came to ask her prayers as credulous. They protested that it was impossible that God should bestow graces on a woman whose life had been so scandalous. Even the Franciscans began to doubt her, and Fr Giunta himself was uncertain of her sincerity. For a time, in distress, she lost her visions; but she prayed steadily for her persecutors and suffered in silence. The Siena provincial chapter of the Friars Minor decided that "for the sake of their consciences no less than of their reputation" they must behave toward her with extreme reserve. Fr Giunta was removed from Cortona and sent to Siena. For seven years Margaret had very little contact with the Franciscans, remaining in her cell and attending Mass at another church because she feared to embarrass them; at last Fr Giunta was permitted to return, and "this venerable religious continued to the end to assist the humble lover of her Saviour in her mission on earth." After a time she experienced a command to go out and bring people to God: she spoke in public, and many people came from neighbouring towns and even from France and Spain to hear her. Fr Giunta complained that his work in hearing Confessions was like the labours of Hercules: "He could not clean out so many stables in one day."

Margaret died in 1297 at the age of fifty, having spent nearly half her life in the most rigorous penance. Pope Leo X approved her feast for the diocese of Cortona from 1522, and she was formally canonized by Pope Benedict XIII in 1728.

Written accounts of Margaret's tragic early life, even fairly recent ones, are highly judgmental. They ignore her unhappy home background, the death of her mother, the rejection by her stepmother, and the acute trauma resulting from the discovery of her lover's body. It is to the credit of the Franciscans of Cortona that, although they were bound to regard her acts as mortal sin, they behaved humanely to a shocked and grieving girl, apart from the period in which local malice forced them to ignore her. The people of Cortona have made amends by erecting a statue of Margaret, accompanied by the dog. There is a painting by Lanfranco in the Pitti Gallery in Florence.

6

OUTCASTS

Women HAVE traditionally lived much more static lives than men. Until the latter part of the nineteenth century they could not travel unless they were rich enough to take an entourage with them, journey with a party, or disguise themselves as men. Women of the merchant classes and poor women generally stayed at home, their horizons bounded by their own town or village. This bore most hardly on social outcasts—women whom nobody wanted to know. Though men could always start a new life elsewhere, women whom their families or the neighbours rejected had little choice but to live with rejection. We should expect to find among them some close to Christ, who was himself "despised and rejected of men, a man of sorrows and acquainted with grief" (a fulfilment of Isaiah 53:2). God became man in humility—a servant to his friends, symbolized by washing their feet; a criminal to his people, symbolized by the marks of the cross.

The *New Jerusalem Bible* translation of the first part of the prophecy from Isaiah is "a *thing* despised and rejected by men." This is the essence of being an outcast: he or she is seen as an object, as less than human. In past centuries women started with what social psychologists call a "spoiled identity," in that they were not men. If they were not beautiful and marriageable they had a double handicap. The passion for a male heir and the rejection of a female infant, particularly if it was the first child, were the rule rather than the exception. The prime consideration for a man of property was the consolidation and transmission of his estates from one generation of males to the next. Girls were useful only for the marriage market: they were expected to be attractive, chaste, healthy, fertile, and obedient to the wishes of their fathers and husbands. An ugly daughter or a sick or disabled one was useless. She was simply damaged property.

Since the American Revolution the ideal of "life, liberty and the pursuit of happiness" has gradually been extended—to slaves, to women, to immigrants, to people of other beliefs. The International Covenant on Economic and Social Rights of 1976 spelled out the aspirations of the great majority of nations to parallel civil liberty with social liberty. Though the signatory nations pledged to order their affairs "without discrimination of any kind as to race, colour, sex, language, religion, political or other opinions, national or social origin, property, birth or other status," there are still many parts of the world in which these aspirations have not yet been fully recognized. Female slavery is still common in parts of Africa and the Middle East, and the idea that a daughter is a father's property dies hard. The *Sunday Times* of 27 July 1997 reported that, as the new constitution for South Africa was being discussed, President Nelson Mandela's commitment to equal rights was challenged by tribal chiefs who argued for the continuation of the practice of *lobola* or brideprice. The traditional offer of cattle in exchange for a bride is apparently now being increasingly replaced by offers of cash, and a bride with a university degree or a cookery diploma commands the highest price. Old habits die hard; but in many countries Catholic organizations have played, and continue to play, a major part in the task of liberating women from such traditional fetters.

Today some universities offer post-graduate diplomas in Disability Studies, and the mechanisms of social rejection are being studied in depth. Historical material is scarce, because the lives of women who suffer from social rejection are seldom recorded in detail; but there is a small group of women saints with social or physical disabilities whose problems have been recorded, and who have been recognized by the Church.

Odilia, the daughter of an eighth-century duke whose estates were close to modern Strasbourg, was born blind. Her father, Adalric, needed an heir, and he reacted to her birth with total fury, proposing to have her killed as though she were a maimed horse or a sick dog. It was given out that the duchess had suffered a stillbirth, and the little girl was brought up by a peasant woman far from home. The story of how Odilia was cured of her blindness, how she returned to her family home and became the abbess of a great monastery must have been frequently recounted in the Middle Ages. The twelfth-century English chronicler John of Worcester told the story in some detail four centuries later.

Eustochium of Padua was the illegitimate daughter of a nun. So great was the scandal attached to her mother's seduction that the child was badly treated, resented, and despised. Her resulting behaviour problems were thought to be the work of the devil, and it was only when a .patient and gentle priest listened to her and enabled her to understand the causes of her distress that she was quietened and able to make her profession in the Benedictine community.

Jeanne de Valois was the daughter of a king and the wife of another, but she was small and plain and had a physical handicap, probably curvature of the spine. Betrothed when she was less than a month old and married at the age of twelve, she never had the carriage or the physical presence to fill the public role of a queen of France. Her husband ignored her existence; she was not present at his coronation as Louis XII; and she was forced to undergo the most distasteful cross-examination in court when she contested his suit of nullity. The king, of course, won his suit. Jeanne's subsequent life as duchess of Bourges and founder of the Order of the Blessed Virgin Mary says much for her faith and her firmness of purpose in the face of long public humiliation.

Germaine Cousin was what we might call a token shepherdess. Occasionally, to balance the queens, princesses, and duchesses who make up most of the roll of women saints, there has been a movement for the sanctification of a humble woman—usually a young girl, usually a virgin, usually from a small village where every detail of her life would be known. Germaine lived an ugly life—suffering from a severe and disfiguring illness, which was probably a tubercular condition, driven out of the house by a harsh stepmother, sleeping under the stairs or in an outhouse. She turned it into a positive affirmation of faith, and the villagers, who had once shunned her, took pity on her. The story of her life has been treated sentimentally by some writers, but it is not a sentimental story and deserves something better than Cinderella treatment.

Josephine Bakhita was an African slave, snatched from her village in the Sudan when she was so young that she never even knew her own name or the name of her tribe. As a slave, she was beaten and brutally ill-treated. Through the help of the Italian consul in Khartoum, who bought her freedom, she was able to travel to Italy, to join the Canossian Sisters in Venice, and to acquire an education. Bakhita wrote her own moving account of her experiences and her prayer life.

All five of these women suffered from "spoiled identity" in the eyes of the world. This is why there are no portraits available of any of them except Josephine Bakhita, who was able to escape to another kind of life where she was treated as fully human. Portrait artists and sculptors through the ages have tended to look instincively for purity of line, harmony, and balance in what they portray and have avoided what is ugly or troubling to the beholder.

That is a very clear example of a rejection mechanism. A blind girl, the distressed daughter of a nun, a tuberculous shepherdess—even a hunchback queen—were simply not paintable; but, like Bakhita, each of them found a dignity of her own through her faith.

172

ODILIA

(? d. 720)

THERE ARE many legends concerning Odilia (also known as Ottilia, Othilia, or Odile). She is said to have been born in Alsace near the end of the seventh century, the daughter of a Frankish nobleman named Adalric and his wife, Bereswind. Adalric, who came of a distinguished line, desperately wanted a son, but their first child was a daughter, and she was blind. Adalric was appalled and quite unable to accept her handicap. Not only was she of the wrong gender, but she was unmarriageable. He regarded the child at first with irritation and then with unreasoning fury. Though his wife tried to persuade him that Odilia's blindness was the will of God, he regarded it as a personal affront and a reflection on the honour of his family. He was determined to have the child killed and spared her life only in answer to his wife's pleas, on condition that she was sent away and that her origins were kept secret.

Bereswind gave the child to a peasant woman who had formerly been in her service, but the secret was difficult to keep. The villagers gossiped about this blind child who was treated with such care. When they discovered that her foster-mother had been in service to Bereswind, the speculations multiplied. Fearful that the stories would reach Adalric, Bereswind had the child moved to the monastery of Baume-les-Dames, near Besançon, where her own aunt was the abbess. Adalric did not know where his daughter had been sent, and nobody dared to mention her in his presence. She was educated by the nuns until she was twelve years old, but at that time she had not yet been baptized.

According to Odilia's tenth-century Life, the saintly Bishop Erhard of Regensburg was told in a dream that he was to go to the monastery near Besançon and baptize a young blind girl, giving her the name of Odilia, and she would receive her sight. He consulted his brother Bishop Hidulf, and together they went to Baume-les-Dames and carried out the baptism by total immersion. Ehrhard plunged the girl in the holy water; Hidulf lifted her out again; Erhard anointed her head, then touched her eyes with the sacred oil, saying, "In the name of Jesus Christ, may the eyes of your body and the eyes of your soul receive light." She became able to see and was baptized Odilia, which means daughter of light. Hidulf, who lived not far from Adalric's castle of Hohenburg, went to see Odilia's father and told him of the miracle. Adalric made a donation to the monastery at Baume but still refused to see his daughter. He told Hidulf that she would be a standing reproach to him, because he had rejected her at birth. He and Bereswind had four sons and another daughter, so his dynastic ambitions were satisfied. Family affection does not seem to have entered into his calculations.

The most distinguished of the sons was Hugh, who grew up to be generous and kind. He corresponded with Odilia, and she asked him to help her to be reconciled to her father. Hugh asked Adalric to bring her home, but Adalric replied brusquely that he had his own reasons for leaving her at Baume, and Hugh did not dare to press him. Somewhat rashly, Hugh secretly sent a carriage and horses to fetch her. Odilia, believing that her father had relented at last, went willingly; Adalric, out walking with Hugh, saw the coach approaching the Hohenberg and asked who was coming. Hugh, fearful of his father's anger, managed to stand his ground, explaining what he had done and insisting that the fault was his, not Odilia's. A violent scene ensued, in which Adalric raised his heavy staff in fury and struck Hugh to the ground. Some accounts say that he killed him. Then, in a complete emotional reversal, he turned to his daughter and was as affectionate as he had formerly been cruel. Perhaps he was at last persuaded that the honour of his family lay in accepting her, not in rejecting her. For a man of strong views and unbridled passions, he was very conscious of his public image.

Odilia stayed with her family for a time, but Adalric was determined that she should marry a German duke, and so she fled from home. She agreed to return only when he promised her his castle of Hohenburg as a monastery and endowed it generously. This castle, which towers over the town of Obernai, stands on a peak formerly called the Odilienberg and now Mont-Sainte-Odile. Odilia became abbess of the new community, where the nuns kept a strict rule of life. She herself lived on bread and vegetables, drank only water, and spent many nights in prayer, sleeping very little. The nuns were devoted to works of mercy, feeding the hungry and caring for the sick and maimed. Many pilgrims came to Hohenburg, and since the steepness of the mountainside made it difficult for sick and elderly people to reach it, Odilia's mother Bereswind endowed an auxiliary convent on the lower slopes, with a hospice attached. After her parents died Odilia cared for patients in the hospice herself, serving them with her own hands. She prayed for her mother and father and is said to have undertaken special penances on her father's behalf. She lived to a great age, and when she was dying she told her community that she looked forward to her soul leaving her body, so that she might enjoy the liberty of the children of God.

Though many of the documents concerning Odilia are historically unreliable, there is a strong local tradition of a rejecting father and a devoted and forgiving daughter who became a great abbess. Her shrine and her abbey were the objects of great devotion throughout the Middle Ages. Charlemagne and other emperors made pilgrimages to Hohenburg, as did the future Pope St Leo IX when he was bishop of Toul and, it is said, King Richard I of England. The pilgrimage was a popular one, and St Odilia was venerated as the patron saint of Alsace before the sixteenth century. The shrine of St Odilia and the remains of her monastery eventually came into the possession of the diocese of Strasbourg, and since the middle of the nineteenth century Mont-Sainte-Odile has again become a place of pilgrimage. Odilia's relics are preserved in the chapel of St John the Baptist, a medieval building now usually called by her name.

The English monk-chronicler John of Worcester, who wrote from 1118 to 1140, reports the story of Odilia under the year 1131, that is, as happening in his own lifetime. Perhaps he heard it from a French monk who visited Worcester and did not realize that it was already some four hundred years old. His version refers to Adalric as "Normannus" but is otherwise substantially the same as that of the tenth-century Life.

EUSTOCHIUM OF PADUA

(? 1443-69)

EUSTOCHIUM, or Eustochia, was a source of scandal from the time she was born, for her mother was a nun. Her story was recorded by the confessor to the Benedictine community of San Prosdocimo in Padua, Fr Girolamo Salicario, who knew her in her adult life and helped her through her troubled life in the community.

Her mother, Sister Maddalena Cavalcabò, was a member of a Benedictine community at Gemola. In 1443 Maddalena was sent to San Prosdocimo for a time—possibly because of some misdemeanour. Discipline there was very lax, and she was seduced by a young man named Bartolomeo Bellini, who was already married. When she realized that she was to bear his child, Maddalena told one of the Sisters. The community attempted to hush the matter up in order to prevent a public scandal—perhaps because there were other irregularities in San Prosdocimo that might have been discovered. The baby was born, baptized Lucrezia, and put out to nurse. Bartolomeo admitted paternity and offered (or was induced) to pay maintenance for the child When she was four years old, he took her to live in his own household.

Lucrezia was said to be " a perfect little angel," but her three-year stay in her father's house was a time of great unhappiness for her. Bartolomeo's wife resented her and ill treated her. She was given little food, dressed in scanty clothing, and cruelly beaten. It is not surprising that she had "seizures" in which she screamed, became disobedient, and was thought to be possessed by the devil. Bartolomeo turned violently against her, and when she was seven he returned her to the convent. There she became again a good, quiet child, loving prayer and study and willingly undertaking manual work.

For some years her life in the convent proceeded without incident. Then the abbess of San Prosdocimo died, and the bishop, who must have been concerned about the laxity of the community, insisted on the election of a new abbess, Mother Giustina di Lazzara, a woman of great fervour and reforming zeal. The other nuns were dispersed and replaced with Sisters from a stricter foundation.

Only Lucrezia, docile and obedient, remained from the previous régime, attending the school run by the nuns. She knew nothing but convent life and had no relatives. She was a pious girl, and when she was seventeen she asked to be admitted to the community. The story of her birth was well known, and the stigma that attached to the mother seems to have been passed on to the daughter. She was the living proof of a scandal the Sisters would have preferred to forget, a child who should never have been born. Also, they were fearful that she had been contaminated by living in the community during its time of laxity. The discussions and the delay must have caused intense mental suffering to a sensitive girl; for a long time, no one would speak to her. In the end, both heredity and environment were counted against her, and when the Sisters voted the majority opposed her admission.

The matter was referred to the bishop of the diocese, who brushed aside the Sisters' fears and ordered that the girl should be admitted. At length she was given the habit and took the name of St Eustochium, who was the daughter of St *Paula; but her clothing, in a community where she was resented and despised, must have been an ordeal. It was reported that when the priest turned to give her the host he dropped it on the floor. Perhaps he too was affected by the tension; but this event was interpreted by members of the community as a sign that the devil was at work again.

No doubt they made this clear to Eustochium. She soon developed what would now be called "behaviour problems." Still shunned and constantly watched for signs of devil-possession, she suffered from explosive emotional attacks. Most of the time she was gentle and obedient, but she would suddenly develop violent moods in which she was rude and disobedient and became uncontrollable. On 1 October 1461—the date was memorable enough to be recorded—she went into a frenzy, shrieking and howling, her hair dishevelled, gnashing her teeth, rolling her eyes, and writhing like a snake. When she picked up a knife, the nuns fell back in horror. Exorcism had no effect. The abbess ordered her to be tied to a pillar for days to restrain her. She returned to normal and went about her duties as before.

The abbess fell ill, and the doctors could make nothing of her malady, ascribing it to poison or the work of the devil. The whole community turned on Eustochium, alleging that she was killing the abbess in revenge for having been tied to the pillar. Word of the community's suspicions travelled from the convent to the town, and at one point a mob gathered round the convent, determined to burn the girl as a witch. The bishop was consulted, and on his orders Eustochium was confined in a small cell and given no food apart from bread and water every other day. The treatment of recalcitrant nuns was not very different from that of lunatics or criminals: near-starvation was a means by which frenzy could be "reduced." In this pitiable condition, Eustochium confessed to everything that she was accused of: to conversing with the devil and to using diabolical arts to kill the abbess. It seems that the only person who suspected that these admissions were false and made under pressure was her confessor, Fr Girolamo Salicario.

The abbess recovered and decided that Eustochium must be induced to leave the convent of her own accord. She asked her own brother, Francesco de Lazzara, "a gentleman of high position and integrity, much respected in

Padua," to talk to the girl. Signor de Lazzara was not unkind. He reminded Eustochium that she had not yet taken her final vows and suggested that her attacks were proof that she was not suited to convent life. He offered to provide her with a husband and a dowry if she would leave, but Eustochium refused, insisting that she was devoted to the religious life and that she must suffer for her vocation. Some of the Sisters were so angry that they wanted to put her out of the convent by force. In this situation of conflict, her condition worsened. She had constant fits of vomiting, coughing up blood. On one occasion she climbed on a high beam. It is not clear whether she was threatening suicide or not, but one false step would have meant her death. She was confined to her cell again and was found lifeless on the floor, stripped of her garments, her throat covered in bruises. Superstitious rumours swept the community: the devil had threatened to let her fall from the beam if her soul was not made over to him, the devil had tried to strangle her. Fr Salicario remonstrated with the nuns for their credulity and their want of charity. He taught them that they had a duty to bear with Eustochium, but they could not understand or cope with her distress.

This wise and gentle confessor spent much time with Eustochium, listening to her patiently, trying to understand her, and quietening her. It says much for his concern and care that she recovered her mental balance and became again the gentle and obedient spirit of her true self. Her noviciate lasted four years, but she finally made her solemn profession.

She was not to live much longer. She was bedridden for some time, endured acute physical pain, and died at the early age of twenty-six. How far her sufferings were caused by the stigma attached to her birth and how far they were due to developing mortal sickness we shall never know. She has long been liturgically honoured in Padua, and her cult was confirmed in 1760—a belated recognition of a troubled servant of God.

JEANNE DE VALOIS
(JOAN OF FRANCE)
(1464-1505)

JEANNE or Jehane (she signed her name as Jehane of France) was the fourth child of Louis XI, king of France, and his queen, Charlotte of Savoy. Two sons, born in 1458 and 1459, had died in infancy. Only a daughter, Anne, born in 1460, survived. The desire for a male heir to the throne was intense. It seems probable that the young queen had miscarriages after Anne's birth, and when she carried a child to full term in 1464, the fact that it was another girl was a deep disappointment to king and court. The succession had to be secured, and when the child Jeanne was only twenty-six days old she was betrothed to the son of the duke of Orléans, who stood next in line to the throne.

There is no evidence on whether Jeanne was physically normal at birth, but when she was only five years old she was sent away from her family and from the court because she had a physical handicap, to be brought up by Baron and Baronne de Linières, an elderly couple whose château was in Berry. At a time when people were pitiless about such conditions, that was enough to make her segregation almost inevitable. The records say that she limped and had a hump on her back. When she later had to wash the feet of the poor, the thirteen poor people were seated on high benches so that she could carry out the ceremony. This suggests that she had a curvature of the spine, which would have made one shoulder higher than the other, caused the limp, and made it difficult for her to bend down to floor level.

She was a good child but plain, pale-skinned, with fair straight hair. When Louis' mother saw her, she fainted and said "Must my son marry this *deformed* girl?" Louis XI insisted that the marriage must take place, and it was celebrated at Monrichard in Anjou in 1476. The young bridegroom was by then duke of Orléans: his father had died in 1465. He was thirteen, handsome and active, and his bride was only twelve. The wedding ceremony was not an auspicious occasion: a double dispensation was necessary, because the king was Louis' second cousin once removed and also his godfather. Both the blood relationship and the spiritual relationship, though remote, were technically considered to be impediments to marriage. The bishop of Orléans, who conducted the ceremony, later made a deposition during the nullity proceedings that Louis had been unwilling to go through with the marriage and had done so only because he was afraid of the king. After the ceremony the bishop expressed his own reservations by not attending either the Nuptial Mass or the banquet that followed.

The young couple went to Blois, where the great castle and the abbey rise impressively above the river Loire, and the people of the city assembled to give them a public acclamation; but Jeanne's taste of popularity was brief. She was sent back to Linières for a further seven years, until she was nineteen. The dowager duchess had made it very plain that she rejected her daughter-in-law, and perhaps this was as well. The court at Blois was known for its immorality and was no place for a gently-reared girl. The king did not want Jeanne at court either. By this time he had a son, the future Charles VIII, and he was openly shocked at the girl's appearance. Jeanne stayed at Linières, but in order to validate the marriage the king insisted that Louis should visit her four times a year. He would arrive with a large party. There would be feasting and merrymaking, and Jeanne would sit silent until they went away the following day. Louis never supported her financially, though the king had provided a generous dowry at the time of the wedding. When the king became parsimonious she lived in very plain circumstances for the daughter of a reigning monarch. She spent much of her time in prayer and meditation.

When she was fifteen, Louis, who was in Bourges, developed smallpox. Jeanne insisted that it was her duty as his wife to go to her him, but when she arrived she found his mother and sisters in charge, and she had to return to Linières. There seemed no limit to the humiliations that were piled upon her—but much worse was to come. In 1483 Louis XI died. Jeanne's young brother became king as Charles VIII, her elder sister Anne acting as regent, and Louis of Orléans became heir to the throne. Anne treated Jeanne well, transferring her to the royal château at Amboise and making her an adequate allowance, but Louis immediately started proceedings for the annulment of the marriage, denying that it had ever been valid.

At twenty, he had had many mistresses and was deep in political intrigue. The only part of France that remained outside the royal jurisdiction was Brittany, and he joined forces with the duke of Brittany with the intention of making a new marriage alliance with the duke's daughter. He was captured and imprisoned at Bourges. Jeanne went to him at once, assuming that it was her duty to do so. For three years she cared for him, obtaining furnishing and kitchen utensils for his rooms, having curtains washed and mattresses re-stuffed, selling her silver and jewels to pay the servants. Louis had an estate in Italy. She arranged to have money sent from there to Bourges and secured oranges, preserved fruits, and olive oil to improve his diet. Then, when her brother King Charles had attained his majority, he visited Bourges. He threw his arms round Louis and forgave him, and the two went off to Italy together, to fight for the kingdom of Naples. Louis showed no gratitude to Jeanne.

He insisted afterwards that his freedom was due not to her but to the magnanimity of her brother.

While Charles and Louis were fighting in Italy, Anne again became regent of France; Jeanne ruled the duchy of Orléans, but Louis still denied that she was his wife. When he wrote to her he signed himself "vostre amye," your friend, not your husband. In 1495 Charles VIII died. Louis of Orléans succeeded him, becoming Louis XII of France, but Jeanne did not become queen. She was not even invited to be present when he was crowned at Reims, nor when he made his ceremonial entry into Paris. An emissary was sent to her, who told her gracefully, "Madame, the king commends himself to you, and has charged me to say that the lady in all the world whom he holds most dear is yourself," but he went on to say that his majesty was "truly grieved" that she was "not disposed to have issue." The marriage was no marriage, and it would be terminated so that he could seek a wife elsewhere.

Jeanne said simply, "I am his wife." She believed implicitly in the validity of her marriage, and she knew that a valid marriage could not be broken. She was very much alone: her brother was dead, her sister Anne was powerless, and her husband—who said he was no husband—was all-powerful. The reigning pope was Alexander Borgia, who had plans for the aggrandizement of his own family and was amenable to offers of honours for his son Cesare. A papal Bull was issued for a suit of nullity. The king had the best legal opinion, and no one was willing to offend him by representing the wife he was proposing to discard. At length the court, headed by two commissioners, the bishops of Mans and Albi, issued an order that the legal faculty of Bourges must represent her. Only one lawyer came to court—and he demanded a safe conduct before he would take the case.

Jeanne had to appear before the court in person to hear the counts on which a decree of nullity was sought. These included the tenuous blood relationship and the even more tenuous spiritual relationship, for which dispensations had been granted before the marriage took place, and two more damaging charges: that Louis had been intimidated at the time of the wedding by threats of violence and that Jeanne was physically incapable of intercourse. When she was interrogated on these two counts, she gave short, firm answers: she had never heard that he had been intimidated; he had never suggested this to her; she did not believe that he had openly tried to repudiate the marriage. She was asked if she knew that she was "not as well formed as other women" and replied that she knew it but did not believe that she was incapable of having a marital relationship and of having children. She protested that the interrogation had been "most distasteful." It must have cost her a good deal, for she was a sensitive girl, and her upbringing had been unusually sheltered.

After that she did not attend the court, but her secretary reported its findings to her every day. She learned, through the relentless piling-up of testimony, that her father had indeed threatened and intimidated Louis and that Louis had long been trying to free himself from what he insisted was a marriage in name only. It seemed that she was the only person who had not known these things. At length the king's counsel demanded that she should undergo a physical examination to determine whether she was still a virgin and whether she was capable of intercourse. This was too much for her to bear, and she refused. At that point, her case was virtually lost.

The final blow was the production of a letter written by her father to a nobleman stating that he had decided to go ahead with the arrangements for the marriage "because I fancy that the children they will have together will not cost them much to rear" and threatening that anyone who opposed it would "have no assurance of life in my Realm." This unpleasant missive arrived suspiciously late in the proceedings, but it is generally regarded as authentic. It was taken to mean that Jeanne could not have children and that Louis had genuinely been intimidated. The verdict of the court was that the marriage was invalid and that Louis XII was free to marry again.

Jeanne had given evidence on oath, and she must genuinely have believed that her marriage to Louis had been consummated; but, given the circumstances of the marriage and his frequently-expressed aversion to her, it seems probable that he told the truth in saying that she was still a virgin. Soon after the hearing, Cesare Borgia went to Valence, bearing the papal decree of nullity. It was handed over to Louis XII on the day he invested Cesare with the dukedom of Valence. The occasion was said to be a very splendid one, with much public rejoicing.

Jeanne's life had been shattered. She was not queen of France. She was not even duchess of Orléans, and officially she had never held either title— though she continued to wear her wedding ring in the belief that her marriage was a true one. Louis, once he had his freedom, was prepared to be generous. He created her duchess of Berry, with all the rights, honours, and prerogatives of the office. She was free to go and live at Bourges and to rule her duchy. At last the small awkward woman with the limp and the crooked shoulder had a life of her own and a place of her own. In March 1499 she entered Bourges and took possession of the château where Louis had been a prisoner. One of her first acts was to pardon all but the worst prisoners in honour of the occasion.

She chose her ministers and advisers well, and she cared for her people. She devoted much time to relieving poverty and distress and went to visit sick people in person, washing and binding their wounds and sores. During an epidemic she refused to leave the city. She had a special care for prostitutes, trying to give them a sense of their own worth and finding respectable places for them. She set up a school for poor boys and supported churches and religious houses. She organized a pageant of the Passion of Our Lord in Bourges, where all the parts were played by clergy, students, and her young scholars, in order to educate the uninstructed.

There was a monastery of Benedictine nuns where the discipline was very lax. Jeanne consulted the archbishop of Bourges and the abbot of Saint Sulpice, visited the abbess, dropped hints, and finally told the abbess outright that the enclosure must be restored. The abbess demurred, saying that if the nuns had entered under the existing Rule, it was not right that they should have to live under a stricter one. Jeanne sent in workmen to close the doors. Furious nuns hammered on the doors and shouted abuse until she went in person to plead with them, telling them that the world had great need of prayer and penance. Six nuns were sent from the abbey of Notre Dame de Charenton, the monastery was reformed, and the nuns became models of zeal and piety.

Jeanne's confessor was the Franciscan Gilbert Nicholas, later better known as Fr Gabriel-Maria. She told him that she wanted to found "an Order of the glorious Virgin Mary," which would be ruled by his own Order, the Franciscans of the Observance. He told her that it was always difficult to found a new Order in the Church, and advised her to follow the Rule of St Clare. A year passed before she told him that she had been convinced from the age of seven (a year or two after she was sent away to Linières) that she must found an Order for the Blessed Virgin. They both prayed long and earnestly and discussed the possibilities. Then he told her that he thought he saw a way: her Order would be distinctive because it would have "no other patron, no kind of life, no pattern other than that of the Virgin Mary herself." He advised her to secure a house near the palace. He would ask a woman teacher at Tours to choose suitable girls and find two friars to train them as postulants. He went to Tours, interviewed the girls himself, and chose eleven of them, reassuring their parents that they would be "spouses of Jesus, religious of the Virgin Mary and daughters of the holy duchess of Berry."

Jeanne devised their daily routine, which was a very stringent one for schoolgirls, involving the full monastic Hours, private devotions, and manual tasks. They were to rise at five o'clock in the morning and to be in bed by seven at night. She went to see them every day, talking to them and inspiring them. Fr Gilbert drew up the Rule, based on the ten Perfections of Mary: Prudence, Purity, Humility, Faith, Prayerfulness, Obedience, Poverty, Patience, Charity, and Compassion. The community was to be called the *Annonciade*, in commemoration of the Annunciation. A site was found for

183

the convent close to the château, and a new building was erected on three sides of a square. In 1502 the Rule was formally approved by the Holy See.

On Whit Sunday 1504 the time had come for the postulants to receive the habit. It consisted of a grey robe, the symbol of poverty common to all Franciscans; a red scapular, symbolizing the love of Christ; a cord of ten knots for the ten perfections; a blue ribbon with a medal of the Blessed Virgin; and a white veil for purity. Red, white, and blue were the colours of the House of Valois—and were later to be the colours of revolutionary France as the *tricouleur*. Jeanne entertained a large company to dinner, took them to hear Fr Gilbert's sermon—and then removed her elaborate velvet and satin robes to show the habit beneath. She had already served her noviciate. Perhaps, since she had endured so much, she can be forgiven this small *coup de théatre*. Fr Gilbert received her profession, and she became the first professed nun of her Order. Then she gave the habit to the new novices.

In November of the same year the town crier was sent out into the streets of Bourges to announce that if any persons wished to see the Sisters, they should do so at once. The first five novices were to be professed on the following day, and the Order would be enclosed. The next day the church was packed, and the archbishop of Bourges preached. The Order was fully established at last. Jeanne could not share the enclosure, though she spent as much time in the convent as possible, because she had duties as duchess of Berry. The convent was connected by a door to her château, and the nuns were given the key, so that she had to knock in order to enter.

She had a close relationship with Fr Gilbert, based on deep prayer and fellowship. Together, they devised two Marian devotions for their friends in the secular world: the devotion of the Ten Ave Marias and the Order of Peace. The first was a prayer invoking the Virgin Mary and naming all the Ten Perfections in turn, to be recited whenever they heard the clocks strike. The second was not in fact an Order, but a confraternity of supporters and fellow spirits.

Jeanne's elaborate court dresses were given to the nuns to be made into vestments for the clergy. She had a great bell cast for the convent, bearing representations of the Annunciation and the Crucifixion. Only two months after the enclosure, in January 1505, she became gravely ill. Fr Gilbert was devoted to her and hardly left her side. She died on 4 February, which was Shrove Tuesday, traditionally a day of carnival, but the streets of Bourges were quiet, for she was much loved and respected. Her body lay in state for eighteen days before burial, and her cult began spontaneously almost immediately. The anniversary of her death was observed as her feast, and twenty years later an Office in her honour was said in Bourges.

Her Order developed: there were houses in Albi, in Bruges, in Rodez within a few years, and others followed. During the Wars of Religion, the Huguenots broke into the convent and the church, wrecking both; Jeanne's silver casket was broken open and her body thrown on a fire. Her cause was initiated in 1604 by the archbishop of Bourges, André Fremyot, brother of *Jane Frances de Chantal, but when differences developed between the French bishops and the Holy See the cause was dropped. The process was started again in 1731, and Jeanne was beatified in 1742. The movement for her canonization stopped during the French Revolution, when all the documents were destroyed, but she is popularly regarded as a saint in France.

Few of the royal women among the women saints and *beatae* paid for their visibility as painfully as Jeanne did—in emotional rejection, in social ostracism, in public humiliation because of a physical handicap. Instead of relapsing into anger or self-pity, she used her experience to help others and gave thanks to the Virgin Mary, who understood the nature of her sorrows.

GERMAINE COUSIN

(c. 1579-1601)

GERMAINE, sometimes known as Germaine of Pibrac, was a poor and sickly child, born with many disadvantages, and she died young; yet the apostolic brief for her beatification described her as one who "shone like a star not only in her native France, but throughout the Catholic Church."

Her family lived in the village of Pibrac near Toulouse, where her father was an agricultural labourer. Her mother died when she was very young. The child had a paralyzed right arm and suffered from scrofula, or the "King's Evil," a condition no longer medically recognized as a specific syndrome. This caused ugly swellings in the neck, which in Germaine's case may have been tuberculous in origin. Her stepmother had no sympathy for her and treated her harshly. She kept her away from her healthier stepbrothers and stepsisters. She was fed on scraps, made to sleep in the stable or under the stairs, and sent out as soon as she was old enough to mind the sheep in the fields.

Germaine accepted this treatment without complaint. Out in the fields she learned to talk directly to God and to live in his presence. The adults of the village tended at first to accept her family's estimate of her as useless and diseased and to treat her with contempt and ridicule. She never mixed with girls of her own age, but she spoke to the younger children, gathering them round her and giving them simple religious teaching. She went to Mass as often as she could and said that when the church bell rang it was as if a thousand cords drew her to the altar. She shared her meagre scraps of food with beggars.

Gradually village opinion changed, and strange stories began to circulate about the girl: how she left her sheep to go to Mass, but they never strayed or fell prey to wolves; how she forded a stream in torrent to get to Mass— some said that the waters parted like the Red Sea before Moses; how two neighbours saw her stepmother pursue her with a stick when the ground was covered with snow, saying that she had stolen bread, and that when Germaine let fall her apron summer flowers fell to the ground. Such stories were indicative of pity and affection for the sickly girl and of growing veneration. The people of Pibrac decided that they had a saint among them. Even her father and stepmother eventually relented and would have taken her into the house, but Germaine continued to live as before until, at the age of twenty-two, she was found lying dead on her pallet under the stairs.

Her body was buried in the church at Pibrac, and a considerable local cult developed, with reports of many miracles and healings. Germaine was beatified in 1854, and the bishop of Poitiers, who gave the eulogy at the ceremony, stressed her essential simplicity and the ways in which, through grace, she learned a wisdom greater than that to be found in books:

> We ask ourselves if she knew how to read, and everything goes to show that she knew nothing of the alphabet except the sign which our fathers never forgot to put at the beginning of the Christian alphabet: I mean the cross of God. But what she learned under the rule of divine grace, in the school of the Saviour's cross, took the place of all the other kinds of knowledge.

She was canonized in 1867. An annual pilgrimage takes place to Pibrac church, where her relics still rest. She is represented in art with a distaff and spindle, sometimes with a sheep at her side and sometimes with roses in her apron.

We know very little about Germaine's life and her sufferings, apart from the pretty tales that have been woven around her. A reviewer in the *Analecta Bollandiana* comments that her chief biographer, Louis Veuillot, has an unrewarding task and that other accounts of her life compensate for the lack of material with picturesque accounts of the life of a shepherdess. If she had entered the religious life, we might have had an account that would stand comparison with that of that great saint Thérèse of Lisieux, who also suffered from tuberculosis and died at the age of twenty-four; but in a remote French village in the sixteenth century there was no one to record it, and only the respect and the sorrow of local people kept her memory alive.

JOSEPHINE BAKHITA

(*c.* 1871-1947)

A SMALL African girl was seized from her village in the Sudan by slave-traders when she was only six or seven years old. She never saw her home or her family again. When she came to write her story in later life she did not know where she came from, which tribe she belonged to, or even what her own name was. She was always called "the little one," but the slave-master gave her a new name, Bakhita, which means "the lucky one." It was the custom to re-name slaves so that they would forget their previous life entirely.

Bakhita knew only that she had lost a loving mother and father, brothers and sisters, a close and affectionate family life in a tribal community. Her uncle was the village chief, and her father owned land and herds of cattle. This peaceful rural life was subject to frequent raids from slave-traders. Although the slave trade had been abolished in Europe, it still flourished in many parts of Africa and the Middle East.

In 1876 or 1877 Bakhita and another girl were playing near the village when two armed men appeared. One asked Bakhita to go a few yards behind some bushes to pick up a parcel. When the child was out of sight of the village she was seized and threatened with a knife and a gun to prevent her from calling out for help. The men marched her away to their own village. They went on all that day and till dawn on the following day, when, exhausted, she was finally pushed into "a hole of a room" in a hut and the door was secured. She stayed in this "hole" for a month before she was brought out and sold to a slave-merchant. Her first reaction was relief: "Seeing the countryside, the sky, the water, and being able to breathe free air." There was another forced march, this time lasting eight days. Three women in the party had chains round their necks, which made deep, bleeding wounds, and it was agony every time they got out of step. Bakhita and another young girl were spared this, though they were chained at night.

They came to a town and a slave market. The weak and sickly were auctioned off first, so that they did not die while they were still in the slave-merchant's hands. The two girls managed to escape and headed for the open country. They had no idea how far they were away from home, and when they saw the huts of a village, each thought that it must be her own village. A man came out, speaking to them kindly, and offered to help them get back to their parents; but this was only a trick, and they were sold again to another slave-merchant. There was another forced march across the great savannah of the Sudan. Some of the slaves in their party had been with their previous owner, and they described his fury at the girls' escape: he had sworn that he would cut them in pieces if he found them. So they went on, lashed by whips to keep them on the move. When a slave stumbled and fell and was not revived by the whip, he or she was left to die or killed on the spot.

At last they reached the city of El Obeid and another slavemarket. Bakhita was sold to an Arab chief as a maid for his daughter. His son beat her unconscious, and she took a month to recover. Then she was sold again, like a piece of property, this time to the household of a Turkish general to wait upon his mother and his wife. She had to dress them, perfume them, fan them, run errands for them. Both carried whips and used them pitilessly on their slaves. "We had to bear it all in silence," Bakhita wrote later; "no one came to dress our wounds, and no one ever dared speak to us. How many of our unhappy friends died as a result of the blows they received!"

There was even worse to come. It was the fashion for slaves to be tattooed with some pattern decided by their owners—a sort of livery on the bare skin. The general's wife decided that all her slaves must be tattooed. Two powerful male slaves held Bakhita down while the woman tattooist made deep cuts in her skin with a razor-blade, and salt was rubbed in the wounds to keep them open. She had a hundred and fourteen cuts and was carried away unconscious. "The scars are still evident on my body," she wrote many years later.

In 1883, after some seven years of brutality and suffering, she was at last rescued. The general and his family were returning to Turkey, and they wanted to get rid of their African slaves. The Italian vice consul in Khartoum bought Bakhita from the general with the intention of freeing her. For the first time since her capture, she was treated with kindness. She was given her first dress to wear and taught European ways. She helped in the house until the vice consul was due to return to Italy, and she begged him to take her with him. He protested that he could not afford the fare, that she would do better to stay in Africa, that she was free to go where she liked, but she persisted. She can have had no idea what Italy was like or how an African girl would manage to live there; but she was convinced that this was her destiny.

They were still in the Sudan when Khartoum fell and General Gordon was killed. The vice consul's house was ransacked by the Mahdi's Dervish followers, but they managed to escape by ship via the Red Sea, the new Suez Canal, and the Mediterranean. When they arrived in Italy the vice consul found a post for Bakhita as nursemaid to the small daughter of a friend of his, Signor Michaeli, who had business interests in the Sudan. Bakhita became very attached to the child, Alice, and travelled back to the Sudan with the family on one occasion. In 1889 it was thought advisable that Alice and Bakhita should stay in a Catholic boarding school run by the Canossian Sisters, the Daughters of Charity, while Alice's parents went to the Sudan again. Bakhita had no formal religion, though she had a great sense of awe at the wonders of creation: "I remembered how, as a child, when I contemplated the sun, the moon, the stars and all the wonderful things of nature, I was wondering 'Who is the master of it all?' And I felt a keen desire to see Him, know Him, and pay Him homage."

The family's trustee, Illuminato Checchini, told her about the Son of God, who had redeemed the world, and gave her a silver crucifix. When she held it she had a strange feeling, which she could not understand. The symbol had power, though she did not yet appreciate what it was.

Bakhita and Alice went to the Canossian house in Venice, and there Bakhita began to learn about the Faith. She asked to be baptized and was instructed by Sister Maria Fabretti, who was later to prepare her for the religious life. In the autumn of 1889, a few weeks before the baptism was to take place, Alice's mother prepared to go to the Sudan again and proposed to take Alice and Bakhita with her. Bakhita said quietly but firmly that she wished to stay with the Sisters. Signora Michaeli evidently still thought of her as a possession, although she was twenty years old, for she cajoled, she pleaded, she became angry, and she threatened. At last she went to see the cardinal patriarch of Venice and asked him to order Bakhita to leave the convent. He consulted the king's procurator, who replied that slavery was illegal in Italy. Bakhita was free to make her own choice. She stayed in Venice.

A few weeks later, in January 1890, Bakhita was baptized and confirmed by the cardinal patriarch himself. Her given names were Josephine Margaret, as well as Bakhita. Her cause had attracted influential support. She had sponsors from the Venetian nobility, and Signor Checchini and his entire family came to support her. Three years later she joined the noviciate.

By 1896, when this unusual novice had completed her noviciate, there was another cardinal patriarch of Venice, the future Pope St Pius X. He questioned her searchingly about her vocation, then smiled and welcomed her to the Order. She was clothed on the feast of the Immaculate Conception and in 1902 was sent to the Canossian house at Schio, north of Padua, where the Sisters ran a school. Bakhita held a series of offices: when she worked in the kitchens, the Sisters noticed that the plates and cups were warmed, so that the food stayed hot; and those with special dietary needs received food prepared with much care. When she took the office of sacristan, she felt honoured by the opportunity to stay "close to Christ" and to prepare the vessels for the Eucharist. When she became porteress she met visitors to the convent and the school as well as the pupils, who called her "Sister Moretta," the little brown sister. They were proud of her: no other Italian school had an African door keeper. Gentle and tranquil, she led a life of strict poverty and attended to her tasks.

It was not until 1902 that the superior of the Canossian community at Schio asked her to write the story of her life. She did so in a document of thirty-one pages, written in Italian, which showed that the illiterate African child had grown into an educated woman with a sensitive power of expression and deep spiritual resources. She described what it was like to be snatched away from her family, to become "a slave, an object, owned by her masters," treated as less than human. She tried hard to recollect details of her childhood, and people who knew the area were able to say that she came from the Darfur region of western Sudan, from the Dafu tribe. The Sudan had suffered many political and economic disasters in the forty years since her capture, and her family was never traced.

In the quiet years at Schio Bakhita had longed to be a missionary. She wrote a poem to express her desire to take the gospel back to her own people:

O dear Lord
Could I but fly to Africa and proclaim aloud to all my people
Your goodness to me!
How many souls would hear my voice
And turn to You.

That was not possible, but in 1935, when she was sixty-five, she was asked if she would visit the other Canossian communities in Italy and tell them her story. She did not like being singled out and "felt that she was sinking into nothingness," but she "did it all for the missions." From 1936 to 1938 she was in the missionary noviciate in Milan—a door keeper again but with the joyous task of welcoming the young women who came to train as missionaries and of reassuring their often anxious parents. Then she went back to Schio, where she remained throughout World War II.

191

When she grew old she meditated on death and expressed her thoughts about the life to come in her writings:

I am going slowly, slowly towards eternity. . . . I carry two bags with me: one contains my sins, the other, much, much heavier, contains the infinite merits of Jesus Christ. When I appear before the tribunal of God, I will cover my ugly bag with the merits of Our Lady. Then I shall open the other, and will present to the Eternal Father the merits of his Son, Jesus. I will tell Him, "Now, judge from what You see." I am sure I shall not be rejected. Then I will turn to St Peter and say, "You can close the door after me, I am here to stay."

In 1947, nearly eighty years of age, she contracted pneumonia. When she was feverish she complained that the chains about her neck were too tight and pleaded with her supposed captors to loosen them, but her last words were calm and rational: "I am so happy. Our Lady . . . Our Lady. . . ."

Her beatification was declared by Pope John Paul II in Rome on 17 May 1992, at the same ceremony as that of Mgr Josemaria Escriva de Balaguer, the founder of Opus Dei. There were three hundred thousand people in St Peter's Square to hear it.

On 10 February 1993, Bakhita at last returned home. Pope John Paul II was in Khartoum, on his tenth Apostolic Pilgrimage to Africa, and the mother general of the Canossian Sisters brought a bust containing her relics to him in the cathedral. In his sermon the pope said, "Rejoice, all of Africa! Bakhita has come back to you: the daughter of the Sudan, sold into slavery as a living piece of merchandise, and yet still free: free with the freedom of the saints."

At the end of the twentieth century slavery still exists in the Sudan. A United Nations report in 1988 states that "the raiders travel south with a military train, then sweep out across the area killing men, burning homes, stealing cattle and taking women and children captive." Christian organizations help local communities to buy back slaves, so that the women and children can be restored to their families. Some of the children taken into slavery are no older than Bakhita was when she was captured, and the conditions of captivity are often no better than those she endured.

7

INNOVATORS

WOMEN who have felt the call to found a new kind of religious organization are usually classified (and honoured) as "foundresses," but there are two reasons for describing them as "innovators" in the present context: first, "foundress" may suggest that they all made the same contribution to the life of the Church. This is not the case. Each found a gap in the existing pattern of religious communities for women, and their contributions were richly diverse. Putting the emphasis on innovation makes it possible to see more clearly what was being introduced, in what way it was new, and why it was needed. The Church has long been reluctant to recognize new religious communities, preferring to assimilate new spiritual insights into existing Orders or Congregations, and some foundresses have faced very great obstacles in doing what they were convinced was the will of God. They have often been told that these trials were necessary. If the innovation is truly the will of God, then it will triumph over all obstacles and all delays. Though the Holy Spirit blows where it lists, the Church has never been in a hurry to recognize that it was blowing in a particular direction, and it has often been notably slower to approve innovations for women religious than for men.

Second, while the Latin languages still insist on feminine forms for women under all circumstances (and for many inanimate objects as well), the English language is rapidly abandoning them. Grammar programmes on computers refuse to accept gender-specific terms such as "poetess" and "authoress." While some of the changes suggested may be dismissed as political correctness of a trivial nature, there is a serious point to be met: a poetess writes verse, a poet (of either sex) writes poetry. An authoress writes sentimental novels for women readers, an author (again, of either sex) writes serious books for general readers. A landlady takes lodgers, a landlord owns property. An usher is a more impressive figure than an usherette. The feminine form often includes an element of denigration. "Innovator" is not gender-specific, and applies equally to founders and foundresses.

The foundress-innovators are all women of deep prayer life and vision. The conviction that they were called to create a new kind of organization usually came slowly over a considerable period of time. Once formed, it proved unshakeable. Some had a social position that ensured them public respect and the assistance of bishops and priests who understood their conviction. Others faced outright opposition from clergy who demanded passivity and unquestioning obedience from women rather than intelligence and energy. The innovators have needed (and exhibited) many gifts: limitless patience; tenacity; diplomacy; leadership to inspire other women; physical, emotional, and spiritual endurance; management skills to run large organizations; skill in counselling and spiritual formation. They have had to be firm enough to assume authority and humble enough to give it up (as most of them did very willingly when the time came). They had to be *gate-keepers*—representing the community to the outside world of Church and secular authorities as well as the outside world to the community. And through all this, their original vision had to be sustained undiminished.

Hilda of Whitby was a princess of the royal house of Northumbria, only a generation after the monks of Iona brought Christianity to northern England. With the help of St Aidan, bishop of Lindisfarne, she founded and ruled a double monastery renowned for its learning and piety. Caedmon was a herdsman on the monastery estate until she recognized the quality of his inspired songs and had him trained in the scriptures. The monastery at Whitby was chosen in 664 as the meeting place for the great ecclesiastical synod at which the Celtic monks finally agreed to accept the Roman practices brought to southern England by St Augustine.

Jane Frances de Chantal, founder of the French Order of the Visitandines, was under the spiritual direction of St Francis de Sales, and they are often described as "co-founders" of the Order. The question has been raised whether this sweet and apparently pliable woman was in fact an innovator at all. One commentator, Henri Brémond, has suggested that she was wax in the hands of Francis de Sales, but Francis was a very sensitive director. The imprint on the wax was not his own image, but the Sacred Heart of Jesus. The Daughters of the Visitation of St Mary became a very different community from the one he had originally envisaged, and Francis had the wisdom to allow it to develop as a contemplative Order. He offered support and encouragement but never intervened in the nuns' search for "the perfection of the divine love."

Margaret d'Youville was left a widow in Montreal, with two young children and a bad reputation. Her husband had been engaged in the illegal liquor trade with the Indians, and people suspected that she was carrying on the commerce. Her small group of women, the Grey Sisters, faced an angry mob and were publicly branded as sinners in church. Their poverty, their hard work, and their compassion for people in need, including Indians and the old and infirm, led to their management of the city hospital and many other enterprises; but the saying in Montreal, "Go to the Grey Nuns: they never refuse anybody or any honest work," was hard-won and is still repeated today.

Madeleine Sophie Barat, the foundress of the Society of the Sacred Heart, came from a farming family in Burgundy. Her brother Louis, a seminarian, taught her and encouraged her vocation. In the aftermath of the French Revolution, there was a great need for women teachers who could provide religious education for future wives and mothers; and there was no shortage of empty convents and monasteries in which to carry out the work. Mother Madeleine Sophie lived to see Sacred Heart foundations in many parts of France, in Canada and the United States, in Britain, and in many of the countries of western Europe. She became a great educationist and an outstanding administrator with an eye equally for detail and broad principles of policy.

Elizabeth Ann Seton, the wife of a New York shipping merchant, was left after his death with no money and five children. She had been a practising Episcopalian, but a period of mourning in Italy led to her reception into the Catholic Church in the face of some social opposition. The story of the foundation of the teaching Order of the Sisters of Charity of St Joseph at Emmitsburg and its development in Canada, the United States, South America, and elsewhere is an astonishing record of an idea that had found its time and place.

Hilda of Whitby and Madeleine Sophie Barat were dedicated virgins. Jane Frances de Chantal, Margaret d'Youville, and Elizabeth Ann Seton were widows who found a new direction for their lives after the death of their husbands. All three maintained their family responsibilities as well as their new commitments.

Accounts of other foundresses will be found elsewhere in this study: *Clare of Assisi, who was inspired by St Francis but was obliged by episcopal decree to continue her work without his support; *Jeanne de Valois, the pathetic, rejected queen of France who found a new dignity in the religious life; *Louise de Marillac, who collaborated with St Vincent de Paul; and four of the women saints in the "Missionaries" section that follows. The lives of these women also provide examples of the personal initiative and endeavour that the women's religious Orders value and honour in their foundresses.

HILDA
OF
WHITBY

(614-80)

Statue in St Hilda's School, Whitby.

"IN THE YEAR of our Lord 680, Hilda, abbess of the monastery of Whitby, a most religious servant of Christ, passed away to receive the reward of eternal life on the seventeenth of November at the age of sixty-six, after a life full of heavenly deeds." So Bede begins his account of Hilda's life, from which most of our direct knowledge of her comes. She was the daughter of Hereric, nephew of King Edwin of Northumbria, and his wife, Breguswitha, a member of the royal family of East Anglia.

Hilda and her parents were driven out of East Anglia by an enemy named Ethelfrith the Fierce and took refuge at Elmete in Yorkshire. Hereric died, thought to have been poisoned by agents of Ethelfrith, so Edwin of Northumbria avenged him, killing Ethelfrith and annexing his lands. Hilda was brought up in the royal Northumbrian household and was baptized when Edwin became a Christian.

Edwin was converted after he proposed a marriage alliance with the daughter of King Ethelbert of Kent, who had first received Augustine and supported his mission. Ethelbert told Edwin that it was not permissible for his daughter, a Christian maiden, to be married to a king who was "wholly ignorant of the worship of the true God." A condition of the alliance was that the princess should be accompanied by Bishop Paulinus, who had instructions to "preserve her and her companions from corruption by their constant association with the heathen." Edwin, evidently an open-minded and thoughtful man, replied that he was willing to listen to the bishop and to adopt his faith if it seemed "more holy and acceptable to God" than his own. Paulinus and the priests of the old religion debated for two years, and eventually Edwin was convinced that Christ was more powerful than the old gods. He and all his household were baptized on Easter Eve 627, when Hilda was thirteen years old.

Bede tells us that Hilda's life fell into two equal parts. Until she was thirty-three she lived the normal life of a noblewoman. As a Christian, she probably carried out works of charity. Then she decided to live the religious life and went to East Anglia, where her mother's family lived, intending to go on to Gaul and enter the royal nunnery of Chelles, near Paris, where her sister Hereswitha was already a professed nun, but Aidan, who had come from Iona to preach the gospel in the northern kingdom and to become bishop of Lindisfarne, persuaded Hilda to return to Northumbria and to follow her vocation there. She was granted a hide of land on the river Wear and lived a secluded life there for a time with a few companions. Then she became abbess of a small monastery at Heruten (Hartlepool) for some years. Aidan and other monks from Lindisfarne often visited the house, and were impressed by her "innate wisdom and love of God."

Hilda must have been in her early forties when she was appointed abbess of Streaneshalch—later called Whitby by the Danes—as superior of a double monastery. The monks were responsible for worship, while the nuns led an enclosed life focused on prayer and contemplation. The sexes were strictly segregated. Hilda was superior of the whole establishment, which also included the administration of a large landed estate. The monastery had to be economically self-sufficient. Like a nobleman's house, it would have had its own farm, its fields of barley and oats, its vegetable gardens, its beehives, and its boats for fishing. Farm labourers, huntsmen, shepherds, butchers, fishermen, carpenters and wood carvers, blacksmiths and leather workers, and other workers from the locality were employed. The monks and nuns did not undertake manual labour, and monasteries did not employ serfs, though they were still commonly to be found in England in the seventh century.

Hilda established a regular pattern of monastic life and "taught the observance of justice, purity and other virtues, but especially peace and charity." No monk or nun retained any personal property: everything was held in common. It seems that she soon became the principal of what was virtually a theological college. She built up a library of manuscripts—all the New Testament and parts of the Old Testament, which were then available in various translations and which had to be copied by hand on parchment or vellum. The vellum came from the skins of the calves on the farm and the parchment from sheepskin. Beeswax provided tablets for writing and candles for worship and for lighting.

Bede tells us that Hilda carried out her task with great energy, insisting that the monks and nuns under her direction should make a thorough study of the scriptures and engage in good works. Five of her monks subsequently became bishops: Bosa of York, Hedda of Dorchester, Oftfor of a diocese in Mercia, John of Hexham, and Wilfrid of York. Whitby became the most celebrated monastery in the north of England. Hilda had a reputation as a wise woman and a sympathetic counsellor, and many people came to her for advice and direction—"ordinary folk" as well as royalty and nobility.

One of the most celebrated events of her period as abbess was her encouragement of the herdsman Caedmon, who was found to have a gift for composing sacred poems and songs. Hilda asked this unlettered farmhand if he wished to become a monk, and when he agreed she directed that he should be trained in the scriptures. He does not appear to have learned Latin, for he devoted his life to writing in the vernacular on great biblical themes. Bede lists these themes, which give a fair illustration of the biblical studies in the monastery in Hilda's day:

> He sang of the creation of the world, the origin of the human race, and the whole story of Genesis. He sang of Israel's departure from Egypt, their entry into the land of promise, and many other events of scriptural history. He sang of the Lord's Incarnation, Passion, Resurrection and Ascension into heaven, the coming of the holy spirit and the teaching of the Apostles. He also made many poems on the terrors of the Last Judgment, the horrible pains of hell, and the joys of the kingdom of heaven. In addition to these, he composed several others on the blessings and judgments of God, by which he sought to turn his hearers from delight in wickedness, and to inspire them to love and do good.

Though much of the work once attributed to Caedmon is now thought to be the work of later writers, his reputation as "the father of English poetry" endures, and his work in the Northumbrian dialect was of great value in spreading knowledge of the gospel among those who knew no Latin. The story of Caedmon must have encouraged other abbots and abbesses to look for spiritual gifts among the humbler members of their establishments.

Whitby, like all the religious houses in the north of England at the time, followed the practices of the Celtic Church, brought to northern Britain by St Columba. The differences between the Celtic system and that of the

Roman Church, brought to southern England by Augustine and his successors, became acute. The main issues were the date of Easter, which was kept at different times, and the degree of authority attaching to the papacy. There was also the issue of the tonsure: the Roman monks shaved the crown of their heads; the Celtic monks, like the Druid priests, shaved the front of their heads, leaving hair only at the back. While this was an intrinsically minor issue it was also a very visible and contentious one.

When the bishops and clergy finally held a synod to determine these questions in 664 they met in Hilda's great monastery. The discussion was a matter of high ecclesiastical politics and bitter debate.

Hilda must have been consulted by many of the bishops and priests who attended. The Celtic Church had its own valued traditions. Aidan had brought the Celtic rite from Iona to Northumbria, and his successor as bishop of Lindisfarne, Cuthbert, maintained the same practices. Cuthbert was Hilda's good friend and adviser, but the debate was heavily influenced by the advocacy of Wilfrid, abbot of Ripon, who had been a monk at Lindisfarne and Whitby before travelling on the Continent and studying in Rome. Wilfred had adopted the Roman rite, and he was convinced that his former superiors and brothers must follow suit. He called the Celtic monks "partners in obstinacy," and many acrimonious words were spoken on both sides before the final decision was taken to adopt the Roman system. Hilda accepted the decision without question, and the rites and practices of the double monastery at Whitby were changed accordingly.

Hilda was ill for the last seven years of her life, first with a racking fever and then with severe internal pains. It is thought that she may have had tuberculosis. She exhorted all members of the community to serve God dutifully when they were in health and to remain grateful to him in adversity or bodily infirmity. Bede tells us that on the last day of her life she received Holy Communion and then summoned all the members of the monastery together. She urged them to maintain the gospel peace among themselves and with others, and then, "while she was still speaking, she joyfully welcomed death, and passed from death into life."

Before Hilda went to Whitby, at the time when she was abbess of Heruten, the infant daughter of King Oswin of Northumbria and his wife, Enfleda, had been dedicated to the religious life as a thanksgiving for Oswin's defeat of Penda of Mercia. The child Elfleda was one year old when she was entrusted to Hilda's care. She grew up at Whitby in Hilda's tradition and became a scholar and a counsellor of repute. When Oswin died in 670 his wife also sought the religious life and entered the community at Whitby. Enfleda became the next abbess and was followed in turn by her daughter Elfleda.

The abbey at Whitby was destroyed during the Danish invasions of the tenth century, and Hilda's relics were lost, though they have at various times been claimed to be held in Glastonbury and Durham. We know that she had an ancient cult: her name occurs in the calendar of St Willibrord (early eighth century), and at least sixteen churches were dedicated to her, nearly all in Yorkshire and Durham. Among the great leaders of the Church in seventh-century England—St Augustine of Canterbury, St Paulinus of York, St Cuthbert, St Aidan, St Wilfrid—this woman scholar and administrator holds a unique place.

Detail from a contemporary portrait, 1636.

JANE FRANCES DE CHANTAL

(1572-1641)

JEANNE Françoise Frémyot de Chantal had a social position that helped her considerably in the early stages of her work in founding the Order of the Visitation. She was the daughter of Benigne Frémyot, president of the *parlement* of Burgundy and a distinguished lawyer; her husband was Baron de Chantal; her brother was the archbishop of Bourges; her spiritual director was St Francis de Sales. All these factors were valuable to her in beginning her chosen work, but her spiritual development and her contribution to the life of the Church were distinctively her own.

She was baptized Jeanne, and took the additional name of Françoise at her confirmation. When she was about twenty she married Christophe de Rabutin, Baron de Chantal, and became the châtelaine of his family seat at Bourbilly. It was a happy marriage. She established good order and management in the house and the estate, which had been neglected since the death of her husband's mother, and bore six children: the first three died soon after birth, to the sorrow of the young parents, but after that they had a boy and two girls who all survived.

In 1601 Christophe de Rabutin was mortally injured in a shooting accident. He survived for nine days, during which he suffered great pain, and he died after receiving the last rites with dignity and resignation. After his death

Jeanne went through three years of deep depression and grief. She tried to conceal her acute sense of bereavement for fear of burdening others and endured repeated consolatory visits from relatives when she would have preferred to be left alone. Every human contact was painful. She was struggling with God—asking him why Christophe had died and what his purpose was for her; but she did not have either the theological or the philosophical equipment for this struggle. When a priest offered to direct her spiritual life she accepted thankfully. His direction turned out to be harsh and insensitive. He weighed her down with prayers, observances, fasts, and austerities that were quite unsuitable for a woman in her distressed state, and he exacted four promises from her: that she would obey him in all things; that she would never go to another director; that she would keep secret all that he said to her; and that she would never speak of her interior life to anyone else. She struggled with this unhappy relationship for three years before she met the bishop of Geneva, Francis de Sales.

Francis had come to preach a Lenten course in the Sainte-Chapelle at Dijon, where Jeanne was staying in her father's home. She followed all his sermons with such concentrated attention that he asked who she was. Francis knew intuitively that she needed spiritual help, but relations between men and women were constrained: etiquette and custom made it difficult for him to help her. They met only in *salons*, and there was no opportunity for conversation in depth. She could have gone to him in the confessional, but she was prevented by her promises to her director, so they exchanged only snatches of conversation in company. When at last she found an opportunity to tell him hesitantly of her promises to her director, he was immediately sympathetic, but he could not lightly take over direction of this young and attractive young noblewoman from another priest, though he felt the strength of her desperation. He arranged a house party at his residence in Anneçy, a few miles from Geneva and then in Switzerland. His mother was present, as were his sister and the abbess of the Puits d'Orbe, providing more than adequate chaperonage. There Jeanne was able to tell him "all that passed within her, which she did with such precision, simplicity and candour as to forget nothing," according to her biographer, Mother de Chaugy. Francis spent a sleepless night, praying for her. In the morning, he sought her out and said, "Madame, shall I say it to you? Needs must, since it is the will of God. All these your former vows have not availed save to destroy your conscience." Jeanne told Mother de Chaugy that he "seemed as though in a trance, so great was his state of recollection." She made her general confession to Francis, and felt a great sense of liberation.

Francis de Sales was a spiritual director who respected the experience of those he directed: he was a good listener, and he refused to play the oracle "for fear of harming souls." At first Jeanne was troubled at not being given firm direction, as she had come to expect, but she came to appreciate the gentle way in which he was leading her. "Never did that blessed one make quick replies," she recalled. He knew that God was working in her and was content to wait. She stayed on at Dijon in her father's house for some time, learning from the religious in the city. She visited the Reformed Carmelites of Dijon and met Anne of Jesus, who had been Teresa of Avila's closest companion among the choir Sisters. She talked to the rector of the Jesuits. She prayed and trusted that God would show her what to do. During this time she had one experience that she cherished: "At daybreak, God made me aware, but almost imperceptibly, of a spark of light in the highest supreme point of my life. All the rest of my soul and its faculties were untouched thereby; but it endured about half an *Ave Maria*." Like Julian of Norwich and other visionaries, she saw "all things in a point."

She corresponded with Francis. All her letters begin with the sign of the cross, and "*Vive Jésus!*" (Jesus lives!). Letters were slow, delayed in winter by snow and storms, but he was a faithful correspondent, and he was still biding his time. They were both learning from the Reformed Carmelites, whose spirituality was still comparatively new to France; but when the Carmelite prioress in Dijon recommended that Jeanne should follow the path of Carmel and suggested more advanced spiritual exercises, Francis wrote, "As regards devotions, I should approve of your still going slow." Three more years passed. It was in 1607, "towards Pentecost," that she finally went to Anneçy to see him and to discuss her future. She put her life in his hands, and he waited patiently while she found her own answers. Should she become a Poor Clare? She was willing, but he pointed out that she was not strong enough to lead a harsh and austere life, and they would not accept her. Should she become a Carmelite? The same held true. When they had exhausted all the other possibilities, she came to the conclusion that she must found a new Congregation. The existing women's Orders would not accept postulants unless they were fit to sing the night offices and endure fasts and harsh food.

There was a need for a new type of community "not too mild for the strong, nor too harsh for the weak," said Francis. It would be a convent for women who were unable to enter the enclosed Orders because of their age, their poor health, or the fact that they had children to care for. It would be particularly suitable for widows. They would keep their links with their families and not be expected to break bonds of affection and concern. They would live in community and give each other mutual support. They would be unenclosed and able to work freely in the community. Francis thought that the new Congregation should be under the supervision of the bishop of the diocese. He wrote to Jeanne later: "Jesus Christ will be your Head and your

Protector. The happiness of your Congregation will not depend on being placed under the government of one superior, but on the fidelity of each Sister individually, and of all together, to unite themselves to God by an exact and punctual observance." She always knelt to read his letters, as a sign that she believed the advice came from God.

The Duc de Nemours gave the Sisters permission to build a house along the canal that runs into the Lake of Anneçy. There was some local opposition. On one occasion, Jeanne wrote to Francis to tell him that the building workers were being threatened; but he carried out negotiations for the Sisters, and on 18 September 1614 he blessed and laid the foundation stone of their convent. There Jeanne and a small group of ladies from aristocratic families formed the first community. None of them had any experience of manual work, because there had never been any lack of servants in their great houses, but they managed their own simple establishment—cooking, tending the orchard and the vegetables, milking the cows. Most of the milk went to the poor children of the neighbourhood. Francis de Sales wrote his famous treatise *On the Love of God* specifically for this group, and he drew up their religious programme—which was not to be as formal as a Rule. They had to learn their Office in Latin—Francis was a celebrated Latinist—but he chose the Little Office of Our Lady as being less taxing than the full Office. He also helped the Sisters to decide on their habit, and no detail was too small for him to consider. There is a story of how he and Jeanne decided that a black muslin veil would be appropriate as a head-covering. Jeanne fetched one of her own former travelling dresses and cut a large square from the voluminous skirt. This was draped over the head of a novice, and the bishop of Geneva, calling for the scissors, trimmed it to shape.

However, the community did not develop on the lines he had expected. Francis thought it would be a community of active workers, serving the sick and poor. His first suggestion was that they should be called *Les Filles de Sainte Marthe*, the daughters of St Martha, stressing their usefulness in the secular world; but these were not young, fit women, and they followed Mary rather than Martha. Jeanne wanted to emphasize the contemplation that would be the centre of communal life. The final decision was that the Sisters would be known as the Daughters of the Visitation of St Mary, or Visitandines—a reference not to their own visiting activities, but to the Blessed Virgin's visit to her cousin Elizabeth and the thanksgiving of the *Magnificat*.

Francis' proposal that the Sisters should take simple vows and dispense with a formal Rule also proved unworkable. The archbishop of Paris pointed out that such an informal organization would be unlikely to receive dowries from parents or other relatives. A degree of permanence and commitment was necessary to ensure financial stability. It was necessary for the Sisters to be fully professed and to have a Rule and Constitutions approved in Rome.

The archbishop was unwilling to dispense with enclosure. The time for that had not yet come, though it was not strictly enforced in France. Many nuns were able to leave their monasteries or convents when they had good reason, as monks did. It was finally agreed that the Order of the Visitation would be technically enclosed. Mother de Chantal was certainly free to leave Anneçy in order to attend to the affairs of her children and to found new houses. The year after she received the habit, on the death of her father, she went to Dijon and stayed there for some months to settle his affairs and to place her son in college. She wrote later that the first period, in which the nuns undertook "outside errands," lasted only about five years, and that "none but the earliest professed" were involved. Then "all at once we found everyone changed, and desirous of enclosure." Gradually the outside work was dropped, and the Order became fully contemplative.

Some ten years after Francis' death his friend and colleague Vincent de Paul was to collaborate with *Louise de Marillac in founding the Sisters of Charity—an organization that had the features Francis had proposed for the "Daughters of St Martha." They served the sick and the poor, took only yearly vows, and were unenclosed; they, however, were strong young country girls who knew how poor people lived, and their work began in the slums of Paris. The older, widowed ladies of the Visitandines would not have been capable of doing such work, and their vocation was to contemplation, not to action. The world needed both.

The Visitandines met a need: there were many would-be postulants, and within a few years houses of the Order were established in Lyons, Moulins, Grenoble, and Bourges. The Sisters lived in "holy simplicity," praying for the world, and the world came to their parlours, seeking advice and counsel. In 1619 a house was established in Paris in spite of much hostility. The Visitandine history of its foundation records:

> The appearance of a humble Institute consecrated to the hidden life, to obedience, and to the interior spirit of Nazareth was looked upon as intolerable in a society given up to pomp and display. Even good people, priests and religious, tried to insist upon Mother de Chantal taking up exterior works.

She resisted these demands At the request of Francis de Sales, Fr Vincent de Paul, then in the early stages of his own work, acted as director to the Paris house. Vincent described her as "one of the holiest souls I have ever met." The abbess of Port-Royal, Angélique Arnaud, was so impressed with the spirituality of the Paris house that she tried, unsuccessfully, to resign her office and to join it.

The death of Francis de Sales in 1622 was a great blow to Jeanne. Five years later, she gave lengthy evidence at the proceedings for the cause of his beatification and canonization, praising him unreservedly. The proceedings were very heavily structured: she was required to give answers to pre-set questions rather than speaking freely of her own experience, but she made some revealing answers. "I know of people," she said, "who were very anxious and harassed—I am one of these myself—and by God's grace, he sometimes restored their peace of soul by a single word." Again, when questioned about his virtues, she described his abandonment to the divine providence and his refusal to try to impose a pattern of his own:

> He said, "From time to time providence wants me to walk along with my eyes shut, and this is a great happiness to my soul, surrendered as it is to God. Why should we want anything that God doesn't want? Happy the soul than lives only in his will!"

Jeanne had many other losses and trials. In 1627 her only son was killed while fighting against the English and the Huguenots in the Île de Ré. He left a young wife and a daughter less than a year old. Jeanne wrote lovingly to her daughter-in-law, telling her to be proud of her husband and to take care of the "dear little girl." This child was later to become celebrated as Madame de Sévigné, one of France's great women writers.

In 1628 a terrible plague raged through France, Savoy, and Piedmont. Jeanne refused to leave Anneçy, offering the resources of the convent for the needs of the sick and spurring the public authorities to greater efforts. The death of a much-loved son-in-law and of Fr Michel Favre, a close and devoted friend of the Visitandines, added to her sense of desolation. As she had told the canonization inquiry, she was by nature anxious and harassed, and the cost to her of meeting all the demands made upon her was very great. She was very much overworked, for the houses of the Visitation had continued to multiply and there were many letters of advice and support to be written to superiors, with care and solicitude for the problems of individuals. She mentions in several letters the "great bustle" in the house at Anneçy. She had entered the religious life to find peace and calm, but now the work all but overwhelmed her. Though she remained firm in faith and resignation, she went through periods of great spiritual dryness and interior anguish, expressed to several correspondents. In one undated fragment, she writes:

You have put me to confusion by asking me about my prayer. Alas! daughter, it is ordinarily nothing but distraction and a little suffering: for what can a poor, pitiful mind filled with all sorts of business do? I tell you plainly, and in confidence, that for about twenty years God has taken away from me all power of the understanding and reflection—that is, meditation—and all I can do is to suffer and hold myself very simply before God, clinging with complete abandonment to his action within me.

She writes to another Sister, "Be content to remain an empty vessel, simply receiving whatever the holy charity of the Saviour may wish to pour in." By 1635 there were sixty-five houses, some of which she had never visited; but she resolved to visit them all, and she did so. Carrying on was an effort of will, an act of faith.

In 1641, when she was sixty-nine, Jeanne was invited to Paris by the queen of France, Anne of Austria, and she was treated there with much distinction and honour. This distressed her, for she had long since chosen the way of silence and contemplation and was not at ease in the artificial atmosphere of the court. On the way back to Annecy she fell ill near her house at Moulins, and there she died on 13 December 1641. Her body was taken to Annecy and buried near that of St Francis de Sales. She was canonized in 1767.

MARGARET D'YOUVILLE

(1701-71)

Margaret hiding a wounded British officer, whose boots can be seen sticking out behind her.
From E. Mitchell, Marguérite d'Youville, Foundress of the Grey Nuns *(1965)*.

THE MARRIAGE of Marguérite Dufrost de Lajemmerais to François d'Youville, Sieur de la Decouverte, in Montreal in August 1722 was a considerable social occasion. The Governor General was present, and the customs and the fashions were Parisian; but this was "New France," a vast uncultivated territory of rivers and forests, where trappers and speculators were more at home than the tight little social circle that attended the wedding. Paris manners were only a thin crust on a rough and often heartless society.

Margaret was twenty. Her father, an army officer of Breton ancestry, had died when she was seven years old, leaving his wife and six children in great poverty. Her great-grandfather, Pierre Boucher, had paid for her education at the Ursuline convent, and she had helped to keep the family by sewing, embroidery, and teaching while assisting in bringing up her younger brothers and sisters. It was a hard apprenticeship. Now she was beginning a new life as Madame d'Youville. François was gay, witty, charming, and well-connected, and she had every reason to expect a happy married life, but three days after the wedding he went away, ostensibly to farm on an island in the St Laurence

River with his brother. Margaret was left to stay with his somewhat tyrannical and parsimonious mother, and this proved to be the first of many such absences. When the periods of absence became longer and more frequent she learned gradually through gossip that his real business was fur trading and that he traded with the Indians by exchanging furs for brandy or whisky. Liquor trading with the Indians was illegal—and dishonourable. The Indians themselves finally brought it into the open when they wrote to the Governor General, complaining that they "could no longer pray God because Youville has given us firewater, and has caused us to drink up all our furs, and when the missionary who teaches us to pray God came, we find ourselves senselessly drunk."

Margaret was appalled, and her compassion for the Indians seems to have dated from this time. She had the very difficult task of trying to be a good wife to a faithless and unscrupulous man. François had no sense of family responsibilities, spending his time with the rougher elements, drinking and gambling and piling up debts. When his mother died he inherited her money, but it was soon gone. Margaret was left alone in poverty much of the time, worrying about his debts, bearing his children, and trying to provide for them. During her eight years of marriage she had four children, of whom only two, François and Charles, survived. The Church was her one source of consolation. In 1727 she joined the Confraternity of the Holy Family and developed a special devotion to the Virgin Mary, spending many hours in prayer and trying to help other people in need. When her husband died of his excesses in 1730 she was pregnant again, but the child, Ignatius, lived only a few months. She opened a small store to pay off her husband's debts and to support herself and her two sons.

The story is told in detail by her younger son Charles, who was later to become the Abbé Dufrost and her principal biographer:

> Her piety had grown since she became a widow; bad weather could not prevent her from attending Mass daily, and in the afternoons, going to adore the Blessed Sacrament whenever her occupations allowed her to do so. . . . From the very first years of her widowhood, she was filled with charity for her neighbour, and considered it as an honour to visit the poor, the sick, the prisoners . . . visiting the poor in the city hospital, and mending the ragged clothing of the destitute.

By 1737, when the young François entered a seminary, Margaret had an aged, blind woman living with her and was accustomed to begging from door to door to help people in more desperate need than herself. On one occasion she begged enough for a funeral for a criminal who had been publicly executed:

209

no one else was prepared to see that he was decently buried. On another she went to the house of a wealthy surgeon and met his daughter, Louise Lasource. Louise, inspired by her example, joined her in her work, and two other women came to share it: Catherine Demers, the daughter of a tailor, and Catherine Cusson, who did home sewing for the tailor's shop. Catherine Cusson was timid but said she was not frightened by hard work—she had known little else since childhood. The four rented a house in the poorer part of Montreal, near the Recollet church, and made a small chapel there, with a statue of Our Lady of Providence on the altar. Charles lived with them until he was old enough to follow his brother to the seminary. It was the custom in French Canadian seminaries for an elder son to take his father's name, and a younger son to take his mother's, which is why Charles took the name of Dufrost rather than d'Youville. He recounts vividly how the small group began to accept poor and sick women into their care. In addition to blind Françoise, they took in a woman who was paralyzed and had to be spoon-fed and one who was mentally disturbed. There was no hospital for women in Montreal. The only hospital, run somewhat incompetently by a dwindling band of the Charon Brothers, was for men only.

The women's project aroused open hostility in the neighbourhood. A petition against the enterprise was sent to the French Minister of Marine, and among the signatories were the husbands of two of Margaret's younger sisters. It was thought that the widow d'Youville and her confederates were carrying on her husband's liquor trade with the Indians. They had left the charmed circle of the respectable, and polite society rejected them. When the four went to church on All Saints Day 1737 they encountered a violent mob, hurling stones and shouting "Down with the *Soeurs Grises*." In French, *gris* means "grey," but it is also slang for "fuddled" or "tipsy." The crowd believed that they were continuing the liquor trade with the Indians and was venting its disapproval. In the Recollet church a packed congregation heard the priest brand the Sisters as public sinners and saw them refused Communion. Margaret reminded her companions that Christ had also been mocked by the crowd.

None of them was afraid of hard work. They put up with the snubs and insults and made an income by sewing uniforms for the French troops and clothes for the explorers who were opening up western Canada—heavy work for women. They did their washing in the St Lawrence River, and in winter they would come back to their house with their hands red and raw and covered with icicles. In December 1737 the four made a private religious profession in the secrecy of the confessional and soon after adopted a simple Rule. By 1740 they had ten old ladies living in the house. Young Charles still lived with them, and François, a lively boy, came home from the seminary to cheer them all up. While it was not an ideal home background for the two boys, their presence brightened the lives of the residents.

Gradually the Grey Nuns won respect. "Let us go to the duties that await us, my Sisters," said Margaret d'Youville, "bearing in mind that in the person of the poor, it is Christ himself we are serving." The vicar general, Fr Normant de Faradon, became convinced that they had been chosen by Providence to take over the hospital run by the Charon Brothers, but his superior, the bishop of Quebec, temporized. It was not possible to take work away from an established religious Order for men and to give it to these untried women—even though they were increasing in numbers and expanding their work.

In 1745 there was a disastrous fire in the house. A log from the fire sent out sparks, which ignited the dry timber dwelling. All the patients were saved except Melanie, the mentally disturbed woman, who insisted on running back into the blazing house to fetch her shoes. The building was gutted, and the Grey Nuns' work lay in ruins. Some onlookers had come to sneer, saying that the fire was a just punishment for their sins; but a surprising number of people came forward to help. The Sulpician Fathers sent them food. Other citizens of Montreal brought blankets, furniture, and pots and pans, and they were offered accommodation. Though they had to move three times in two or three years, the work went on. Margaret said: "God will provide, since it is to shelter his poor," and her faith was justified. In that same year the Grey Nuns demonstrated their commitment by signing an act of total renunciation and self-dedication known as the Original Commitment (*engagements primitifs*) drawn up by Fr Normant. This document is still signed by every Grey Sister on the day of her profession.

The negotiations between the church authorities and the city authorities over the future of the hospital continued. For a time there were only three elderly Charon Brothers left, and then two of them died. The Order decided to concentrate its work in the Quebec hospital, which would have left Montreal without any resources for the care of the sick poor. In 1747, following a long battle between church and city authorities, the Grey Nuns were finally allowed to take over the work and to provide hospital care for both men and women. They were officially designated as the Sisters of Charity of the General Hospital, but Margaret preferred the older name. She said, "Keeping the name of the Grey Nuns will remind us of the insults of the beginnings, and keep us humble." They took over a debt of £38,000, a commitment to pay the annuity of Brother Dellermé, the last of the Charon Brothers, who was returning to France, and a dilapidated building in urgent need of repairs. The furniture was rickety, worn, and damaged. The front doorsteps had disappeared, so that the way in was by climbing over wooden crates. Their assets were £786 a year and two farms, which should have been producing crops for sale but which had been left uncultivated for years. Fr Normant told them, "In short, the task is humanly above your possibilities, but our faith will obtain all from God." Margaret's reply was "Ruins are quickly rebuilt when God takes a hand, and what he builds is made to last."

The Grey Nuns had to borrow a further £10,000, but with that and voluntary help from the citizens of Montreal the hospital was put to rights. The front doorsteps were mended. Major repairs were undertaken to doors and windows, and no less than 1,226 panes of glass were put into the broken windows. The wards were painted and decorated, and the farms were put under cultivation again to provide food and income. By 1748 there were sixty-five patients, and even Margaret's relatives were supporting her work. When Charles came home in 1752 before his Ordination he was shown the candle shop, the cobbler's shop, the bakery, the brewery, the tailor's shop. The hospital and the hospice wards for old people were expanded. In 1753 Letters Patent arrived from France bearing the signature of the king, Louis XV, and in 1755 Bishop de Pontbriand of Quebec formally confirmed the Rule with Mother Margaret as superior. The Grey Nuns received their grey habits on the feast of St Louis of France, 25 August. They broke with tradition by deciding to wear plain bonnets instead of veils, explaining that they did heavy work and that veils would get in the way.

When there was a smallpox epidemic, Margaret and other Sisters went out to nurse the sick. The Indians were badly affected, and Margaret went to them herself, feeling a sense of obligation because of the way in which her husband had corrupted and cheated them. It was a desperate time for French Canada. In the Franco-British struggle that culminated in Wolfe's storming of Quebec and the surrender of Montreal in 1759 the Grey Nuns continued their work, nursing military as well as civilian casualties. There was a ward for English prisoners as well as one for French soldiers, and Mother Margaret insisted on treating patients in both in the same manner, saying, "He died for all without distinction of race or colour."

When she heard that Indians were torturing an English prisoner she paid a ransom of £200 for him. He had already been tied to the stake, and the flames were lit when he was rescued. He was brought in more dead than alive, but when he was able to speak he said in good French, "I am your prisoner, Madame, your prisoner for life. Would you have some work to give me?" His name was John, and he proved invaluable as an interpreter, since the Grey Sisters spoke no English and the English prisoners spoke no French. On another occasion an English fugitive burst into a room where Margaret and two other Sisters were making a tent for the Army. He dived under the folds of the tent, and when a group of Indians followed, the leader brandishing a tomahawk, Margaret merely pointed to another door. The Indians rushed out, and the fugitive emerged to thank them, telling them that his name was Southworth. Four more British prisoners escaped the Indians wearing the capes of Grey Nuns—though their boots would have given them away to a close observer.

The hospital was short of beds, short of medicine, short of food. The Sisters knitted woollen stockings for the troops but wrapped their own legs in strips of cloth to keep warm. Sometimes they were near starvation. Margaret's prayer was "Give us this day our daily bread—or if not to us, at least to the poor." Cattle were set to graze on the farms, and English prisoners helped to plough and sow crops to keep them all alive. When Montreal finally fell to Wolfe's troops in 1759 they expected the worst; but a polite delegation of officers called and left them to their work. They were told afterwards that they were spared because of the intervention of "Southworth," who had hidden under the tent and who must have been an officer of some standing.

Margaret's loyalty was to "our masters, the poor," showing mercy and justice to people of all races, classes and conditions. When the war was over—and Louis XV had shrugged off his lost Canadian possessions as "a few acres of snow"—the hospital and its associated enterprises continued to grow. On one occasion Margaret found an abandoned baby in the snow, and she took this as a sign that she should open an orphanage for foundlings. As the years passed the Grey Nuns developed schools as well as orphanages. They worked with prisoners, with negro slaves, with the Indians, with mentally-handicapped and epileptic people, and with prostitutes.

In May 1765, when Margaret was sixty-four years old, disaster struck again: a fire in a nearby house spread rapidly in a high wind, and the General Hospital was engulfed. It seemed that her life's work was in ruins; but the *Hospitalières* of St Joseph offered shelter and hospitality, the new English governor general sent rations, and offers of help came from all sides—even from two Indian tribes, who remembered Margaret's work in the smallpox epidemic. The spokesman for the Indians said, through an interpreter, "You came to us when sickness entered our tents, when death was claiming our members. You closed the eyes of our old people, and healed our children. Now misfortune has befallen you in turn. Fire has destroyed your house, and you have nothing left. . . . To prove to you that we have not forgotten your kindness, we are bringing you our offering."

They had brought what they had—blankets, moccasins, knives, beads, and a few coins. Eventually the British Government paid compensation, and the hospital was rebuilt. A precious possession was the small statue of Our Lady of Providence, which had escaped the flames for a second time.

213

Margaret once told her niece "We need crosses in order to reach heaven," and her life provided many—poverty, insecurity, sickness, and ceaseless toil in a harsh environment—but she was always ready to reach out to those whose lot was worse than her own. When she died in 1771 Sister Louise de Lasource, who had been with her from the beginning, spoke her epitaph: "She loved greatly, Jesus Christ and the poor."

At her beatification in 1959, Pope John XXIII called Margaret "the Mother of Universal Charity." She was canonized on 9 December 1990, becoming the first native-born Canadian saint.

ELIZABETH ANN SETON

(1774-1821)

The Filicchi Portrait, c. 1804.

Artist unknown: now in St Joseph's Provincial House archives, Emmitsburg.

ELIZABETH Bayley was born in New York two years before the American Declaration of Independence. Her parents were members of the English establishment that then dominated the city and devout Episcopalians. Her father, Dr Richard Bayley, was a professor at King's College, which later became part of Columbia University, and New York's first port health officer. Her mother, Catherine, was the daughter of the Episcopal rector of St Andrew's church, Staten Island.

Richard Bayley supported the British cause and served as a surgeon to the British troops during the American Revolution. Catherine died in 1777, when the war was still raging and Elizabeth was only three years old. She would have known little of the loss of her mother, for Dr Bayley soon remarried. His second wife was Charlotte Barclay, daughter of Andrew Barclay and Helen Roosevelt, whom Elizabeth called "a woman of rare and sweet attainments." Elizabeth was educated partly at a private school and partly by her father. She had the run of his extensive library, where she read voraciously and developed an ambition to work with the sick and poor.

In January 1794, at the age of nineteen, she married William Magee Seton, son of a wealthy shipping merchant, who came from a very similar social and religious background. William Seton had been educated in England and had travelled in Europe for his father's firm. In 1795 the young couple spent the summer on Staten Island and saw something of Dr Bayley's work in the Quarantine Hospital, where he was medical superintendent. Immigrants were already coming from Europe in search of work and a better way of life, and Elizabeth was touched by their poverty, particularly the plight of women and children. In the next nine years she and William had five children of their own, but she found time and energy for welfare work in the poorer quarters of New York City. With her husband's backing she founded a society with the somewhat cumbersome title of the Society for the Relief of Poor Widows with Small Children and became known as "The Protestant Sister of Charity."

Shipping was a risky business during the French wars, and William became bankrupt in 1800. The shock of losing his family wealth must have been compounded by the humiliation of having all his family possessions, furniture, and even clothing, listed and taken to pay his debts. William, who had been under great strain, developed tuberculosis, which often proved fatal at that time. He needed a southern climate and was advised to spend the winter of 1803 in Italy, where he had business associates, the noble and wealthy Filicchi family, who lived in Tuscany. Elizabeth had only just recovered from the birth of her fifth child, Rebecca, but she would not let her husband go alone. Her first duty was to him. On 2 October they sailed for Italy with their eldest daughter, Anna, leaving the other four children, William, Catherine, Richard, and six-week-old Rebecca, with relatives. The journey was a dangerous one, since they could have been stopped by English or French warships or the many privateers who preyed on ships at that time. It is interesting to note that, twenty-seven years after the Declaration of Independence, William carried a British passport, signed by "His Majesty's Consul-General for the American Colonies," for their protection. The Bayleys and the Setons still had their roots in England.

The voyage took eight weeks. They landed on 18 November in Legnano (Leghorn), where they faced unexpected privation. Though their friends the Filicchis were ready to receive them and care for them, they were not allowed to proceed. There was yellow fever in New York, and they required a bill of health. William, by then seriously ill with tuberculosis, had to go into quarantine. Elizabeth went with him to the *lazaretto*, where at first he was left to lie on a bare floor, cold, and without food. It was due to her astonishing courage and to the support of the Filicchis that he was made reasonably comfortable. Elizabeth nursed him until he was allowed out of quarantine on 19 December, but by then the end was near, and he died eight days later.

Elizabeth was only twenty-eight. She had been through the shattering experience of William's illness and death, and she was left in a strange country. She stayed on in Italy with the Filicchis, trying to sort out her life and find what meaning she could in it. There were two Filicchi brothers, Filippi, a merchant who had extensive business contacts in the United States and knew the Seton family well, and Antonio, a notary with a large civil and ecclesiastical practice. Elizabeth and her small daughter stayed with Antonio and his wife, Amabilia, and their seven children. When Elizabeth turned to the Church, help came from Catholics, not from the Episcopalians with whom she had been brought up. A week after William's death she wrote to a friend, "I am hard pushed by these charitable Romans, who wish that so much goodness should be improved by conversion," and professed herself "willing to hear their enlightened conversation," Christian worship as she knew it was solidly Protestant. Catholic practice was unknown in the Church of England and the Episcopal Church of America until the time of the Oxford (Tractarian) Movement of the 1840s. The Filicchis lent Elizabeth books by Francis de Sales and Bossuet. She went with them to daily Mass. In order to distract her from her grief they took her to Florence, where she was overwhelmed by the ancient splendour of the churches and began to understand the doctrine of the Real Presence. When a procession passed her window carrying the Blessed Sacrament she found herself falling to her knees. She had to be taught how to make the sign of the Cross and what it meant, why Catholics fasted, the liturgy of the Church's year. She wrote home to her sister repeatedly, appreciating all that the Filicchis were doing for her: "Oh my! The patience and more than human kindness of these dear Filicchis for us! You would say it was our Saviour himself they received in his poor and sick strangers." Before long she was writing, "My God! How happy would I be, even so far away from all so dear, if I could find you in the Church as they do."

When she returned to New York it was with the determination to become a Catholic. This was a great shock to the Bayleys and the Setons. Elizabeth's sister-in-law wrote: "Catholics—! Dirty, filthy, red-faced: the church a horrid place of spits and pushing—ragged etc. etc.," and Elizabeth's comment was, "Alas, I found that indeed." In New York at that time Catholics were mostly Italian, Irish, or Central European immigrants—the kind of poor people she had been trying to help when she was William's wife. Now she needed a sacramental life, and she was impressed when she went to a Catholic church and found "old men and women and young women, kneeling about the altar." There were heated discussions with her relatives. Both the Bayleys and the Setons withdrew all financial support, and she was left in very straitened financial circumstances. Former friends no longer wished to know her. Her uncle and godmother cut her out of their wills, and there was "contemptuous laughter" when her name was mentioned at respectable New York dinner tables. She was distressed and became very thin, but she persisted in her decision, took instruction, and was received into the Catholic Church on 14 March 1805.

Elizabeth had herself become one of the Poor Widows who had aroused her compassion when she was happily married and wealthy. She wrote to Antonio Filicchi:

> My daily object is to keep close to your first advice (with St Francis): to take every event gently and quietly, and oppose good nature and cheerfulness to every contradiction . . . but Mrs William Seton is obliged to watch every moment to keep up appearances. You know, Filicchi, what it costs to be always humble and satisfied.

She had to earn her living, and she determined to keep the children with her. Her best asset was her education. For a time she ran a school, but the parents withdrew their children when they found that they were receiving Catholic teaching. She started a boarding house for boys who went to schools in the city, cooking, sewing, and cleaning for them, but the numbers dwindled. She thought of moving to Montreal, where she could escape the anti-Catholic prejudice that surrounded her on all sides and where living would be cheaper than in New York, but then she received an invitation from a priest in Baltimore, Fr Dubourg, to found a Catholic school for girls there. She sailed with her children from New York to Baltimore and was disconcerted on landing to find that there was no one to meet her, but she was told that Fr Dubourg's chapel was being consecrated that morning. She went to the chapel. As the organ pealed and the service began the chapel door flew open to admit a small black-clad widow with five children.

Once she started work she found herself the centre of a group of women with similar aims and ideals, and it soon became clear that this group would found the nucleus of a new religious Order. On 25 March 1809 Elizabeth, by then thirty-five years old, took her first vows in religion with the blessing of the bishop of Baltimore. Other members of the community followed, and in July 1809 they moved to the Stone House at Emmitsburg, near Baltimore, taking the name of the Sisters of St Joseph. It seems that this title, which they took from St Joseph's Valley where the Stone House was situated, was intended to be only temporary. They meant to adopt the Rule of the French Daughters of Charity. This Order, founded by Vincent de Paul and *Louise de Marillac, the first superior, was devoted to the relief of the poor and to teaching in parish schools. Some French nuns were promised for the new foundation, but they were prevented from going to Baltimore by the religious persecution of the Napoleonic régime.

In any case, the Rule of the French Daughters of Charity had to be modified: it specified that widows who joined the Order must send their children elsewhere, and Elizabeth had every intention of keeping her children with her. In consequence, the Sisters at Emmitsburg became known as the Daughters of Charity of St Joseph, or the American Daughters of Charity. Unusually, they kept their surnames—possibly because two of the early Sisters were called Cecilia and it was decided that they should not have to change their baptismal name. Elizabeth was elected superior and known from the first as Mother Seton. She was the head of the school, which accepted poor children without tuition fees, and she had her own children under the same roof.

The first school at Emmitsburg, for girls, was opened in 1810. The curriculum was an exacting one: "Chapel from six until eight; school at nine, dinner at one, school at three, chapel at six and a half, examination of conscience and Rosary." Elizabeth's educational initiative met a real need as more and more Catholic immigrants came to the United States from Europe with ambitions for their children's education.

Mother Seton was much respected. She wrote to her old friend Julia Scott in September 1809:

> You will hear a thousand reports of nonsense about our community. The truth is, we have the best ingredients of happiness—order, peace and solitude. . . . I am a name to keep up regularity and say that there is a head of the house. The chief work I do is to walk about with my knitting in my hands, give my opinion, see that everyone is in their place, write letters and give good advice.

But this homespun approach concealed a good mind and a talent for organization. A school for boys followed in 1818 and a separate school for German Catholic children in the same year. Mother Seton's own children grew up in the Stone House. Anna and Rebecca both joined the American Daughters of Charity. Catherine joined the Sisters of Mercy and became Mother Catherine Seton. Richard died young, trying to save the life of a priest. William went into the American Navy. He was a midshipman, abroad with his ship, when his mother died at the age of forty-seven. She was planning yet another school, in New York, and this was completed after her death.

On 3 October 1808, Elizabeth had written to Julia Scott, "It is expected that I shall be the mother of many daughters." Her Order grew very rapidly and is today one of the largest and most influential of its kind. It owes much to its foundress, who broke class barriers to start building an education system for the first generation of American-born Catholics. Elizabeth's lively and animated letters form a unique record of this process.

Elizabeth was beatified by Pope John XXIII and canonized by Pope Paul VI in 1975. A thousand nuns of her Order were present at the canonization, from North and South America, Italy, and the "missionary countries," and Pope Paul stressed her contribution to the Faith as mother, widow, and consecrated nun. He emphasized her "dynamic and authentic service for future generations" and her "affirmation of spirituality in a land where spiritual values were becoming obscured by temporal prosperity."

MADELEINE SOPHIE BARAT

(1779-1865)

Artist's impression based on a photograph taken after her death.

THE FOUNDER of the Society of the Sacred Heart was born in dramatic circumstances that were to shape her whole life. On the night of her birth in Joigny, Burgundy, there was a fire in the old timbered houses of the town. The child was two months premature, and she was so frail that she was not expected to survive. She was taken through the confusion and excitement by a neighbour, accompanied by her eleven-year-old brother, Louis, for immediate baptism by the curé. All the men of the town were busy with the fire and its aftermath, and so Louis became her godfather. The double emergency—the flames and the smoke and his mother's unexpected labour—made a deep impression on the boy. The solemnity of the promises he made at Madeleine Sophie's baptism led to an intense sense of responsibility for the child.

Their father was a cooper, who owned a small vineyard. Louis went away to train for the priesthood, and when he came home from the seminary at Sens Sophie was ten. He had completed his theological education but was too young to be ordained, so he obtained a post in the college at Joigny as a teacher of mathematics. He had become a very severe young man. He disapproved of Sophie's high spirits and her emotional approach to life, and he resolved to educate her through a taxing programme of studies. Every day started with an early Mass, and the child spent long hours studying Latin, Greek, mathematics, history, and botany. She wept over the *Iliad*. After a time, as a recreation, she was allowed to read *Don Quixote* (in Spanish) and Dante (in Italian). Louis taught her rigorously, without praise or encouragement, endlessly pointing out and correcting her faults. The

221

neighbours said that no good would come of educating a girl; but while many girls would have been unable to sustain such a régime, Sophie seems to have flourished under it.

The teaching went on for the first four years of the French Revolution. Louis was ordained and at first followed the lead of his diocesan, the bishop of Sens, in taking the oath to the Civil Constitution of the Clergy, as demanded by the revolutionary government; he was not to know that his bishop would become a Jacobin and an atheist. When Pope Pius VI condemned the oath Louis withdrew his pledge, as did many other clergy and religious. Their lives were at risk in the steadily-mounting persecution. The priests in the neighbouring town of Auxerre were killed and their bodies thrown on a dunghill. Louis decided that he must go to Paris. This cannot have been for his own safety: perhaps he thought of martyrdom. A year later a former schoolfellow recognized him and denounced him to the Committee of Public Safety. Before he was thrown into prison in the *Conciergerie* he managed to send tokens to his family in Joigny: the Sacred Heart of Jesus and the Immaculate Heart of Mary, embroidered on linen. The Visitandines were making these tokens by the thousand for the faithful to wear in secret.

Louis was fortunate to escape the guillotine. It seems that another former schoolfellow was responsible for making up the rota of those to be executed each day, and he was successful in keeping Louis' name off the lists. Louis was released in 1795 and returned to Joigny, to find that his sixteen-year-old sister had continued her studies on her own. She wanted to enter a religious Order, but there were no religious Orders left. The monasteries and convents were pillaged and derelict. He determined that Sophie must accompany him to Paris. It was a dangerous prospect: priests who had refused to accept the oath were still proscribed, and bloodshed might break out again, but though their mother wept, their father agreed that this unusual child must continue her education. Louis took her to Paris to lodge in the house of an elderly lady, a staunch Catholic who kept a chapel for non-juring priests on the top floor of her house, and there Sophie embarked on a stiff course of theological training. Louis was not interested in female emancipation: he simply taught his sister what he himself had been taught in the seminary because that represented knowledge—he knew no other. Sophie still received no encouragement or affection from him. When she made shirts as a present for his feast-day he gave them away to a beggar; when she started a piece of embroidery he threw it away, saying that it was a waste of time, but in his determination to teach the full Faith to his god-daughter he produced a unique person—a woman with the seminary education strictly reserved to men and to which women normally had no access.

During the years of the Revolution, Christian education had been abolished in France. In 1789 there had been about sixty thousand clergy and religious. Many died by the guillotine, including *Madeleine Fontaine and the nuns of Arras, and others died of want or existed in penury. When the terror and the madness were over it was time for a fresh start. One of the surviving priests who saw the need for the reconstruction of Christian education was Abbé Léonor de Tournély. The Society of Jesus had been suppressed in 1773. De Tournély planned a Society of the Sacred Heart on Jesuit principles, which might be united with the older Society when the ban was finally lifted. Though the Jesuits were a strictly male Order, he planned an equivalent Order for women. When he died in 1797 he gave his plans to Abbé Varin. The men's Order was destined to be short-lived, but the women's Order was to find its leader in Sophie Barat.

By 1801 the men's Order was established, and Louis wished to join it (he was eventually to become a Jesuit when the ban was lifted). When Fr Varin asked him if anything held him back he mentioned his responsibility for his sister, and Fr Varin asked to meet her. She was still a diffident peasant girl, and her only ambition was to become a Carmelite tertiary, but Fr Varin soon realized that she was ideal for his purpose. There were plenty of diffident peasant girls, but only this one had the necessary qualities of character—plus the exhaustive training of a seminarian. He told her: "The gifts that God has given you, the education that you have received, are not meant to be kept in a cloister." Sophie said later: "I knew nothing. I foresaw nothing. I accepted everything."

In 1801 the first house of the new Society for women was founded at Amiens, with Sophie and four companions, and a school was established. The first superior, who was elderly, proved unsuitable and left within a year, saying distractedly, "I really don't know what will become of this house. Sister Grosier can't even sweep her room; Sister Deshayes trots and trots around, and that's all; Sister Sophie can't put two words together." The high-spirited emotional girl had become a silent and reserved young woman, but at the age of twenty-three she was appointed superior, and the qualities of heart and mind that Fr Varin had appreciated gained full expression. She had to give up teaching, which she enjoyed, but she became totally absorbed in the work of building up the Society and its schools. There were many would-be novices, and she would accept only the best. When Fr Varin told her that she must take sparrows as well as eagles, she replied that she wanted eagles: "We could not accept complete nonentities." She wanted first-class teachers with the gift of bringing the Faith alive.

There was no shortage of empty convents and abbeys. The second house was founded at Grenoble in 1804, where there was already a small group of

Sisters led by *Philippine Duchesne. The third was in the old Abbaye des Feuillants at Poitiers, formerly a Cistercian monastery. Sophie arrived there on the back of a farmer's cart, because there was no room in the public stagecoach. She was told that Fr Enfantin of Bordeaux had preached so well on the subject of vocations that he had over thirty young girls ready to go to Poitiers. Sophie—now Mother Barat—interviewed them all. "The numbers increased daily, until I had not a moment's rest," she wrote. There were novices to be educated and trained and schools to be set up—boarding schools for those who could pay fees, and day schools or day places for poor girls. Educational equipment had to be bought and syllabuses planned.

All this work took its toll. The triangular journeys across France from Amiens to Grenoble to Poitiers by public stagecoach, which often ended in the mud or in ditches, were exhausting. She had two serious illnesses, thought to be either cancer or tuberculosis, in the early days of the Society, but she simply continued to work, trusting that she would have the time to do what she must. For its first six years the Society had no name, because it was dangerous to be too specific, but on 10 March 1807 Emperor Napoleon signed a document (in a tent, while on campaign) that made it officially the Society of the Sacred Heart. The request came from the bishop of Amiens and the emperor's own mother, Letitzia Buonaparte, a firm Catholic who never accepted the French spelling of her own name. Napoleon was in favour of Christian education for girls for distinctly idiosyncratic reasons: he said, "I want to see women who are believers, not reasoners, sure that by that very fact they will be attractive women."

The girls in the Sacred Heart schools were both believers and reasoners. Mother Barat's aim was "to give personal worth to each child, worth of character, strength of principles, anchorage in faith." The curriculum she designed was broad—somehow she had escaped the constrictions of her brother Louis' teaching. The girls learned Latin, the Bible, and the classics, but they were also taught literature, the work of "the great writers of Spain, Italy, and even England" in addition to those of France, and they were taught history and geography. The history syllabus included Bible history, sacred history, and also world history. Mother Barat disapproved of history syllabuses that taught short periods of history in depth and insisted that the girls must appreciate the whole sweep of human development. There were two kinds of geography—physical geography, covering the whole world, and "astronomical geography," dealing with the cosmos, the planets, and the stars. Thus, bravely, she set out to teach the girls about God's world in God's universe.

It was, of course, early-nineteenth-century teaching. There was a considerable emphasis on precision of language and grammar, a good deal of memory work, and an emphasis on good handwriting (though Mother Barat did tell her teachers that when they had corrected the handwriting and grammar of one page of a composition, they should pay attention to the contents). The discipline was strict by modern standards, but for girls at that time it was an excellent education—as demanding as the best education for boys and broader in concept. She said, "We must know how to inspire in our pupils a passion for the beautiful."

There were trials and tribulations of the kind that so often seem to test the work of any new Order, including a bizarre episode when the superior of the first house at Amiens and her chaplain, Abbé Étienne de Saint Estève, developed their own modifications of the Rule and the customs of the house. They swept away all devotion to the Sacred Heart and circulated their own Constitution to all the other houses. In 1813 Saint Estève, a supporter of Napoleon, was appointed secretary to the French embassy in Rome, where he used his position to try to secure approval of his Constitution from the Vatican. He established a house in Rome, claiming to have founded a new Order and to have the ear of the Pope. The superior and two Sisters from Amiens went to join it. Fr Varin and Mother Barat were informed that when Fr de Saint Estève's new Constitution received papal approval, a superior general would be appointed for ten years only and Mother Barat would be deposed. Instead of combating this attack, the two prayed and waited, and eventually Fr de Saint Estève went too far: Mother Barat had sent an appeal for support to the Jesuits in Italy, and she received what appeared to be a reply stating that she and her "accomplices" would have to join the new Order on pain of excommunication. This letter was signed "Stephanelli." Enquiries in Rome showed there was no Cardinal Stephanelli, and that this was merely an Italianization of Saint Estève's own name. When this forgery was exposed the breakaway movement collapsed.

After Napoleon's defeat at Waterloo, when the Church in France was restored to some of its former standing, the second General Congregation of the Society adopted a revised Constitution, a new habit, and a new Rule, and the Sisters renewed their vows. The Society received the first papal approval from Pope Pius VII: its members were "to continue to form young girls in the virtues of Christian piety in peace and perfect tranquillity" and "to pay no attention to false rumours."

The diffident peasant girl had become not only a scholar but a talented administrator. In 1816 a new motherhouse was set up in Paris, and the demands increased. The Russian ambassador was interested in Russian converts; a reception had to be organized on the feast of the Sacred Heart for the cardinal archbishop and the grand almoner of France; and "bishop after bishop" came to see Mother Barat, all wanting schools in their dioceses.

There were new premises in Paris, in the Hôtel Biron, once part of the abbey of Saint Germain. There were royal visitors, and King Louis XVIII made a personal gift of a hundred thousand francs for the chapel; but despite the attention of the fashionable world and an increasing number of girls from aristocratic families, Mother Barat kept to simplicity of heart and simplicity of manners. A novice wrote: "She is lively, gay and intelligent. She is only forty years old. The youngest of the novices speaks to her as easily as one of her Sisters. She is always among us." In the schools the children were plainly dressed and taught obedience. When she heard a group of girls laughing at her peasant origins (for her name was plain Barat, without the *de* signifying aristocratic connections) she gathered up her books and said quietly that she would leave. There was immediate contrition.

There were long delays in securing final approval from Rome, though Pope Leo XII sent encouraging messages. At length a commission of cardinals was set up. Some cardinals raised difficulties because the Sisters were not enclosed, but Solemn Approbation was finally granted on 22 December 1826. Meanwhile Mother Barat was more than ever on the move, as the number of foundations increased. In 1818 *Philippine Duchesne, who had welcomed her at Grenoble, was at last able to fulfill her dream of founding a mission in Louisiana, from which many foundations followed in the United States. Houses were founded in Turin and Rome and at Perpignan, near the Spanish border.

Mother Barat was repeatedly ill. In 1829 she fell off a table and damaged her side and her foot. She could not walk for a year and had to be dragged about on "a sort of sled" on wheels. She had haemorrhages. She told one correspondent that her writing looked "like a wind shaking the trees," but the seven-months child who had nearly died at birth was a survivor. Despite her infirmities she continued to visit every house in France, and in 1832 she went to visit the Rome house. It was functioning, but the workmen were very slow. "Business in this country moves like a tortoise," she complained, "We Frenchwomen could die of it. We need the patience of saints." She was so respected in Rome that a marchessa urged Pope Gregory XVI to keep her there: "Holy Father, the Mother General must be chained to Rome, and you must give me the key." The Pope's reply was: "The generals of Orders are not chained."

She was not fit enough to visit the new houses that were founded in Poland, in New York, in Canada, in Ireland, in Holland, in England—at first at Berrymead Priory and later at Roehampton. As she grew older she complained, "I am nailed to France," and she would have travelled the world if she could.

There was another policy crisis in 1839, when the Sixth General Congregation of the Order met in Rome to discuss a re-drawing of the Constitution. The Order had developed so rapidly that some revision was needed. After bitter opposition to Mother Barat's very limited suggestions for change, the Congregation decided for radical revision. The reformers wanted no less than forty-six changes to the Constitution. Fr Varin, much distressed, wrote to her, "Where is our dear Society of the Sacred Heart? I no longer ask that question, having no strength to reply." Though Mother Barat was equally distressed, she did not oppose the changes. She said, "I like to leave liberty to those who deserve my confidence," but she suggested that the new system might be implemented for a three-year experimental period. The Society was in turmoil: some houses accepted the new draft Constitution, while others did not. Mother Barat had to stay in Rome, where Pope Gregory XVI wisely refrained from pronouncement until the situation was clear. At the end of three years, a committee of cardinals unanimously decided to restore the earlier Constitution.

Mother Barat was not afraid of change—she believed that her Order had been divinely inspired and that she must be faithful to its foundation—but she was an educational innovator. As educational standards and methods changed, the study-plan had to change: it was revised every six years. She learned much from the Salesian Brothers, and her influence in turn affected education for girls in many countries. "Administration, by its very nature, means dealing with difficulties," she wrote in a letter. A stream of letters went out to all her houses, guiding, advising, passing on information, helping individuals. A letter to Philippine Duchesne illustrates her capacity for detail:

> The Society, though very poor at the moment, has united all its little efforts to collect some presents for you. Beauvais and Paris are sending you a piano. Sister de Marboeuf has got the seeds and the candelabra. Mesdemoiselles de Cassini and de Saint Marc are sending you all that is wanted to teach drawing: models, paint-boxes, crayons etc. Grenoble will send you silk and flowers. Poitiers, paper. Amiens, 100 francs. All ask your prayers.

"I have such a need for solitude," she wrote in another letter, but her only solitude was an occasional brief silent retreat to strengthen her prayer life and renew her energies. She wrote to another correspondent, "I am like the secretary of some minister. I have no time to breathe. When visits and business come, is Jesus there in the midst of them? Can he be there in peace? I doubt it, and how painful are these doubts to a soul that seeks him and finds everything but him."

In her later life she was able to travel by train, which was a great relief after the jolting coaches. She liked to sit on station platforms, eating her lunch from a bag and making friends with passers-by. Another helpful invention was the telegraph, which made it possible for her to be in contact with all her far-flung houses. As the pace of her life became slower she found more time for children, whose company she always enjoyed, and for animals. There was a lamb, Robin, in the garden of the motherhouse, which followed her from place to place. She liked birds and was able to free a dove that had flown into the chapel. When the nuns regretfully decided to drown a litter of kittens, the mother cat took them carefully one by one into Mother Barat's room, and their lives were spared.

Fr Varin died shortly before the Golden Jubilee of the Society in 1849. Mother Barat deeply missed his support and told the assembled delegates of her trust that "from the height of heaven, he will protect this little Society which, after God, owes its existence to him." Much honour was paid to her at the Jubilee, but she still insisted that she was not a foundress, saying, "The Sacred Heart is the Founder of this little Society." In 1854 Mother de Rousier, who had been superior of the Turin house until the Italian *Risorgimento*, was sent to visit all the North American houses. She was with Mother Philippine Duchesne when Philippine died and gave her a final blessing in the name of Mother Barat. When she had toured North America, Mother de Rousier was asked to go on to Chile, where the archbishop of Santiago wanted foundations. She had "an unspeakable journey" over the Isthmus of Panama, travelling by mule and by canoe, and at one point fell over a precipice. Her fall was stopped by some bushes and she was rescued with ropes. She went on to make foundations in Santiago and Talco.

When Mother Barat was eighty-five she asked the Eighth General Congregation to relieve her of the post of superior general. In affection, her Sisters refused, but they gave her a vicar general, Mother Goertz, to relieve her of many burdens. Less than a year later she died, on Ascension Day, 25 May 1865. She had ruled the Society for sixty-four years. There were eighty-six houses (a further twenty-five had been closed or confiscated by hostile governments) and 3,500 Sisters in many countries.

There are no photographs of Mother Barat when she was alive. In 1853 she was induced to sit before a camera, then a new invention, but when she saw it she said, "Take away your machine. You don't understand. It's not my face that should be reproduced, but my affection for you all. Then you would have something worthwhile." The only artists' impressions of her are based on a photograph taken after her death.

Madeleine Sophie Barat was beatified in 1908 and canonized in Rome on 12 May 1925, when thousands of girls and women who had been educated in

Sacred Heart schools filled the basilica of St Peter. In his address Pope Pius X compared the life of this peasant girl from Burgundy to Christ's parable of the Mustard Seed, "which is indeed the least of all seeds, but when it is grown up is greater than all herbs, and becomes a tree, so that the birds of the air may dwell in the branches thereof."

8

MISSIONARIES

UNTIL Christopher Columbus sailed out of Seville to discover the New World across the seas, civilization centred on the Mediterranean basin and the land routes to the East, but within thirty years of that epic voyage Vasco da Gama had taken the Portuguese flag across the Indian Ocean and Hernán Cortés had overthrown the Aztec Empire in Mexico. The oceans beyond the Mediterranean were crossed by sailing ships, explorers and traders opened up new territories. Within fifty years Francis Xavier had begun the missionary work that was to take him to the East Indies, Malaysia, China, and Japan. Jesuits, Franciscans, Augustinians, and others took the gospel into new lands, facing unknown dangers and often sacrificing their lives for their beliefs.

Until the nineteenth century missionary work was exclusively the prerogative of the male religious Orders. Women religious read about missions in the Americas, the Far East, Africa, and later Australia. They listened to missionary priests, prayed for missions, and collected money for missions; but these were enterprises for men, in which they could have no part. The work involved danger, discomfort, hardship, and a considerable lack of the privacy and protection women were thought to require. Missionaries did not travel as the wealthy travelled. On land they went by public stagecoach or by mule (horses were expensive); at sea, they travelled steerage. It was unthinkable that frail women should be subjected to these conditions.

The logic of sending out dedicated groups of women with skills in teaching, nursing, and social care was first perceived in France after the Napoleonic Wars. In time the case for women missionaries became unanswerable. The European nations began to understand that colonies were not simply sources of plunder or commercial assets. Many colonial populations, whether indigenous or immigrant, had desperate needs. As the sense of responsibility for colonial territories grew it became clear that women religious were needed as well as men, whatever the hazards of travel.

Anne Javouhey and the Sisters of the Congregation of St Joseph of Cluny went out to the French colonies in the days of sailing ships. The first Sisters sailed for Réunion in 1817, taking nearly six months to make the journey. There were not many French colonies left, and those that remained were in urgent need of assistance. They had been neglected through the long years of the French Revolution and the Napoleonic Wars, and under the terms of the Treaty of Vienna the victorious Allies demanded that France should emancipate her slaves. Mother Javouhey realized that freed slaves of both sexes needed clothes, shoes, work, and accommodation. Shoes in particular became symbols of freedom. In her lifetime her Congregation went on to found missions in West Africa, the Caribbean, Newfoundland, and India, rehabilitating slaves, setting up schools and workshops, running hospitals. A woman of large sympathies, she even went into Sierra Leone, at the invitation of the British governor, to run a hospital for France's former enemy.

Philippine Duchesne of the Sisters of the Sacred Heart sailed to Louisiana from France in 1818. Her letters to her home community contain vivid descriptions of the journey across the Atlantic, of storms at sea, of contrary winds that repeatedly drove the ship off course, of cabins deluged by sea water, culminating in a heartfelt comment: "Land is more attractive than water." The journey up the Mississippi to St Louis took the first group a further six weeks. They had to learn self-sufficiency like other American pioneer women, milking cows, growing vegetables, storing their winter provisions. They set up schools for Indian and Negro children and dispensaries. Since the Louisiana Purchase in 1803, the territory was no longer a French colony but part of the United States. Until the steamships started a regular mail service, the Sisters were often desperately lonely for contacts with France, and Philippine never saw her native country again.

Frances Cabrini went out to the United States in 1889 to care for the "poor Italians" of the first waves of American immigration, often exploited and crowded into tenements, working in the unregulated factories of New York, Boston, Chicago, and other developing cities. Though she became a naturalized American, Italy was her homeland, and her Sisters were trained in the Italian houses of her Institute, the Missionary Sisters of the Sacred Heart. She crossed the Atlantic back to Italy nine times, made a mission to Nicaragua by river-boat, and crossed South America from Valparaiso through the Andes to Buenos Aires and Rio de Janeiro.

Mary MacKillop began her work in Australia in the 1860s, at a time when the cities into which the new immigrants crowded were virtually cut off from one another: a journey from Adelaide to Sydney or Brisbane involved taking a ship round the coast. She set up schools in the poor quarters of the cities, where many children were illiterate and barefoot, and when the development of free state schooling affected the work of Catholic schools she diversified the work of the Sisters of St Joseph of the Sacred Heart into nursing, welfare, and running foundling homes. She and her Sisters met the needs as they arose. She often travelled on her own, because there was not enough money for her to take a companion, and sometimes she did not even have the fare to complete her journey, let alone the fare home. On her journey to Europe, she went on to Rome alone, to England and Scotland alone, and she scandalized the bishop of Waterford by her unchaperoned arrival in his diocese, though he later appreciated her sense of vocation and her determination. Her dealings with the bishops of the scattered Australian dioceses were difficult and complicated. In the pioneering days, the work of women was not highly valued.

By the time **Katharine Drexel** founded the Order of the Sisters of the Blessed Sacrament, travel was much easier. Her first trip to the north-west United States was as an honoured guest of the new North Pacific Railroad Company, in a private railcar, with her banker father. Though the conditions were comparatively luxurious, the journey was not without risk, for the train narrowly escaped a hold-up by a gang of robbers. On her later journeys the Indian war-dances she witnessed were still too realistic for comfort. In her travels across the United States, setting up schools, colleges and dispensaries, she took many risks, and she faced threats from the Klu Klux Klan in the South. A champion of human rights for Indians and Blacks long before these became popular causes, she was fearless and outspoken in her criticism of racial discrimination. Despite the great wealth she inherited (which she disposed of to her many charities), she always travelled by the cheapest class, taking her food in a carpet bag, which became well known to the bishops and clergy she visited.

These five women are representative of many others who have taken the Christian message into new territory. In the days of easy air travel we can only try to imagine the delays, the discomfort, and the very real dangers they faced. Their courage came from their faith. Many of the difficulties they encountered in their work came from poor communications with their ecclesiastical superiors. Though Philippine Duchesne and Katharine Drexel worked in response to requests from bishops and clergy who had learned the value of missionary Sisters, Frances Cabrini, Anne Javouhey, and Mary MacKillop faced considerable prejudice from bishops who thought the work unsuitable for women, or that it should be undertaken only under their own control. Frances Cabrini was told to go back to Italy by the archbishop of New York: the ship on which she had come was still in the harbour, and she was advised to sail back with it. Her reply, "I have letters from the pope," has become a classic of women's emancipation in the Church. Anne Javouhey was threatened with excommunication. Mary MacKillop was actually excommunicated for a period of about four months, though in a ceremony that was technically invalid.

These attacks on their work must have been harder for the women to bear than hazardous voyages, drought, flood, snakes, yellow fever, poverty, and loneliness. They bore them with great courage. They also bore them with outstanding patience and great humility—even with a sense of humour. It was the work that mattered.

ANNE-MARIE JAVOUHEY
(1779-1851)

*Statue by Fr M. Bernard
at the motherhouse of
the Sisters of St Joseph of Cluny
in Paris.*

ANNE was twenty-one, a postulant at the house of the Sisters of Charity in Besançon, France, when she told a priest that she "seemed to see—was it a dream? Or just my imagination?—a multitude of children, poor, sick, weeping. . . . What especially struck me was a multitude of Blacks, men, women and children, calling me 'Dear Mother.'" Whether it was a dream or imagination, the experience was remarkably prophetic. She may have known of the existence of other races—though her biographers suggest that she did not—but in 1800 women could not be missionaries. She could not even have imagined that she would become the foundress of an Order that stretched in her lifetime from the Americas to India.

Her background was solid, bourgeois, and conventional. She was born in Chamblanc, Burgundy, the fifth child of a well-to-do farmer, Balthazar Javouhey, and his wife, Claudine. She was twelve years old in 1792, when the worst excesses of the French Revolution flared up in Burgundy. A spirited child, she rescued people from a blazing chapel when the revolutionaries set fire to it, warned priests in danger of the approach of spies, and cheerfully misdirected the mob when they came to hunt them out. She collected local children together, taught them the Catechism, and presented them to the priest for First Communion—which they had to receive secretly in one of her father's barns, with the windows shuttered.

234

She was seventeen or eighteen when the conviction grew that she was to found a Society for the education of young girls. Her father thought she should stay at home: he owned several farms, and she had the makings of an excellent manager. She wrote to him about this time saying, "My dear father, I hear you were intending to send me to Pluvot to manage men," and protesting that this would be unsuitable because of her desire for the religious life. She must have learned about planting and harvesting, hiring and supervising labour, account-keeping, and buying and selling land on the family farms—knowledge she was to put to good use later in her missions.

She had very little formal education, no more than that of the local village school, but she was a born organizer. She developed a Rule for herself and her younger sisters, keeping periods of silence, and reciting the Hours. Her father, alternately impressed and exasperated, said, "I don't know why, but I've got children not like others—in fact, they're the very opposite." On one occasion he broke into the schoolroom, kicked the chairs over, and threw the books about. On another he took the clock they used to keep the Hours and removed the weights. Her mother was a pious woman, but she could not understand this lively daughter and lamented: "Nanette will always be a trouble to us."

By 1800 the wave of religious persecution was over: her parents sent her to the Sisters of Charity, and she bent her will to the obedience required of her but went through a period of spiritual desolation and great anguish. She told her confessor of her dream on the evening before she was due to take her vows. He thought she should not proceed to her clothing. Her parents had already arrived for the ceremony, but she went home with them.

For a time her life was empty: she lacked direction. Then two priests suggested that she should start a small school in a nearby village. She had the backing of a Trappist abbot, Dom Augustin de l'Estrange, and her father bought a small house for it. The school was not a success: a traditional farming community did not see much point in educating girls. After a time she went, on Dom Augustin's advice, to the Trappistine house at La Val-Sainte in Switzerland. Dom Augustin seems to have hoped that she could become a Trappistine, though the Trappist way of life was very alien to her active temperament. He rebuked her in the confessional, telling her that she was deluded and suffered from "the demon of Pride," but she held fast to her dream. Again she came to the eve of her clothing. Then he told her that she must be free to follow the call of God and sent her home.

There was another period of confusion and lack of purpose. Life was not easy for a girl who was regarded as a twice-failed nun. She made two other attempts to set up village schools, but there was no demand for her services. She and her sisters lived near starvation level: on one occasion, when they had no food at all, her father and brothers arrived with a cartload of provisions. Her father complained that she was ruining him and that he was becoming exhausted with the frequent journeys to look after her, but he continued to support her and eventually took her and her sisters and the younger children under her care back to his own home, where he built an extension for them. His wife was quite right: Nanette was proving a trouble to them.

In 1805 she had an opportunity to secure the support she longed for. Pope Pius VII stopped at Chalon, not far from Chamblanc, on his way from Napoleon's coronation in Paris. Anne and her sisters went to the papal Mass, received Communion from the hands of the pontiff himself, and asked for an audience. Pope Pius, confronted by four young girls in blue dresses and white caps, gave them his blessing and told Anne to persevere in her vocation. Then a priest at Chalon offered them a house and some support. Anne went to see the bishop of Autun: he was doubtful about the project but gave them ten francs. She went to see the mayor of Chalon. At this time all schools in France and many premises that had formerly belonged to the Church were regulated by the civil authorities. The mayor gave her part of what had been the diocesan seminary and provided beds and tables and other furniture. Two of her sisters and their brother Pierre came to join in the work: Pierre was thinking of seeking ordination, and Anne dreamed of parallel Orders for men and women. The municipal council voted a grant of a thousand crowns a year. Within a year or two Pierre and a colleague were managing a school for eighty boys, while Anne and her eight colleagues had a school of 123 girls, of whom thirty-four were boarders.

In June 1804 an imperial decree required that all religious communities should be placed on a legal basis under the new Napoleonic constitution. By this time Napoleon's accord with the pope was broken, and all religious bodies were made answerable to the civil power. A provisional decree was given for "the religious association formed in the diocese of Autun and called by the name of St Joseph, with the purpose of forming children of either sex to work, good morality and Christian virtue."

The clothing took place in the church of Saint Pierre in Chalon on 12 May 1807. The new venture had caught the imagination of the people of Chalon: there were processions and banners and cheers from the crowds as they went to their clothing. Anne was elected as the first superior of the Congregation.

Thereafter the work prospered. There were many opportunities as the process of educational reconstruction developed. Like *Madeleine Sophie Barat, who was born not far from the Javouhey home in the same year as Anne, she took full advantage of them. There were empty properties to be filled, and many requests came for assistance in re-building a Catholic educational framework for France. Anne set up workshops, a hostel for the poor, a boys' school run by a relative, a preparatory seminary, houses in the dioceses of Franche-Comté and Champagne. The community moved to a disused seminary in Autun on a three-year lease. Before long the community's work became over-extended. Some of the smaller houses had to close, and the community was heavily in debt. Balthazar Javouhey came to the rescue again. He paid the creditors and employed the town crier to restore the community's financial reputation. If he upbraided his daughter for her "rashness and want of prudence," he was always there when he was needed.

In 1811 France was at war with Spain. The public authorities requisitioned most of the seminary at Autun for army officers and their families, and the great hall which had been the Sisters' refectory was used as a hospital for the wounded. Anne and the other Sisters nursed the sick men and put up with considerable hardship. On one occasion four Austrian soldiers arrived, sick and hungry, when there was literally no food. Anne took the community clock, a gift from her father, and pawned it, reappearing with a long French loaf and two bottles of wine for the soldiers.

In 1812 the lease on the seminary expired, and the community had to move again. Balthazar Javouhey (who was splendidly atoning for his early irritation with his daughter) bought them a former monastery at Cluny, a Franciscan house of great antiquity. It had been the site of a Benedictine monastery founded in 910, a forerunner of Cîteaux. From that time on, the Congregation became known as the Congregation of St Joseph of Cluny.

Anne founded two schools at Cluny, one for poor pupils and one for fee-paying pupils, and when Louis XVIII was restored to the throne of France in 1814 she went with two or three Sisters to Paris. They were so poor at first that they had to fetch water from the Seine and live on bruised fruit and vegetables from the gutters of Les Halles, the great market; but, as before, persistence and endurance produced results. She opened a small school, and after a time the administrator of the diocese of Paris entrusted a government school to the Sisters. There was a good deal of interest—and some criticism, because Anne instituted the "Lancastrian" teaching system, which was then new to France. Joseph Lancaster had pioneered a system by which the teachers taught a group of monitors, and the monitors taught the pupils. Parisians considered this shocking because Lancaster was English and not a Catholic (he was a Quaker), but, irrespective of nationality and creed, the system made good sense when teachers were in short supply.

Anne had become a very good communicator: she kept both the civil authorities and the diocesan authorities fully informed of her plans and never acted without their approval. She convinced the Prefect of the Seine and a Cabinet minister, M. Laîné, of the value of the schools. M. Laîné became Minister of the Interior for all France and gave her full support. He also introduced her to his kinsman, the deputy governor of the Isle of Bourbon, later renamed Réunion, east of Madagascar. The colonial missions suddenly became a possibility.

The long war that ended with Napoleon's defeat had left France exhausted and the French colonies depleted and run-down. Some had been occupied by the British forces; some had been blockaded; others had been left to their own devices, without government policy or finance. The Treaty of Vienna in 1815 restored some colonies to France, but the new government of Louis XVIII had to agree to abolish the slave trade over a five-year transition period. While there were many in France who demanded liberty for the oppressed, the white colonists resisted strongly, forecasting a "black revolution" and insisting that they could not afford to pay "white wages" to their black labourers. There was a need for schools, for hospitals, and for a programme of resettlement for emancipated slaves.

Anne wanted to lead this mission herself, but she was needed in France, where new foundations were being made. Four Sisters of the Congregation of St Joseph of Cluny sailed for Réunion on 10 January 1817. The voyage took five months and eighteen days. They started a school, then four more Sisters joined them and they started another. The Colonial Minister was enthusiastic about their work and asked for a group to go to Senegal in West Africa. This time Anne's sister Rosalie went as superior, with their brother Pierre as escort to the party. They sailed with the vicar apostolic (the equivalent of a bishop for an area not yet constituted a diocese). They were fêted in Tenerife with flowers and banquets, but they finally arrived in Senegal to find "a desolate scrub" with no church, no school, and a demoralized local population. The vicar apostolic left after two months, saying that the situation was impossible and he would make representations in Paris. The nuns stayed, and for eighteen months they had no priest to say Mass. Then at last a new vicar apostolic arrived, with five crates of much-needed potatoes. The nuns' joy over both the priest and the potatoes speaks volumes for the hardships they had endured.

M. Laîné, as Minister of the Interior, proposed that a contingent of Sisters should be assembled in readiness for work in other colonial settlements, and Anne decided to concentrate the work of the Congregation on the missions. She assembled nineteen Sisters: seven for Senegal, six for Guadeloupe, three for Cayenne (Guiana) and three for Réunion. In 1822 she sailed for Senegal herself, leaving her niece Clotilde as acting superior general. She sent her sister Rosalie home to France to become superior of the motherhouse at Cluny and took her place, running the school and the hospital.

Anne had malaria, but every white settler in West Africa had malaria, and she was soon up and about again, teaching, nursing, planning, organizing.

"As for the sick," she wrote of the white colonists, "most of them are bad lads, and most of them won't listen to a word about religion, whether in life or when they are dying." The Senegalese were friendly but inclined to indolence, and they were all Muslims. They saw her praying and invited her to make her *salaams* with them, saying that the whites did not pray. At first this impressed her, but she soon concluded that Islam was only a covering for a mass of ignorance and superstition. After a time she asked the authorities for a tract of land in the interior. She developed a settlement of huts, surrounded by a thorn hedge to keep the lions out, and bought twelve cows. She started agriculture, inducing the Senegalese to plant maize and rice and beans and manioc.

The governor of the British colony of Sierra Leone and the Gambia asked Anne to start work there. She was remarkably free of racial or political prejudice: she took people, black or white, African or French or English, as she found them. So she went to help France's old enemy. "The English have no idea of what a well-equipped hospital should be," she reported. They lived in comparative luxury, and were "very zealous Protestants," frequently singing hymns at five o'clock in the morning. The governor was so grateful for her work that when she was ill he insisted that she should be nursed in his own residence.

In 1822 Anne had to return to France, partly because of repeated illness and partly because there was a crisis in relation to the community in Réunion. The superior, Mother Marie-Joseph Vernon, died. Anne appointed another superior, but a Sister named Thaïs, exploiting both the slow communications with the motherhouse and the almost total lack of communication between the Vatican and the French bishops, obtained recognition from Rome. She then declared that all the other houses of the Congregation were "irregular" and that Anne, the other superiors, and the other Sisters were not entitled to call themselves "of Cluny," or to wear the habit. The matter dragged on for a long time but was eventually settled in favour of the original Congregation by the intervention of the archbishop of Paris.

There were demands for more Sisters in Guiana. They went out and opened another school, in spite of great difficulties. There was a cyclone, and the superior was killed by a falling building. In the chaos that followed the cyclone there was an epidemic of yellow fever, but still the Sisters stayed, and the governor described them as "the consolation of this land."

Between 1825 and 1828 there were eight new foundations in France. The Congregation was asked to take over two lunatic asylums—one near Rouen and one near Alençon. Anne arrived at the latter alone to find naked lunatics, some violent and some crouching under the straw "like dogs," screaming and howling. Seventeen Sisters came in the next day to wash the patients, to cut the men's beards, and to set them to work in house and garden. There were new colonial foundations in Martinique, in Saint Pierre and Miquelon, south of Newfoundland, and two workshops in Pondicherry, India. Anne appointed her sister Marie-Thérèse to make visitations to all the houses in the colonies. In 1828 the Congregation finally received full recognition from the Vatican and the royal assent from Louis XVIII of France. By that time Anne had gone abroad again, on a government-sponsored mission to Guiana.

She made two trips to Guiana to create a new settlement, Nouvelle Angoulême, in a district along the river Mana. It needed settlers and services—a school for the many orphans left from the Napoleonic Wars, a church, a hospital. Anne recruited settlers with the necessary skills—farm labourers, mechanics, and craftsmen. They went out on contract for three years, during which time they were guaranteed food, lodging, and a living wage. They were promised land if they stayed after that. The expedition sailed with forty Sisters, twelve lay assistants, a doctor, a chaplain, and Pierre Javouhey, who continued to escort his sisters on their long and hazardous journeys.

The soil was fertile, but the climate was unhealthy. Some settlers were homesick, and many were ill. The priest did not stay—the community had long periods without one—but the workshops were set up and the fields tilled. The white colonists were slow to free their slaves. Anne bought slaves when she could and set them free. There is a letter from her second Guiana trip that describes vividly how this was done. Shoes had great symbolic importance as signs of free status, so the Sisters collected large piles of old shoes, and the former slaves forced their feet, often injured, malformed, or maimed, into these ill-fitting emblems of freedom before hobbling off to emancipation. She took over the administration of a leper settlement on the island of Saint, north of Cayenne, and she sent some young Guianians to France to train for the priesthood. This was not a great success: the cultural gap was too great, and few of them persisted. Of those who did, few returned to Guiana.

When Anne returned to France in 1830, it was to a very different situation. There was another revolution, and the *Orléaniste* Louis-Philippe had become king. The new government withdrew support from the Order for a time, and there was a new and hostile bishop of Autun, the marquis de Trousset d'Héricourt. Mgr d'Héricourt had been ordained after a brilliant military career and appointed bishop at the age of thirty-two after only four years in Holy Orders. He had very firm views on the management of a women's Order. As Fr Martindale comments, he thought "a man's hand was needed, and that hand was his." He appointed a male superior, the abbé Josserand, to the motherhouse at Cluny and announced that he himself was the superior general. He demanded an exhaustive statement of all the colonial establishments—their revenue, their lands, their property, the methods of instruction used in the schools, the numbers of pupils and of patients in the hospitals. He stopped a new building at Senlis, north of Paris, and required Anne to go back to Cluny. Anne had to explain that she could not hand over decision-making to him: under the Constitutions of the Order, decisions were taken by the Council. Further, many of the houses of the community were in the dioceses of other bishops, or in colonial territories with their own vicars apostolic. The bishop of Autun could not possibly claim jurisdiction over all the work of the Congregation. The Ministry for Public Worship and the Ministry for Colonies supported her, and the king himself had a Mass said for her in his private chapel, but the new archbishop of Paris resisted any secular intervention in the affairs of the Church and was unwilling to take action against the bishop of Autun.

Even on Anne's second trip to Guiana, Mgr d'Héricourt pursued her, asserting his own authority. He sent out a priest to the settlement, who declared that he was the superior of the Congregation, made high-handed and unwise decisions, refused Anne absolution, and passed her over at Communion. The bishop even wrote to threaten her with excommunication.

When she returned to France she went to Paris to see officials of the Ministry of Public Worship. It was 1848, and the barricades were up again in the streets, but the revolutionaries recognized her, and there were cries of "It's Mother Javouhey! Make way for General Javouhey!" The bishop of Autun was informed that the Constitutions could not be altered in his favour. She went to Fontainebleau, where the bishop of Meaux admitted her to the sacraments. She returned to Cluny and was honoured by the local clergy— but not by Mgr d'Héricourt. He sent a lengthy memorandum to the Ministry of Public Worship, alleging that she had defied his authority, that her powers as superior general had expired years earlier (though it was common practice for a foundress to remain in office without re-election), and that her temporal affairs were in a state of disorder. He complained that everything seemed to be in the hands of her relatives, "sisters and nieces." In fact, she had two sisters in the Order, and one niece. In 1845 he attempted to close the motherhouse at Cluny. The Sisters were informed that it was a sin to support Anne as superior general. Anne told them roundly that it was a sin not to support her: many other bishops were prepared to receive them if the bishop of Autun persisted in his actions against them. The archbishop of Paris appointed a commission of three priests to examine the state of the Congregation, and they reported in her favour, but Mgr d'Héricourt continued his campaign. The papal nuncio, now reinstated in France, assured Anne that she was the superior general; that she could give the habit to

Sisters in any country with the approval of the local diocesan; and that Rome did not recognize any bishop as superior general of a women's Congregation. It is likely that pressure from the nuncio and other bishops led Mgr d'Héricourt to refrain from the drastic act of closing the motherhouse.

Toward the end of her life Anne resolved to go to Rome at last and lay her statutes and ideas before the pope. It was too late: in June 1851 she was thought to be dying, but she recovered sufficiently to be told of the death of Mgr d'Héricourt on 14 June. She said: "So he's gone, that good bishop. God rest his soul." When the priest who told her had left she added to the Sisters who were with her, "We all but met, he and I, on that very day, before the judgment seat of God." She was a woman of humour and also of great charity. She expressed a wish that all the papers concerned with the conflict with the bishop should be burned, and there is no mention of this searing and long-drawn-out struggle in the Congregation's account of her life.

Anne died a month after Mgr d'Héricourt, on 15 July, and was buried in the Congregation's chapel at Senlis. She once said, *"Je n'aime pas les femmelettes,"* I don't care for silly, weak women. Certainly *femmelettes* of the kind the bishop of Autun apparently preferred would have been of little use in the gruelling circumstances of the early colonial missions. The celebrated French writer-diplomat, Chateaubriand, doubtless intending to be complimentary, called Anne *"Un grand homme,"* but she was not a man, even a great one. She was a woman of great faith, of remarkable courage, and considerable administrative ability. It was nearly a century before her sanctity was formally recognized, but her beatification took place in 1950.

PHILIPPINE DUCHESNE

(1769-1853)

Painting in the convent of St Charles, near St Louis, Missouri.

ROSE PHILIPPINE DUCHESNE grew up in France when Louisiana was still a French colony. Her family—merchants, lawyers, and politicians who lived in the wealthy quarter of Grenoble—frequently encountered the Jesuits who came back from the New World to talk of their work in evangelizing the Indians. Philippine's confessor, attached to the church of Saint André, was a former Louisiana missionary.

Philippine was sent for a time to the Visitandine convent of Sainte Marie-en-Haut, founded by *St Jane Frances de Chantal, where she took a great interest in geography, studying maps and following the missionaries' journeys. She had a devotion to St Francis Xavier—venerated as the greatest missionary since St Paul—who had founded missions in the East Indies, India, and Japan before dying on the coast of China. For a time she was taught with her brothers; but when she was eighteen she determined to enter the religious life and went back to Sainte Marie-en-Haut. Her mother and sisters went to the convent to beg her to return home, but she stayed. She had been there for nearly two years when the French Revolution broke out.

There were riots in Grenoble, and anticlerical feeling ran high. It was too dangerous for her to make her profession. In 1790 Sainte Marie-en-Haut was closed and the Sisters were disbanded. Philippine had to go home, and she accompanied her family to their country house at Grannes, where there was less risk of attack. After a time she lived quietly with a former nun under a simple Rule. They had to support themselves by embroidery and plain sewing because the Duchesnes' property had been sequestrated. The convent at Sainte Marie-en-Haut had become a prison, and many clergy were incarcerated there. Priests were hiding in the rural areas, and Philippine became a "priest hunter"—one of the many women who found them, gave them shelter, and took them to attend the sick and dying.

Eventually the political oppression ceased, and in 1800, when the French government made a Concordat with Pope Pius VII, Philippine was free to resume the religious life. She started by educating local children, who had simply run wild during the revolutionary period. Then she resolved to buy back Sainte Marie-en-Haut from the government. How she did this is not clear, for when she took it over she had no money to maintain a community, but she got it cheaply because it was in a very dilapidated state. It was "open to the winds"—the doors were off their hinges, the windows were broken, tiles were missing from the roof; but it was a time when women who wanted to live the religious life were coming together again, and a few other former nuns came to join her. They adopted a simple habit and found a priest to celebrate Mass for them on Christmas Eve. Philippine was inexperienced in community life; at the age of thirty-three she was still a novice. She compensated for her inexperience by introducing a very rigid system of administration: not the gentle and relaxed Rule of the Visitandines, but something closer to the Rule of the Society of Jesus (then proscribed), including the full Ignatian exercises. This was combined with total enclosure and extreme austerity. Her own austerities were many. She even sprinkled her meagre food with wormwood so that she would not enjoy eating it. She did not have the authority to impose this extreme system on the other members of the community. Some of the Sisters became alienated and left.

Two priests, Fr Rivet and Fr Varin, were concerned about the risk of failure in this small community. Fr Varin had worked with *Madeleine Sophie Barat in founding the Society of the Sacred Heart in Amiens in 1801, and it was agreed that the community at Grenoble should become the second house of that Society. Mother Barat, still only twenty-five, visited Grenoble to establish the Rule, and Philippine, ten years older, found the strength to acknowledge her own inadequacies and to welcome her new superior with an open heart. Mother Barat saw her privately, enlisted her sympathies, and heard about her desire to become a missionary, promising to help when she could. The nuns were told to eat properly and to concentrate on the liturgy and periods of private devotion rather than indulging in endless prayers. If they were going to teach, Mother Barat told them, they needed to be physically fit and energetic. Grilles and gratings were thrown away, and a noviciate was established. Fr Rivet's sister became the local superior.

Philippine, freed from the responsibilities of managing Sainte Marie-en-Haut, was more than ever convinced that she must go to the mission field. She wrote many letters to Mother Barat, telling her of her self-examination, her prayers, her conviction that she must offer herself "for the foreign missions, to teach the pagans of China or any other distant land." Philippine received much sympathy and counsel from her superior, but she had to learn patience: it was twelve years before the opportunity arose. During that time she taught in the school, managed the community's finances, and nursed the sick—all skills she would need in Louisiana. She became secretary general at the motherhouse in Paris, but her heart was still with her "poor savages." China was forgotten. She was convinced that she had a vocation to go to Louisiana to work with the American Indians. She wrote: "I have shed many tears over America before the statue of Our Lady."

Mother Barat found that her secretary general was a woman of one idea. She wrote to Mother Josephine Bigeu, one of her counsellors:

> I begged her not to speak to me about it any more, since no door was opening to us for missions. "What?" she would say, "don't you want me to think of my plans any more?". . . "Very well, dear Philippine," I said, "let's talk sense. If I should give you the obedience to go and convert the savages, what would you do without companions, without money, without support, without any means of leaving? Do you think God would work a miracle in your favour, and give you the privilege of walking on the waters?". . . As I had not such strong faith as hers, I would not say the word that she awaited so insistently.

At last the door opened. In 1817 Bishop Valentine Louis Du Bourg of Louisiana visited the convent. At the time Philippine was the porteress, and she must have been the first to welcome him. The United States had bought Louisiana from France in 1803, when it became the eighteenth state of the Union. Bishop Du Bourg wanted foundations and was determined that they should come from France. Mother Barat was at first doubtful about such a venture and then wanted to lead the expedition herself, but she was needed in France, and Philippine pleaded to be allowed to go. There was already a convent of Ursulines in New Orleans, but the new community was to work far up the Mississippi River. After long negotiations the project was agreed, and she was appointed superior of the new community—against her wishes, for by this time she no longer wanted to hold authority. A teacher was engaged to teach the five missionary nuns the language of their new country.

Philippine struggled with the unfamiliar tongue, though she never became fluent in English.

The five set out by stagecoach across France for Bordeaux. It was a difficult journey, for they had to share the coach with two drunken, anticlerical army officers who sang disreputable drinking songs. The solitary Jesuit travelling with them tried to drown the noise with hymns and canticles, which must have made matters worse, but at Bordeaux Fr Louis Barat was waiting for them, to help them on their way. Philippine wrote to Mother Barat:

> I leave in France so much that I love, and I shall always be bound to my native land by the strongest ties. . . . You desired this privilege for yourself. . . . God makes use of you where you are, but since I could do nothing, he will try me out elsewhere. . . . The whole merit of our mission will be yours: the peril, both to body and to soul, will be ours.

Perils to the body followed soon after they set sail on Holy Saturday, 1818. The ship ran into a storm in the Bay of Biscay, and another off the Azores. Though it was only April, the heat was intense. At times they were becalmed and at others the winds were contrary—they were driven five times over the Tropic of Cancer on their journey. It was too rough for Mass to be celebrated. The Sisters were sea-sick, and had no privacy in the small, malodorous, bucketing vessel. Philippine wrote afterwards, in one of her regular letters, "For fifty-two days, we saw nothing but the sea and the sky," and gave a vivid picture of their terrors: "The star-studded sky disappears behind mountains of water. The sea, nearly black during a storm, seems to gape, revealing a bottomless abyss. Twice during the night the high sea forced open our portholes and flooded our berths."

It was not until 25 May that they entered the Mississippi Delta and saw the mud-banks and swamps of a new continent. They were finally deposited at the Ursuline convent in New Orleans at half-past two in the morning. There they were hospitably welcomed, and Philippine found that the Ursulines were teaching three hundred children. There were catechumen classes for Negro and Indian children, and she wrote to Fr Varin, "I feel my soul dilating with hope." The Sisters' thick French habits were almost unbearable in the heat, and they were badly troubled by mosquitoes: the local men helpfully offered them plug tobacco to drive the mosquitoes away. Philippine had scurvy as a result of a poor diet during the weeks at sea, but she was ready to start teaching. She was to open a college for girls and one for boys. She wrote back to her Society asking for "the Rule of the School, the plan of studies, an astronomy, an atlas . . . a geography, the poem *La Religion* by Louis Racine, and *Esther*, a breviary, the definite formulary of vows, and the Summary of the Constitution of the Society . . . also a beautiful embroidered flounce for an alb."

On 12 July the Sisters started up river for St Louis. By this time they had adopted a simple black cotton habit, which made the climate more bearable. They were astonished to see the first steamboats, which were plying the Mississippi. They sailed through the bayou, where the trees were draped with Spanish moss, the vultures waited on rotting tree-trunks, and the alligators crawled, past rice swamps, past orange groves and sugar plantations. The journey took them six weeks—as long as crossing the Atlantic. It was 21 August when they finally arrived in St Louis, then a frontier town. The streets were unpaved, the cathedral was a wooden building, and the bishop lived very frugally. They had no money. In all the time since they had left Grenoble they had had no letters or packages from their Society in France, and the mail did not reach them until 8 October, when three deliveries came at once.

By early 1819 they had begun their school for girls, but there were only three boarders. They had a single cow, which produced milk for the boarders but none for the Sisters. They lived largely on salt fish and meal until the Ursulines sent them provisions. Even water was scarce. The well dried up, and it cost the community twelve cents to send a boy down to bring two small buckets from the Missouri. Philippine wrote back to France—lively, detailed letters telling of their privations and asking for supplies: seeds, plants, tools, altar wine, and olive oil. "The only edible oil to be had is bear grease, which is revolting."

Her "poor savages" were something of a disappointment, for many of the Indians had been corrupted by their contact with white settlers and were not particularly grateful for the teaching offered by the Sisters. "We sweetly dream," wrote Philippine, "of giving instruction to docile and innocent Indians, whereas the women, no less than the men, are afflicted with drunkenness and indolence." As so often in schools attached to new foundations, there was no shortage of poor children, who came in winter "famished and barefoot to school along frozen roads, and wearing only the lightest of dresses," but fee-paying boarders were slow in coming.

The bishop gave the community his full support and spent a retreat with the Sisters, raising their spirits and strengthening their resolve. They moved from their first house at St Charles, where the lease was expensive, to another where there were new log cabins and a farm with cows, calves, and chickens. "We had to appease the cows with cabbages," wrote Philippine, "for they were at first very obstinate." She and her companions learned self-sufficiency like the pioneer families, picking berries and fruits, storing apples, gathering nuts, and stacking wood for the winter. It was a far cry from her comfortable childhood in Grenoble and even from her self-imposed austerities at Sainte Marie-en-Haut.

By 1820 there were twenty-one girls in the boarding school, and the classes for Indians and poor white children were put on a regular basis. In time there was a new church and a priest to say daily Mass for the community. The first American postulants were beginning to come forward. There were very hard times ahead, coping with drought, flood, cyclones, and on one occasion with an epidemic of yellow fever. Philippine—now Mother Duchesne—often longed for support. On one occasion she wrote: "All consolation has gone. My heart yearns for someone to lean on. . . . I must lean on God, and on him alone," but the mission was a success. The first of many Sacred Heart convents in the New World had been established. By 1848 there were six houses, and the missions were still expanding.

In her thirty-four years in the United States, Philippine never saw France again. The mail improved as steamboats began to cross the Atlantic, and letters flew back and forth from Louisiana to the motherhouse in Paris. She wrote of her achievements, but also of her difficulties and her self-doubt. In 1834 she wrote: "I feel that I am an outworn instrument that is fit only to be hid in a dark corner. God allows everything to deepen this impression in my soul. I have never at any time attracted people's confidence and the same is true here." Mother Barat's replies were bracing: "You have indeed suffered much, but God has endowed you with a strong constitution, so I trust that you will recover your strength, and that we shall have the consolation of keeping you for a long time to perfect your own sanctification and consolidate the mission that you have founded."

Philippine was never content with what she had achieved. She had not been endowed with the administrative ability and the warmth of temperament of her talented and capable superior general. Less certain in her judgment, she agonized over her decisions. Less outgoing, she often felt herself to be isolated and, as she said, "wept among the cabbages," but she gave all she had. She shared the courage and the endurance of the American pioneers. Life was often hard and sometimes dangerous, but sacrifice and hardship were essential parts of her calling. She continued to push into new territory. She was seventy when she founded a school for Indian children in Kansas, and she had to be dissuaded when she planned a new venture in the foothills of the Rocky Mountains; but by that time she was worn out and exhausted by hard work. In 1840, when she was seventy-one, she had to be relieved of her office as Provincial of America. Mother Barat had dreaded taking this step, but the responsibilities had simply grown too great for Philippine to manage. The nature of the Society's work had changed. It was no longer a matter of establishing small missions but of managing schools with high standards in the developing cities. By then there were others to carry on this work, and the railroads were opening up routes across the continent.

Philippine died at the convent at St Charles in 1852, at the age of eighty-three. Mother de Rousier, sent by the seventh general congregation of the Society to visit the American houses, saw her shortly before her death and gave her a blessing in Mother Barat's name. When Mother de Rousier asked a blessing in return, Philippine feebly traced a cross on her visitor's forehead and said, "I give you my heart and my soul and my life—O yes, my life, generously." She died a few days later. She had indeed given generously from the moment she agreed to join the Society of the Sacred Heart.

Her tomb was first enclosed in a small chapel in the convent garden at St Charles. Later, a memorial church was built on the site, and this has become a place of pilgrimage. She was beatified in 1940.

MARY
MACKILLOP
(1842-1909)

MARY MACKILLOP's parents were both Highland Scots who emigrated to Australia. Alexander MacKillop, the son of a farmer from Inverness-shire, was a former seminarian, well-trained in philosophy and theology. He kept quiet about his background, because failed priests were not popular in Catholic circles. He arrived in Sydney in 1838, and his bride, Flora McDonald, travelled out with her mother and brother in 1840. They met and married in the same year, and Mary, their eldest child, was born in 1842

Australia was regarded as a land of opportunity by new immigrants, but Alexander never achieved the success he hoped for. He took a post as a clerk for a time, then became involved in a series of schemes involving land speculation. Mortgages were unpaid, projects failed, and he was repeatedly bankrupted. A born optimist, he persisted in his belief that he was on the brink of making his fortune; meanwhile, his family grew, and the debts multiplied. Mary had very little formal education, because the MacKillops moved from place to place, and there was seldom money for school fees, but she learned from her father and from the Church. For a time she attended the academy opened in Sydney by the Sisters of Mercy, and when she was old enough they were prepared to accept her as a postulant, but Mary felt a responsibility to help her mother and the six younger children. Her father was often away from home on his schemes, on one occasion going to New Zealand to look for gold.

Mary became governess to a family living near Penola, in what is now the State of South Australia. Penola was then a straggling village. There was one Catholic priest, Fr Julian Tenison Woods, who had a parish of a few hundred people, mostly farmers, scattered over a vast territory. Fr Woods, a charismatic personality of huge enthusiasms, supported Mary in her aims. When she was barely twenty she went to Portland in Victoria, secured a post as a salaried teacher for a time, then rented a large house for her family to live in, hoping to start a Catholic school of her own. Things went badly wrong, chiefly owing to her father's lack of discretion and to the fact that he spent the money sent by her grandfather to buy the school a piano. Mary left Portland with debts of £100 and went back to Penola, where Fr Woods told her, "I dread very much the pressure of your father to break up your little home again if you make one. I think you should make it understood that he is not to come." So Mary started again, in a cheap rented cottage. It was no more than a shack, and their only water supply came from catching rainwater. She found a dilapidated stable for a school house, and her brother John, who had been found work in a surveyors' camp and was embarking on a career as a surveyor, came and renovated it for her. Within two or three months she and her sister Annie were teaching thirty-three children. Gradually, with some help from Fr Woods and their MacKillop relatives, the affairs of the family were sorted out. Their younger sister, Lexie, came to live with Mary and Annie; their mother went to a boarding house in Portland, taking the two youngest children, both boys; their sister Maggie went to live with an uncle's family; and their father to live with his brother in Hamilton, Victoria. A friend of Mary's from Portland, Blanche Amsinck, and a young governess named Rose Cunningham came to join her. Several other suitable young women were also attracted to the possibility of a teaching Institute.

Fr Woods gave Mary much spiritual and moral support, but he had no money. He talked of a new religious foundation and laid down a rule of life for the teachers, encouraging them to wear plain black dresses and hats as the first step toward a habit; but many local people were hostile to the enterprise: they thought that if Mary wanted to enter the religious life she should join an existing Order. Fr Woods continued to be highly optimistic. He bought the school a statue of St Joseph but expected Mary to collect the money for it. This was difficult: her own household was desperately poor, their diet often being no more than bread and treacle, and the parents of the children who came to their school often could not afford even the small weekly fees.

By this time Fr Woods had been transferred to Adelaide and had acquired the high-sounding titles of Director General of Religious Education, Inspector of Schools, and Chairman of the Diocesan Board of Education, but he was proving a liability to the small community: the clergy were deeply disturbed by his lack of practical planning. He had enormous enthusiasms but no head for detail and no grasp of financial issues. Hostility grew when he shut down a number of small parochial schools, saying that the teachers were unqualified and that the new Institute would provide properly trained teachers in time.

When the bishop of Adelaide paid the Penola school a visit he was impressed by the standards of teaching, discipline, and cleanliness despite the dilapidated premises. Mary kissed his ring, and he said, "God bless you, Sister Mary," which implied approval of plans for the Institute.

In 1867 there was a new development: Fr Woods called Mary and Rose Cunningham to Adelaide, where they were to be clothed and start a new school. Miss Josephine McMullen, who ran a private school in the city, had been a novice of the Sisters of Mercy in Ireland. She was prepared to join the Institute and to hand over her premises to it. The two embarked by ship for Adelaide on what seemed like a risky venture, but they arrived safely, spent some days of retreat with Josephine McMullen, had their simple black habits blessed, and began to teach. Adelaide was a shock—a shanty town with holes in the road and filthy gutters—and the children were even poorer than those in Penola. Many of them came to school barefoot, but sixty children attended, and Mary charmed the parents. She was young and smiling, and she never patronized them. She talked to them simply and directly, so that they did not feel ashamed of their poverty. Soon the school roll reached two hundred children between the ages of eight and sixteen, many of them completely illiterate when they enrolled.

On 15 August 1867 Mary was professed in an elaborate ceremony devised by Fr Woods. She made the three vows of poverty, chastity, and obedience and a fourth, "to promote to the utmost of my power the love of Jesus Christ in the hearts of little children." She adopted the name of Sister Mary of the Cross. She now had three novices in Adelaide, all experienced teachers.

The Sisters had no money except the fees, which had to be kept very low and did little more than pay the rent, but the parents brought them gifts—a clutch of eggs, a lump of home-churned butter, a sack of potatoes. Their mattresses were filled with straw, and they drank from tin cups. The floors were scrubbed but had no mats. They rose at five in the morning and recited the Office Hours, said Prime and Terce, and attended Mass before breakfast three hours later—and breakfast was bread and dripping. When the Sisters travelled they went third class. A parishioner told Fr Woods that this was dangerous, because there were "very low blackguards" about. They continued to travel third class.

The quality of the Sisters' spiritual life and their evident dedication brought postulants. Before long there were thirty. Fr Woods, who had constituted himself director of the Institute, undertook all the training, but Mary soon became doubtful about his approach. He was often domineering and unkind to the postulants. Even more worrying was his enthusiasm in encouraging two hysterical novices, who declared that they had visions and heard voices. He was convinced they were great mystics, comparable to those of the Middle Ages. Though he had done much to help in the founding of the Institute, his insistence on his own absolute control and his lack of judgment meant that he was increasingly proving a liability.

Mary's own work went well. Within two years of her arrival in Adelaide the Sisters of St Joseph were teaching in seventeen separate schools. Often the schools were only shanties, and many of the children were so badly clothed that the Sisters had to beg cast-off clothes for them from the better-off. The Sisters themselves had changed from their original black habits to brown. Brown alpaca was cheap and cool, and it did not fade as badly in the fierce Australian sun. Mary began to branch out into other activities: she visited the sick, making no distinction between Catholics and non-Catholics as she reckoned that both needed help and consolation. She started a House of Providence for homeless women, from very young girls without families to the old and deserted. She opened a refuge for unmarried mothers. For all these enterprises the Sisters begged from door to door, carrying a large carpetbag and hoping to fill it with donations from the new rich class that was growing up in the city.

The bishop of Adelaide, who was in Rome, wrote to Fr Woods reminding him that he had promised to send Sisters to Queensland. There was no money for their passages, but the bishop assumed that they would be able to beg. He expected Fr Woods to head a small party, but Fr Woods stayed in Adelaide. Mary had to ask her relatives for money for this journey of 1,600 miles, and she had to go alone. She left with enough money to take her only as far as Sydney. In Sydney she stayed for nine days with the Sisters of the Good Samaritan, who were housed in a crumbling debtors' prison, and the Benedictine nuns found money for her passage to Brisbane.

She arrived in Brisbane on the last day of 1869, only to be told by the vicar general that there was no need for her services. The Australian States were gradually introducing free and compulsory state education. While in South Australia religious instruction in state schools was limited to readings from the Authorized or Douai versions of the Bible, the syllabus in Queensland was less restricted, and the diocese had decided that all Catholic schools would accept the state grant.

In spite of this unpromising beginning, Mary stayed, believing that there was room for schools that offered full Catholic teaching. She established three schools in the face of considerable misunderstandings with the diocesan authorities, and in 1872 a foundation was made in the Bathurst diocese at the request of the bishop. When she returned to Adelaide, however, she found that the situation there had deteriorated in her absence. Fr Woods' memory had grown patchy, he had become intensely suspicious of those who disagreed with him, and he had delusions. He made dramatic prophecies of impending deaths—chiefly of those clergy who were opposing him. The archdeacon and other senior clergy were seriously concerned about the Institute. The Rule, drawn up by Fr Woods, forbade the ownership of property, so that its members had no security. They did not even own their own convent, and they had considerable debts. They did not teach in state schools, though other Catholic teaching organizations found it possible to do so, and there was increasing concern about mysterious happenings in the convent, where the two "mystic" sisters were becoming extravagant in their claims to extraordinary spiritual experiences. Fr Woods nominated one of them as superior of the Adelaide house and the other as novice-mistress.

The Sisters of St Joseph had proved the value of their work, but they were totally dependent on Fr Woods, and he in turn was dependent on the good will of Bishop Shiel of Adelaide, who had spent most of the previous three years in Rome, seeking support for his diocese. The response had been disappointing. During this time Fr Woods had sent him many enthusiastic letters, assuring him of the progress of the Institute, but when he finally returned to his diocese, without the funds and the priests and nuns he had hoped for, it was to be confronted with a sorry tale of maladministration and incompetence. Fr Woods, who had required unquestioning obedience from Mary and the Sisters, should have been the person to answer for the Institute, but he was not available for questioning. He was involved in an accident, he was said to be dying, and when it emerged that he had only broken two ribs he left Adelaide, avoiding a confrontation. The full force of episcopal indignation, fuelled by complaints from senior clergy, fell on Mary. A clerical commission was set up to investigate the affairs of the Institute. Its main conclusions were that each convent should be autonomous, subject to the direction of the parish priest, and that any Sisters who objected would be required to leave. Mary was told—indirectly, since she was not regarded as either foundress or superior—that she must leave the motherhouse within three weeks. No doubt years of clerical frustration with Fr Woods went into these strictures.

Bishop Shiel was a very sick man, and his illness must have made a bad situation worse. He was also reported to be drinking heavily. Mary asked to see him but was refused an interview. The bishop, without inquiring further, sent a message ordering her to an outlying convent on pain of excommunication. She stayed, still asking to see him. On 22 September 1871 he arrived at the convent, was vested with mitre and crozier, and, in front of the astonished and terrified Sisters, excommunicated her. He was unable to carry out the procedure properly, and he omitted some of the necessary formalities.

Mary went away quietly, saying nothing. She wore lay dress and stayed outside Adelaide while the affair subsided. The Sisters of St Joseph were disbanded in the Adelaide diocese. Some went to teaching posts and some back to their parents. There were wild stories in the anti-Catholic newspapers, but many of the clergy were sympathetic, regarding the situation as a terrible miscarriage of justice brought about by two very sick men. Mary continued to receive Communion in private from priests who regarded the excommunication as not only unjust but technically ineffective.

Bishop Shiel was dying; in January 1872 he realized that he had been misled by his advisers and rescinded the sentence. He died only a week later, and the Sisters of St Joseph watched and prayed round his coffin.

The archbishop of Sydney set up an Apostolic Commission, consisting of the bishops of Hobart and Bathurst, to investigate the Institute's work. They recognized its value and decisively severed Fr Woods' connection with it, so that Mary became superior for the first time. The schools reopened, and there was a new friendliness from the clergy, but the Institute needed a formal status to protect its work in the future. This meant seeking the approbation of the Holy See for a suitable Rule.

On 28 March 1873 Mary sailed for Italy. Again she was alone. The Institute could not afford more than one fare, and she had no idea how she was going to finance her return passage. She knew little about Italy, but she was told that the Papal States had been seized by an anticlerical government, and it was thought advisable that she should conceal her religious identity. She travelled as Mrs McDonald, a widow, and when the purser asked her how many children she had (she was still only just over thirty) she replied, "Oh, a great many." She had a male relative to escort her as far as Brindisi, but when she finally landed after a very rough voyage, she still had three hundred miles to travel by train. This was a novelty, because all her travel in Australia had been by sea, round the coast. Rome was a culture-shock. She did not speak the language, and the customs were strange, but she went straight to the churches. To be able to worship in the Gesù, in the church of St Ignatius, and in St Peter's was an almost unbelievable gift to a woman who had practised her faith in tin shacks and wooden shanties.

The clergy to whom she had letters of introduction were away during the heat of the Roman summer, so she had plenty of time to visit the churches. Her funds were exhausted. She was down to her last few lire when she saw Fr Anderledy, assistant to the Jesuit Father General. He found accommodation for her in a convent and arranged for her to see cardinals who could deal with her application. They were encouraging; but the Vatican tends to move slowly, and everybody was preoccupied with the acute political situation. Mary was fatigued by the heat, which she thought was worse than in Queensland, and like many others she caught Roman fever. Even when she recovered she was subject to serious migraines, which disabled her for two or three days at a time, but she prayed at the shrines of the saints with a great sense of privilege and then, being told that she would have months to wait, decided to go to Britain to seek postulants.

The Jesuits helped her with money. She travelled overland, visiting schools in Italy and Germany on the way, sitting up all night on trains and in station waiting-rooms. London was a disappointment. Though she met a duchess and a marchioness, they gave her little help, and there were no postulants. Friends provided enough money for her to go to Scotland, and she toured the Catholic Highlands, going to the places from which her parents had emigrated. There were relatives in the Braes of Lochaber. The parish priest recommended her work from the pulpit, and she met many friendly people. Some thought she was a girl of sixteen; others thought she was "a little old lady in black."

In March 1874, a year after her arrival in Italy, she was back in Rome—for a few days only, she wrote to her Sisters; five weeks later she was still waiting. She wrote in her diary that she felt united to God's will but sad: "Bodily health bad but mental distress worst of all." Then at last the Rule was agreed. The official notification came to her: "Sister Mary of the Cross, Superioress of the Sisters of St Joseph in Australia." This was recognition at last.

Before returning to Australia Mary went to Ireland to seek postulants and, if possible, priests. She met some opposition—notably from the bishop of Waterford, who told her that he was "shocked to find so young a woman engaged alone on such important business" and that the sooner she went back to Australia the better, but when he got to know her he helped her with introductions to other bishops and influential people. When she finally returned to Australia she was accompanied by fifteen postulants and two priests. They sailed on 5 November, and the postulants were given their new names on the feast of the Immaculate Conception. They arrived back in Australia on Christmas Day. Both priests insisted on saying the three Masses of Christmas, so the nuns attended six Masses before they could land. When they reached the motherhouse they were greeted by their Sisters and nearly a hundred new postulants.

This might be thought a triumphant ending to the story of Mary MacKillop's difficulties as a foundress, but Australia was over six weeks' journey from Rome, communications were slow, and the battle lines were being re-drawn. Though Mary was recognized in Rome as "Superioress of the Sisters of St Joseph *in Australia*," the bishops of Queensland and Bathurst, the brothers James and Matthew Quinn, both opposed a form of organization beyond their own diocesan authority. The bishop of Queensland called Mary "an obstinate and ambitious woman." She made repeated visits to the houses in both dioceses but was eventually forced to withdraw her Sisters from Queensland. The Sisters of St Joseph continued in the Bathurst diocese under the control of the bishop of the diocese. Later, a new bishop of Adelaide also refused to recognize her jurisdiction. Mary wrote sadly, "I often think that rest will come to my dear Sisters when I am gone; many prejudices are directed against myself, for bishops and priests think me some extraordinary and bold woman." She received, however, a warm welcome from the archbishop of Sydney, and the bishop of Armidale also welcomed her, so that for some years her work was focused on New South Wales, with the Sisters expelled from Brisbane and Bathurst and those who came from Adelaide. She opened a new noviciate in Sydney.

The matter was not finally settled until 1885, when Archbishop Moran of Sydney went to Rome on being created a cardinal. He returned with the judgment that the Institute should have extra-diocesan status but that Mary should resign as superior. She did so gladly. She had not wished to stand at the previous chapter, but her Sisters had insisted and had indeed wanted her to be superior for life.

Mary's resignation and the statement from Rome should have been enough to quieten the dissident bishops. It was not. In November 1885 the plenary council of the synod of bishops of Australia and New Zealand carried the following resolution against the wishes of Cardinal Moran:

> As regards the Congregation which is called "The Sisters of St Joseph of the Sacred Heart," the bishops think it opportune that the convents or religious houses should be subject, like those of the Sisters of Mercy, to the Ordinaries of the dioceses in which they exist.

Again, Rome moved slowly. It was not until 15 July 1888 that Pope Leo XIII made the Institute of St Joseph a canonical Congregation with the motherhouse based in Sydney. At the same time Cardinal Moran appointed Mother Bernard as Mother General for a period of ten years.

Mary was forty-seven years old. She thought the change was a wise one. She was still Mother Foundress, and she was glad to be out of the line of episcopal fire. She devoted herself to training the novices for a few months, then became acting superior of the motherhouse. In 1890 she was appointed the Mother General's representative, making canonical visitations to all the houses, opening new convents, and visiting schools. Now that the railways had developed she travelled by train, not in the little coastal ships. She travelled many thousands of miles in Australia, saying her Rosary on the journeys, praying for the people she knew and the people she met; in 1894 she made the first of three visits to New Zealand, where the work of the Institute was already developing. She wrote back to Sydney of volcanoes and magnificent mountains, of rats on the roof, of the three Sisters who taught Maoris in their own language, of the joy of seeing Maoris coming to Mass and Benediction.

On 7 August 1898 Mother Bernard died suddenly, and the subsequent general chapter unanimously voted Mary back as Mother General. She carried on all her activities with her usual disregard for her own health or comfort. She was in New Zealand in 1901 when she had a stroke, which left her with partial paralysis, but her mind was clear, and she continued to work from a wheelchair, typing her own letters. It was not until the summer of 1909 that she found the effort too great, and she died quietly on 8 August.

There were seventy-three priests at Mary's Requiem Mass, presided over by her champion, Archbishop Moran. By then the Institute of St Joseph comprised 106 convents and 750 nuns. It had come of age. So had the Catholic Church in Australia. Mary was beatified by Pope John Paul II in 1995.

FRANCES XAVIER CABRINI

(1850-1917)

From a photograph.

FRANCESCA SAVERIO CABRINI was an improbable missionary—a young Italian primary teacher, less than five feet tall and in chronically poor health—but she had been named for the great St Francis Xavier, and she was determined to follow him into the mission field. It seemed an ambition unlikely to be fulfilled, for attitudes to women in her native Tuscany were highly conservative, and girls were expected to stay at home.

Frances was born at the village of Sant'Angelo, south of Milan, on 15 June 1850. Her father was a farmer. Her mother bore at least eleven children, but most of them died young, and one who survived was mentally handicapped. Frances was taught for a time by her elder sister, Rose, who was the village schoolteacher, and then sent as a boarder to the convent school of the Daughters of the Sacred Heart at Arluno. She stayed there until she was eighteen, by which time she had passed her examinations as a primary schoolteacher. She was appointed as the teacher in a neighbouring village, Vidardo. At that time, soon after the unification of Italy, there was a wave of anticlerical sentiment, and the teaching of religion in state schools was forbidden. When the mayor of Vidardo objected to her teaching religion during the school day, she gave the children religious instruction after school hours and led them to the Mass in the village church on Sunday.

At this time Frances wanted to join a religious Order, and she applied to the Society of the Sacred Heart, but her small size and her physical frailty counted against her, and she was told that she was not strong enough for the rigours of convent life. She went to the Canossian Sisters at Crema, but they took the same view. There was a smallpox epidemic in Tuscany in 1872, and she followed the example of her uncle, Fr Louis Oldini, in nursing the sick. She contracted smallpox herself but recovered without scars thanks to the devoted nursing of her sister Rose. Her parish priest, Fr Antonio Serrati, knowing of her dedication and her determination to work for the Church, recommended her for appointment as the head of a Catholic orphanage for girls, the House of Providence in Cadogno. Frances took on this work with enthusiasm. She managed the orphanage successfully, set up a workshop for the girls when they were old enough to be employed, and recruited and trained a small group of assistants. It was not her fault that the scheme failed: it was under-funded and badly organized, and she had no control over the resources. Its failure was a blow to her, but she had learned many valuable lessons, which she would use later in her work.

Her heart was set on missionary work in the Far East. If men were able to go on foreign missions, why should women not do the same? There were women and girls to be taught and brought to the Faith in these far-off and unimaginable lands. She sought permission to found a house devoted to foreign missions, perhaps to work in China, which had recently become open to European influence. Other young women came to join her. There was a good deal of resistance from the church authorities on the grounds that missionary work was unsuitable for women, but at last Frances was allowed to found the *Missionarie del Sacro Cuoro* (Missionary Sisters of the Sacred Heart) for her small group.

Her aims were initially modest: she realized that the work would have to be thoroughly tested and approved in the diocese before it was thought suitable for a foreign mission. Her Rule was a sensible and pragmatic one. She expected the Sisters to work hard, but there were no extreme austerities. She thought that if they were giving all they could to the poor and needy (of whom there were many in northern Italy) that was hard enough. They spent four hours in prayer, worship, and meditation each day and kept times of silence. It was a mixed vocation, part active and part contemplative, and the keynotes were humility and simplicity. Frances was always willing to undertake the most humble tasks herself, and her example inspired the others. She worked strictly under the guidance of her ecclesiastical superiors, and made no demands that would alarm them or cause them concern. In 1881 her Rule was approved by the bishop of Lodi, and as the reputation of the

Missionary Sisters of the Sacred Heart grew, other houses were set up in the diocese.

Seven years later, in the autumn of 1887, she was ready to ask for a wider recognition of her Institute. The bishop of Lodi was seriously ill, and when she approached the archbishop of Milan, he three times refused to see her. At the fourth attempt she saw him but was told to go back to her diocese and to be content with diocesan approval. She records the next step drily in her diary notes, writing of herself in the third person, as she always did:

> Frances Cabrini had always cherished a fervent desire to engage in foreign mission work, but she did not want to go herself or to send any of her Sisters until she had obtained the approval and blessings of Christ's Vicar on earth, the Supreme Pontiff. For this purpose, she went to Rome in 1887.

Her aims were to start a house in Rome and to explore the possibilities of foreign missions. When she saw the vicar general at the end of September he was dismissive. She had no money, no powerful allies among the clergy or the nobility, nothing but her own determination. He said there were enough nuns in Rome, no need for a new Order, and she should be content with the work she was doing. She went back in October and asked him again. Impressed by her steady resolution, the vicar general spoke to the pope. She was given more than she had hoped for: approval of her Rule, and not one foundation in Rome, but two; she was to start a free school for the poor and manage an orphanage outside the city in the Sabine hills. Five Sisters joined her. She walked the streets hunting for suitable premises for the school and bought second-hand furniture from bargain sales and junk shops. She literally begged for support, and she got it. Four months later her Institute received the papal Decree of Commendation, a mark of confidence for a women's Institute. She began to plan for the Italian houses to become training institutions for the mission in China.

Her Institute was not to start work in China: the immediate need for Italian missionaries was in the United States, which was then classified by the Church as mission territory. There was a deep economic depression in Italy in the 1870s and 1880s. Many families scraped together the passage money and set out, crammed in the small, heaving cargo boats, for the promise of the New World. Those who could not manage to pay for their passages accepted indentures: they were advanced the passage money but had to pay it back at exorbitant rates of interest after their arrival in the United States. Several hundreds of thousands of Italian immigrants crossed the Atlantic each year, looking for work in New York, in Chicago, in the cities of the Eastern seaboard. They left one sort of poverty and squalor for another: when they reached their adopted country it was to find that the only work available was in factories and foundries, where they were often exploited and lowly paid, and they had to crowd into insanitary tenements in districts that soon became known as "Little Italies." They did not speak the language, and they did not understand the customs of this still predominantly Anglo-Saxon society. Clinging to what they knew, they formed an underclass—poor, alien, and often despised.

The bishop of Piacenza, Giovanni Battista Scalabrini, had seen the crowds of emigrants queuing for trains at Milan railway station, poorly dressed, loaded with their worldly belongings, and hoping for a better life. He sent some mission priests out to New York and contributed articles for the Italian press on the problems. One immigrant wrote, "We are like mere animals. We live and die without priests, without teachers, without doctors." Bishop Scalabrini sympathized with Mother Cabrini's plea that women had much to offer as missionaries. He suggested that the Sisters of the Sacred Heart should go to America and not to China, but Mother Cabrini's mind was still set on China.

A year later he tried again. He told her about the high rate of industrial accidents in the American industrial plants, of families left without a breadwinner, of ragged children roaming the streets without education or religious instruction. He also told her that had received calls from Archbishop Michael Corrigan of New York for Italian mission priests, and that the wife of the director of the Metropolitan Museum of Art in New York, Countess Palma di Cernola, had raised the sum of $5,000 toward the cost of a home for Italian orphans. Mother Cabrini, torn between America and China, decided to leave the decision on the future of her Institute to Pope Leo XIII. *Propaganda Fide* had recently published a report on the urgent need for action by the Church to help Italians in the United States. The pope listened to Mother Cabrini for some time, thought quietly, and then gave his decision in a phrase which the Cabrini Sisters still quote: "Not to the East but to the West."

The small party, consisting of the superior and six Sisters, sailed from Le Havre on 23 March 1889 for New York. There were 1,500 immigrants on the same ship, and it was an uncomfortable and very rough voyage. When they finally landed in New York in a heavy downpour there was no one there to meet them. The city seemed huge and noisy, full of flashing lights, and they had to walk the streets soaked to the skin, to find shelter for the night. The only place available was in an evil-smelling basement in a rough quarter, where they were assailed by bedbugs and cockroaches. Mother Cabrini was up at dawn and went to see Archbishop Corrigan, but the archbishop told her bluntly that he wanted priests, not nuns. He had written to Italy, refusing to accept the Sisters, but they had sailed before his letter was received. The $5,000 for an orphanage was no longer available, and in any case he thought missionary work was quite unsuitable for women. He pointed out that the ship on which the seven had come was still in the harbour and advised them to board it again and sail back to Italy. There was nothing for them to do in New York. Mother Cabrini replied with as much dignity as a very small woman could muster, "I have letters from the pope." The Sisters stayed.

They had no money, and the diocese and the major religious Orders refused to give them any assistance. They had to beg from door to door for money to survive, and for a time they had to stay in a dirty tenement room. Then other women religious—the Sisters of Charity and the Bon Secours Sisters, who knew of the archbishop's lack of sympathy for women—came to their aid. They found decent lodgings and started a school in the church of St Joachim, off Roosevelt Street. They washed and de-loused the children and began to teach them, understanding when they ran off to earn a few dimes by shining shoes or selling newspapers because their families needed the money. Mother Cabrini went to visit the Countess Palma di Cernola, to find out the truth about the $5,000. She found that the countess and the archbishop had disagreed about the site of an orphanage. The countess wanted it to be in the wealthy part of New York, where people could afford to support it, and the sight of the orphans would touch their consciences. The archbishop thought that anti-Catholic feeling was so strong that it would be wiser to site it among the poor. He also objected that $5,000 was not enough: it would provide only running costs for a year. He was probably right on both counts, but a compromise was worked out: the countess accepted his views on the site, and the archbishop agreed to allow the project to go ahead, trusting that funds would become available to maintain it. In April 1859 the Asylum of the Angels was opened on 59th Street. It was a success, and Archbishop Corrigan changed his mind about the Cabrini Sisters—helped, it is said, by a "salty letter" from Bishop Scalabrini back in Italy.

As well as running the school and the orphanage, the Sisters started visiting the sick and feeding the hungry, and the warm-hearted Italians supported their own. The small shopkeepers in Little Italy gave them what they could spare—a cabbage, a string of garlic, a packet of sausage, a pumpkin—as they went about their concerns. Mother Cabrini's mission was to "our poor Italians, who are abandoned and very much looked down on by the English-speaking public." She was an Italian first, last, and always. Though she learned English, she never spoke it fluently. As the Italian immigrants became established in the city some of them became wealthy, and they had confidence in the Sisters who had come to America in poverty, as they had. Before long the Institute was offered a large house in upstate New

York as a base for its work. From that time on Mother Cabrini's life was devoted to reconciling requests for help and offers of assistance.

Early in 1892 she was invited to go to Nicaragua to found a school for the daughters of descendants of the Spanish conquerors. She went there with only one Nicaraguan girl as an interpreter, braving the steamy heat, the filthy river boats, and the tropical rainstorms. She founded a college for the daughters of the nobility, sending for fourteen Sisters from her training houses in Italy to staff it, but her main interest was in the Indians, who flocked to hear her preach the gospel. This was real evangelism, of the sort that she had hoped to carry out in China, but when she contracted yellow fever the Indians melted away very quickly. She often said, "I must go back, I must go back," but the demands on her time were such that it was never possible.

Before the end of 1892 she had recovered, and she went to New Orleans, where the Italian community was involved in an ugly incident. The chief of police was assassinated, and thirteen Italians were charged with the crime. The jail was attacked by a mob, and eleven of the prisoners were lynched, their bodies being hung from lamp posts. Only two escaped. In New Orleans, the Italians were called "Wops" and "white-skinned niggers," and as racial hatred rose, there was fear in the Negro-Italian quarter, where both minorities lived in poverty and squalor. Mother Cabrini went into the noise and the dirt and the heat. She rallied Italian support, bought a tenement building, and roofed the courtyard to make a school. Though she had little time for Anglo-Saxon Protestants, she did develop a respect for the Salvation Army. They were the only people, apart from her and her Sisters, who would go into the seedy bars and the dark alleys quite fearlessly, bringing some sort of order into the lives of the most helpless and the most degenerate.

She was invited to start foundations in other cities: Cincinnatti, Pittsburg, Buffalo, St Louis, Missouri, Denver, San Francisco. She set up schools and orphanages and workshops with unquenchable energy. In Seattle a site had to be cleared before the builder could start work. The Sisters did not know how to begin. Mother Cabrini took up a pick and showed them how to use it, saying, "A missionary must be able to do any kind of work."

A large fresco in the chapel of the former St Antony's Orphanage in Carney, New Jersey, commemorates a dream that gave a new direction to her work. There was an epidemic, and she was asked to start a hospital in New York. There had been a small Garibaldi Hospital for Italians, but its funds had been mismanaged, and the medical and nursing care had almost come to a standstill. At first she refused, saying that the Missionary Sisters of the Sacred Heart were teachers, not nurses, and already overburdened with work. In her dream, she saw the Blessed Virgin Mary helping the sick, and she was told that this was because she, Frances Cabrini, had refused to do the work on Mary's behalf. She started the hospital.

She and her Sisters began with no more than the building, the patients, a few mattresses, and some bottles of medicine. There was no gas, no running water, and no money. The Sisters had to go begging on the first afternoon, but help came. Money was given; gifts were donated; medical consultants offered their services. Before long there was an efficient hospital with a medical board. She named it the Columbus Hospital, because it was founded in 1892, four hundred years after the discovery of the New World. She wanted to remind the United States that Christopher Columbus was not Cristobal Colón, as the Hispanic population called him, but an Italian from Genoa named Cristofero Colombo. Other Columbus Hospitals developed in other great American cities.

All this work could not be undertaken without large numbers of trained Sisters, and one of the most remarkable aspects of Mother Cabrini's work is the way in which she kept in touch with her bases in Italy. In all, she made nine voyages back to Italy—organizing training programmes for her Sisters, explaining her work to the Catholic hierarchy, describing the needs of the immigrant Italians, and obtaining approval for her work.

She was asked to make foundations in Argentina and Brazil, where waves of Italian emigration had followed those to North America. On the way to Argentina she and her assistant, Mother Clara, stopped at Panama City. The Sisters who had staffed the college in Nicaragua had been driven out by a revolution, but they had transferred their work to Panama and ran a flourishing school. After four months in Panama City Mother Cabrini and Mother Clara sailed on in a banana boat to Valparaiso and then went through the Andes by train, over flimsy bridges slung across gorges, past towering mountain ranges. Careless of snow and cold and hunger and thin, rarefied air, Mother Cabrini brushed aside the fears of Mother Clara:

> Difficulties, difficulties! What are our difficulties, my daughter? They are childish fantasies, enlarged by the vividness of imaginations not yet accustomed to being enclosed and immersed in the omnipotent God. Dangers, dangers! What are dangers? These are phantoms that ambush the souls of those completely consecrated to God, or those imagining themselves so to be.

She set up a school in Buenos Aires—developing blisters on her hands and feet from sweeping out the premises herself. Then she toured Argentina, setting up new schools and orphanages, and went on to Brazil, where Cardinal Arcoverde, archbishop of Rio de Janeiro, had appealed to her: "Mother, I have a million souls to save. Come and help me!" But she was an

Italian; she did not even speak Spanish or Portuguese. She realized that if the work of her Institute was to become truly international, she had to have a broader training-base in Europe.

In 1896 she was in Italy, working with the training houses and involved in litigation over a bequest. She eventually won her case. Then she went to Paris, where she was asked to found a home for wealthy old ladies, who were apparently thought to be more respectable than orphans. She was offered a former palace, with wall-to-wall carpeting and mirrors everywhere. She accepted, and the Sisters draped curtains over the mirrors. One of the residents was a wealthy and powerful American dowager who supported her plea for an orphanage, so she got the orphanage as well. She made a foundation in London, and was fascinated by the Italian waiters—a new sort of Italian for her, courteous and sophisticated. Back in Rome in 1898 she had an audience with Pope Leo XIII, who told her to "hurry all over the earth if possible, in order to take the holy name of Jesus everywhere."

So she hurried over all the earth: to New York; to Chicago; to Spain, where she surprised the Queen Regent by refusing to allow two of her Sisters to be in attendance at court, saying firmly that they were "not of this world"; to the West Coast of America, where she was remembered standing in the hot sun wearing her habit and a Stetson, watching the builders at work; on by train to New Orleans, narrowly missing injury in a train hold-up. The Rule of the Missionary Sisters of the Sacred Heart was given definitive approval in 1907, when she was fifty-seven years old. By that time, there were foundations across the United States and across South America, and the movement in Europe had developed in France and Spain as well as Italy. There were sixty-seven houses on three continents, running schools, hospitals, college hostels, general hospitals, and foundling homes. Mother Cabrini determined to visit them all, and she did so. While she was in Argentina she founded a second college. There was a smallpox epidemic in Rio de Janeiro, and she nursed the sick Sisters herself.

Back in the United States she started a new enterprise: Sisters who would work in the prisons, helping the prisoners, including condemned prisoners on Death Row. They also helped prisoners' relatives and ran a rehabilitation programme for discharged prisoners. She visited Sing Sing and addressed the Italian prisoners in their own language as "*Mi buoni amici,*" my good friends.

In 1910 the second general chapter, held in Rome, made her superior general for life. She had not wished this honour, but she was told that it would be sheer foolishness for anyone else to take the tiller while the pilot was still in the boat. Many of her Sisters said that they would be prepared to offer the remainder of their own lives if she could stay alive. "What would be the good of the lot of you dying?" demanded their beloved Cabrini. "What should I do all alone? No, no. Live on, and do some work."

In 1916 she was at last able to take a six months' spiritual retreat. Her work was nearly completed. Just over a year later she was wrapping Christmas presents for the children of a church school in Chicago when she collapsed, and she died on the following day.

Mother Cabrini became a naturalized American in 1907—not because she had abandoned Italy but for a purely pragmatic reason: under federal corporation law, the many properties of her Institute were required to be in the hands of American citizens. She was canonized in 1946 by Pope Pius XII and formally proclaimed "the patroness of immigrants." She is known as the "first citizen saint" of the United States. She is commemorated in the Immigration Museum at the foot of the Statue of Liberty; on the bronze doors of St Patrick's Cathedral, New York; in the National Shrine of the Immaculate Conception in Washington, D. C.; and by a statue in St Peter's Basilica in the Vatican.

KATHARINE DREXEL

(1858-1955)

From a photograph.

KATHARINE DREXEL, founder of the Order of the Most Holy Sacrament, was a banker's daughter who inherited great wealth. The contrast between the life she inherited and the life she chose is striking, for she gave not only her money but her whole life and energy to the care of two neglected groups: American Indians and American coloured people. The sheer scale of her achievements is becoming apparent only with the development in the late twentieth century of a respect for human rights.

When Katharine was born, on 26 November 1858, her family had been in Philadelphia for two generations. Her grandfather, Francis Martin Drexel, was an Austrian portrait painter from the Tyrol who, like many other immigrants of his time, arrived in New York sea-sick and travelling steerage. He became a very successful businessman. At that time there were many local currencies in paper money, issued by banks. He set up a brokerage business, trading in these currencies. When the business prospered, he opened a bank, which became Drexel and Sons, and at the time of the Gold Rush he had a branch in California. In the American Civil War he provided gold for the Union government. The Drexels of Philadelphia were wealthy and respected, part of the American success story.

Katharine was the second child of Francis, son of Francis Martin Drexel. Her mother died at her birth. Two years later Francis married Emma Bouvier, daughter of a wealthy French family, who became a much-loved stepmother. There were three Drexel girls—Elizabeth, the eldest; Katharine; and Louise, daughter of the second marriage. The family was Catholic, and the girls had a very devout nurse, Johanna Ryan, who was to stay with them for forty years. The girls also had a governess and tutors to teach them Latin, French, and music.

A frequent visitor was Dr James O'Connor, pastor of St Dominic's church in Holmesburg, near their country house. Katharine heard him speaking about the plight of the American Indians and their need for education. Dr O'Connor had some forthright views: he told the Drexels that if the whites had respected their obligations under the Indian treaties and the agreements for Indian reservations, Custer's Last Stand would never have been necessary: the Indians had been repeatedly forced back out of their territories by the greed of the frontiersmen. Later, when he became vicar general of Nebraska, he wrote to the Drexels about the Benedictine Abbot Marty, who had gone to see Chief Sitting Bull, knowing that the chief had sworn to kill the first white man he saw. Abbot Marty survived and persuaded Sitting Bull to agree to a truce. Katharine's imagination was fired by such stories.

As a young girl she had to complete her education and take part in the social round of Philadelphia. She was fifteen when she made her first trip with her family to Europe, and she already showed a strong individuality in her likes and dislikes. She thought Westminster Abbey was "gloomy" and disapproved of the royal tombs. At the Tower of London she asked to see the cell in which Fr John Gerard had been imprisoned and was indignant to find that it was not open to the public. In the British Museum she saw Martin Luther's signature and thought it "a mean, scrawny bit of writing." In Florence she visited Elizabeth Barrett Browning's grave and thought about Savanarola. In Switzerland she went across Lake Geneva to Ferney with her stepmother to see Voltaire's château, and they wondered that he could have been "such an old cynic" when everything around him spoke of the power of God.

Back in Philadelphia the girls were kept busy. Katharine "came out" in 1878, and there were dresses to be chosen and fitted, balls to attend, relatives to be visited; but there were also more serious activities. Mrs Drexel ran a private social service agency and spent over $20,000 a year of her own money on grants and food parcels for the poor of the city. Elizabeth, Katharine, and Louise helped in this work, and during the summer they taught in a small school at St Michel, near their country home. It was an excellent training for the work that Katharine increasingly felt she was called to do.

Mrs Drexel died in 1883, and Francis took his daughters to Europe again. Katharine was greatly impressed by a visit to Siena, where she visited the home of her name-saint, *Catherine of Siena. When she returned to Philadelphia she told Dr O'Connor that she had a vocation and wanted to enter a contemplative Order. He counselled her to wait: she was still only twenty-five, and he thought her enthusiasms might change. In 1884 she made her first trip to the developing north-west of the United States: Drexel and Co. were considering investment in the new North Pacific Railroad, and Francis took his daughters on a long trip by private rail car.

In Montana they were nearly ambushed by a bandit gang determined to hold up the "rich bankers from the East" but managed to escape. Katharine must have seen Indian settlements from that rail car.

In 1885 Francis Drexel died in Philadelphia. The terms of his will were detailed and were to have a considerable effect on Katharine's benefactions later. His estate totalled the then enormous sum of over $15 million. This was to be held in trust for his three daughters, who were to receive the income in equal shares. When a daughter died the income was to go to the survivors or survivor. Their children, if any, were eventually to have the capital. If there were no children, the capital was to go to charities of the testator's specification. In the event, none of the three daughters had a live child, and Katharine lived longest. She eventually inherited all the income.

Fr O'Connor, now bishop of Nebraska, sent two mission priests to see Katharine: one was from Dakota and the other from the Indian Bureau in Washington, D.C. They told Katharine that the Canadians had solved the problem of the Indians by honouring their agreements with them and setting up guaranteed reservations for as long as they were needed. If the Indians in the United States were still killing white settlers, it was because the whites had not kept faith with them, and many more Indians had been massacred than whites. Katharine was much impressed by these arguments and by Helen Hunt Jackson's book *Ramona*, in which she read: "The Indian is perhaps a heathen, but he bows before a Great Spirit, he believes in immortality, is brave and fearless, and keeps his word until he is betrayed."

Katharine went to Europe again, with Elizabeth and their nurse Johanna. This time she had a definite purpose. She was received by Pope Leo XIII in private audience, and asked him what she should make her vocation. Pope Leo was well aware of the needs of the developing United States: only a few months later, he was to send *Frances Cabrini "not to the East, but to the West." His reply to Katharine's questions was, "Why not become a missionary yourself, my child?"

When she returned to the United States Katharine accepted an invitation from Bishop O'Connor to visit the missions in the north-west. Again she travelled by train. She awoke one morning in Dakota in a log cabin without window curtains to find a group of Sioux children, their noses pressed to the glass, gravely looking at the stranger. She visited a number of missions, some of which she was already supporting, went to Indian feasts, and watched war dances, which must have taken some courage. She met Chief Red Cloud, whose braves had wiped out a whole corps of the United States Army back in 1866, but who had since made a treaty of peace. She went on to Wisconsin, Minnesota, and Buffalo Bay on Lake Superior. By this time she knew her vocation.

Her sisters had both married, and they also had their good causes. Elizabeth had founded the St Francis Industrial School with the Christian Brothers, and Louise was supporting the Mill Hill Fathers' work with Americans of Afro-Caribbean descent. The three combined to found the Francis A. Drexel Chair of Moral Theology at the Catholic University of Washington. In 1888 Katharine entered the convent of the Sisters of Mary in Pittsburg to begin her religious training. Her intention, supported by Bishop O'Connor and Archbishop Ryan of Philadelphia, was to found a new Order, but she had to start by serving her noviciate in an established one. She described her structured day in letters to her sisters, and she behaved with such humility and diligence that the other novices did not know that she had a special vocation. She told her sisters that the hardest problem was learning to walk upstairs slowly. She was used to running.

At her clothing she kept her own name, signifying her devotion to Catherine of Siena. She worked in the Mercy Hospital, learning nursing care. Now that others knew of her intention to work with the Indians, postulants came with the intention of joining her Congregation. In February 1891 she took her vows, and by then she had twelve postulants.

Katharine wanted to start work in the West, but the archbishop and her superior held her back. Her Sisters were still young and untried, and although she made a trip to the Sioux in Wyoming and another to the Pueblos of New Mexico by train and stagecoach, she saw the importance of consolidating the Congregation before she made new foundations. In January 1895 she took her final vows. The Congregation was to be known as the Sisters of the Blessed Sacrament for Indians and Negroes. Though the life would be active rather than contemplative, it would focus on bringing the sacraments to these under-privileged peoples. The Rule was basically that of the Sisters of Mercy, with some borrowings from the Holy Ghost Fathers, who were also engaged in missions.

By this time demands were flooding in from all over the south and west of the United States. Katharine was giving money away freely for missions, for schools, for orphanages. In 1897 she was asked to compile a list of her donations before a Decree of Praise was issued from Rome for the Congregation: she was reluctant to do so, because she thought that Rome would think they were well financed: her list covered substantial donations to twenty-six different dioceses.

In 1900 she went to Arizona to visit the Navajos, a peaceful agrarian people who were known as "The Bedouin of the South-West." She paid all the costs for a Navajo mission. This visit involved a five-day rail journey: she no longer travelled in a private rail car but in a public coach, and she took a basket of food with her to save on the cost of meals. She had learned to travel as cheaply as possible, but she always tipped the porters well, saying, "These poor coloured men have to sit all night on hard seats, and often in the aisle, while we passengers sleep comfortably."

Katharine returned from her trip full of information about the Navajos—their striking looks, their artistic designs on blankets and rugs, their iron and silver work, the Spanish influence on their clothes—but when she went back to visit the mission building project a year later she found everything covered with dust and none of the work finished. She galvanized the contractors and got them working hard. She wanted to make a permanent endowment for the Navajos, but under the terms of her father's will this was not possible. She was already spending $50,000 a year on schools, and an endowment would cost more than $1 million.

1904 found her in Nashville, Tennessee, planning a school for Negro children. It was a city of strong racial prejudice and bigotry, where coloured children went to shanty schools and received poor teaching. Like the Indians, the coloured population knew that education was the means to a better way or life and welcomed all the help that she could give them.

In 1907 the Constitutions of her Congregation came up for revision. There was considerable delay in getting answers from Rome, and one day Katharine had a visit from a small, determined Italian woman who knew the problem. It was *Mother Cabrini. Her advice was that Katharine should go to Rome and conduct the negotiations herself. Things sometimes got overlooked in Rome unless one kept up the pressure. So Katharine sailed for Rome. There she called on cardinals with letters of introduction, had an audience with the pope—and waited. The preliminary work had been well done, however, and her reputation as a benefactor was well known in Rome. In a little over a month she received approval for her Constitutions for a probationary period of five years. Final approval came in 1913, when a reference to "Negroes" in the title of the Order was changed to "the coloured population," a wider and more acceptable term.

The Sisters of the Blessed Sacrament were being sent to missions all over the United States. There were calls to help the coloured communities in Columbus, Chicago, New York, and Boston. Mother Katharine tramped the streets herself, looking for suitable premises. There was a school in Atlantis, a house in St Louis, a mission in Cincinnati, a new convent in Harlem. Wherever she and her companions went they took a carpetbag containing sandwiches and fruit. Money was to be spent on those in real need, not on themselves.

Then came a call from New Orleans. The archbishop asked her to make a foundation, a high school or a training college for teachers, to provide higher education for coloured students. The old Southern University had moved to Baton Rouge, and its campus was for sale. It cost $18,000. Mother Katharine bought it, and it became Xavier Academy, now Xavier University, the first Catholic university in the American South for coloured students

Some years later Mother Katharine took a trip up the Mississippi on a paddle steamer, visiting all the rural schools she had helped to found in the delta, to see how they were progressing. The demand for education was tremendous, and much of it was being met by Xavier graduates. Katharine was prepared to do any kind of work and to face any kind of opposition. When she founded the Catholic Indian Bureau in Washington, D.C. she swept the floors and carried furniture herself. In Beaumont, Texas, she ran into opposition from the Klu Klux Klan: the Sisters went to Mass one morning to find a sheet of paper nailed to the church door. It read: "We want an end to services here. We will not stand by while white priests consort with nigger wenches in the face of our families. Suppress it in one week, or flogging and tar and feathers will follow." On the following day there was a threat to dynamite the church. The matter was resolved by what looked very much like divine intervention: during a Klan meeting there was a heavy thunderstorm. The most prominent Klansman was struck by lightning and killed.

Mother Katharine disliked public speaking but drove herself to it. She was years ahead of her time in opposing segregation, demanding educational opportunities for the coloured population, exposing biased reportage in the press. When she made a new foundation in South Dakota in 1922 she spent all her money, commenting, "Right now, I am $100 ahead." The foundation grew into a large establishment with a school, houses for teachers, a farm, a post office, and its own newspaper, but she needed more money. When a special Act of Congress was passed freeing from taxes the income of anyone who gave more than 90 percent to charity she was the main beneficiary, and the extra money went to her foundations.

By the end of the 1920s Mother Katharine was over seventy but still continuing to visit her missions and schools. By that time there were 190 teaching Sisters and eighty lay teachers in the schools. Teachers were properly trained and accredited. They were sent to regular classes at universities, and special lecturers came to them from New York and elsewhere. Xavier College acquired new premises in the coloured quarter of New Orleans and was renamed Xavier University. The cost of land, buildings, equipment, and a first-class sports stadium was over $650,000, but Katharine found the money, contributing much of it herself. She refused to mix with the celebrities at the opening ceremony but watched from a window in the science block. Pope Pius XI sent her a special commendation and a blessing.

At seventy-four she was working with the Navajos again, setting up a new mission and a dispensary in Arizona, moving on to Santa Fé and setting up a centre for Indian catechists in New Mexico. She was with the Sisters in Holbrook when they were told that the papal Secretary of State was landing at the local airport for refuelling. Cardinal Pacelli emerged from his aeroplane, astonished to find three nuns waiting for him in the middle of the desert. He blessed them and flew on his way. Later, as Pope Pius XII, he was to make a statement on human rights in his first encyclical, *Summa Pontificatus*: all human beings are children of God, sharing a supernatural fellowship in the Kingdom of Christ.

The journeys continued. Mother Katharine insisted on making a yearly visitation of all her foundations. She was seventy-six when she had a cerebral haemorrhage; she was advised to take life more easily, but she continued to deal with mounds of correspondence and to be consulted on all major projects. In 1937, when her term as superior general came to an end, she wanted to give up all authority, but her Sisters elected her vicar general, and named her *prima soror*—a fitting title for a foundress.

When her sister Louise died in 1945 the entire income from the Drexel trust came to Katharine, and she used it. Many new foundations were made— in California, Indiana, Louisiana, and other states in the south and west. By this time Katharine was confined to a wheel chair. The Holy Ghost Fathers came to her room to celebrate Mass daily. She prayed constantly for justice for the Indians and the coloured people she had served for so long, and she kept up her correspondence for many years. She was to live to the age of ninety-seven. In her last years she could only scrawl notes: "Lord Jesus, hear us"; "Mary, pray for us who have received Him"; and "The deeper the darkness. . . ." When she died her coffin was carried by six men: two Indian, two coloured, and two white. The *New York Times* wrote: "She gave her millions as cheerfully as she devoted her life."

Ironically, she had no money to bequeath. The capital of the Drexel Trust reverted to the causes that Francis Drexel had specified in 1885, and these did not include any of her many ventures, which had been set up after that date; but few people of either sex or any race can have left so great a legacy in human capital. She was beatified on 29 November 1988.

Appendix I
WOMEN IN MALE DRESS

IN THE ancient and medieval worlds a popular theme in accounts of saints was that of a woman who entered a monastery disguised as a man. These accounts, like those of courtesans, are often discounted or edited out by biographers. This may be because the early traditions are oral and not supported by contemporary documentary evidence, or because the subject is regarded as potentially scandalous. In earlier centuries, however, there were often circumstances in which a woman would find it advisable to dress as a man for purely practical reasons. It gave her the freedom to travel or live alone without fear of violence or sexual harassment. Such women were not transvestites, transsexuals, or male impersonators: their adoption of male attire was simply a matter of convenience and caution. The clothes of men and women were not very different: laymen wore long robes or tunics, monks wore habits, and both wore cloaks. The chief distinguishing marks of women were their long hair and their veils, and these were easily dispensed with.

In none of the stories of women who dressed as men is there any suggestion that the women themselves caused any kind of scandal. They lived austerely, often as solitaries or in the kind of monastic foundation where the monks came together only for meals and divine service. They kept their Rule. They died in the Faith. The fact that they concealed their gender (and were able to do so) suggests a considerable modesty and physical reticence in these communities. A woman who wished to live in a Christian community may not have been able to find a community of women she could join—the monastic movement for men developed well in advance of the corresponding movement for women. If a woman wished to live as a solitary, giving the impression that she was a man would have been an obvious precaution. Some at least of these women seem simply to have chosen a way of life in which their gender would not be a barrier to religious devotion.

Below are some of the stories about women who passed as monks that found a place in the Society of Bollandists' *Acta Sanctorum* in the second half of the seventeenth century. Feast-days are appended to distinguish these women from others of the same name with whom their stories may have been confused.

Euphrosyne (1 Jan.), otherwise Ephrosyna or Euphrasia, was the daughter of a pious and wealthy citizen of Alexandria named Paphnutius—possibly named after St Paphnutius the Great, who died in 350. Paphnutius betrothed his daughter to a young man of great wealth, but she refused to marry him. She tore off all her jewellery and gave it to the poor and ceased to wash her face, "even with cold water." She talked to an old monk who had prayed for her ever since her childhood and told him that her father was so determined on the marriage that he would seek her out and carry her off by force. While her father was away she changed into men's clothing and went to the monastery where her father sometimes observed a retreat. She told the abbot that her name was Smaragdus (Emerald) and was accepted. The appearance of the handsome Smaragdus so distracted the other monks that she moved to a solitary cell, where she remained in prayer for thirty-eight years. Pilgrims came to consult the holy Smaragdus: one of them was her own father. She gave him instruction but kept her face hidden from him, and he did not recognize her. She was in any case much changed by her austerities. When she was dying she revealed her identity. After her death her father retired from the world and was given permission to occupy her cell for ten years before his own death.

Marina (12 Feb.): this story is attributed to Antioch in Pisidia, Asia Minor, not to the better-known Antioch in Syria, some three hundred miles distant. A man named Eugenius decided to retire to a monastery after the death of his wife. Since there was no one to care for his young daughter Marina he took her with him, telling the abbot that she was a boy named Marinus. They both remained in the monastery until Marina was twenty-seven years old and Eugenius was dying. He told Marina to remain in the monastery and never to reveal that she was a woman.

Marinus was asked to collect goods for the monastery from the port. This involved staying overnight at an inn, and when the innkeeper's daughter became pregnant, she accused Marinus of being the father of her child. Rather than revealing her true gender, Marina accepted the accusation. She was dismissed from the monastery and lived at the gates as a beggar for five years, caring for the child. She was re-admitted to the monastery after five years and ordered to undergo severe penances. The mother of the child confessed when Marina was dying, and the monks realized the extent of her sacrifice. Then they fell to their knees, confessing that they had been harsh and cruel to the handmaid of God, and Marina was buried with honour in the monastery chapel.

Theodora of Alexandria (11 Sept.) is sometimes confused with another Theodora of Alexandria (28 April), a virgin martyr. The Theodora whose feast-day falls on 11 September was the wife of Gregory, prefect of Egypt. She was said to be deceived by a sorceress into committing adultery, and she fled, dressed as a man, to expiate her sin in a monastery in the Thebaïd. There she was accepted and lived a life of great austerity. On one occasion she was sent into Alexandria in charge of a camel train, and her husband recognized her, but she insisted on returning to the monastery, where she stayed for about eight years before her death.

Like Marina, Theodora was accused of being the father of a male child, who grew up in the monastery and is said eventually to have become the abbot. After she died, her husband came and stayed in her cell for two years.

Reparata of Caesarea (8 Oct.) is described in an ancient Life as a virgin martyr whose original name was Margaret. She may be the same as, or have been confused with, Margaret of Antioch (formerly 20 July), whose miraculous legends are now thought to be unreliable. The Reparata story is that of a girl forced into marriage, who ran away on her wedding night, disguised herself as a man, and entered a monastery under the name of Pelagius. She was accused of seducing a nun and bore her punishment without complaint. Her innocence was discovered only after her death.

Eugenia (25 Dec.), a virgin martyr of Rome, was buried in the cemetery of Apronian on the Via Latina. A basilica was later built in her honour and restored during the eighth century. As in the case of Reparata, a legend about a woman who passed as a monk has been grafted on to the original story. According to the legend, Eugenia was accepted in the monastery as "Eugenius." A woman named Melanthia, believing her to be a man, made advances to her and was "energetically repulsed." In revenge she charged Eugenius with sexual misconduct. The governor was appalled by what he thought to be the laxity of the monastic establishment, and all the monks were condemned to death. When Eugenia revealed that she was a woman the monastery was spared, and Melanthia was struck by a thunderbolt.

These stories come from different cities: Alexandria, Antioch in Pisidia, Caesarea, Rome. In all five cases a woman dresses as a man and enters a monastery for men. Four of the women are virgins: Theodora is a married woman. Four of them have good reasons for assuming a male identity: Euphrosyne and Reparata are escaping from forced marriages; Marina is taken to the monastery by her father and lives there by his direction; Theodora is escaping from an angry husband and seeking a place where she can do penance for her single act of adultery. Only in the story of Eugenia is no reason given for entering a male monastery, and since the story is attributed to Rome, where there were groups of holy women from the earliest Christian period, there would have been no reason for her to do so. This story is said to have oriental origins and looks very much like a graft from the Middle Eastern stories. The story of Reparata-Margaret similarly looks like a combination of borrowings from elsewhere, probably the result of fairly muddled discussions by weary travellers.

Euphrosyne, Marina, and Theodora are worth taking more seriously. All three maintain silence until their death. Euphrosyne's father and Theodora's husband come to occupy their cells, which suggests that they wanted to do penance for the behaviour that drove the women into the monasteries. It also suggests that the monks respected their sentiments and helped them to do so. There is no hint of scandal: only of a sober desire to make reparation for a sorry situation. In the case of Marina, like that of *Pelagia the Penitent, the monks do not discover the truth until the body is prepared for burial, and they are neither shocked nor horrified. They fall to their knees and pray; they are moved to tears; and the body is interred gently and with reverence.

Marina and Theodora are falsely accused of sexual intercourse with a woman, and this may well be the origin of similar themes in the stories of Eugenia and Reparata. Marina cares for the child personally; Theodora does not, but the boy remains in the monastery and grows up to become the abbot. The details of these two stories are very different. It is possible that such a false accusation was made at least twice—and then copied elsewhere. The borrowing may have been satisfying to male story-tellers. The thought that a woman could lead a man's life *and not be detected as different* would have been very disturbing. The ancient male world would not expect women to breach the gender barrier without dire consequences.

There is no evidence that the stories of Euphrosyne, Marina, and Theodora had a single origin or that they were borrowings from the story of Pelagia the Penitent. They are difficult to date; they are spread over the cities of the Middle East; and the saints' names, being common ones for the period, are easily confused; but behind them all is the shadowy, but probably genuine, experience of real women finding sanctuary in celibate male communities where they could escape from the problems of being feminine.

There is also the curious but well attested case of a twelfth-century woman, which suggests that the experience represented by the early stories was not unknown in the medieval world:

Hildegunda of Schönau (April 20) is said to have died in 1158. She has never been formally canonized, but this true of most of the saints of her period, and her name occurs in German martyrologies. A Life by the monk Philip Harveng, who died shortly after 1180, is said to be based on contemporary accounts, including Hildegunda's own. Caesarius of Heisterbach (1170-1240) wrote another Life, based on stories circulating about her in his day.

Hildegunda was born at Neuss on the Rhine, and her mother died when she and her twin sister were very young. Her father, left with the problem of caring for two young daughters, might have married again, but he determined to go to the Holy Land. He cut Hildegunda's hair short, dressed her as a boy, and took her with him to the Holy Land, giving her name as Joseph, and leaving her twin, Agnes, in the convent at Neuss. When they were in Jerusalem he died, and Hildegunda's clothes and money were stolen. She continued to pass as a boy for her own protection and was taken to the hostel of the Knights Templar. A relative found her there, and they started back for Germany, but the relative died on the way. By this time Hildegunda was a tall and handsome stripling, bronzed by the Eastern sun and "so attached was she to the freedom of this dress and the protection it afforded her that she still concealed her sex."

On reaching Cologne she was engaged as a servant boy by an old canon of the cathedral, and she gave thanks to God for "having protected her in cold and heat, from the violence of men and savage beasts, and kept her innocence in the midst of so many and great dangers." She accompanied the canon on a journey to Rome, but when they left Zusmarshausen they were separated, and she was accused of being a thief. She gave evidence against the real thief, and he was hanged, but in revenge his confederates captured her, thinking she was a young man, and strung her up on a tree next to the corpse before making their escape. Hildegunda had a vision and was rescued by a knight, still in the character of "Joseph." She went to Rome for a time with a pious elderly female recluse, then met an old knight who wanted to be a lay brother at Schönau and accompanied him. She was accepted without question at the monastery and lived among the brethren. According to Caesarius of Heisterbach, she was diligent and hardworking:

> reading, studying, day and night observing the discipline of the house exactly, and as it pleased God, making daily advances. And to tell the truth, in or out, Joseph conducted himself irreproachably, making himself liked by all for his amiability, not regarding his delicacy of constitution, but subjecting himself to hard labour, carrying stones and timber from the forest, fasting and watching, and conducting himself as a stout man rather than as a tender woman.

Tiring of the monastery, Hildegunda tried to go back to the old roving life. Twice she was physically restrained from doing so on the orders of the abbot, and once illness prevented her from leaving. Then she died. When they discovered that she was a woman, Caesarius tells us that not one of the monks could refrain from tears, and when the abbot recited the prayers for the dead, they could not find their voices to sing Amen. "Joseph" had often talked about his sister Agnes at Neuss. The monks at Schönau sent to Neuss and discovered that Agnes was dead; but it was remembered that her twin Hildegunda had gone to the Holy Land with her father, and had not been heard of since.

It is notable that Hildegunda was wise enough to choose elderly travelling companions, so that she could be free from sexual advances. The monks at Schönau clearly had no suspicion of her true identity, and she fulfilled all the requirements of the monastic life.

Appendix II

INVISIBLE WOMEN

THE WRITER of the preface to *A New Dictionary of Saints* (1993) comments that the people who have been canonized or beatified include "far more clergy and religious than lay people, and also far more bishops than priests and men than women":

> Canonization and beatification are exterior marks, "certificates" if the expression may be allowed, with which the Church honours certain individuals, a selection from among those many holy ones who contribute to its holiness. And in the making of that selection some purely natural factors come into play. Men, as opposed to women, have by their very gender greater opportunities of notable achievement and of the fame of their virtues becoming widespread in the world.

The "invisibility" of women in the past is a frequent theme of feminist literature. Often, it seems, they were not deliberately ignored: in a world dominated by male concepts and male values, they were simply not noticed.

We are accustomed to think of the apostles as lonely men, travelling single-handed to the cities of the Middle East to proclaim the gospel; but St Paul tells us quite clearly in 1 Corinthians 4-5 that he and Barnabas were the only ones among the apostles who did not have wives to accompany them on their travels. Children, if any, could have been left with the extended family, but the wives went with their husbands. Can we at least hope that the wives of the apostles were women who were worthy of them and shared their faith, not mere concessions to the flesh? St Philip the Deacon, we are told in Acts 21: 8-9, had four virgin daughters, who were prophets. They are all rated as saints in Eastern martyrologies; but we know nothing at all about their mother.

Here are some examples of other women of whom we know very little, though the men with whom they shared their lives have been publicly recognized:

Valeria and her husband Vitalis were martyred in Ravenna in the persecutions of Marcus Aurelius, about the year 171. According to the Roman

Martyrology, a physician named Ursicinius was about to be martyred, and his courage nearly failed. Vitalis "cried out to him to play the man." If injunctions of this kind were common, one wonders how women martyrs were expected to die. Both Ursicinius and Vitalis were martyred. After their deaths Valeria was also arrested and tried. When she refused to sacrifice to the Roman gods she was beaten to death. She and Vitalis are both recognized as saints, but he is commemorated by the magnificent basilica of San Vitale in Ravenna and named in the Ambrosian Mass. There appears to be no commemoration of Valeria, who showed equal courage with that of her husband, witnessed his death, and then followed him in martyrdom. Later, Vitalis was said to be the father of the mysterious SS Gervase and Protase, whose bodies were discovered by St Ambrose. No mention was made of their mother.

Teresia, the wife of Paulinus of Nola, was a wealthy and patrician Spanish lady. Paulinus, who died in 431, was the son of the Roman prefect in Gaul. We have no details of Teresia's ancestry. Between them, they owned large estates in Gaul, Spain, and Italy, and after some years during which Paulinus, who was an advocate, held public office, they retired to Teresia's Spanish estates near Barcelona. They had been childless for years and longed for a son and heir. When Teresia found that she was expecting a child it must have seemed like the beginning of a new life for them both, but the child lived only a week. They had become Christians: it is thought that Teresia was converted first and that she encouraged Paulinus to follow suit. They decided to live very simply and gave Teresia's Spanish wealth and property to the people of Barcelona. The result was that there was a popular clamour for Paulinus to become a priest, and he was ordained by the bishop in 393.

It seems clear that they shared their property and made their decisions together. They moved to Paulinus' estates in southern Italy, near Naples. There they gave more property to the people of the area, built a church and an aqueduct, and kept a small estate where they could give shelter to pilgrims, other travellers, and poor and sick people. Evidently they had both decided to become celibate recluses, for they each had a hermit's cell in the grounds, coming out of seclusion only to say their daily Office with their visitors. They spent more than twenty-five years in Nola following this way of life until about 409, when Paulinus was made bishop of Nola. St Augustine of Hippo wrote to Paulinus, praising Teresia "not as one leading her husband into luxury, but rather as leading him back to strength in his innermost being. We salute her also . . . because she is joined in close union with you, and is attached to you by spiritual bonds which are as strong as they are chaste."

The wife of Vulflagius: this story may have legendary elements, but the relics of St Vulflagius (d. 643) are still venerated at Montreuil-sur-mer in France, and the view of women that underlies the accounts was evidently acceptable to the Church in medieval France. Vulflagius, whom the Franks called Wulphy, was a layman who married an intelligent and pious girl. They were happy together and had three daughters. The people of Rue, near Abbeville, where they lived, thought their way of life so exemplary that they asked for Vulflagius to be ordained as their parish priest. The bishop of Amiens agreed but stipulated that the couple must live in continence. Secular priests were usually allowed to marry at this time, but celibacy was valued and encouraged. Vulflagius and his wife promised the bishop that, though they would continue to live together in the same house, they would be continent, but after years of happy married life they were accustomed to sleep together, and they broke their promise. Vulflagius was so horrified at his failure to remain celibate that he went on a pilgrimage of penitence to the Holy Land and, even on his return, insisted on living alone as a hermit. The three daughters also withdrew from the world and took monastic vows. There is no information at all on what happened to Vulflagius' pious and intelligent wife, and we do not even know her name.

The wife of "King Richard": Richard of Wessex is traditionally recognized as a saint, and is venerated as "King Richard" in Lucca, Italy, where he died in 720. His wife, Winna, was the sister of St Boniface, and they were the parents of three well-known saints: Willibald, bishop of Eichstätt; Winnibald, abbot of Heidenheim; and Walburga, abbess of Heidenheim, who followed her brother in ruling the double monastery. When Willibald was very young and thought likely to die from sickness, Richard and Winna took him to a great stone cross near their home and laid him at the foot of it, promising that they would offer his life to God if he recovered. After the children had grown up Richard set off on a pilgrimage to Jerusalem, taking Winnibald and Willibald with him, and he died at Lucca in Italy, where tradition says that he was king of England. Winnibald went on to the Holy Land, and on his return to Italy he was sent to join St Boniface in Germany. Willibald and Walburga subsequently joined him there, becoming successively abbot and abbess of the double monastery at Heidenheim. We have no further information about Winna, who was the sister of a saint, the wife of a saint, and the mother of three others.

Lady (Cecilia) Stonor: when Edmund Campion, saint and martyr, came from Rome with Fr Persons in the first wave of the English Mission in 1580, he published his celebrated *Decem Rationes*, a challenge to the Elizabethan Settlement, distributing four hundred copies in the university church of St Mary the Virgin, Oxford. The pamphlet was secretly printed at Stonor Park in Berkshire with the help of its owner, Lady Stonor. The printers came to the Hall "disguised as gentlemen" in order to keep the project secret from the people of the locality. Campion was arrested soon after and martyred at

Tyburn in 1581. Lady Stonor was arrested for her part in what was regarded as a conspiracy and died in prison. It is not known whether her cause has ever been put forward.

Mrs Swithin Wells: following a stricter enforcement of the laws against Catholics, seven men, known as the London Martyrs of 1591, were executed in London on 10 December of that year. They were St Edmund Gennings, St Polydore Plasden, St Swithin Wells, St Eustace White, Bd John Mason, Bd Sidney Hodgson, and Bd Brian Lacey. They were beatified in 1929, and the first four were canonized in 1970, to be numbered among the Forty English Martyrs.

The seven were arrested during a celebration of Mass at the house of Mr and Mrs Swithin Wells at Gray's Inn Fields. They were accused of high treason and subsequently executed. Mrs Wells was also arrested and stood trial with her husband. She was condemned to death but subsequently reprieved, and she spent eleven years in prison before she died there. Her cause has been promoted but has not been determined.

Appendix III
OUT OF THE CLOISTER

MARY
WARD
(1585-1644)

The earliest portrait, 1621.

In the I.B.M.V. convent in Augsburg.

THE CAUSE of Mary Ward, the founder of the Institute of the Blessed Virgin Mary, has not yet been approved, though Pope Pius XII referred to her at the World Congress of Catholic Action in 1956 as "Mary Ward, that woman beyond compare, given to the Church by England in its most sombre and blood-stained hour." More recently, Pope John Paul II is on record as saying on two occasions that he hoped that approval would come in his lifetime. She is included here for two reasons: she is the only major English foundress; and her life illuminates a central issue in the history of religious Orders for women: their freedom to undertake an active life of service as nurses, teachers, social workers, and missionaries. Monks have always had the choice between the active and the contemplative life, but enclosure was the rule for women. Mary Ward wanted a women's Order that would parallel the ministry of the Society of Jesus—teaching and preaching in the community and free of episcopal control.

She was well ahead of her time. Francis de Sales had proposed an Institute to be named The Daughters of St Martha some years earlier, but this had not developed, partly because of opposition from the hierarchy and partly because *Jane Frances de Chantal and her companions were drawn to the contemplative life. Vincent de Paul and *Louise de Marillac did not found the Daughters (later Sisters) of Charity until 1633, and even with Fr Vincent's support they were not a full Order: they were only permitted to take vows for a year at a time. Mary Ward, born in 1585, had a singularly clear vision of the teaching work that women might undertake for the Faith. In England, when she was growing up, Catholicism was proscribed, and priests on the English Mission were few in number, moving from one country house to another in danger of their lives. Though a priest was needed to celebrate Mass and dispense the sacraments, women, out of sheer necessity, were taking on much of the pastoral ministry that had been traditionally reserved to priests. They taught the children, prepared candidates for baptism and confirmation, made pastoral visits to the sick and dying, took non-liturgical services, and made everything ready for the Mass. Mary, who came of an old Catholic family in Yorkshire, knew nothing of Catholic bishops, for there had been none in England since Henry VIII's Act of Supremacy in 1534. Diocesan organization and discipline had ceased to exist in the time of her great-grandparents. She had no experience of the women's religious Orders, for they had ceased to operate in 1536, when the monasteries were dissolved. She had been brought up in a heroic tradition of loyalty to Rome and opposition to the civil power. Many priests had been executed on the Knavesmire at York, and *Margaret Clitherow had met her death in York Prison. Bd Francis Ingleby of Ripley Castle, a secular priest executed in 1586, was Mary's cousin. She was related to seven of the nine men implicated in the Gunpowder Plot of 1605, and her own father was arrested for complicity, though he was subsequently released.

In the year of the Gunpowder Plot, at the age of twenty, she went to the English College at Saint Omer to try her vocation. The priests she had met in their hurried and dangerous visits were Jesuit priests of the English Mission, such as Fr John Mush, who had been confessor to Margaret Clitherow, and Fr John Gerard. She hoped to be trained for the work she had already begun to do in teaching girls and women. It was probably not until she reached the English College at Saint Omer that she encountered the Jesuit attitude to women. The Society of Jesus was an Order for men. Its founder, St Ignatius of Loyola, had specifically stipulated that women were not to be admitted.

Mary had been taught by Jesuits and in the Jesuit tradition. All she understood was the ministry of the priests she knew—their devotion, their courage, and their freedom of action; but she found that women's Orders in Saint Omer, the Benedictines, the Augustinian Canonesses and the Poor Clares, were all enclosed. All that the Jesuits could suggest was that she should work as an outsister for the Poor Clares, begging food for the convent and alms for the poor, while the nuns remained shut away from the world. She did this for a year, eating coarse food such as black bread and herrings, washed down with black beer, and doing heavy work in the laundry. All the other outsisters were Walloon-speaking, and she could not communicate with them. She did not mind the hardships, but this work was not what she felt called to do, and she left at the end of her noviciate to find a more appropriate way of serving God.

Mary had all the assurance of an English gentlewoman abroad and, at this stage in her life, no shortage of money. She talked to the rector of the English College, to superiors of the religious Orders for both men and women, and to the bishop of the diocese about her plans. Bishop Blaes approved her proposal for a community on three conditions: the convent should be sited in a fortified town, for safety; the Sisters should not "quest or be mendicant"; and they should obey the bishop of the diocese. When he told her that she would need the permission of the archduke of the Netherlands, she went to court to ask the archduke herself. The archduchess Isabella was enthusiastic about her project and kept Mary at court for some weeks. She was to support Mary's work financially for many years, and from this time on Mary sought the support of secular rulers and their wives to establish her foundations. Catholic kingdoms were fighting for survival in the struggle against Protestantism, and the rulers and their wives understood, better than the Vatican, the importance of training the next generation of Catholic women.

Mary had a house built at Gravelines, a town with stout defences. She started with nine other Englishwomen, including her sister Frances, and five professed Poor Clare Sisters were sent from the Walloon convent at Saint Omer to train them. Again Mary came to the point of profession. She was a choir sister by this time, and she loved the peace and seclusion of the Rule; but on 2 May 1609 she had an overwhelming religious experience. She felt that, like Abraham, she was being called to leave what she knew and to go where she did not know. She said that the experience came with such force "that it annihilated and reduced me to nothing." After some months of counselling and discussion her confessor, Fr Roger Lee, S.J., advised her to go back to England to the work she knew and to prepare herself to do God's will. She made a vow of chastity to him and a vow that she would obey him if he ever directed her to enter an established Order.

Back in England Mary settled in London, in the prosperous quarter of St Clement's churchyard, near her friends and relatives. She wore fashionable clothes (as did the priests on the English Mission: it was a good disguise), but when she went to visit Catholics in prison she dressed like a domestic servant. She taught when she could and converted a dying woman to Catholicism. It was in London that she had what is known as "the Gloria Vision." She said afterwards that "something very supernatural befell me." She was given to understand that she was not to enter a closed Order, and her whole being was filled with the glory of God. "Some other thing was to be done by me, but what in particular was not shown."

She gathered round her a group of young women, who would become the core of her Institute. They were all related to one another, and they set out for Saint Omer to start a school for English girls. This was a new venture: there were schools for boys in both England and the Netherlands but not for girls. The "English Ladies," as they became known, had all had governesses. Mary bought a house in Saint Omer, and they all worked hard to become proficient in teaching. They taught the Catholic faith, Latin, reading, writing, needlework, music, and dancing. The main problem was that they had very limited finances. The Institute had no canonical standing, and the parents of postulants were reluctant to hand over their daughters' dowries to a project that might fail.

Bishop Blaes and Fr Lee pleaded with Mary to accept one of the four main Rules—Benedictine, Franciscan, Augustinian, or Carmelite Reformed. She merely replied that "they seemed not what God would have." Her Institute was to do the work women were doing in England. Its members were not to be outsisters or tertiaries; they were to be fully professed religious, working in society as men worked. In fact this kind of apostolate was not unknown on the Continent. There were many small foundations in France and the Netherlands that were not strictly enclosed and whose members taught and worked in their own locality. Bishops often allowed this without protest, and some encouraged the Sisters in their work. There were even a few houses for women under the Ignatian Rule, though not officially recognized by the Society of Jesus; but Mary wanted official recognition of women's right to work outside enclosure, and she wanted her Institute to be free of episcopal control, because it would work in many countries, not just in a single diocese. She was inspired by the idea of mission—even of going to convert the Turks, or to work in India.

Other women's Orders were trying to become free of enclosure at the same time, but the directive from Rome was explicit: women religious could work only in closed communities. This rule might be tacitly ignored outside Italy, but only in a particular diocese with the consent of the bishop. Mary must have had the problems explained to her, but her sense of vocation was unaffected. In 1612, when she was recovering from an illness, she had another "illumination." She wrote to Fr John Gerard, who was at the English College, that he must understand what she had been told "as it is writ, without changing one syllable." The message she received was *"Take the same of the Society. Father General will never permit it. Go to him."* The Society was the Society of Jesus. She was to work on the same lines. The Jesuit General would not allow it—indeed, he could not, under the Ignatian Rule—but nevertheless she was to make representations to him and to continue her work, whatever the opposition.

289

Bishop Blaes, Fr Gerard, and Fr Lee all laboured to draw up Constitutions that would satisfy Mary, but she would have none of them. She had received her instructions: "Take the same of the Society," and nothing else would do, impossible though it was. Fr Lee was gradually convinced that she was genuinely inspired and that she must follow her inspiration, but opposition to the work of the English Ladies was gathering in Saint Omer. They were known as "the Galloping Girls" because they would not live quietly in enclosure. In 1615 an anonymous paper accused them of "gadding about hither and thither" and enticing postulants away from other religious houses. They were being called "Jesuitesses," and the Jesuits—themselves under attack for their active engagement with society—were embarrassed. Fr Lee was forbidden to communicate with the English Ladies, and in the English College there were cries of *"regulario regularibus"*—send them all back to the cloister. Bishop Blaes wrote an open letter defending them, stressing their courage and the relevance of their work to the new situation, in which Protestantism was taking hold in so many parts of Europe. This was the time of the Thirty Years' War, when Lutheranism seemed to be sweeping across the western world. A new situation, Bishop Blaes argued, needed new structures. He commended the English Ladies and "their angelic way of life which has been suggested by the Holy Spirit for the evident advantage of the English Church and of the English convents." However, he was careful to commend them as a teaching Institute, not a religious Order.

Mary sent a petition to Pope Paul V in Rome. The pope instructed Bishop Blaes to care for "the said virgins," and promised that the Apostolic See would "deliberate." Meanwhile Mary visited Liège and decided to found a house for novices there, on land next to the Jesuits. Her old ally Fr John Gerard was there, and the Jesuits were trying to be helpful. Fr Gerard's finances were always complicated, and he had many mortgages, but he somehow secured the money, though Mary was to find herself heavily in debt later as a result. It was a time of much worry and some privation—her own funds were exhausted, and parents still would not pay their daughters' dowries.

Mary went back to England to see her six colleagues who were all "working secretly in Catholic houses." While she was there she was outraged to hear a Jesuit say, "They are but women." He went on to say that he "would not for a thousand of worlds be a woman, because they could not apprehend God." She said nothing at the time but afterwards wrote one of her most celebrated statements on the subject of women's rights:

There is no such difference between men and women that women may not do great things. And I hope in time to come it will be seen that women will do much. What think you of this word, "but women"? But as if we were in all things inferior to some other creature which I suppose to be man!

On a later visit to London, to collect money owing to the Institute, she was arrested and brought before the magistrates at the London Guildhall. One of them insulted the Virgin Mary, and she exploded from the dock, "What! a miserable man . . . to blaspheme and revile the most holy and divine Mother, the Queen and Lady of all creatures!" She was sentenced to death but freed "by her friends paying down money," whether as fines or bribes, and went back to Liège, where she went into retreat, meditating on the kingdom of Christ and renewing her devotion to God's will.

The financial situation grew worse. There was a time when the English Ladies in Saint Omer were forced to stay indoors because the bailiffs were likely to arrest them in the street. In Liège they faced huge debts and went hungry. Mary told Cardinal Bandini that they could not survive unless they received "the means for the most urgent necessities of life"; yet she founded two more houses at Cologne and Trier, hopeful that Pope Paul V would at last approve her plans. When he died in 1621 she went to Rome, realizing that she must start again with his successor, the elderly Gregory XV. Mary always believed in hitting a problem head on.

Incredibly, she and her small party walked to Rome, with two packhorses for their baggage, setting out on 21 October 1621 and crossing the Alps in winter. They covered thirty miles a day, ignoring, cold, snow, the threat of robbers, and the devastation and risks of war. They started early each day, so that they could reach the gates of a city before they closed at sunset, and they came down through Milan, Parma, Modena, and Loreto to reach Rome as the bells rang out on Christmas Day. Mary went to St Peter's to venerate the tomb of Peter, and to the Gesù, the Jesuit church, to pray for two hours at the tomb of St Ignatius. Then, wasting no time, she arranged an audience with the pope, which took place on Holy Innocents' Day, 28 December. Gregory XV was fatherly and benign, and he promised that the work of the Institute would be "immediately taken into consideration."

Mary can have had no idea of the slow processes of decision-making in the Vatican. Eleven days later she expressed surprise that a decision had not yet been reached. Nor did she realize the enormity, from the Italian point of view, of what she was asking. Both Pope Gregory and the Jesuit Father General had received complaints about the extraordinary behaviour of the English Ladies: they preached in church, when St Paul had said clearly that women should be silent; they went about in "various costumes," creating scandal; they wandered hither and thither, unchaperoned; they were altogether uncontrollable; and their finances were in a parlous state.

291

Mary thought she had only to convince God's vice regent on earth that her plans were God's will, and he would approve them. She understood nothing of the complexities of Vatican organization and Vatican politics. When she realized that she must lobby supporters she stayed in Rome, writing endless letters and memoranda, visiting anyone who might back her cause, besieging cardinal after cardinal. A malicious observer said, "Everybody is laughing at her," but if she knew she took no notice. She asked the Curia for permission to start a school for girls in Rome—and opened the school before she got it. Eight of the English Ladies from the Netherlands came to staff the school.

Early in 1623 she was still waiting for the pope's approval of her plans. She had had a year of disappointments and humiliation. She worked hard to set up the school in Rome, and there were plenty of poor girls who wanted to be pupils; but the rich sent their daughters to established convents, and the English Ladies did not receive the fees they had hoped for. They were practically destitute, begging for alms. Desperate, Mary decided to go to Naples, which was a Spanish kingdom. Again the party walked—this time without even packhorses to carry their baggage. Italy was in turmoil, and there was famine and plague in the cities they passed through. Mary suffered acutely from gallstones, often lying on straw in a barn or at the side of the road until the attack passed. When they arrived in Naples a preacher appealed for help for them, and the Neapolitans were generous. When the school was established Mary returned to Rome. Pope Gregory had died, and the new pontiff was Cardinal Matthew Barberini, who took the title of Urban VIII.

Her first attempts to see Pope Urban were unsuccessful. When she finally secured an audience at Frascati, all the frustrations came out. She told him point-blank that her Institute had already been "confirmed in heaven"; that those who had been charged to deliberate its status had been "adverse" and had misunderstood; and that he should "recommend the matter to God, for to God and his Holiness did we wholly commit it." She gave him yet another document, "a long memorial." Pope Urban was benign but offered nothing. The complaints were multiplying—"foul memorials full of horrible lies," Mary called them on one occasion. Though she did not realize it, the movement had already been set in train to have the Institute suppressed.

Mary was told bluntly by Cardinal Millini that the pope would not approve her Institute, that the houses in Italy would be shut, and that the English Ladies would have to go home. On 11 April 1625 a decree from the Congregation of Bishops and Regulars (which must have had the pope's approval) informed the Italian bishops that the English Ladies were forbidden to live together, to wear a uniform, or to teach in schools. Mary received no official notice of the decree. The Vatican did not deal with women. She only heard rumours and saw her school in Rome and a new one in Perugia closed, the members of her Institute dispersed. In November the landlord of their house in Rome was given three days to evict them, and they were informed that if they did not leave the building they would go to prison. The Naples foundation held out for two or three years, but eventually that also closed. Mary spent much time praying at the tombs of the saints, asking for the strength to bear suffering and defeat, resolving to love her enemies. At length, she was given permission to found houses (though only for teaching purposes, not those of a religious Order), "in Germany and other lands beyond the Alps." It was at least understood in Rome that in these far northern places, women were accustomed to "gad about," to speak to men as equals, and to practise other freedoms unthinkable in Italy.

Mary and her party walked to Munich, where the Elector Maximilian was prepared to welcome them. They arrived on 7 January 1627 and were treated well. They were given a property, and it was furnished for them. The Electress Elizabeth befriended them and gave them twenty thousand florins for their work. Fr John Gerard, with whom Mary was still corresponding regularly, wrote: "God Almighty reward that worthy duke and duchess for their charity." He advised Mary to consolidate her work and not to attempt any more foundations. Those at Liège and Saint Omer were collapsing, the older members dying, the younger ones leaving, and the debts rising; but Mary saw a great need and a great opportunity. She heard that, after a victory in Bohemia, the Emperor Ferdinand was restoring Catholicism in his territories, so she went to Vienna and asked for his support. Ferdinand approved her project and gave her a choice of two houses in the city. Her school opened in September 1627.

At first all went well, with 425 pupils enrolled. Another school was opened at Pressburg (now Bratislava), and one was planned in Prague, but Fr Gerard's warnings proved correct: the Institute did not have the resources for expansion. The school was badly understaffed, and the English Ladies were largely untrained. Most of them did not even speak German. Further, reassured by the emperor's support, Mary had made a fatal mistake in not seeking the approval of the bishop of Vienna. Perhaps she avoided this because she knew that Bishop Kleisl had earlier been exiled by the emperor— and had spent his exile in Rome, where he would have heard a good deal about the activities of the English Ladies. When he complained to the pope the German venture was doomed.

Mary went to see the papal nuncio, who made it clear that he wanted the English Ladies out of Austria. At one point he threatened her with excommunication, but Mary merely brushed the threat aside, saying that excommunication would not be valid. "Now," he wrote afterwards, "I fear her more than ever, for it seems to me that she is more than woman, and she is reputed to be more than man." Letters flew from place to place: the English Ladies were accused of light living and gossiping, of inventing miracles and revelations, of stealing dowries. Mary went back to Rome, struggling through war-torn Europe. She saw Pope Urban, who was still benign and said that the matter would be examined. She stayed fourteen months, while the houses at Saint Omer and Naples and in Flanders all closed. Then she went back to Munich, still trusting in the pope, still writing letters telling him that God had given her "assurance that this Institute shall remain in the Church of God until the end of the world."

In January 1631 the papal Bull *Pastoralis Romani Pontificus* decreed that the Institute was to be "suppressed, extinct, uprooted and abolished." In February Mary was arrested as "a heretic, schismatic and rebel to the Holy Church" and placed under lock and key in the Anger convent of the Order of St Clare. She was not allowed to take leave of her community, but before she left she turned to them and said: "Mortification and suffering are best when most complete." She was denied the sacraments for seven weeks and near death when she was released after ten, on the personal order of the pope. Some other members of the Institute were imprisoned, and all were forced to leave without resources, though the elector provided for those in Munich for a time. In October 1631 Mary went back to Rome to see Pope Urban. The pope clearly felt that the authorities had over-reacted, for he treated her kindly, agreed that she was not a heretic, and told her that she must "exercise the endurance of the servants of God." These trials, he told her, were a way of proving her calling. Twenty-three other faithful members of the Institute found their way to Rome, and they were allowed to live as a community. Pilgrims flocked to see them, and when the pope was told, he said, "I am very glad to hear it." He gave Mary a pension, put one of his coaches at her disposal, and sent his own doctor to see her when she was ill.

At last, in September 1637, she decided to go back to England. This time she had to travel by litter and coach because of her poor health. On the way she visited the graves of her friends at Liège and witnessed the final destruction of her work in the Netherlands, but when she arrived in London, on 20 May 1639, she was courageously prepared to start all over again. She had letters of introduction to King Charles I's Catholic queen, Henrietta Maria. She met many influential people and began plans for a new school, but it was too late. Charles I was already locked in conflict with Parliament, and in 1642 the Civil War broke out. The king was captured and eventually executed. The queen escaped to the Netherlands. Mary had to leave London and go back to Yorkshire. In 1644, when York was besieged by twenty thousand of General Fairfax's Roundheads, she had to move into the city;

when the siege was over she settled at Hewarth Manor, only a mile from the walls.

Mary told her companions: "I have much to do, do not beg our Lord to take me," but she was very ill. When they knew she was dying she rallied them: "Fye, fye, still look sad on it! Come, let us rather sing and praise God joyfully for his infinite loving-kindness." So she departed, calling on the name of Jesus. Mary was buried in St Thomas's church, Osbaldwick, near Hewarth. Her tombstone is still in the church, though Mother Mary Salome records that in a letter from York, written in 1727, a member of the Institute recorded that the grave was opened "many years ago," and nothing was found in it but the engraving of her name. Her Institute survived: in 1685 a benefactor gave the superior the sum of £450 to buy a house and garden in York for the community, and the Bar Convent stands today on the same site. A house in Hammersmith was supported by James II's Catholic queen, Mary of Modena. In 1703 Pope Clement IX approved the Rule but not the Institute, since there was still strong opposition in the Vatican both to the concept of an unenclosed Order of women, and to the proposal that they should be free of diocesan control. In the aftermath of the French Revolution *Madeleine Sophie Barat lived to see her Order established in nine countries but faced episcopal opposition, and even in the second half of the nineteenth century, *Anne Javouhey and *Mary MacKillop endured bitter and acrimonious disputes with bishops.

Full papal approval was not given to the Institute of the Blessed Virgin Mary until 1877, though the Institute and its schools had become highly respected in many countries. Mary Ward's battles were not over even then. Her challenge to the hierarchy's view of women was still remembered in Rome, and she was not officially declared to be the foundress until 1909. In 1978—333 years after Mary's death—the Society of Jesus at last granted the Jesuit Constitution to the Order, welcoming the Sisters as fellow workers. Today the Institute of the Blessed Virgin Mary is what Mary Ward's "illumination" led her to work for. She attempted the seemingly impossible. She suffered humiliation and apparent defeat in her lifetime, but the strength and clarity of her vision in the end moved mountains.

Alphabetical Index

Chronological Index

by date of death

References

General texts: abbreviations as listed are used in the individual references that follow.

A.A.S.	*Acta Apostolicae Sedis, Commentarium officiale*, Rome, 1908 - .
AA.SS.	*Acta Sanctorum*, 64 vols., Rome, Paris, and Antwerp, 1643 - .
Anal.Boll.	*Analecta Bollandiana*, Brussels, 1882 - .
Bibl.SS.	*Bibliotheca Sanctorum*, 12 vols., Rome, 1960-70; Suppl. 1, 1987.
Butler	*Butler's Lives of the Saints*, new full edition 12 vols., 1995-9.
D.A.C.L.	F. Cabrol and H. Leclercq, eds., *Dictionnaire d'archéologie chrétienne et de liturgie*, Paris, 1907-36.
D.C.B.	W. Smith and H. Wace (eds.), *Dictionary of Christian Biography*, 4 vols., London, 1877-87.
Delehaye	H. Delehaye, *Légendes hagiographiques*, Paris, 1905, trans. and ed. D. Attwater, *Legends of the Saints*, 1962.
D.H.G.E.	A. Baudrillart *et al.*, eds., *Dictionnaire d'histoire et de géographie écclésiastique*, Paris, 1907-36.
Dict.Sp.	M. Viller *et al.*, eds., *Dictionnaire de spiritualité*, 2 vols., Paris, 1937.
Distant Echoes	J. A. Nichols and L. T. Shank, eds., *Distant Echoes: Mediaeval Religious Women*, 1984.
D.N.B.	*Dictionary of National Biography*, ed. Leslie Stephen *et al*, 1885-.
D.T.C.	A. Vacant, A. Mangenot, and E.Amann, eds., *Dictionnaire de théologie catholique*, 15 vols., Paris, 1903-50.
Golden Legend	Jacobus de Voragine, *The Golden Legend*, trans. W. G. Ryan. Princeton ed., 2 vols., 1993.
H.E.	*Historia Ecclesiastica*, denoted by the name of the chronicler, e.g. Bede, *H.E.*
Hutton	Hutton, Olwen, *The Prospect before Her: the History of Women in Western Europe, 1600-1800*, 1996.
Lib.Pont	*Liber Pontificalis*, ed. L. Duchesne, 1886.
N.C.E.	*New Catholic Encyclopaedia*, 15 vols., New York, 1967.
N.P.N.F.	P. Schaff and H. Wace, eds., The Nicene and Post-Nicene Fathers, 1887-1900, 2d series reprint, 1979.
P. B.	F. Guérin, ed., Vie des saints des Petits Bollandistes, 17 vols., Paris, 1880.
Petersen	Joan Petersen, trans. and ed., *Handmaids of the Lord: Holy Women in Antiquity and the Middle Ages*, 1996.
P.G.	J. P. Migne, ed., *Patrologia Graeca*, 162 vols., Paris, 1857- 60.
P.L.	J. P. Migne, ed., *Patrologia Latina*, 221 vols., Paris, 1844-64.

Introductions to chapters:

Visionaries: Dionysius, *The Divine Names and Mystical Theology,* trans. and ed. John D. Jones (1980); *The Cloud of Unknowing,* trans. and ed. Clifford Wolters (1961); *Julian of Norwich: the Revelations of Divine Love,* trans. and ed. Grace Warrack (1901, 2d ed. 1907); *Teresa of Avila, the Interior Castle,* trans. and ed. Halcyon Backhouse (1988); *The Complete Works of St John of the Cross,* trans. and ed. E. Allison Peers (1951); *The Revelations of Mechtild of Magdeburg,* or, *The Flowing Light of the Godhead,* trans. and ed. Lucy Menzies (1953); F. von Hügel, *The Mystical Element in Religion as studied in St Catherine of Genoa and her Friends* (1908, rp. 1952); Thomas Merton, *The Ascent to Truth* (1951, rp. 1994); *N.C.E.* 10, Fr T. Corbishley on "Mysticism," pp. 175-9, and Fr J. Aumann on "Mystical Phenomena," pp. 171-4.

Martyrs: Ambrose, De *Virginibus* 1, 5, 10, N.P.N.F., 10, pp. 361-90; Jerome, *Letter 22 to Eustochium,* N.P.N.F., 6, pp. 22-41; Chris Jones, "Women, Death and the Law" in *Martyrs and Martyrologies,* ed. Diana Wood (1993), Studies in Church History no. 30; Aldhelm, *De Virginitate* in *Aldhelm:The Prose Works,* ed. M. Lapidge and M. Herren (1979), p. 112; Eusebius, *H.E.*, 5, N.P.N.F., 1, pp. 211-20; Palladius, *Historia Lausiaca,* trans. and ed. Cuthbert Butler (1904), bk. 3.

Collaborators: Encyclicals of Pope Pius XII, *A.A.S.* 37 (1948) 285-98; *A.A.S.* 48 (1956) 782; *The Destiny of Modern Woman in the Light of Papal Teaching,* ed. W. B. Faherty, (1950); *The Woman in the Modern World,* ed. E. Firkel, Eng. trans. H. C. Graef, (1959). Addresses of Pope Pius XII, "Women's Duties in Social and Political Life," address to Catholic women's organizations (1945), C.T.S. pamphlet, London; "Woman's Place in the World," address to the women of Rome (1946), C.T.S. pamphlet, Dublin. See also L. F. Cervantes, "Woman," *N.C.E.*, 10, pp. 991-7; W. B. Faherty, "Woman (Catholic Teaching on)," *N.C.E.*, 10, pp. 998-1000; P. Schine Gold, "Male/Female Collaboration: the example of Fontrevault," *Distant Echoes,* pp. 151-68.

Wives and Mothers: Ambrose, *De Virginibus,* 1, 5, 10, N.P.N.F., 10, pp. 361-90; Jerome, *Letter 22 to Eustochium,* N.P.N.F., 6, pp. 22-41; Thierry Lelièvre, *100 nouveaux saints et bienheureux de 1963 à 1984* (1985), pp. 12-16; Hutton, chs. 1-5, pp. 25-216.

Penitents: Delehaye, pp. 3-9, 49-65, 86-92, 150-5. John Chrysostom, *Homiliae in Matthaeum,* trans. and ed. F. Field (3 vols., 1839), 67; Hutton, ch.8, pp.299-31; E. H. Peters and T. R. Heath, "Eve," *N.C.E.*, 5, pp. 655-9.

Outcasts: E. Goffman, *Stigma: Notes on the Management of Spoiled Identity* (1963); P. Hunt, *Stigma: the Experience of Disability* (1966); M. Blaxter, *The Meaning of Disability* (1976); E. Gerhardt and M. E. Wadsworth, *Stress and*

Disability (1985): C. Barnes, G. Mercer and T. Shakespeare, *An Introduction to the Study of Disability* (1996); I. Brownlie, *Human Rights* (1981), pp. 106-112.

Innovators: J. Adair, *The Skills of Leadership* (1984); C. Handy, *Understanding Organizations* (1985, rp. 1993); M. A. Chemers and R. Aman, *Leadership Theory and Research* (1993).

Missionaries: G. Goyau, *La femme dans les missions* (1946).

Individual saints

AGNES: Jerome, *Letter 22 to Eustochium*, N.P.N.F., 6, pp. 22-41; Ambrose, *Sermon 48, P.L.*, 17, 701-6; Ambrose, *De Virginibus*, 1, 2, N.P.N.F., 10; Prudentius, *Peristephanon* 14; *AA.SS.*, Jan., 2, pp. 714-28; *Lib. Pont.* 1, 196; *Golden Legend*, 1, pp. 101-4; *D.A.C.L.* 1, 905-18, contains a summary of Agnes's Life. Cols. 918-65 provide detailed archaeological evidence, with illustrations; *D.H.G.E.* 1, 909-10; Lucy Menzies, *The Saints in Italy* (1924), pp. 4-5; F. Jubaru, *Sainte Agnès de la Voie Nomentane d'après les nouvelles recherches* (1907); *Sainte Agnès vierge et martyre* (1909); A. J. Denomy, *The Old French Lives of St Agnes* (1938); Life: L. André-Delastre, trans. R. Sheed (1963).

ANNA MARIA TAIGI: There are many Lives, of which Mgr C. Salotti's *La vénérable servante de Dieu, Anna-Maria Taigi* (1865, rp. 1922) is the fullest. Others, in English, are G. Bouffier (1865); E. Healy Thompson (1873); A. Bessières, S.J., trans. S. Rigby, *Wife, Mother and Mystic* (1952). A Life was published by Burns & Oates in 1874, with no details of authorship. See also *D.H.G.E.*, 3, 355; *Bibl.SS.*, 11, 99-101; *A.A.S.*, 12 (1920), pp. 240-5; *Anal.Boll.* 55 (1935), pp. 195-6; 56 (1936), pp. 229-30).

ANNE JAVOUHEY: Lives in French include V. Caillard (1909); F. Delaplace (1914); G. Goyau (1934); G. Bernoville (1942); and in English, C. C. Martindale, S. J. (1953); G. D. Kittler, *The Woman God Loved* (1958). There is an English version of the anonymous Life from the Congregation of St Joseph of Cluny, trans. J. B. Cullen (1912), but this has notable omissions relating to the conflicts with the Sisters in Réunion and the bishop of Autun. See also *Anal.Boll.* 30 (1909), pp. 132-3; 33 (1915), pp. 373-4; 70 (1936), p. 370.

ANUARITE NENGAPETA: *Osservatore Romano*, 9 Sept. 1985; James Fanning, *Clementine Anuarite* (1986); Thierry Lelièvre, *100 nouveaux saints et bienheureux de 1963 à 1984* (1985), pp. 73-5.

BARBE ACARIE: André Duval, *La vie admirable de Soeur Marie de l'Incarnation*, was published only three years after her death (1621). See also Fr Bruno de Jésus-Marie, *La Belle Acarie* (1942); L. C. Sheppard, *Barbe Acarie, Wife* *and Mystic* (1953); H. Brémond, *Histoire littéraire du sentiment religieux en France*, vol. 2, *L'Invasion mystique* (1930), ch. 4, pp. 193-262, and vol. 6, *La conquête mystique* (1929), pt 1, pp. 3-226. Eng. trans. K. L. Montgomery, *The Coming of Mysticism* (1930) and *The Triumph of Mysticism* (1936); *N.C.E.*, 3, p. 122; 9, p. 219; 13, p. 597; Two short popular works are Emily Bowles, *A Gracious Life* (1879), and E. de Broglie, *La Bienheureuse Marie de l'Incarnation, Madame Acarie* (1903).

CATHERINE OF GENOA: The *Libra de la vita miracle e dottrina santa de la beata Caterinetta da Genoa* (commonly referred to as the *Vita e Dottrina*) ed. Cattaneo Marabotto and Ettore Vernuzza (1551). A French translation (1616) was reprinted in 1960. Umile Bonzi da Genova, in *S. Caterina Fieschi Adorno* (1961-2) summarizes arguments that Catherine's own writings are difficult to distinguish from the comments. Lives by P. Garvin (1874); J. Sertorius (1939); L. de Lapérouse (1948). F. von Hügel, *The Mystical Element of Religion as studied in St Catherine of Genoa and her Friends* (1908, rp. 1952). See also *AA.SS.*, Sept., 5, pp. 123-95; *Dict.Spir.* 2, pp. 290-324; *D.H.G.E.*, 11, 1506-15; *Summa Theologica* III, supplem. quaest. 6.3. Writings: *Treatise on Purgatory and the Dialogue*, trans. and ed. C. Balfour and H. D. Irvine (1946); *Catherine of Genoa: Purgation and Purgatory, The Spiritual Dialogue*, trans. and ed. Serge Hughes, intro. Benedict J. Groeschel (1979).

CATHERINE OF SIENA: The most important primary materials for Catherine's Life are the *Leggenda Major* of Raymond di Capua, the *Supplementum* and the *Leggenda Minor* of Thomas Caffarini, and the documents for her canonization in 1461, together with her letters. The letters present many difficulties of transcription and dating. Lives: Raymond di Capua, trans. G. Lamb (1960); E. G. Gardner (1950); A. Levasti, *My Servant Catherine*, trans. D. M. White (1954); J. Jorgensen, trans. I. Lund (1938); A. Curtayne (1929, 2d ed 1935); G. Cavallini (1999). The radical criticisms of R. Fawtier, *Ste Catherine de Siene et la critique des sources* (2 vols., 1921-30) have been examined by E. Jordan in *Anal.Boll.* 40 (1922), pp. 365-411, and in the appendix to Alice Curtayne's Life. Works: *The Dialogue*, trans. and intro. Suzanne Noltke (1980). *Saint Catherine of Siena as seen in her Letters*, trans. and ed. V. D. Scudder (1905).

CLARE OF ASSISI: The Life by Thomas of Celano is in *AA.SS.*, Aug., 2, pp. 754-67. Eng. trans. by Paschal Robinson (1910, revised ed. 1953) from the edition of P. Pennacchi, and C. Balfour (1910) from the sixteenth-century French edition by Bro Francis Du Puis. The latter includes four letters from Clare to Agnes of Bohemia. Modern Lives by E. Gilliat Smith (1914); M. Fassbinder (1934); R. M. Pierazzi (1937); N. de Robeck, (1951); P. Casolini (1953); Ingrid Peterson (1993); R. Brooke and C. N. L. Brooke in D. Baker (ed.) *Mediaeval Women* (1978), pp. 273-88. See also *Archivium Franciscanum Historicum* 13 (1920), pp. 403-57; R. W. Chambers and W. W. Seaton, *The Rewle of Sustris Menoresses Enclosid*,

E.E.T.S. 148 (1914, rp. 1962); J. R. H. Moorman, *The Franciscan Order from its Origins to the Year 1517* (1968), pp. 211-5, 274 ff.; *Bibl. SS.*, 3, 1201-17.

EDITH STEIN: Life by Teresa Renata de Spiritu Sanctu Posselt, trans. C. Hastings and D. Nicholl (1952). This biography, written by Benedicta's novice-mistress and later prioress, is the basic text, together with Fr Erich Przywara's "Edith Stein zu ihrem zehnten Todestag," *Die Besinnung* (1952), pp. 238 ff. H. C. Graef, *The Scholar and the Cross* (1955), draws on both and also on a number of other sources such as letters and interviews with Edith Stein's friends and colleagues. There is another biography in English by Waltrud Herbstrith (1971). *N.C.E.*, 12, pp. 686-7, contains a short summary by H. C. Graef. Works, ed. L. Gelber and R. Leuven: vol. 1, *Kreuzeswissenschaft*; vol. 2, *Endlich und Ewiges Sein*; vol. 3, *Des hl. Thomas von Aquino Untersuchungen über die Wahrheit* (1950-); Suzanne H. Batsdorff, *Edith Stein: Selected Writings, by her niece* (1990).

ELIZABETH ANN SETON: Lives by A. M. Melville (1960); J. I. Dirwin (1962); J. F. Hindman (1976); E. M. Stone (1993). For a broader view, see H. de Barbéry, *Elizabeth Seton et les commencements de l'Église Catholique aux États-Unis* (1868). Original letters and papers are preserved at St Joseph's Central House, Emmitsburg, Pennsylvania, with copies at the Catholic University of America, Washington, D.C., and the archives of the archdiocese of Baltimore. For writings, see J. B. Code (ed.), *Letters of Mother Seton to Mrs Juliana Scott* (2d ed. 1969); E. Kelly and A. Melville (eds.) *Elizabeth Seton: Selected Writings* (1987); *Memoirs, Letters and Journals of Elizabeth Seton*, ed. R. Seton (1869).

EUDOXIA: *AA.SS.*, Mar., 1, pp. 875-83; *P. B.*, 2, p. 151; S. Baring Gould, *Lives of the Saints*, March (1872, rp. 1907), pp. 2-8.

EUSTOCHIUM OF PADUA: *AA.SS.*, Feb, 2, p. 643 contains an account written by Peter Barozzi, bishop of Padua, in 1487, less than twenty years after Eustochium's death. A Life by the Jesuit historian Giulio Cordara, published in 1765, is based on a manuscript by Fr Girolamo Salicario, confessor to the community, then preserved at San Prosdocimo. See also Fr Thurston's account, "A Cinderella of the Cloister," in *The Month* (1926, 1), pp 138-48.

FRANCES XAVIER CABRINI: The Life by Mary Louise Sullivan, M.S.C., (1992) contains much material from the Cabrini archives, an essay on sources and a full bibliography. Other lives by C. C. Martindale (1931); E. J. McCarthy (1937); A Benedictine of Stanbrook (1944); L. Borden (1945); E. Macadam (1946); E. V. Daily (1947); M. A. Farnum (1947); T. Maynard, *Too Small a World* (1948); P. di Donato (1960); S. C. Lorit, trans. Jerry Hearne (1988). Mother Cabrini's writings include *Escortatione della Cabrini* (1954) and *Diario spirituale* (1957); also *Viaggi della Madre Francesca Saverio Cabrini . . . narrati in variae sue lettere* (1935).

GERMAINE COUSIN (OF PIBRAC): There is a Life by Louis Veuillot, revised by his nephew François Veuillot (1894) in the series Les saints, and another by E. Duplessis (1894). See also H. Bartolini, *La Bergère au pays des Loups: Ste Germaine de Pibrac (c. 1579-1601)*. Lady (Georgiana) Fullerton wrote a play, *Germaine Cousin, The Shepherdess of Pibrac*, published by Burns & Oates in the early years of the twentieth century.

HELENA: Eusebius *H.E.*, bk 3, and *Life of Constantine*; Socrates, *H.E.*, 1, 17; Sozomen, *H.E.*, 2, 1; Theodoret, *H.E.*, bk 1; *AA.SS.*, Aug., 3, pp. 548-654; Geoffrey of Monmouth, *History of the Kings of Britain*, trans. Lewis Thomas. (1966), pp. 132, 233; *Anal.Boll.* 57 (1940), pp. 199-205; Cynewulf, *Elene*, ed. P. O. E. Gradon (1958); Evelyn Waugh, *Helena* (1950, rp. 1963).

HERMINA GRIVOT: M. T. de Blazer, *Vie de la Mère Marie-Hermine de Jésus et de ses compagnes*, is published in two versions: the full edition (Rome, 1902) and an abbreviated edition (Quebec, 1910; Paris, 1946). See also G. Goyau, *Valiant Women: Mother Mary of the Passion and the Franciscan Missionaries of Mary*, trans. G. Telford (1946); *N.C.E.*, under "China: Martyrs of," 3, p. 629; Irving Weinstein, *The Boxer Rebellion* (1971).

HILDA OF WHITBY: Bede, *H. E.*, trans. and ed. L. Sherley-Price (1952), 3, 24; 4, 25-34; Eddius Stephanus, *Life of Wilfrid*, Eng. trans. ed. B. M. Colgrave (1927), 10, 54; Lansdowne ms., *Vie de Ste Hilde* (fourteenth-century) in the British Museum, Lansdowne 436, fol. 105v-107r; A. Warren (1989). See also *D.N.B.*, 9, pp. 832-3; *D.H.G.E.*, fasc. 139-40, 480-2; *N.C.E.*, 6, p. 1116; Dame Etheldreda Hession, "St Hilda and St Etheldreda," in *Benedict's Disciples*, ed. D. H. Farmer (1980, new ed. 1995), pp. 70-85; *Butler*, November, rev. Sarah Fawcett Thomas (1997), pp. 157-9.

HILDEGARD OF BINGEN: Life by Gottfreid of Disibodenberg and Dieter of Echtenberg, with additions by Guibert of Gembloux (all three were contemporaries): *P.L.*, 197, 91-40; The *P.L.* vol. 197 also includes *Scivias* and other works, and a number of letters (in Latin). The *AA.SS.* version of the Life (Sept., 5, pp. 629-701) has been translated into English by J. H. McGrath as *The Life of the Holy Hildegard* (1980). Modern Lives and commentaries: S. Flanagan (1989); B. Newman, *Sisters of Wisdom: St Hildegard's Theology of the Feminine* (1987); F. Bowie and O. Davies (eds.), *Hildegard of Bingen: An Anthology*, with new translations of her writings by R. Carver (1990); *Hildegard of Bingen's Scivias*, trans. B. Hozeski (1986); H. Schipperges, trans. J. Cumming, *The World of Hildegard of Bingen: Her Life, Times, and Visions* (1998). Among many audiotapes of her music for women's voices are Hyperion KA66039, *A Feather on the Breath of God*, and Harmonia Music HMU 407200, *11,000 Virgins: Chants for the Feast of St Ursula*.

JANE FRANCES DE CHANTAL: F. M. de Chaugy, *Mémoires sur la vie et les vertus de sainte Jeanne-Françoise Frémyot de Chantal*, 8 vols. (1874-9): Eng. trans. *The Life of St Jane Frances de Chantal* (1882); L. V. E. Bougaud, *Histoire de sainte Chantal et des origines de la Visitation*, 2 vols. (1861, Eng. trans. 1895); *The Spirit of St Jane Frances de Chantal as shown in her Letters*, trans. and ed. Sisters of the Visitation, Harrow-on-the Hill (1922); A. Gazier, *Jeanne de Chantal et Angélique Arnaud d'après leur correspondance* (1915), reviewed in *Anal. Boll.* 40 (1922), p. 228; St *Francis de Sales: a testimony by St Chantal*, trans. and ed. E. C. V. Stopp (1967). Lives by H. Brémond (1912); Ella King Sanders, *Sainte Chantal*, 1572-1641 (1918); J. M. Scott (1948); E. C. V. Stopp, *Madame de Chantal: portrait of a saint* (1962); Hutton, pp. 380-1.

JEANNE DE VALOIS: J. F. Bonnefoy (1941) bases his Life on the chronicles of the Annonciade; Mgr Hebbard, *Saint Jeanne de Valois et l'ordre de l'Annonciade* (1878); A. M. C. Forster, *The Good Duchess: Joan of France* (1950); A. Redier, *Joan of France* (1946); *N. C. E.*, 7, p. 993; *Anal. Boll.* 10 (1892), p. 473; 16 (1898), p. 535; 59 (1942), p. 371.

JOSEPHINE BAKHITA: Maria Luisa Dagnino, *Bakhita Tells Her Story* (1991, 3d ed. 1993); Mother Agnes, F.D.C.C., *The Lucky One* (1970); *Vita più Speciale: Communicazioni de Vita Canossiana* no. 3 (1992); Christian Service International Report, October 1998.

JULIANA OF MOUNT CORNILLON: *AA. SS.*, April, 1, pp. 435-77, has an account originally written by John of Lausanne in French, but translated into Latin; *Golden Legend*, 1, pp. 160-1. See also Clotilde de Sainte-Julienne, *Sainte Julienne de Cornillon* (1928); E. Denis, *La vraie histoire de Ste Julienne. . .* (1938); C. Lambert, "L'Office de la Fîte-Dieu," *Rev. Bén.* 54 (1942), pp. 61-123; *N. C. E.*, 4, pp. 345-7; Michael Walsh, *A Dictionary of Devotions* (1993), pp. 77-8.

KATHARINE DREXEL: *Annals* of the Sisters of the Blessed Sacrament; Katherine Burton, *The Golden Door* (1957, rp. 1961); *N. C. E.*, 4, pp. 1059-60.

LOUISE DE MARILLAC: M. Gobillon, *Vie de Mlle le Gras* (1676); Mgr Baunard (1898); E. de Broglie (Eng. trans. 1933); panegyric on her canonization by Pope Pius XII, reprinted from the *Irish Ecclesistical Record*, 1945. Popular Lives of this saint tend to be slight and not always accurate. There is useful material in the Lives of St Vincent de Paul: P. Coste, C. Bassau, and G. Goyau (1932, Eng. trans. 1934-5, 3 vols.); J. Calvet (1948); M. Purcell (1963). See also *The Conferences of St Vincent de Paul to the Sisters of Charity*, ed. P. Coste, trans. J. Leonard (4 vols., 1938-40); Hutton, pp. 382-4; and for general background H. Brémond, *Hist. littéraire du sentiment religieux en France*, 3 (1921), pp. 222-57.

MACRINA THE YOUNGER: Gregory of Nyssa's *Vitae Sanctae Macriniae* in Latin, *AA.SS.*, July, 4, pp. 589-604, and in *Gregorii Nysseni Opera*, 8, ed. V. W. Callahan, 1, 347-414 (series ed. W. Jaeger, 1960-); *The Life of St Macrina* in English, trans. and ed. W. K. Lowther Clarke (1916); *On the Soul and the Resurrection* (the *Macriniae*), N.P.N.F., 5, pp. 428-68; for a new translation and commentary see Petersen, pp. 41-86; modern Life by P. Maraval (1977).

MADELEINE SOPHIE BARAT: Mgr Baunard (Eng. trans. Georgiana Fullerton, 2 vols., 1876); G. de Grandmaison (1909); Margaret Ward (1911); M. Monahan (1925); C. E. Maguire (1960); M. Williams (1965) contains many of Mother Barat's letters; J. W. Saul (1968).

MADELEINE FONTAINE: L. Misermont, *Les Bienheureuses Filles de la Charité d'Arras* (1920), in the series Les saints; A. Lovat, *The Sisters of Charity Martyred at Arras in 1794* (1920); J. McManners, *The French Revolution and the Church* (1969); M. Voyelle, *Religion et Révolution: le déchristianisme de l'An II* (1976); C. S. Philips, *The Church in France, 1789-1848: A Study in Revival* (1929); J. Le Goff and R. Brémond, *Histoire de la France religieuse*, vol. 3 (1991); *Anal.Boll.* 105 (1956), pp. 409-23.

MARGARET CLITHEROW: John Mush, *A True Report of the Life and Martyrdom of Mrs Margaret Clitherow* (1619). The original manuscript is in York Minster Library. There are transcripts in *English Recusant Literature*, vol. 393, 1, and in *The Life and Death of Margaret Clitherow of York*, ed. William Nicolson (1849). Katharine Mary Longley, *Saint Margaret Clitherow* (1986) is an improved and up-dated version of the author's *Margaret Clitherow, 1556-86* (1966), written under the pseudonym of Mary Claridge. The same author's "In His Image: St Margaret Clitherow, 1556-86," *Canadian Catholic Review* (Jan. 1988), pp. 10-16, contains further revision. See also Margaret T. Monro, *Margaret Clitherow* (1947); Claire Cross, "An Elizabethan Martyrologist and his Martyr: John Mush and Margaret Clitherow," in *Martyrs and Martyrologies*, ed. Diana Wood, Studies in Church History no. 30 (1993).

MARGARET D'YOUVILLE: The *Vie de Mme d'Youville* by Abbé Charles Dufrost is preserved in the general archives of the Grey Nuns in Montreal, together with his edited version of the *Mémoire pour servir à la vie de Mme d'Youville*, consisting of statements by her Sisters. Lives by A. Sattin (1829); E.-M. Faillon (1852). A. Ferland-Angers (1945) includes extensive correspondence and documentation relating to the foundress. Sister Estelle Mitchell is the author of three modern texts: *Elle a beaucoup aimé* (1959), Eng. trans. *Marguérite d'Youville, Foundress of the Grey Nuns* (1965); *Father Charles Dufrost and his Mother* (1991), and *The Spiritual Portrait of Saint Marguérite d'Youville* (1993). See also *Osservatore Romano*, 10 Dec. 1990, p. 6; *D.C.B.*, p. 1216; *Catholic Work*, 61 (Jan.-Feb. 1994), p. 8.

MARGARET OF CORTONA: Margaret's confessor, Fr Giunta Bevegnati, left an account of her life while he knew her, but this glosses over her earlier experiences: *AA.SS.* Feb., 3, pp. 302-63, Eng trans. F. M. Mahoney, *The Life and Revelations of St Margaret of Cortona* (1883). Other Lives by Fr Cuthbert, S.S.F. (Lawrence Anthony Hess), *A Tuscan Penitent* (1907); F. Mauriac, trans. B. Wall (1948); R. M. Pierazzi, trans. B. Davies (1939). Franciscan sources are summarized in Mgr. Léon's *Auréole Séraphique*, Eng. trans., *Lives of the Saints and Blessed of the Three Orders of Saint Francis*, 1 (1883), pp. 272-312. See also P.B., 2, pp. 618-23; *Bibl.SS.*, 8, 757-73; *Anal.Boll.* 27 (1908), pp. 500-1.

MARGARET OF SCOTLAND: Turgot's Life (badly damaged by fire) is in the British Museum: Ms. Cotton Tiberius D III. There are reproductions (in Latin) in *AA.SS.*, June, 2, pp. 320- 40; J. Pinkerton, *Lives of the Scottish Saints* (1889), pp. 159-82; and an English translation by W. Forbes-Leith, S.J. (1884). Mediaeval chronicles that deal with Margaret's life include the *Anglo-Saxon Chronicle*, trans. and ed. G. N. Garmonsway (1972), pp. 201, 202, 236; William of Malmesbury, *Gesta Regum*, v, 400 ; Eadmer, pp. 126-7. Modern Lives by Lucy Menzies (1925, 1947); T. Ratcliffe Barnett (1926); Margaret Gordon (1934); J. H. B. MacPhail (1947); D. M. Roberts (1960). D. Baker (ed.), *Mediaeval Women* (1978), pp. 119-41; *D.N.B.*, 12, pp. 1017-9.

MARY MACKILLOP: Osmund Thorpe, C. P. (1957); W. Moodystack (1982); D. Lyne (1982); P. Gardiner, S. J. (1993); *N.C.E.*, 9, p. 37; *Butler*, August, rev. John Cumming (1998), pp. 70-2.

MARY OF EGYPT: St John Chrysostom, *Homily in Matthew*, 67; *AA.SS.* Apr., 1, pp. 68-90; Cyril of Scythopolis, *Life of St Cyriacus*, in *The Lives of the Monks of Egypt*, trans. R. M. Price, ed. John Binns (1991), pp. 256-8. See also Baluze-Mansi 13, p. 100; *Golden Legend*, 1, pp. 227-9; A. B. Bujila, *La vie de sainte Marie l'Égyptienne* (a reprint of the ancient Life, 1949); D.A.C.L. (H. Leclercq), 10, 2, 2128-36; *D.C.B.* 3, 830; S. Baring Gould, *Lives of the Saints: April* (1872. rp. 1907), pp. 15-24.

MONICA: St Augustine, *Confessions* (1991), trans. Henry Chadwick, esp. bks 3, 6, 9; L. André-Delastre, *Sainte Monique* (1960); V. E. Bougaud, trans. Lady (Mary Elizabeth) Herbert (1894); M. E. Procter (1931); W. Sherren (1949); *D.A.C.L.*, 11, 2, 2232-56.

ODILIA: There is a tenth-century Life of St Odilia, ed. W. Levison, in *Monumenta Germaniae Historiae, Scriptures Merov.*, (1839-1921) 6, pp. 24-50; cf. *Anal.Boll.* 13 (1894), pp. 5-32, 196-287. In the judgment of Levison, hardly any of the material can be accepted as reliable history. There is a considerable literature on St Odilia, but the devotional Lives are for the most part unreliable. For the account in the *Chronicle of John of Worcester*, see J. R. H. Weaver's edition (1908), pp. 34-6. See also P.B., Dec., pp. 252-63, from *Les saints de Franche-Comté*; *D.A.C.L.*, 12, 1921- 34, lists a number of medieval manuscripts. On St Odilia in art, see C. Champion, *Ste Odile* (1931).

OLYMPIAS: Palladius, *Historia Lausiaca*, trans. and ed. W. K. Lowther Clarke (1918), pp. 161-2, 168; Sozomen, *H.E.*, bk. 8, ch. 9; Socrates, *H.E.*, bk. 6, chs. 3-5, 15-18. The letters of St John Chrysostom to St Olympias have been translated into French by Anne-Marie Malingrey (1947) and into English in E. A. Clark, *Jerome, Chrysostom and Friends: Essays and Translations* (1979). The Life was printed for the first time in *Anal.Boll.* 15 (1896), pp. 400-23. One chapter, the eleventh, appears to be a later interpolation by another hand. There is also an account of the translation of her remains in *Anal.Boll.* 16, pp. 44-51, written much later. See also J. Bousquet, "Vie d'Olympias la diaconesse," *Revue de l'Orient Chrétien*, second series, 1 (1906), pp. 225-50, and 2 (1907), pp. 255-68; H. Leclercq in *D.A.C.L.*, 12, 2064-71, lists many medieval manuscripts; D. Attwater *St John Chrysostom, Pastor and Preacher* (1939, rp. 1959).

PAULA: *AA.SS.*, Jan., 3, pp. 326-37; Jerome, *Letters*, 39, 45, 108, N.P.N.F., 6, pp. 49-54, 58-60, 195- 232. There is a new translation of Letter 108, to Paula, in Petersen, pp. 126-67; *Golden Legend*, 1, pp. 121-6; F. Lagrange, *Histoire de Sainte Paule* (1868), Eng. trans. Lady (Mary Elizabeth) Herbert, *Wives, Mothers and Sisters of Olden Times*, vol. 1; vol. 2, pp. 1-129; R. Genier, *Sainte Paule* (1917); J. N. D. Kelly, *Jerome, His Life, Writings and Controversies* (1975).

PELAGIA THE PENITENT: *AA.SS.*, Oct., 4, pp. 248-68; *Golden Legend*, 2, pp. 230-2. Helen Waddell, *The Desert Fathers* (1936), pp. 285-302, gives the account of "James the Deacon" in full in her own excellent translation from the *Vitae Patrum* (Rosweyde, 1614). Delehaye, pp. 150-5; *Bibl.SS.*, 10, 432-7.

PHILIPPINE DUCHESNE: Lives by M. T. Kelly, *A Life's Ambition* (1910); M. Erskine (1926); M. K. Richardson, *Redskin Trail* (1952); L. Callan (1957); L. Callan, *The Sisters of the Sacred Heart in America* (1937). See also Margaret Williams, *St Madeleine Sophie: her Life and Letters* (1965), pp. 76-8, 155-60, 332-3, 531-3.

SALOME: *AA.SS.*, June, 7, pp. 451-6, contains an account ascribed to Abbot Walter of Aitach; Asser, *Life of King Alfred*, various editions including a Penguin edition trans. and intro. Simon Keynes and Michael Lapidge (1983), chs. 14-15; William of Malmesbury, *Gesta Regum Anglorum*, bk. 2, ed. T. D. Hardy (1840), pp. 169-70; *The Annals of Roger de Hoveden*, ed. H. T. Riley (1853), pp. 19-20; R. M. Wilson, *The Lost Literature of Medieval England* (1952), pp. 37-8.

APPENDIX I

Euphrosyne: P.B. 1, pp. 249; D.C.B. 1, p. 297; *Anal.Boll.* 51 (1933), p. 268. **Marina:** *AA.SS.*, July, 4, pp. 278-87; *P.G.*, 115, 348 ff; *Golden Legend*, 1, pp. 324-5; *D.C.B.*, 3, 831. **Theodora:** *Golden Legend*, 1, pp. 365-8; *P.G.*, 115, 665-89; P.B., 5, p. 58; *Anal.Boll.* 28 (1909), p. 363. **Reparata:** *AA.SS.*, Oct., 4, p. 24; Delehaye, p. 151. **Eugenia:** H. Delehaye, *Étude sur le légendier romain* (1936), pp. 171-86; *Butler*, 25 December. For the legends on Eugenia, see the Sanctuarius of Mombritius, printed in Rosweyde, *Vitae Patrum*, and *P.L.*, 21, 1107-22. Two or three different Greek versions are known in manuscript, and that of the Metaphrast is printed in *P.G.*, 116, 609-52. There are also Syriac and Armenian versions: the former translated into English by A. Smith-Lewis in *Studia Sinaitica* 9 and 10, and the latter by F. C. Conybeare in *The Armenian Apology of Appolonius* (1912). **Hildegunda:** the Life by Philip Harveng, abbot of Bonne-Esperance, *AA.SS.*, April, 2, pp. 778-85, is said to be based on contemporary accounts, including her own. S. Baring Gould, *Lives of the Saints, April* (1872, rp. 1907), pp. 254-9.

APPENDIX II

The wife of Philip the Deacon: see Philip, *AA.SS.*, June, 1, pp. 608-10; P.B. 6, pp. 472-4; *N.C.E.*, 11, p. 275.
Valeria: see Vitalis. *AA.SS.*, Apr., 3, pp. 568-71.
Teresia: see Paulinus of Nola. *P.L.*, 99, 18-152; Jerome, *Lives of Illustrious Men*, ch. 99, N.P.N.F., 3, p. 394. *AA.SS.*, June, 5, pp. 167-204. Modern biographies of Paulinus by A. Baudrillart (1903) and P. Fabré (1948-9). See also *D.C.B.*, 4, pp. 234-45; *D.T.C.*, 12, 68-71.
The wife of Vulflagius: see Vulflagius or Wulphy, *AA.SS.*, June, 2, pp. 29-34; *Anal.Boll.* 17 (1898), p. 307; 21 (1902), p. 43; P.B., 6, pp. 510-14, from the *Historia Abbavillana* (1480); S. Baring Gould, *Lives of the Saints*, June (1872, rp. 1907), pp. 71-2.
The wife of "King Richard": see Richard. M. Coens, "Légende et Miracles du roi S Richard," *Anal.Boll.* 49 (1931), pp. 353-97; A. Stanton, *A Menology of England and Wales* (1892), p. 600; For Winnibald and Willibald, see C. H. Talbot, *Anglo-Saxon Missionaries in Germany* (1954).
Lady Stonor: see Edmund Campion. R. Persons, *On the Life and Martyrdom of Father Edmund Campion*, facsimile edition, ed. T. Allfield (1970); Cardinal William Allen, *A Brief Historie of the Glorious Martyrdom of twelve reverend Priests*, ed. J. H. Pollen (1908); Henry More, *Historia Missionis Anglicanus Societatis Jesu* (1660), published as *The Elizabethan Jesuits*, trans. and intro. Francis Edwards (1981), bks 2 and 3. For a modern biography see Evelyn Waugh, *Edmund Campion* (1935), especially the bibliography, pp. 224-5. For general background see J. Bossy, *The English Catholic Community 1570-1850* (1975).

Mrs Swithin Wells: see Swithin Wells, London Martyrs of 1591. Catholic Record Society, 5 (1908), *passim*: see especially pp. 131ff., pp. 204ff. See also Bede Camm, *Nine Martyr Monks* (rp. 1931), pp. 60-72; J. H. Pollen, *Acts of the English Martyrs* (1891), pp. 98-126; G. Anstruther, O.P., *The Seminary Priests*, vol. 1 (1968), pp. 128-9, 278-9, 377-8.

APPENDIX III

Mary Ward: M. Chambers, ed. J. Coleridge, S.J. (2 vols., 1882); Henrietta Peters, trans. H. Butterworth (1994). M. M. Littlehales, I.B.V.M., *Mary Ward: Pilgrim and Mystic* (1998). The Painted Life series of illustrations of the Life of Mary Ward is in the I.B.V.M. convent at Augsburg, Germany, and there are copies in the Bar Convent Museum at York.

ADVANCE PRAISE for *PERFORMANCE WITHOUT PAIN*

Performance without Pain is a must-read for musicians, athletes, dancers, and anyone who wants good health and long life. Kathryne Pirtle's personal journey from a near career-ending injury to vibrant health will inspire you to take responsibility for your health.

> Jordan S. Rubin, NMD
> *New York Times* bestselling author of
> *The Maker's Diet, Patient Heal Thyself* and
> *Restoring Your Digestive Health*;
> Founder of Garden of Life Company

I have read Ms. Pirtle's book, *Performance without Pain,* with shock and disbelief at the ill-considered judgments of the food industry and our government's decisions concerning it. The history of milk set forth in Chapter 5 is *jaw-dropping!* Frankly, it's a wonder any American is well today! The book is a must-read if you care at all about your family's health and is, without doubt, one of the most important books I have ever read.

> Barbara Haffner
> Assistant Principal Cellist, Lyric Opera of Chicago

One person through personal experience, another through professional study—put them together and a stark picture of nutritional marketing emerges. Kathy Pirtle, John Turner and Sally Fallon have written an insightful book revealing some of the myths propagated by the food industry while revealing to readers a roadmap for better health and pain-free living. Having competed in the NBA and suffering many of the symptoms Kathy, John and Sally discuss, I find myself appreciative of their work and wanting to share their findings with others. Reading the book and the subsequent change in my diet have resulted in my life being more productive, less stressful, and most important—pain-free. I encourage you to see for yourself.

> Ron deVries,
> Former NBA basketball player

As a professional ballet dancer, teacher, choreographer, and serious flutist all my life, I find that Ms. Pirtle's story resonates deeply with me. Like Ms. Pirtle, during the course of my career I have sought remedies for injuries and ailments; some of those remedies have been highly successful, while others have left much to be desired. In my opinion, Ms. Pirtle's extensive research and her resultant discoveries open up a whole new world of hope for healing and health for performing artists. I am grateful for the magnificent and caring effort she has put into sharing her knowledge, including her practical, easy-to-follow instructions for applying it. Ms. Pirtle's book is important for anyone seeking complete health as well as for anyone seeking optimal performance capacity.

Daniel Duell
Artistic Director, Ballet Chicago
Former Principal Dancer, New York City Ballet

Ms. Pirtle, Ms. Fallon and Dr. Turner have written an informative and extremely important text for all performing artists that is especially relevant today, when performers are seeking more and more medical attention for performance-related injuries. Many performance-related injuries are very difficult to diagnose, and the nutritional aspect to injury provides a valuable piece of this highly complicated puzzle. I have spent much of my professional career examining and treating individuals with performing arts-related injuries and have recently realized the huge importance nutrition plays in the healing and health of the musculoskeletal system. Many of the musicians I see have food allergies and many poor nutrition habits—fast foods, unbalanced, etc. Many have chronic pain conditions, often diagnosed as fibromyalgia-type pain. This text may very likely provide the help that many of these individuals need for full recovery and continuation of long, uninterrupted musical and dance careers.

Nicholas F Quarrier, MHS, PT, OCS
Clinical Associate Professor of Physical Therapy
Ithaca College, Ithaca, NY
Director of *The Healthy Musician: Care and Prevention of Music-Related Injuries* Summer Workshop